AF758351

Business Services in European Economic Growth

Also by Luis Rubalcaba

BUSINESS SERVICES IN EUROPEAN INDUSTRY: Growth Employment and Competitiveness

TRADING SERVICES IN A GLOBAL ECONOMY (*co-edited with J.R. Cuadrado and J.R. Bryson*)

THE NEW SERVICES ECONOMY: Challenges and Policy Implications for Europe

Also by Henk Kox

GROWTH CHALLENGES FOR THE DUTCH BUSINESS-SERVICES INDUSTRY: International Comparison and Policy Issues

THE FREE MOVEMENT OF SERVICES WITHIN THE EU (*with A. Lejour and R. Montizaan*)

Business Services in European Economic Growth

Edited by

Luis Rubalcaba and Henk Kox

palgrave
macmillan

Selection and editorial matter © Luis Rubalcaba, Henk L. M. Kox 2007
Foreword © William J. Baumol 2007
Chapters © their authors 2007

All rights reserved. No reproduction, copy or transmission of this publication may be made without written permission.

No paragraph of this publication may be reproduced, copied or transmitted save with written permission or in accordance with the provisions of the Copyright, Designs and Patents Act 1988, or under the terms of any licence permitting limited copying issued by the Copyright Licensing Agency, 90 Tottenham Court Road, London W1T 4LP.

Any person who does any unauthorised act in relation to this publication may be liable to criminal prosecution and civil claims for damages.

The authors have asserted their rights to be identified as the authors of this work in accordance with the Copyright, Designs and Patents Act 1988.

First published 2007 by
PALGRAVE MACMILLAN
Houndmills, Basingstoke, Hampshire RG21 6XS and
175 Fifth Avenue, New York, N.Y. 10010
Companies and representatives throughout the world

PALGRAVE MACMILLAN is the global academic imprint of the Palgrave Macmillan division of St. Martin's Press, LLC and of Palgrave Macmillan Ltd. Macmillan® is a registered trademark in the United States, United Kingdom and other countries. Palgrave is a registered trademark in the European Union and other countries.

ISBN-13: 978-0-230-00202-9 hardback
ISBN-10: 0-230-00202-1 hardback

This book is printed on paper suitable for recycling and made from fully managed and sustained forest sources. Logging, pulping and manufacturing processes are expected to conform to the environmental regulations of the country of origin.

A catalogue record for this book is available from the British Library.

Library of Congress Cataloging-in-Publication Data

Business services in European economic growth / edited by
Luis Rubalcaba and Henk Kox.
p. cm.
Includes bibliographical references and index.
ISBN 0-230-00202-1 (alk. paper)
1. Service industries–Europe. 2. Europe–Economic conditions–21st century. I. Rubalcaba-Bermejo, Luis. II. Knox, Henk.

HD9986.A2B87 2007
338.4094–dc22 2007025506

10 9 8 7 6 5 4 3 2 1
16 15 14 13 12 11 10 09 08 07

Printed and bound in Great Britain by
Antony Rowe Ltd, Chippenham and Eastbourne

Contents

List of Figures and Tables

Figures

Tables

Notes on the Contributors

Paul Baker is Director, Baker Research & Consulting, Brussels, Belgium and Associate Consultant at ECORYS Nederland, Macro and Sector Policies Division, Rotterdam, The Netherlands.

John R. Bryson is Professor of Enterprises and Economic Geography, School of Geography, Earth and Environmental Sciences, The University of Birmingham, UK. Vice-President of the European Association for Research on Services (RESER).

José A. Camacho is Titular Professor. Department of Applied Economics, University of Granada, Campus Universitario de Cartuja, Granada, Spain. Secretary of the Regional Development Institute.

Francesco Crespi is Postdoctoral Fellow in the Department of Economics, University of Rome III, Italy.

Peter W. Daniels is Professor of Geography and Co-Director Service Sector Research Unit, School of Geography, Earth and Environmental Sciences, Dean of Physical Sciences and Engineering. University of Birmingham, UK.

Werner Hölzl is researcher at the Austrian Institute for Economic Research (WIFO), Vienna.

Jeremy Howells is Professor and Executive Director of Manchester Institute of Innovation Research, Manchester Business School. University of Manchester, UK.

Henk L.M. Kox is Senior Economist with CPB Netherlands Bureau for Economic Policy Analysis, The Hague, The Netherlands.

George van Leeuwen is a Researcher with Statistics Netherlands, Voorburg, The Netherlands.

Aija Leiponen is Assistant Professor of Applied Economics and Management, Cornell University, New York, USA.

Arjan Lejour is Programme Manager of European Analysis at the sector International Economics with CPB Netherlands Bureau for Economic Policy Analysis, The Hague, The Netherlands.

Ian Miles is Professor of Technological Innovation and Social Change, Manchester Institute of Innovation Research, Manchester Business School, University of Manchester, UK.

Dirk Pilat is Head of the OECD Science and Technology Policy Division.

Andreas Reinstaller is a Researcher at the Austrian Institute for Economic Research (WIFO), Vienna, Austria.

Mercedes Rodríguez is Assistant Professor, Department of Applied Economics. University of Granada. Campus Universitario de Cartuja, Granada, Spain.

Luis Rubalcaba is Professor of Applied Economics at the University of Alcalá, Madrid, Spain. He is also President of the European Association for Research on Services (RESER) and Director of the Services, innovation and competitiveness area at the SERVILAB, Spain.

Bruce S. Tether is Professor at the Manchester Institute of Innovation Research, Manchester Business School, University of Manchester, UK. Ghoshal Fellow, Advanced Institute of Management Research, London, UK.

Elvira Uyarra is a Researcher at the Manchester Institute of Innovation Research, Manchester Business School. University of Manchester, UK.

Desirée van Welsum works at the OECD Directorate for Science, Technology and Industry; Information, Computer and Communications Policy Division.

Henry van der Wiel is Senior Economist, Programme Manager with CPB Netherlands Bureau for Economic Policy Analysis, The Hague, The Netherlands. Associated with CentER/University of Tilburg, The Netherlands.

Paul Windrum is Deputy Director of the Centre for International Business and Innovation (CIBI), Reader at Manchester Metropolitan University Business School, and Visiting Professor at Max Planck Institute for Economics, Jena.

Foreword

William J. Baumol

This book is a major contribution to our understanding of the current growth process. Well written, and based on careful research and defensible reasoning, it should be required reading for anyone who wishes to understand the intricacies of the growth process. And given the substantial role played by the business-service sector, it is an arena that has been inadequately explored, giving the authors of the essays that make up this book the scope to contribute substantially to the literature.

The magnitude of the influence of the business-services sector is not generally appreciated. Let me cite some of the indicative observations from the book: Business services constitute one of the fastest growing sectors of the economy. '. . .over the period 1979 and 2001 the sector accounted for 54 per cent of total EU employment growth, and for 18 per cent of income (value-added) growth'; '. . .more than 19 million workers in business services generate more than 1,000 billion euro and . . . account in relative terms for more than 11 per cent of the total EU15 economy. Between 1979 and 2003, value-added growth in business services (4.2 per cent) was higher than in any other sector except telecommunications. In terms of employment, the growth of business services (4.4 per cent) far outstripped the growth of any other major sector' (Introduction and Chapter 1).

Yet the sector has a record of relatively slow productivity growth, being composed, to a substantial extent, of services drawn from what I have elsewhere called 'the (productivity) stagnant sector' of the economy. These are items with a significant handicraft component, including R&D, software creation, consulting and accounting, and whose labour component is not easily reducible.

The surprising part of the story is the evidence that the growth of this relatively stagnant sector tends to accelerate the productivity growth of the economy as a whole, and does so to a significant degree. This is why the sector is so important for those who study the performance of the entire economy rather than concentrating their attention on some one of its relatively limited components, for its own sake. The explanation, rather straightforward in retrospect, stems from an earlier misapprehension of the author of this preface, one that was subsequently corrected by Nicholas Oulton and others. Oversimplifying the argument, consider an industry whose productivity is growing rapidly, and that uses two inputs, labour and business services, and steadily increases the productivity of each of these, say at 3 per cent a year. If at the same time the business-service suppliers are increasing the productivity of their labour input at an annual rate of one per cent, then the transfer of labour from the first industry to the second reduces the amount of labour undergoing a 3 per cent productivity growth, but adds to the labour first subject to a one per cent productivity growth, *to which is subsequently added the 3 per cent growth experienced by its reincarnation in the form of a utilized business service*.

It is this simple explanation of the slow growth–rapid growth paradox in the utilization of business services that goes far in accounting for their critical role in the performance of the macroeconomy. This book, however, is not confined to theory and goes on to explore the associated reality, casting needed light in an important subject that has previously too much been kept in the dark.

William J. Baumol
Berkley Center for Entrepreneurial Studies, New York University

Acknowledgements

The authors thank the support of Foundation Rafael del Pino and the technical layout performed by Stefano Visintin, Jorge Gallego and Gisela Di Meglio.

FUNDACIÓN
RAFAEL
DEL PINO

Introduction

Henk Kox and Luis Rubalcaba

The European economy is in a process of structural change. Two major trends have characterized the period of the past two decades. One is that the share of manufacturing in the overall economy is shrinking. The other trend is that services, and particularly business services, account for a monotonically increasing share of the European economy. Both structural shifts are linked to each other in several ways. The fabric of inter-industry relations is being woven in a new way as a result of the growing specialization in knowledge services, the exploitation of scale economies for human capital, lowered costs of outsourcing in-house services, and the growing tertiarization of all production processes, including that of the manufacturing industry. The business-services industry plays a key role in many of these processes. Many links between the development of the business-services industry, and its role in economic growth, remain under-explored in the literature. With this book we hope to fill some of the gaps in the knowledge.

This book provides insight into the economy of the business-services industry and its contribution to levels of overall economic growth in Europe. We present a rich set of original and coherent contributions that cover three aspects of the position of business services in the European economy:

- the rapid growth of the European business-services industry itself;
- the contribution of business services to the competitiveness and growth of other parts of the European economy; and
- the market characteristics and dynamics of business-services markets, at a local, European and global level.

We will argue that business services contributed heavily to European economic growth, in terms of employment, productivity and innovation.

The container concept *business services* covers a broad spectrum of services that are mainly traded in business-to-business transactions. These intermediary services range from software development to temporary-labour agencies, from equipment rental to economic consultancy, and from translation services to accountancy. Business services form a most dynamic group of activities that over the last two decades accounted for about half of the growth in European employment. As a consequence, this sector is by now in terms of employment larger than the total manufacturing industry in several EU countries.

Business services are linked intimately to the production of all economic sectors as a supplier of intermediary inputs, often of a knowledge-intensive nature. The business-services industry adds value and provides important inputs to different economic products and processes. Recent years have reinforced the economic linkages between services and goods, between tangible and intangibles, between services industries and goods industries, between service markets and goods markets. While most business-service firms are still oriented at national markets, other sections of this industry are rapidly globalizing through international trade and direct investment activities. Some parts of the business-services industry even are at the very heart of new services-offshoring trends. Business services are both active players and active catalysers for global change, changing physiognomy and borders of the markets in which they operate. If we disregard transport and travel, business services form the main component of intra-European services trade.

Business services: a young concept

Interest in the business-services industry is relatively new within economic theory. The surge in attention is to a large extent a by-product of structural change in the economy. Classical economists such as Smith and Ricardo used to regard services as an unproductive activity having more to do with the distribution and consumption of wealth than with its production. An exception was sometimes made for transport. The implicit association of production with material goods production disappeared with the ascent of neo-classical economic theory from the early 1870s onwards. But in the century to follow, theoretical interest in the service sector's contributions to growth was little more than half-hearted. A gap remained between acknowledging theoretically that value could be created through both material and non-material production, and empirical research in which the emphasis remained on material production.

Service activities were initially part of more vertically integrated production activities. Agriculture and manufacturing already included service functions like planning, management, administration, assessment of quantity and quality of products and inputs, product improvement, labour recruitment, learning and education, marketing, transport, storage and distribution. Service professions gradually took over part of these business functions, running them as specialized and commercially independent activities. This went along with process and product innovations that further developed these service functions. It took some time before this specialization was recognised as a new phase in the social division of labour. Colin Clark pointed out in 1938 that no less than 50 per cent of the British and US labour populations worked in professions other than mining, agriculture, manufacturing and crafts. He framed the catchword 'tertiary production' for this no longer negligible category. However, it still was treated as a heterogeneous residual of goods production.[1]

In the 1960s the American economist Baumol pointed out that growth of the service sector could function as a drag on macroeconomic growth because of the limited potential for productivity increase (Baumol, 1967). Ensuing discussion soon led to the conclusion that at least an analytical distinction had to be made between government services, consumer-oriented market services and producer-oriented market services. Theoretical interest in producer services as a specific economic sector thus dates back to the 1970s.[2]

It was not before another decade had passed that business services – a subset of producer services – received any real theoretical and empirical appreciation. The interest was triggered by the industry's high growth rates and the complexity of its relationship with outsourcing, innovation and productivity tendencies elsewhere in the economy. Moreover, the high rate of human capital input in business services made the industry an interesting case from the perspective of modern growth theory and the economics of technical change. The general shift of economic activities away from the primary and secondary sectors and towards the tertiary sector has recently seen a specific focus on knowledge-based services.

From Adam Smith's times onwards, services were defined by what they are *not* – no goods, no material, no agriculture, no manufacturing. Hill (1977), in a seminal article, did away with the negative approach towards services. In '*On Goods and Services*' he emphasized that a difference exists between goods and services. Goods are physical objects that are appropriated and therefore transferable between economic units. However, a service provided by an economic unit, represents '*a change to the condition of*' a person or goods belonging to another economic unit. The service is defined as a positive result.[3]

Business services are predominantly delivered to companies, other production organizations and government agencies. Hence, viewed from the angle of their destination, business services are primarily intermediate inputs, even though some business services – such as notary or architectural services – supply part of their production to individual consumers. Often the business service is co-produced interactively with the client. Building on Hill's definition of services we define business services by their role for clients:

Business services is a set of service activities that – through their use as intermediary inputs – affect the quality and efficiency of the production activities, by complementing or substituting the in-house service functions.

The definition implies that business-services firms supply activities that in many cases could also have been produced in-house by the client. Service elements are pervasive in any production process, indeed functional services lie at the very heart of *any* production process. Such functional services can be provided by employees on a firm's own payroll, or they can be bought from outside providers. In the latter case, we speak of business services as an independent industry. At the end of this introduction we present an operational taxonomy of business services based on the aforementioned definition.

For reasons of brevity and to avoid endless repetition, we will use the abbreviation 'BSS' for business services in the rest of this introductory chapter.

A brief overview of the book

The book is organized in three sections. Part I deals with the central issues related to the contribution of BSS to European economic growth. Crucial for the growth contribution are the expansion of the BSS industry itself, its own productivity performance, and the growth spillover effects it generates for other parts of the European economy. Part II zooms in more specifically on the dynamic spillover effects that BSS industry creates for the productivity and innovation in other economic sectors. Finally, the performance and spillover effects of the BSS industry depend to an important degree on the efficient operation of markets in business services. This is the topical item of Part III. It focuses on the characteristics and dynamics of BSS markets at European, global and regional level.

Part I of the book analyses the causes of the strong BSS growth and its effects on the European economy. The first chapter produced by the editors presents evidence concerning the growth causes of the business-service sector itself, showing what part of income and employment growth in the EU can be attributed to the growth of BSS industry itself. The chapter concludes that the growth of BSS is only partly caused by the fact that other industries simply outsource existing in-house services to BSS industry. Rather, the evidence indicates that a bigger role is played by an explosive growth in service specialisations, product innovations and new technologies like ICT.

In Chapter 2, Ian Miles reviews the literature regarding the role of BSS for the performance of its client firms. He pays attention to the roles of different types of BSS, in particular the knowledge-intensive business services (the so-called KIBS).

A standard view is that the growth of BSS employment is related to the sector's relatively weak productivity performance. This is analysed by Dirk Pilat (Chapter 3). He analyses the development of BSS productivity, showing differences by country and by sub-sector. He also discusses the possible role of measurement problems.

Chapter 4, by Rubalcaba and Kox, analyses the impact of BSS industry on the overall growth of the European economy. BSS industry has a relatively weak productivity performance and at the same time represent a growing share in the European economy. It begs the question of whether or not this development carries the seeds of stagnationist tendencies, the so-called 'Baumol disease'. The chapter argues that as long as the positive spillovers from BSS to innovation and productivity growth in other sectors are large enough, there is no reason to expect such stagnation tendencies in general terms.

The second part of the book investigates various aspects of growth spillovers generated by the BSS industry. The emphasis is on dynamic spillovers in the form of knowledge dissemination, innovation, and productivity-growth impacts.

Three related chapters apply input–output analysis to investigate the existence and magnitude of inter-sectoral growth spillovers that stem from BSS use. Paul Baker in Chapter 5 identifies the sectors that are the most important and most intensive users of BSS. The productivity performance of intensive users of BSS inputs was better than that of 'intermediate' users and of the BSS industry itself. Baker estimates the returns in term of production and productivity that sectors derive from using BSS inputs.

The BSS industry includes the software and computer-services industry, which has had a profound impact on the nature of production and distribution in many ways. In Chapter 6, Francesco Crespi investigates the hypothesis that increased use of computer and related services by a sector has a positive impact on a sector's productivity performance. He finds that the diffusion of IT services has indeed had a strong and positive role in shaping productivity in European industries in the period 1995–2000. In Chapter 7, José Camacho and Mercedes Rodriguez estimate for a number of EU countries how the use of inputs from knowledge-intensive services affects production and productivity of client industries. They also find evidence for knowledge spill-overs related to the use of knowledge-intensive services.

In Chapter 8, Howells, Tether and Uyarra draw on a firm survey to examine the patterns and drivers of innovation in four knowledge-intensive services sectors, exploring the behavioural aspects of BSS innovation. Innovation by services firms tend to involve complementary changes across a number of dimensions like organizational structure, technology and skills.

Aija Leiponen in Chapter 9 assesses empirically how incentives in the contracts between knowledge-intensive BSS providers and their client may affect innovation outcomes. Using data for Finland she shows which types of contractual arrangements (material versus non-material incentives, pricing rules, property rights on innovations) are most inductive to create knowledge spillovers to client firms.

Using a new type of model, Hölzl, Reinstaller and Windrum (Chapter 10) show the limits of 'outsourcing-for-cost-cutting' strategy. After discussing different outsourcing motivations, they discuss potential costs and benefits of outsourcing in-house services to BSS firms. Short-term cost advantages may in the long term have a negative impact on the potential innovation capacity and competitiveness of firms.

Part III of the book analyses the market characteristics in the BSS industry from an economic and from a spatial perspective. Business services is mostly a small-scale sector, but we also find global players. Do they actually compete with each other, or are small and large firms operating in segmented sub-markets? What is the role played by government regulation?

Chapter 11 by Kox, Van Leeuwen and Van der Wiel, using data from 11 EU countries, find that firm scale and regulation of market entry by governments affect labour productivity in this industry. They also find that market segmentation between small and large firms has a negative impact on productivity performance in the BSS industry.

BSS industry appears to have been an important facilitator of globalization tendencies. Rubalcaba and van Welsum in Chapter 12 investigate the role of globalization and especially international outsourcing in the BSS industry. They estimate the maximum effects that BSS outsourcing might have on employment. The potential employment affected by offshoring is impressive.

While the freedom to provide services across borders is one of the four 'freedoms' outlined in the EU Treaty, the econometric results by Kox and Lejour in Chapter 13 show that national borders are still obstacles for intra-EU exports of commercial (business) services. This is to a large extent due to differences in national regulations.

Bryson and Daniels (Chapter 14) review the literature on the role of geographical segmentation and hierarchy in the markets for business and professional services. Also building on a case study they conclude that dichotomy exists between a large majority of BSS firms that are mostly locally engaged and a small group of firms that operates beyond the regional marketplace.

Finally, Chapter 15 by the two editors of this volume discusses a number of possible policy implications – at a national and at an EU level – from the findings on market structure.

Main lessons learned

Using the research results of this book, we offer directions for future research and suggestions for policy makers.[4]

1. *Strong growth of the business services industry*. By its own strong growth, BSS industry contributed forcefully to economic growth in recent decades. The dynamism of BSS industry itself was such that, over the period 1979–2001, the sector accounted for 54 per cent of total EU employment growth, and for 18 per cent of income (value-added) growth.
2. *Productivity growth in BSS industry itself is sluggish*. . . . Although measurement problems may play a role, the productivity-growth record of BSS industry itself is weak. In some countries BSS sectors present negative contributions to productivity growth. The differentiation in productivity growth between countries and between sub-sectors suggests that not all possibilities for productivity improvement in the BSS industry are exhausted.

3. *. . . but the BSS industry' indirect contributions economic growth still dominate.* Several chapters in our book demonstrate that the input of business services in other industries gives rise to measurable positive impacts on firm efficiency, innovation and productivity. The inputs of computer-related services have more or less revolutionized production. Other parts of BSS industry had a less spectacular, but still important role for efficiency and innovation. By creating and diffusing knowledge, KIBS firms are drivers and facilitators of innovation in many industries.[5] The increased availability of business services has removed many scale indivisibilities for human capital and knowledge assets. It thus improves the position of small and medium-sized firms, and, hence, the structural flexibility of the economy. These indirect contributions to aggregate productivity growth and aggregate economic growth may compensate for the weak productivity performance of BSS industry itself. The challenge for the future is whether the indirect growth contribution of the BSS sector will remain strong enough to future productivity growth.
4. *The growth of the BSS industry is only partly caused by outsourcing of existing in-house services jobs.* The growth of the BSS industry is not an optical illusion caused by the outsourcing of existing jobs. Though such simple outsourcing does play a role (cleaning, catering, maintenance, security, call centres), it represents only part of the story. Even for the relatively simple services, new knowledge-intensive elements are added, like total facility management by cleaning firms, security management by private security agencies, and customer-relations management by call centres. The growth of the BSS industry is first and foremost the expression of a more complex social division of labour, especially related to knowledge functions in production. From this perspective, the current tertiarization of production inputs is a process that can be compared to the way that manufacturing industry has developed out of the agricultural and craft sector. Many current BSS products are new specializations and new services that can hardly be compared to the 'pre-existing' in-house services functions.
5. *The knowledge spillover effects by BSS firms are often related to tacit and embedded types of knowledge.* Circulation of knowledge is difficult to control once the knowledge is available. Knowledge-intensive BSS firms have a role in conceptualizing and disseminating tacit forms of production and market knowledge. By being able to look in the 'knowledge kitchen' of clients, KIBS firms may select best-practice information with regard to different competence areas. Such knowledge is subsequently used for dissemination, thus helping other firms to get closer to the efficiency frontier in specific competence areas.
6. *Contractual arrangements may influence BSS contributions with regard to innovation and knowledge transfer.* Contracts between the BSS firms and clients often are incompletely specified, because of transaction costs and outcomes that sometimes are a priori uncertain. BSS firms that regularly transfer

service-related intellectual property rights to their clients or sign exclusivity arrangements with clients tend to be significantly less innovative.

7. *The role of spatial proximity for standardized business services is declining. . .* Standardized, off-the-shelf business services involving codified knowledge have become increasingly 'footloose' due to improved information and communication technologies (ICT). It allows off-site or even offshore provision of standardized services like invoicing and other administrative tasks, technical testing, software debugging, design, simple customer relations and even security surveillance. ICT progress and standardization of service jobs will only further strengthen this 'death of distance' tendency. On-line provision of such business services may become more important in international trade between countries. One of the estimates in the book is that offshoring of standardized BSS jobs could have substantial effects on employment. The analysis of occupational employment data for selected countries shows that close to 20 per cent of total employment could potentially be affected by the international sourcing of IT- and ICT-enabled services.
8. *. . .but proximity remains vital for a large part of the BSS industry.* Face-to-face interactions with client firms will remain very important for those BSS activities that are tailor-made for clients, involving tacit knowledge, learning processes, management interaction and quality reputation issues. International provision of such business services will either mean that BSS firms either operate through local subsidiaries or send their employees temporarily to foreign customers.
9. *Competition in business services is weakly developed due to market segmentation and lack of market transparency.* Several chapters in the book demonstrate that European BSS markets are segmented: along national border lines, according to regional differences, according to the size-class of firms, and even according to the different service varieties that BSS firms offer to their clients. An implication is that many firms, even in the same subsector and country, are not each other's competitors. The lack of competition due to segmentation and market opacity weakens the incentive for BSS firms to operate in an efficient and cost-effective way. The degree of market segmentation is found to have a negative impact on productivity performance of firms. This is, of course, only valid as a broad picture. At a more disaggregate and local level we also find more complex competitive situations. Sometimes, small firms in specialist niche markets are able to compete successfully with even large, more generalist firms at home and in foreign countries.
10. *Large numbers of BSS firms are smaller than the minimum-efficient firm size.* Although the BSS industry has a small number of large multinational firms, in most EU countries the great majority (90–95 per cent) of BSS firms has fewer than ten employed persons. Business services is one of the economic sectors with the highest firm start-up rates. This has given

rise to a popular view according to which scale economies do not play a role in the BSS industry. It is shown in the book that this is a fallacy. Though there are differences by subsector, it is shown that firms with fewer than 20 employed persons on average have significant scale-related productivity disadvantages. Below this minimum-efficient firm size, BSS firms apparently have fewer opportunities for internal labour division and for using their often high-skilled personnel (human capital) in an efficient way. It is only the existence of weak competition that allows a majority of firms to operate at a less-than-efficient firm size.

11. *Government policies may affect competition between BSS firms (and, hence, efficiency incentives) in a negative way by suppressing potential market entry.* A market mechanism that forces incumbent BSS firms to operate in a more cost-effective way, is the pressure coming from newly-entering firms. If domestic regulations make market entry more expensive, this will lower the number of start-up firms, and thereby reduce efficiency incentives for incumbent BSS firms. Chapter 11 finds that the level of start-up costs caused by regulation has a significant negative impact on productivity performance. Another source of potential competitive pressure comes from foreign (import) competition. Although the Rome Treaty speak of the freedom to provide services in other EU member states, the 'Single European Market for Services' is still far cry from being realized. Each country has its own set of – often historically grown – rules for product-markets in services. The differences in national regulations imply that exporting BSS firms in each export country incur additional fixed costs for complying with the national product-market rules. Policy heterogeneity between EU countries thus creates market-entry costs that lower the BSS imports from other EU member states, with a negative impact on competition intensity in domestic markets.
12. *Business services have become a strategic sector in advanced economies.*[6] Weak competition lowers the contribution of the BSS industry to aggregate economic growth. Since the BSS industry has become a major source of intermediary inputs for all sectors in the EU economy, a lack of competition and cost efficiency in BSS industry has economy-wide repercussions. Improving overall competitiveness and efficiency of BSS industry may therefore strengthen this industry's contribution to overall European economic growth. Policy actions towards BSS industry are still at a embryonic step so far.[7]
13. *Need for more research and better statistics.* Finally, our book has shown how much the BSS economy still needs more research. Given its size (about the same as manufacturing in some countries), its dynamism, and its function in economic growth, the BSS industry is still 'under-researched'. The market organization and competition in BSS industry certainly requires more research. This also holds for the complex relation between in-house service production, outsourcing and offshoring.

The lack of research in these fields is partly caused by the deficient quality and quantity of statistical data on the BSS industry, even though recently the situation is improving. Further research should be based on better statistics. Some categories of business services are still too aggregate and further research would require more breakdowns by kind of activity.

Annex: business services in economic statistics

Business services are part of the so-called producer services, a group of service activities that supply a considerable part of their production to other companies as intermediary inputs. Figure 0.1 shows some conceptual relations between the most used services aggregates. Business-services sectors consist of two broad groups, the operational services that supply relatively standardized services, and the knowledge-intensive services (KIBS) that generally produce client-specific services with high knowledge content. The wider group of producer services includes business services, but also sectors like transport, logistics, construction, wholesale trade, banking, insurance, and telecommunication.

The characteristic that business services could also have been produced in-house by the client distinguishes them from other producer services such as network services (transport, energy), banking and insurance. It is hardly possible for client firms to internally provide the latter type of producer services. At a micro level, the boundaries between service sectors are often much more blurred, as firms may have secondary activities in other service sectors or even outside the service industry.

From the statistics point of view, the European Union's NACE classification, Section K represents most of the business-services sub-sectors. It includes five main categories at the 2-digit level of business services: 70 Real Estate; 71 Renting and Leasing; 72 Computer Activities; 73 Research and Development (contract research); and 74 Other Business Services. The 2-digit NACE categories correspond with the International Standard Industry Classification (ISIC) of the United Nations. The group of business services is normally understood to consist of the NACE categories 71, 72, 73 and 74. In terms of employees and number of firms, most business services firms are found in the last of these categories.[8] Chapter 2 by Ian Miles presents the statistical categories usually considered as knowledge-intensive services.

Statistical classification problems for business services are much greater than for services as a whole, or for some traditional services like banking, trade, transport or tourism. The newness of the sector, the continuous development of new activities, the proximity of one activity to another and also the lack of interest shown by statisticians have made for a multiplicity of classifications

Producer services	**Business-related services**	**Business services**	**Knowledge intensive-business services (K.I.B.S.)**	• Software and computer services
				• Strategy and management consultancy
				• Accountancy, tax and legal advise
				• Marketing services, opinion polling
				• Technical services, engineering
				• Personnel training, headhunting
			Operational business services	• Security services,
				• Facility management, cleaning
				• Administration, bookkeeping
				• Temporary labour recruitment
				• Other operational services (e.g catering, photography, translating, call centres)
		Distribution and trade services		
		Transport and logistics		
		Banking, insurance, stock exchange		
		Telecommunication, courIers		
		Energy services		
	Consumer services partly used by enterprises (business travel, company health services, social insurance services)			

Figure 0.1 Defining business services as part of producer services

and a lack, even today, of criteria for the study of business services. The fact that most business services nowadays can be found in the residual category *Other Business Services* (NACE 74) exemplifies the relatively short history of business services as an independent economic sector. The functional industry classifications (NACE, ISIC) do not start from a positive definition of business services. They use a negative statistical approach based on classification as residual (what is not in. . ., not elsewhere classified). We prefer a positive taxonomy as proposed in Figure 0.1. Here business services are classified according the type of in-house service functions they develop, complement or substitute in client firms.

The chapters presented in this book do not always use exactly the same concept of business services and sometimes concentrate on some sub-aggregates (like knowledge-intensive business services) or prefer to approach a broader range of producer services for comparative purposes.

Notes

1. Clark (1938). Later on, Clark dropped 'tertiary' and instead referred to the 'service' sector. Cf. Fisher (1939) and Maddison (2004).
2. Browning and Singelmann (1978) came up with a useful disaggregation of tertiary services, distinguishing four categories: distributive services (trade, transport and communication), producer services (banking, insurance, business services), social services (government, health, education, non-profit organizations) and personal services.
3. See also Martini (1990), Rubalcaba (1999) and Gadrey and Gallouj (1998) for positive definitions of services.
4. These lessons apply to the whole set of BSS, as well as to most of their branches. However, BSS are quite heterogeneous and some conclusions may apply more to certain BSS than others. This is particularly true when considering differences between knowledge-intensive BSS and operational BSS.
5. Guerrieri *et al.* (2005) find evidence that international trade in BSS products also goes along with international knowledge spillovers, as measured through patent citations.
6. This has been recognised by the European Commission (1998, 2003a). Studies by Arnold *et al.* (2006) and Rutherford *et al.* (2005) confirm that improved productivity in intermediary services may be a crucial factor for productivity growth in other sectors of the economy.
7. This assessment is valid for many other services as well. EU policies related to services are analysed in Rubalcaba (2007a).
8. In the latter group, most of the typical business services activities can be found at 3 or 4-digit level, namely: 74.1 Legal, auditing, market research, management consulting, etc.; 74.2 Architecture and engineering; 74.3 Technical analysis and tests; 74.4 Advertising; 74.5 Selection and supply of personnel; 74.6 Investigation and security activities; 74.7 Office Industrial Cleaning; 74.8 Other business activities (not elsewhere classified).

Part I

Business Services and Economic Growth

1
The Growth of European Business Services

Luis Rubalcaba and Henk Kox

Introduction

The most direct contribution of the business-services sector to economic growth comes from its own dynamism and expansion. The present chapter discusses the stylized facts about business-services growth in the European Union. We discuss explanatory factors and we also differentiate between business-cycle and structural elements in the sector's growth. Separate explanations will be offered for the cyclical volatility and for the structural component in the growth of business-services industry. In the final part of the chapter we analyse the characteristics of business services employment.

1.1 The magnitude of business-services growth

The business-services sector (BSS) has experienced a remarkably strong growth process during the past two decades, in terms of both employment and value added. Business services nowadays count as one of the largest economic sectors in the European economy, larger than such sectors as transport, communication, hotels and restaurants taken together. As shown in Table 1.1, more than 19 million workers in business services generate more than 1,000 billion euro, and the sector's employment and value added account for some 11 per cent of the total EU15 economy. Between 1979 and 2003, value-added growth in business services (4.2 per cent) was higher than in any other sector except telecommunications. In terms of employment, the growth of business services (4.4 per cent) far outstripped the growth of all other major sectors.

Table 1.2 provides further insight into the differences between EU countries.[1] The BSS value-added share in EU member states ranges from 3 per cent in Greece to 13–14 per cent in Ireland, France and the UK. In terms of the BSS employment shares, the intra-EU differences are somewhat smaller. The annual growth of both value added and employment in the EU15 has been more than 4 per cent. Countries with consistent high growth rates are Austria, Ireland, Luxemburg and Spain, while France, Belgium and Denmark have witnessed relatively low

Table 1.1 Key data on the growth of business services, European Union (EU15), 2003

Sector	*Value added*			*Employment*		
	Billion euro[1]	*% relative shares*	*Growth rates*[2] *1979/03*	*Thousands*	*% relative shares*	*Growth rates*[2] *1979/03*
Business services	**1,067**	**11.2**	**4.2**	**19,460**	**11.4**	**4.4**
– Renting of equipment	90	0.9	5.0	563	0.3	3.4
– Computer and related activities	183	1.9	6.6	2,450	1.4	6.1
– Research and development	37	0.4	2.4	632	0.4	1.8
– Legal, technical, advertising	472	4.9	3.8	7,037	4.1	3.8
– Other business activities, n.e.c.	286	3.0	3.9	8,778	5.1	4.8
For comparison						
All sectors	9,540	100.0	2.2	171,167	100	0.6
– Manufacturing	2,516	26.4	2.2	42,055	24.6	−1.0
– Distributive trades	937	9.8	2.3	25,943	15.2	0.9
– Transport	455	4.8	2.4	7,191	4.2	0.5
– Financial services	576	6.0	2.5	5,392	3.2	1.3

Notes: 1. Current prices. 2. Annual exponential growth rates. Value added at constant prices 1995.
Sources: Based on OECD National Accounts data (STAN), and data compiled by Groningen Growth and Development Centre GGDC (cf. O'Mahony and Van Ark, 2003).

growth rates for value added and employment. Interestingly, the EU15 countries and the USA had similar employment growth rates in business services over this long period, but the average value-added growth in the USA was higher. This differences implies that productivity growth in the EU business-services sector was weaker than in the USA.

We find a clear correlation between the share of business services and GDP per capita in Europe. Figure 1.1 plots a correlation between GDP per capita and the employment share of the BSS sector. The average values for the EU25 are used as the basis for comparison (index = 100). We indeed find the expected pattern, even within Europe. EU member states with a low income per capita all have a less developed BSS sector, while in none of the richer countries do we find a low share of BSS jobs. Countries like Portugal, Lithuania, Latvia or Slovakia are below 60 per cent of the EU25 average. Luxemburg is an outlier. The correlation coefficient is 0.75 for the whole set of 30 countries presented here. This increases to 0.85 if Luxemburg is excluded from the sample. The results imply no direction of causation, but we may infer that the development of the BSS sector is associated with a process of structural change in the economy as average income goes up.

Table 1.2 The growth rate and the share of business services value added and employment. Selected countries, 1979–2003

Country	*Relative shares in total economy, 2003*[1]		*Annual growth rates, 1979–2003*[2]	
	Value added	*Employment*	*Value added*	*Employment*
EU15	11.2	11.4	4.2	4.4
Austria	9.2	9.4	5.7	5.3
Belgium	–	14.2	3.8	3.5
Denmark	7.8	9.7	4.1	3.1
Finland	7.2	8.5	4.8	5.2
France	13.3	13.7	2.9	3.5
Germany	12.3	11.4	4.4	5.1
Greece	3.4	6.4	3.5	4.5
Ireland	14.3	7.8	5.2	6.0
Italy	11.7	10.5	4.4	6.3
Luxembourg	7.6	15.6	8.6	7.5
Netherlands	11.2	14.2	4.5	4.3
Portugal	6.5	6.6	3.6	6.6
Spain	7.1	7.4	5.3	5.4
Sweden	10.3	9.8	4.3	4.2
UK	13.5	13.7	4.6	3.2
PM: USA	11.0	11.8	4.6	4.3

Notes: 1. Current prices. 2. Annual exponential growth rates. Value added at constant prices 1995.
Sources: Based on OECD National Accounts data (STAN), extended and compiled by GGDC, see Table 1.1.

There is a second interesting finding on the basis of this empirical analysis. The four quadrants of the graph are derived from the EU25 average for both variables. If we confine ourselves to the country sample in the upper right quadrant of Figure 1.1, it appears that there is no longer a significant correlation between GDP per capita and the employment share of the BSS sector. This suggests the existence of some threshold level in the relation between both variables. The correlation does not say anything about the direction of causality with regard to this threshold level.[2]

Summarizing, the empirical evidence in this section shows that over the past decades employment in business services grew faster than in the total European economy and also faster than in the rest of the European services sector. The countries of northern and central Europe display stronger employment growth in business services than those in southern Europe. In absolute terms, job creation in the business-services sector in all countries represented a major shift in market-sector employment. The growth difference between business services and the rest of the economy was smaller for value added than for employment. Finally, for European countries we find a significant and strong positive

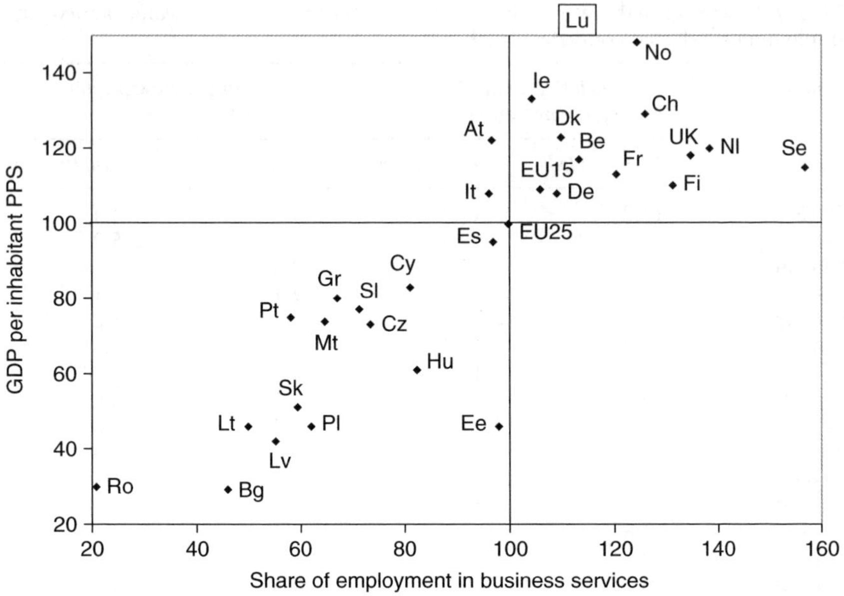

Figure 1.1 Correlation between GDP per capita and the share of business services in total employment in Europe, 2000
Source: Eurostat national account data for GDP, PPS (standardized PPP-purchasing power parity).

correlation between the average income per capita and the share of business services in total employment. This correlation holds up to some threshold level of business-services employment.

1.2 Causes for structural growth of the business-services sector

The rather spectacular growth of the business-services industry may have several explanations. A literature survey may yield a panoply of factors, related to different aspects (technology, institutions, social preferences, organizational developments). The explanations operate at different levels of analysis (micro, meso, macro). Several factors can operate at the same time, although at different levels of analysis. Other factors may hold for particular periods, for particular branches, or for countries in a particular stage of development. Rubalcaba (1999), Aiginger (2001), Kox (2001) and Miles (Chapter 2, this book) present comprehensive literature surveys on the growth factors.

Here we focus exclusively on two dominant explanations for the structural growth of business services. The first theory, defended *inter alia* by Rajan (1987) and Lewis (1988), states that the growth is an optical illusion, because existing activities and jobs in other industries are simply replaced by similar activities in business-services industry.[3] The second theory defends that structural growth of business services is a new development phase in the social division of labour. It builds on Adam Smith's classic view that specialization and scale effects form the very heart of economic progress.[4] We subsequently deal with both explanations.

Structural growth or optical illusion? If the entire growth of business-services industry would be based on a simple shift of existing in-house services jobs from other sectors to business-services firms then we could indeed speak of a purely administrative shift: a 'changing of nameplates'. It is inherent in our definition of business services that many services supplied by business-services firms *could* also have been produced *internally* by firms in other industries.[5] On average, about 40 per cent of all persons employed in manufacturing work in occupations that are more or less (business)service-related.[6] Table 1.3 sketches a range of intra-company service functions that may or may not be up for outsourcing to business-services firms.

The proposition that the growth of business services represents only an administrative change can be analysed in the same way as an analogue problem in international trade theory. Viner (1950) investigated whether economic integration between countries leads to additional trade (trade creation) or whether it represents a re-channelling of trade patterns (trade diversion).[7] Following Viner's distinction, we can distinguish two types of business-services growth:

- *Displacement growth* (trade diversion) occurs when services hitherto produced in-house by other industries are outsourced to business-services firms, with no change in the nature of the services.
- *Trade creation* occurs when business-services firms provide products to client firms that are different (higher quality, more specialized) from the in-house services that the client firms produced in-house beforehand, or that are even completely new.

It is an empirical question which of these growth-types accounts for most of the recent growth in business services. Given the heterogeneity of firms and their in-house services this in fact requires a broad survey-based research method using firm-level microdata. To our knowledge such a study does not yet exist. We therefore turn to second-best research methods based on sector-level data.

A first test is whether the share of services jobs in manufacturing has diminished over time. Figure 1.2 shows that since 1995 it has indeed declined in the UK, Denmark and France. However, it has increased in all the other EU countries, especially in Spain, Italy and Germany. These data therefore do not confirm the existence of an overall trend towards a lower share of service-related jobs in manufacturing. The test is not conclusive because the data on employment structure in manufacturing may be subject to other tendencies that affect the number of services jobs. An increasing number of manufacturing

Table 1.3 Internal service functions and externally delivered producer services

Major functions in enterprises	*Corresponding external producer services*
1. Strategy and new markets	– Management consultancy – Market research – Fairs and exhibitions
2. Information management (IT services and infrastructure)	– Computer services – Consultancy on information technologies – Telecommunication services
3. Personnel	– Selection and provision of personnel – Professional training
4. Production and technical function	– Engineering and technical services – Tests and quality control – Maintenance service and repair of equipment
5. Design functions	– Research and development – Industrial design
6. Marketing	– Advertising – Direct marketing – Public relations
7. Purchases and sales	– Distributive trades (incl. after sales services)
8. Financial resources	– Banking – Insurance – Renting and leasing
9. Administration and accounting	– Accounting and auditing – Legal services
10. Transport and logistics	– Logistics – Transport services (persons) – Transport services (merchandises) – Express courier – Real estate
11. Facility management services	– Security services – Building maintenance – Cleaning services – Catering – Environmental services / waste disposal – Energy and water services

products are nowadays sold 'encapsulated in a service jacket' (Howells 2002).[8] This in itself could cause a persistent increase in the number of service jobs in manufacturing.

A further test to establish the growth sources of the business-services sector can be based on input-output analysis. A rough approximation method is the following. Suppose we divide the total economy into three parts: *Business*

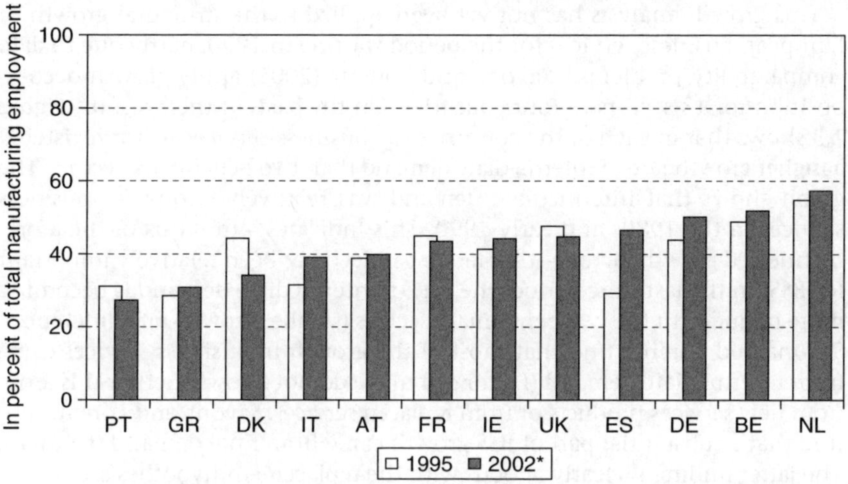

Figure 1.2 Share of employment in service-related occupations in the manufacturing sector (as % of total employment of manufacturing, 1995 and 2002)
Note: Services-related occupations cover ISCO classes 100–500, 830, 910, 933. Data for Germany are from 2001.
Source: EU Labour Force Survey 1995, 2002 (figure reproduced from Pilat and Wölfl, 2005).

Services; Other Industries (all other market sectors); and *Government* (non-markets sectors). Using decomposition methods we may break down the sources of structural growth for *Business Services,* and thus answer the question of why it has a larger share of total production and employment over time. Specifically, it may give the relative importance of the following structural growth sources:

(a) final demand in *Business Services* grows faster than in both other sectors;
(b) *Business Services* benefits most of both markets sectors from privatization (public services procurement) in the *Government* sector;
(c) the *Business Services* sector gets a larger share in total intermediary deliveries of *Other Industries;*
(d) comparing the change in value added of *Other Industries* with the change in *Business Services'* intermediary deliveries to *Other Industries*. In case of replacement growth both must be about equal.

If replacement growth were indeed the dominant reason for the growth of business services then we should find that the last two conditions (*c, d*) are satisfied. Moreover, the importance of growth source *c* for *Business Services* must be larger than that of the growth sources *a* and *b* together. A more technical description of the growth decomposition method is added as Annex at the end of this chapter.

This growth analysis has not yet been applied to the structural growth of European business services for the period starting in 1990, partly due to data comparability problems.[9] Savona and Lorentz (2005) apply growth decomposition for 13 sectors in four countries. On the basis of their results, Figure 1.3 shows that in each of the countries the business-services sector registered a higher growth rate of intermediate demand than two benchmark sectors. The graph shows that intermediate demand was relatively strong for business services in the 1980s and early 1990. This indicates – in terms of the aforementioned growth factors – that factor *c* indeed has been relatively important for BSS. In the last time period, the role of intermediate demand is becoming more in line with the two benchmark sectors (smaller growth-rate difference). Savona and Lorentz find that most of the growth in business services came from intermediate demand (factor *c*), but we do not know whether this arose from new services products or from replaced services. Savona and Lorentz also find that a substantial part of BSS growth came from final demand (factor *a*). The latter finding is clearly at odds with the replacement hypothesis.

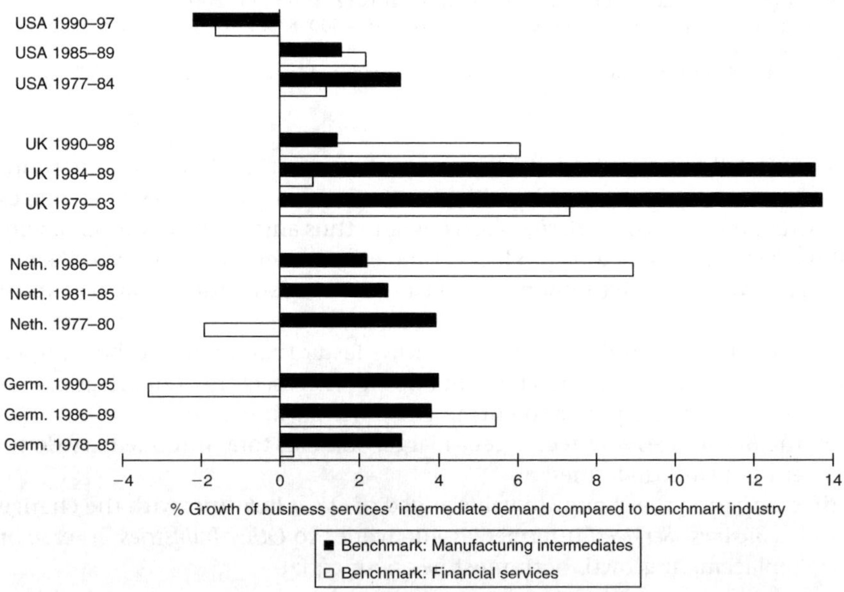

Figure 1.3 Growth rate difference of the share of intermediate demand in total output: business services compared to manufacturing industries[1)] and financial services (Germany, UK, Netherlands and USA, three sub-periods)
Note: 1) For manufacturing we used two subsectors (machinery industry and electrical-equipment industry) that both have substantial intermediate deliveries.
Source: Calculated from data in Savona and Lorentz (2006).

Since the late 1980s many empirical studies have applied some form of input–output analysis to analyse growth factors for services sectors, often at a rather high aggregation level and mostly for one specific country.[10] Most of the intermediate deliveries from business services appear to go to manufacturing, the business-services industry itself, and the public sector (for example, ECORYS-NEI 2004). The finding that the business-services industry itself has become the most intensive user of business-service inputs can hardly be reconciled with the proposition that the growth of business services is mostly due to displacement growth. This suggests that displacement growth can at best explain only a limited part of business-services growth.

Ruyssen (1990), in a study for the European Commission, found that the role of BSS subcontracting is seldom simply a transfer of employment between sectors. It often involves a new division of work between the client company and the service company providing the services. Several studies indicate that a shift has taken place from pure replacement outsourcing to service-upgrading, particularly with regard to the human-capital content of the services product.[11]

In the early 1980s most outsourced services were either low- or medium-skilled (cleaning, catering, internal and external transport, building maintenance). In the next period, from the mid-1980s until the late 1990s, many standardized in-house services became subject to outsourcing, including security services, training of personnel, administration, storage, technical testing, computer services and recruitment. Especially wage costs and scale effects derived from standardization played a dominant role in this stage of outsourcing. If replacement growth took place, it was probably most relevant in this period. Before the turn of the twenty-first century, almost all authors took it for granted that the outsourcing of in-house services from manufacturing and other industries came to the benefit of *domestic* business-services industry.[12] Since this time developments in ICT have lowered communication and coordination costs to such an extent that the international outsourcing of in-house services tasks has become more than an exotic exception (cf. Chapters 10 and 13 in this book). Due to this development a new range of standardized in-house services can be sourced from low-wage countries, including knowledge-intensive jobs of a standardized nature (cf. Van Welsum *et al.* 2006 a, b). The offshoring of standardized services tasks to low-wage countries could weaken the market position of domestic firms that produce standardized business services.[13] If anything, the offshoring tendency will therefore make the displacement-growth hypothesis less relevant for explaining the structural growth of domestic business services in Europe.

At a national level this process goes along with a change in the composition of the total labour force. Figure 1.4 illustrates the shift away from routinised jobs that is taking place in the total labour force of the USA.[14]

From the mid-1990s onwards the process of domestic outsourcing has changed gradually. Even specialist and close-to-management service activities – that to this date were considered to be the core company domains – became

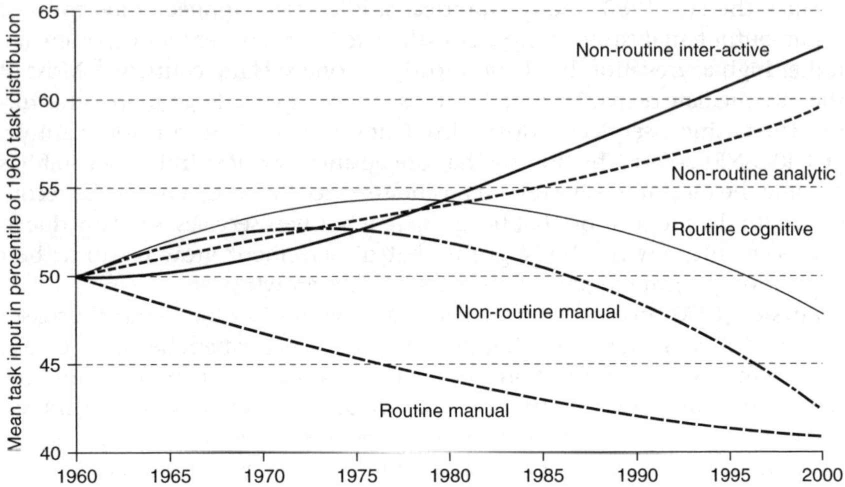

Figure 1.4 Trends in routine and non-routine task inputs in US labour force
Note: The picture is based on an analysis of the occupational structure, using census data and Current Population Survey data, using the mean 1960 task input structure as point of reference. Plotted variables depict the employment-weighted mean of each assigned percentile in the indicated year.
Source: Autor, Levy and Murnane (2003).

eligible for outsourcing. Typically, these were non-routine jobs. Knowledge-intensive services with high skill inputs gained strongly in this most recent wave of outsourcing (cf. Miles, Chapter 2 in the present book). Outsourcing of knowledge-intensive services went along with product innovation and product differentiation, generating demand for specialized services products. Since the mid-1990s, subsectors that mostly produce client-specific business services have gained most. The professional specialization and the quality of knowledge inputs of knowledge-intensive business services firms became a dominant reason for outsourcing in this stage (Kox 2002).

We may now summarize the evidence to date. Leaving international outsourcing (offshoring) apart, the available evidence suggests that *trade creation* is probably more important than *displacement growth* (trade diversion) in explaining the domestic structural growth of business services. Business services play a key role in the growing complexity and 'intermediarization' of the social division of labour.[15]

To date we have presented a helicopter-view discussion of the reasons for the structural growth of the business-services sector, thereby abstracting from various other factors that may play a role in specific sectors, countries, and subsectors. To correct for this simplification Figure 1.5 offers an integrative framework that gives a place to other explanatory factors and sub-factors

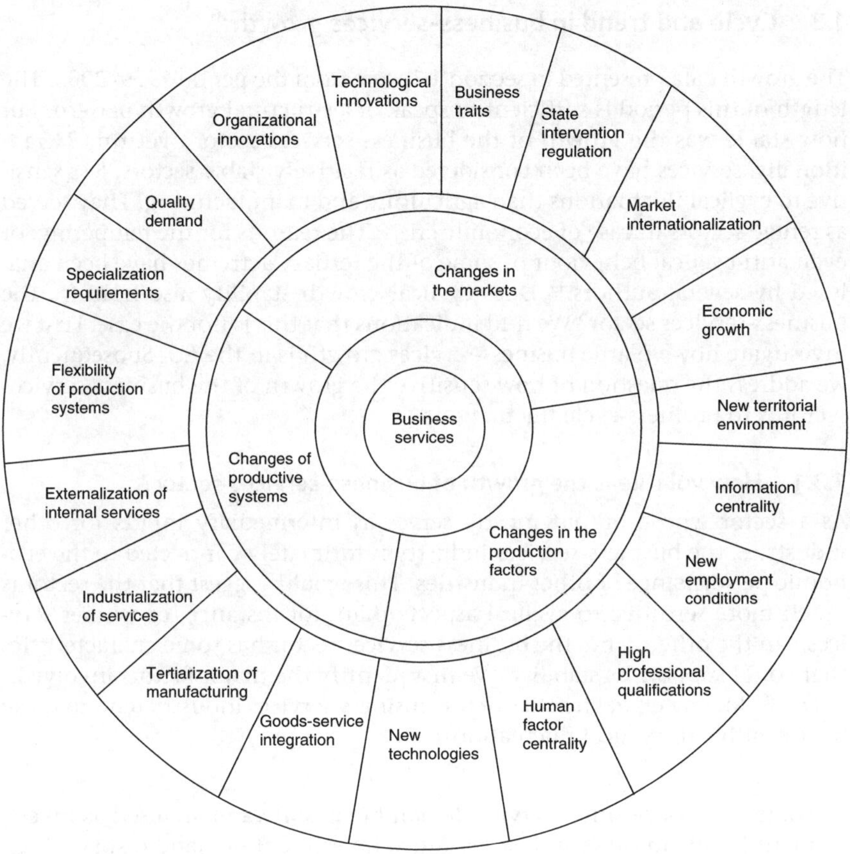

Figure 1.5 The causes that explain the emergence of business services

relating to the emergence of business services (Rubalcaba 1999). The main growth factors have been grouped into three aspects: changes in productive systems, changes in the factors of production and changes in the markets. These three aspects are pictured in the inner ring of Figure 1.5. There is a relationship between these three aspects and each of the 18 explanatory sub-factors represented in the outer ring. These 18 sub-factors include a wide range of economic and social changes that may explain the growing role of services: new consumer and productive needs and demands, income growth, technological changes, outsourcing, upskilling, the integration of markets and globalization, inter-sectoral differences in productivity growth and the role of the state and public services. The diagram allows for the possible relationships between the two rings.

1.3 Cycle and trend in business-services growth[16]

The growth data presented in section 1.1 were from the period 1979–2003. The length of this period is sufficient to speak of a structural growth pattern. But how stable was the growth of the business-services sector over time? Traditionally, services have been considered as relatively stable sectors, less sensitive to cyclical fluctuations than agriculture and manufacturing. They served as refuge sectors in case of economic crisis. The reasons for the tempering, or even anti-cyclical behaviour of some of the tertiary activities have been analysed by several authors.[17] Does cyclical growth stability also hold for the business-services sector? We find indications that this is not the case. First we investigate how volatile business-services growth is in the EU. Subsequently, we address the question of how sensitive the growth of the business-services sector is to business-cycle fluctuations.

1.3.1 How volatile is the growth of business-services sector?

As a sector whose output mostly serves as intermediary inputs for other industries, the business-services industry is intimately connected to the economic performance of other industries. This would suggest that the sector is much more sensitive to cyclical aspects than, for instance, consumer services. On the other hand, the business-services sector has some characteristics that could support its stability. We first identify the major factors involved.

The following characteristics of the business-services industry tend to make it susceptible to cyclical fluctuations:

- Some parts of business service demand (e.g. software) are used as investment inputs in other industries. Since investment demand displays high cyclical fluctuations, this exposes some parts of business services to cyclical patterns.
- The sector's high degree of integration with the manufacturing industry may increase volatility.
- Compared to other service sectors, business services have a higher exposure to international competition, which could expose the sector to more cyclical effects.
- The business-services sector employs more part-time, temporary and self-employed workers than is the average in the other main economic sectors. This segment of the labour market tends to be most seriously affected by cyclical effects.
- The business-services industry has high birth (entry) and death (exit) rates for firms.[18] In the downturn of the cycle, a relatively large group of firms that entered during the upswing are 'shaken out'. In the upswing, many start-ups enter this sector as self-employed firms.

- Flexibility arises from the fact that the labour market for business services is, in many cases, more liberalized than that of its products, so that employment may be more volatile than value added.
- The business-services industry is a strong client of itself; this means that a cyclical downturn in other client industries will be multiplied.

Apart from these factors, the business-services sector also has some characteristics that could contribute to growth stability over time:

- Job market characteristics: the on-average high qualification of workers in business services may produce a high degree of labour hoarding during the downswing of the business cycle.
- Sharp cyclical fluctuations are often found in sectors whose products can easily be stocked. As with other service sectors, this does not apply, thus contributing to limited business cycle sensitivity.
- Some 25 per cent of the intermediate outputs of the business-services industry go to sectors (public sector, trade, utilities) that are relatively stable over the business cycle.[19]
- The fact that some professions and activities are still relatively heavily regulated (e.g. European Commission 2002a) could dampen the effect of business fluctuations.

As far as business services are concerned, we can expect them to behave differently from the services sector as a whole. The aforementioned factors suggest that the business-services sector has a higher exposure to cyclical effects than most service sectors, but there are also some compensatory characteristics. Moreover, the level of business-cycle volatility may be different in various parts of the business-services industry. The behaviour, for instance, of advanced and personalized services, where labour hoarding can be important, may be very different from that of operational and standardized services, where labour can be hired and fired more easily. It is a matter for empirical analysis to determine whether pro-cyclical or anti-cyclical effects dominate in the behaviour of business-services growth in the EU member states.

1.3.2 Trend estimation and cyclical components in business-services growth

The present section breaks down the growth of the business-services industry into cyclical and trend effects. This is done by applying the most widespread practice of decomposing, i.e. the procedure adopted by Hodrick and Prescott (1980). They propose a filter (henceforth referred to as the HP filter) for decomposing cyclical and trend effects. Advantages of the filter are its flexibility, simplicity and reproducibility.[20] Figure 1.6 shows the development over the business cycle of value added for business services (and – separately – also computer services), manufacturing and the total economy.

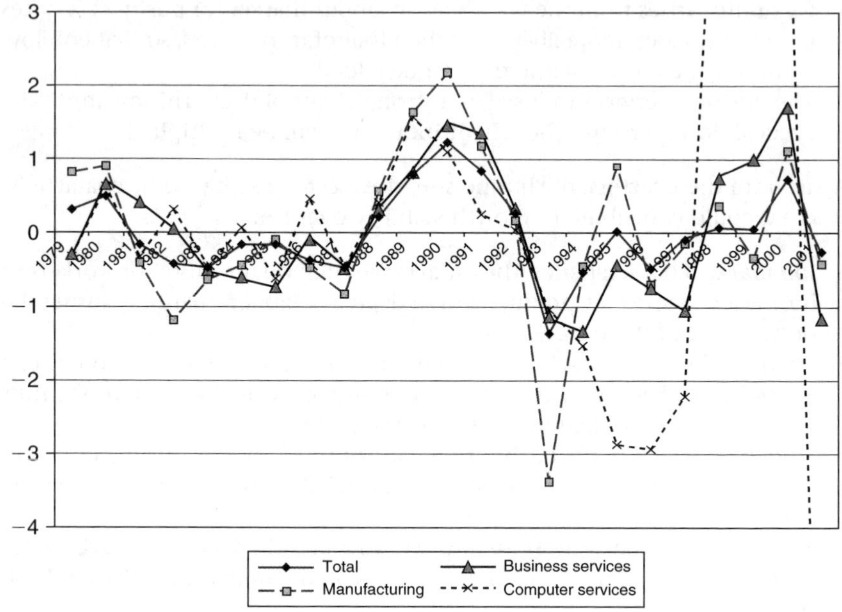

Figure 1.6 Cyclical growth as annual deviation from long-term value-added growth, EU15, 1979–2001 (percentage of deviation)
Note: The Y-axis is derived from total value added minus structural trend in value added (derived from HP filter). Data: based on National Accounts data (STAN) and data by GGDC (cf. O'Mahony and Van Ark 2003).

In contrast to many other service activities, business services displayed consistently pro-cyclical behaviour between 1979 and 2001. They behaved similarly to manufacturing, growing more than other sectors in expansion phases (1978–80, 1988–91 and 1997–2000) and suffering more the effects of economic crisis (1981–84, 1991–94, 1996–97 and 2000–02). The tendencies towards a closer link between the manufacturing cycle and the value added of business services contribute to the progressive inter-relation of the sector with the other industrial branches and the growing globalization of the service markets. However, there is a difference between manufacturing and business services. From 1995 onwards manufacturing appeared to become less cyclical than in the preceding period (1979–95), while in business services we see the opposite development: they became more pro-cyclical than manufacturing. The separate data for computer services show that this may be due to the influence of ICT-related services such as computer services during the boom and crisis of the new 'e-economy' starting in 2000.

Figure 1.7 shows that the high volatility of business-services employment with respect to the cycle contrasts with that of most other service sectors. Some

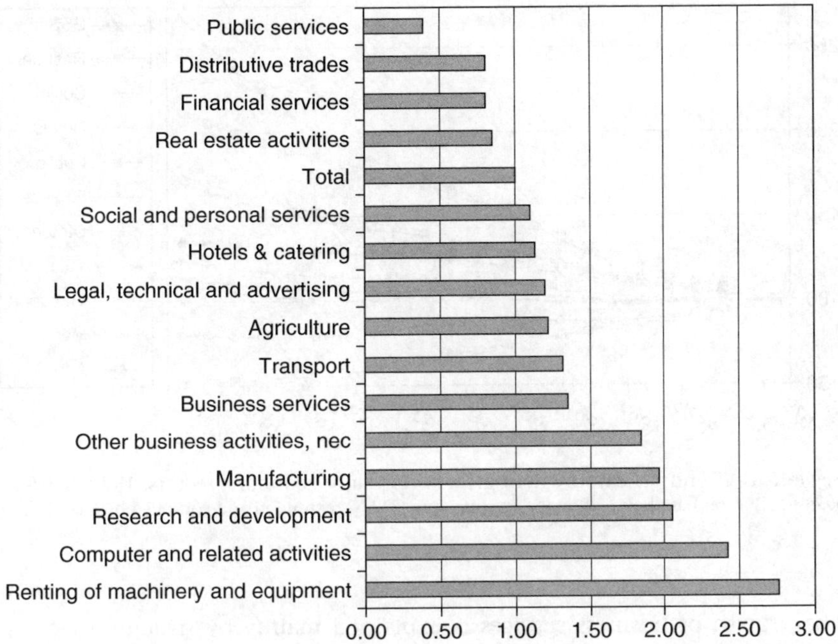

Figure 1.7 Relative volatility in business-services employment and other major economic sectors, 1979–2001
Sources: HP filter based on National Accounts data (STAN). extended and compiled by GGDC.

sectors (public services, distributive trade and financial services) display less volatility than the economy average. Employment fluctuations in business services are particularly strong. This indicator is marked by labour flexibility and by the growing integration of services in manufacturing industry. Advanced services such as computer services and R&D services are more volatile than those operational services included under the category 'other business services'.

These empirical results demonstrate that the sector has a strong pro-cyclical influence on employment, with much more volatility than the economy average. High integration with industry and labour flexibility may be two explanatory factors.[21] However, the strong sensitivity of business services to economic cycle could also be understood as a weakness because of the 'temporary' character of business services: when things go wrong, enterprises reduce their costs and cancel many business-services contracts, but when they go right, enterprises decide to expand, and more business services are contracted. The cyclical behaviour of business services cannot explain the continuous growth of the sector in both absolute and relative terms during the last quarter century.

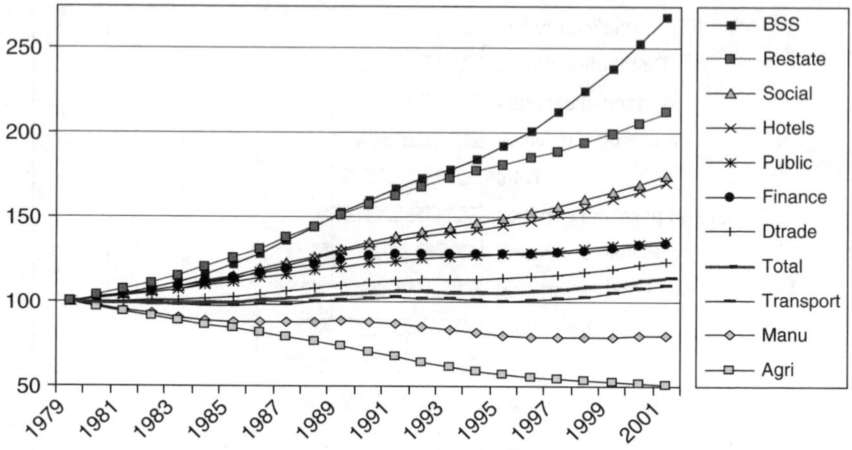

Figure 1.8 Trends in employment growth for major economic sectors, 1979–2001
Sources: HP filter based on National Accounts data (STAN). extended and compiled by GGDC.

The growth of business services is explained mainly by structural factors, absorbing most of the recession effects. That explains why only in few countries and few sub-sectors recessions have absolute negative influences in business services.

Figure 1.8 depicts development trends in employment for major economic sectors. The difference between the structural growth of business services and the rest of the sectors is marked, even though the business-services sector starts from a relatively small absolute size.

We conclude that to date the structural growth trend for the business-services industry has dominated its relatively high cyclical volatility. The flipside of the coin is that once the structural growth of the business-services falters, the larger weight of business services in the total could increase the intensity of cyclical volatility across the entire economy. In several European countries, the cyclical prospects of the business-services sector are already being used as an early warning indicator for cyclical developments throughout the entire economy. It must be stressed, however, that the structural growth of business services in many EU member states does not yet seem to be exhausted.

1.4 Employment and jobs profiles in business services

Business-services employment in Europe has grown at an impressive annual rate of 4.5 per cent between 1979 and 2001, a higher growth rate than in any other major economic sector. In this section we offer further discussion of the characteristics of employment in business services, based on data from the

European Labour Force Surveys. First, the section analyses whether business-service jobs are different from jobs in other industries. Secondly, we pay some attention to country differences in employment profiles. Finally, there is a special subsection on education and training.

Anything special in business-service jobs? Business services are sometimes considered to be a source of flexible employment, providing new opportunities for women, young people, part-time workers, tele-workers and so on. In some sub-sectors, such as consultancy services or ICT services, all these assumptions hold to a large extent. However, when one considers business services as a whole – including operational services and professional services – the sector is so different from other economic sectors. Table 1.4 provides a comparison between business services and other economic sectors in terms of job profiles.

Apart from the very high rates of self-employment, business services do not lead in any of the relevant employment characteristics. The employment profile is very similar to that observed in the economy as a whole. Business services offer slightly more opportunities for women, young people and part-time jobs than other economic sectors, but less than in the case of hotels, restaurants and personal and social services. Compared with manufacturing industries, business services employ many more women, young workers and part-time workers, but the results are similar to those observed in other service activities. In terms of temporary work or the number of hours worked, the sector also presents a situation similar to the total economy, but slightly 'better' in the sense of there being less temporary work and fewer hours worked. The only clear characteristic specific to business-service jobs is the rate of self-employment, which is significantly higher than for other major economic sectors. This is explained by the presence of professional services and ICT professionals working independently.

Country employment profiles. Analysing differences between countries, the employment profile of large countries such as Germany, France or the United Kingdom deviate hardly at all from the EU total. There is a significant share of women and young workers in countries as different as Luxembourg, Portugal, Cyprus and Spain. There are more older workers in some new EU member states such as the Czech Republic, Poland or Estonia, but other Eastern EU countries have higher percentages than for EU15. Greece, Italy and the Czech Republic lead the self-employment rates, while Lithuania, Luxembourg, Finland, Norway or Rumania have the lowest rates. Spain and Portugal have the highest temporary employment shares (28–9 per cent), followed by Slovenia and Poland. On the opposite side we find Austria, Hungary, Belgium, Denmark, the Slovak Republic and the UK with low rates of temporary employment (6–8 per cent).

Remarkable intra-EU differences exist with regard to the part-/full-time composition of employment. Part-time employment can be considered as an indicator of labour market flexibility. The leading country in part-time schemes

Table 1.4 Characteristics of labour markets by economic sector, EU25, 2003

	% women in total	*% 15–39 people*	*% self-employment*	*% part-time jobs*	*% temporary work*	*Average hours first job*	*Average hours second job*
Business services	44.6	54.3	**21.4**	18.5	12.5	37.2	11.8
PM							
Total all sectors	43.7	50.1	14.7	17.0	12.7	37.4	12.4
Manufacturing	30.1	52.2	7.4	6.7	9.9	38.8	12.8
Services	53.0	50.1	13.1	19.8	12.5	36.5	11.5
Distributive trades	48.4	56.0	20.6	19.8	11.5	38.0	12.8
Hotels & restaurants	54.5	**60.6**	20.1	24.4	**19.2**	39.4	13.5
Transport & communications	25.8	47.9	11.1	9.1	7.7	**40.2**	**14.0**
Finance	50.7	53.4	7.4	12.5	5.7	37.3	10.4
Public administration	44.4	44.1	0.0	11.7	10.6	36.7	11.8
Other services	**70.3**	44.8	9.2	**26.5**	15.1	33.5	10.6

Source: Eurostat, Labour Force Survey, 2004.

is the Netherlands, where close to half the employment in business services is part-time. In Germany, Austria, the UK, Sweden and Denmark, part-time working in services is also much higher than in industry, but shares are 20–30 per cent of the total working population. In Italy, Spain, Portugal and Greece, the part-time shares are extremely low in all sectors. In computer services, part-time shares are not much larger than in industry, even in countries such as the Netherlands or Denmark.

Between 1996 and 2003, part-time working increased hardly in all EU15 business services. The use of female part-time employment is nearly twice that of men and women jointly (32 per cent versus 18 per cent at the EU15 level), with some countries (for example Denmark) far outstripping that picture. However, trends do not show a marked increase in the use of this working arrangement in business services.

Country differences with regard to the average number of hours worked may reflect national variations in labour legislation and collective bargaining systems. In 2003, the average worker in EU business services worked 37.2 hours. For full-time workers, the United Kingdom emerges as the country where workers (in NACE sector K) work longest, with 44.3 hours, followed by Germany (43.9) and Greece (43.7). Most countries report figures above the 'standard' 40 hours. Overall we find that the gap between the number of working hours for part-timers and for full-timers has become smaller between 1996 and 2003.[22]

Education and training profile of business services. The sector, in general, has a very strong orientation towards higher education, much more than most other industrial or service sectors. This can be seen in Figure 1.9. In manufacturing and total services, the education profile is dominated by the intermediate educational level, while there are more workers with low education levels, particularly in manufacturing.

The business-services sector consists of equipment renting, ICT services, contract R&D and *Other Business Services*. In the sectors of computer services and R&D services, the share of highly educated people is impressive, particularly, in R&D services. It is also high in *Other Business Services*, despite the fact that this aggregate also includes sub-sectors such as cleaning or security services, which employ many low-skilled workers. *Other Business Services accounts for the majority* of business-services employment. In equipment renting and real estate the educational profiles are similar to the total services average.

In order to add a time dimension, Figure 1.9 also pictures the employment share of highly educated workers in 1996. In all economic sectors, the share of highly educated increased between 1996 and 2003. This also holds for the business-services sectors, even if they were already very much geared towards this high profile in 1996.

A further indication of the high educational profile in business services can be derived from the percentage of business-services enterprises that provide their workers with any type of training. It may reflect the extent to which workers are

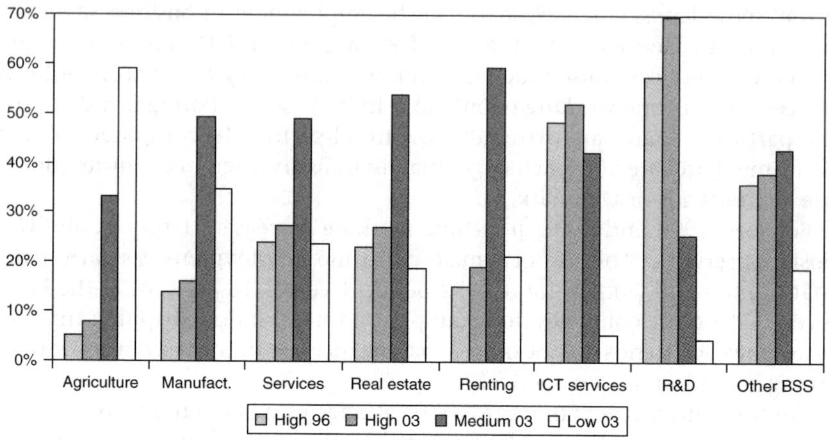

Figure 1.9 Education attainment levels by major economic activity and business services, EU15 countries, 2003
Source: Based on Eurostat data. Labour Force Survey 2004.

prepared to adapt to new requirements and manage to deal with increasing organizational and work complexity. Data for 2000 from the European Labour Force Survey indicate that in all EU15 countries, business services invests more in providing Continuous Vocational Training (CVT) to their workers than the average for the total economy. Moreover, it also appears that the average costs of CVT courses are much higher in business services than in the rest of the economy. This may reflect a higher level of specialization and knowledge input in these courses. There are strong differences among European countries in terms of the percentage of business-services firms that use CVT training for their employees. For example, the percentage of Spanish and Portuguese enterprises spending resources on training is less than 50 per cent that of their Dutch or Danish counterparts. In the countries where the percentage of enterprises providing courses is higher (Denmark, Ireland and Netherlands), the training costs per course is also higher.

1.5 Conclusions

The business-services sector has experienced a remarkably strong growth process over the course of the past two decades, in terms of both employment and value added. Business services today count as one of the largest economic sectors in the European economy – larger than such sectors as transport, communication, hotels and restaurants taken together. The sector's employment and value added account for 11 per cent and 12 per cent, respectively of the total EU15 economy. Value-added growth during the last two decades was higher than in any other sector except telecommunications.

Regarding employment, the growth of business- services far outstripped the growth of any other sector. For European countries we find a significant and strong positive correlation between the average income per capita and the share of business services in total employment. This correlation holds up to some threshold level of business-services employment.

This chapter considered the causes of structural growth in the business-services industry. Partly, the growth may have been caused by outsourcing of existing in-house services jobs from other sectors to the business-services industry, especially in the 1980s and in the early 1990s. Subsectors that produce standardized business services contributed most to the growth process in this period. Since the mid-1990s, a shift has occurred. The growth of business services especially reflects a growing complexity and specialization in the social division of labour between industries. In this stage, many knowledge-intensive and non-routine services tasks became eligible for outsourcing to independent services firms. However, this was seldom a simple substitution of pre-existing in-house services jobs. Professional specialization and product innovation often also caused the nature of the service product to change. Since the mid-1990s, those subsectors that predominantly produce client-specific services products contributed most to the structural growth of business-services industry.

The recent tendency to 'offshore' some standardized services tasks from suppliers in low-wage countries may weaken the market position of domestic firms that produce standardized business services. As a consequence, the displacement-growth hypothesis will become even less relevant for explaining the present structural growth of business services in Europe.

We have also paid ample attention to the relation between structural and cyclical elements in the growth of the business-services industry in Europe. Traditionally, services were considered as relatively stable sectors, less sensitive to cyclical fluctuations than agriculture and manufacturing. They served as refuge sectors in case of economic crisis. Closer analysis shows that the business-services sector has a higher exposure to cyclical effects than most service sectors, but there are also some compensatory characteristics. Moreover, the business-cycle volatility may be different in various parts of the business-services industry. The empirical analysis concludes that the structural growth trend for the business-services industry has until now dominated its relatively high cyclical volatility.

Business-services jobs on average appear to have no special characteristics compared with other economic sectors. There are two major characteristics of business-services which can – to a certain extent – be considered 'special'. The first is the high incidence of self-employment, especially in professional and knowledge-intensive business services. The second is the high profile of educational attainment levels and the relatively strong importance of professional training in the sector. The importance of know-how in business services is epitomized by the large number of enterprises providing their staff with continuous vocational training courses, as well as the greater amount of resources used on those courses.

Annex: Accounting for decomposition of structural growth of the business-services sector

In order to analyse the causes of the structural growth of business services compared to the rest of the economy, a simple input-output system may do, as described in Kox (2001). We distinguish three sectors: business-services (BSS) industry, other market industries and non-market sectors, represented by the suffices B, M and Q, respectively. The input–output system is:

$$x = Ry \tag{1.1}$$

in which x is a vector of gross production, R is the Leontief inverse matrix (3×3 dimension) of intermediate deliveries, and y is a vector of final demand. The growth of gross production between period 1 and period 0 is given by:

$$\Delta x = x_1 - x_o = R_1 y_1 - R_o y_o = \Delta R\, y_o + R_o \Delta y + \Delta R\, \Delta y \tag{1.2}$$

The change in final demand can be expressed in terms of the initial final demand and a row vector (f) that gives growth percentages of total final demand per sector, so that:

$$\Delta x = \Delta R\, y_o + R_o\, f y_o + \Delta R\, f y_o \tag{1.3}$$

The base year shares of final demand are used as weights for the growth rates. The framework so far can be applied straightforwardly for tracing the causes of the structural growth rate difference between the B sector and the M sector:

$$\dot{x}_B - \dot{x}_M = \frac{\Delta x_B}{x_{Bo}} - \frac{\Delta x_M}{x_{Mo}} \tag{1.4}$$

After filling in all elements from the full i/o system, the structural growth rate difference between the B sector and the M sector can be decomposed like in equation (1.3):

$$\begin{aligned}
\dot{x}_B - \dot{x}_M = {} & \dot{y}_B\, y_{Bo}\left[\frac{r_{BBo} + \Delta r_{BB}}{x_{Bo}} - \frac{r_{MBo} + \Delta x_{MB}}{x_{Mo}}\right] + y_{Bo}\left[\frac{\Delta r_{BB}}{x_{Bo}} - \frac{\Delta r_{MB}}{x_{Mo}}\right] \\
& + \dot{y}_M\, y_{Mo}\left[\frac{r_{BMo} + \Delta r_{BM}}{x_{Bo}} - \frac{r_{MMo} + \Delta x_{MM}}{x_{Mo}}\right] + y_{Mo}\left[\frac{\Delta r_{BM}}{x_{Bo}} - \frac{\Delta r_{MM}}{x_{Mo}}\right] \\
& + \dot{y}_Q\, y_{Qo}\left[\frac{r_{BQo} + \Delta r_{BQ}}{x_{Bo}} - \frac{r_{MQo} + \Delta x_{MQ}}{x_{Mo}}\right] + y_{Qo}\left[\frac{\Delta r_{BQo}}{x_{Bo}} - \frac{\Delta r_{MQo}}{x_{Mo}}\right]
\end{aligned} \tag{1.5}$$

Using this growth decomposition equation we may distinguish between three factors that could explain structural growth of the business-services industry:

- final demand in B sector grows faster than in both other sectors ($\dot{y}_B > \dot{y}_M, \dot{y}_Q$);
- the B sector benefits most from privatization in Q sector ($\Delta r_{BQ} > \Delta r_{MQ}$);

- the B sector gets a larger share in the intermediary deliveries of the M sector ($[\Delta r_{BM} - \Delta r_{MM}]y_{Mo} > 0$), which could be replacement growth if it goes along with an at least equivalent shrinking of value added in the M sector.

Notes

1. Apart from possible statistical biases, the country results may also reflect different market situations and sectoral specialisations.
2. Either there is a level of BSS employment beyond which income growth per capita depends on other factors, or there is a level of income per capita beyond which economic wealth may be derived as well from BSS as from other economic sectors.
3. Rajan (1987) and Lewis (1988) find empirically that business-services growth is due to employment substitution inside the companies as a result of subcontracting the required services outside the company. The characteristics and significance of their statistical results have, however, been called into question by Perry (1992).
4. The theory has been developed further by, *inter alia*, Stigler (1951), Edwards and Starr (1987) and Francois (1990).
5. For our definition of business services see the Introduction of this book.
6. The following count as services-related occupations are: legislators, senior officials and managers, professionals and associate professionals, clerks, service workers and shop and market sales workers, as well as drivers, sales and services elementary occupations and transport workers (Wölfl 2004).
7. Cf. also Meade (1955).
8. For instance, producers of photocopying machines now sell x months of problem-free photocopying instead of only the hardware, just as producers of airplane engines sell y hours of problem-free flying. This means an increase of manufacturing jobs into downstream production stages (sales, consulting, maintenance, insurance, leasing).
9. Amounts must be expressed in constant prices and a correction is necessary for that part of growth that is due to growth in final output of *Other Industries*. The test can be done for most EU countries as soon as comparable input-output tables in constant prices for the 1990s are available. A large ongoing EU project, EUKLEMS (http://www.euklems.net), in which many national statistical and research institutes co-operate, may yield these results in some years.
10. Cf. the empirical growth studies on producer and business services by Beyers and Lindahl (1996a), Kutscher (1988), Tschetter (1987), Fontaine (1988), Oosterhaven and Hoen (1998), Klodt *et al.* (1997), Peneder *et al.* (2000), Wölfl (2004), Perry (1990), De Bandt (1995a, 1999), Kox (2001), Pilat and Wölfl (2005), Coe (2000), Savona and Lorentz (2005).
11. For example, Peneder *et al.* (2000), Beyers and Lindahl (1996), De Bandt (1995a; 1999); Coe (2000); Kox (2002; 2001).
12. An exception was Feenstra and Hanson (1999) who also looked at international dimensions of outsourcing.
13. Recent trends towards the offshoring of some business services such as call centres and ICT services have led to fears in the US and Europe about the migration of jobs to low-wages countries like India. Some estimates say that more than two million jobs in the US and one million in Europe will move to developing countries (e.g. McCarthy 2002). See chapter 12 in this volume.

14. As more routinized manual jobs and standardized knowledge-intesive jobs are sourced from low-wage countries this reduces the scope for future replacement growth by the domestic business-services industry smaller. An increasing part of the remaining jobs will be characterized by non-routinized services tasks.
15. In Chapter 4 we elaborate further on this issue.
16. The authors thank Pilar Bengoechea of DG ECFIN (European Commission), for her contribution on this section.
17. For example, Elfring (1988); Cuadrado and del Río (1993); Lee (1996); Filardo (1997); Petersen and Strongin (1996).
18. This reinforces the 'lame duck' effect or the increase of productivity during recessions (Caballero and Hammour, 1991).
19. However, the anti-cyclical part played by the public sector may have declined over the past decade, as the result of the control over the public deficit and less use of open-ended contracts by the national administrations.
20. Modern dynamic general equilibrium theory advises against making a distinction between trend and cyclical effects, based upon the argument that both growth and business cycles are determined by fundamentally the same factors. In this section we use the HP trend and cycle decomposition for descriptive purposes rather than for separate explanations of trend and cycle developments.
21. Thus, it is unsurprising that the volatility of business services is consistently higher from the beginning of the eighties onwards. Since then, processes of market flexibilisation and inter-industrial integration have taken place, which have had a very powerful influence on business services.
22. The average EU part-timer in NACE sector K worked 18.6 hours in 2000, around seven minutes less to working tasks than was the case in 1995. On the other hand, the average number of hours worked under the full-time regime in sector K was 42.6 in 2000, which represents a 20 minute decrease with respect to the figure reported five years earlier (42.9). Hence, the gap between the number of hours worked under full-time and part-time regimes appears to have diminished during the last five years (data from Eurostat Labour Force Surveys).

2

Business Services and Their Users: A Literature Review

Ian Miles

Introduction

This chapter reviews the literature regarding the relationship between business service (BSS) firms and their clients, especially in terms of the ways in which BSS contribute to client performance. The literature is very widely scattered, and unevenly developed – some BSS have received little attention, others a great deal, and various aspects of performance receive different amounts of emphasis. The literature contains much evidence and argument as to the positive contributions of BSS to client performance. With the caveats mentioned before about differential focus, there have been many studies that attempt to provide solid evidence for BSS contributions, and some analysis of how they are effected. There has been relatively little attention to the conditions which help – or hinder – the realization of these positive outcomes: a wealth of practical experience on this matter has not been complemented by much systematic research. Issues such as the capacity of clients to make effective use of BSS, and the dangers associated with outsourcing of core functions, have received some attention, and further research needs to explore the determinants of more and less successful BSS use in more depth. This is highly policy-relevant, given the important role that BSS play in national and local innovation systems.

2.1 The range and rise of business services

BSS are services that are contributing to the *business processes* of organizations – including public and voluntary bodies as well as enterprises in the private sector. The contribution of BSS to other enterprises attracts particular interest, but public sectors are often major users of certain BSS. BSS cover a wide range of activities, which is recognised in recent elaborations of industrial classification schemes. Statistically, BSS sectors are identified in NACE (Rev.1) as falling within section K (real estate, renting and business activities – often statistics are only presented at this fairly high level of aggregation). The range of activities is rather wide. NACE 71.1 and 71.21–23 cover *Leasing & renting*: Renting of transport and construction equipment; Renting of office machinery incl. computers.

Then we move into more knowledge-intensive business services (KIBS), marked by a high level of graduate employment. *Computer Services* are covered by NACE 72.1–6: Hardware consultancy; Software consultancy; Data processing; Database activities. NACE 73.1, 73.2 cover *Research and Development* services, on natural sciences and engineering, and on social sciences and humanities. Other more technology-related activities are captured in NACE 74.2, 74.3 *Technical Services*: Architectural; and Technical testing and analysis. Less technology-oriented services are classified in NACE 74.11–.12, 74.14 *Professional Services*: Legal activities; Accounting & tax consultancy; Management consulting; and in NACE 74.13, 74.4 *Marketing* services: Market research; Advertising.

The remaining BSS are typically less knowledge-intensive, though there are firms and probably subsectors with high levels of graduate employment within some of these. They are classified as *Labour recruitment* NACE 74.5 (Labour recruitment and provision of personnel); *Operational services* NACE 74.6, 74.7 (Security activities; Industrial cleaning) and (inevitably) *Other* NACE 74.81–84 (Secretarial and translation activities; Packing; Fairs & exhibitions).

When Harry Greenfield (1966) wrote his pioneering study of producer services, innovation featured hardly at all as a driver of outsourcing. He would have found examples of computer and R&D service companies being employed by the private sector. But new technologies and changing products and markets have led firms to realize that they need to acquire new capabilities. BSS have come to the fore as a way of negotiating these challenges. The interrelationships between BSS in general and other economic activities remain poorly understood, and the relevant literature is very scattered.[1] For example, management research has examined the role of business services in terms of outsourcing – seen positively as enabling enterprises to concentrate on their core competencies, seen more critically in terms of loss of organizational memory. Innovation researchers and regional geographers have examined the role of business services in innovation networks and in the diffusion of knowledge. Studies of knowledge management and intellectual property systems have examined how business services tackle these issues. The present volume draws together many of these perspectives.

2.2 Externalization and outsourcing

The terms 'outsourcing' and 'externalization' can be misleading. Using a BSS does not necessarily mean that a previously in-house service function is now being sourced externally. A great deal of the growth of BSS is not a matter of switching to more efficient external supply of functions, but a matter of organizations responding to external challenges that require capabilities that did not exist in-house. While in principle the client can be seen as deciding between in-house provision and the external sourcing of a service, rapidly establishing or acquiring in-house capabilities to deal with a major technical or environmental challenge is often impractical, at least in the short term.[2] Indeed, it may even be difficult to develop capabilities to manage the support that a BSS may be employed to provide. The contexts, processes and consequences of outsourcing are themselves evolving as the business environment changes. Even the more routine operations, whose 'outsourcing' or 'offshoring' to remote data processing and call centre services was associated with the first wave of research interest in this topic, are now providing services that are significantly different from those yielded by earlier generations of offshore services, let alone earlier, in-house, sales, marketing and after-sales departments. Simplistic models of economic rationality fail to take account of the considerable learning processes (and thus investments of time and energy) required to undertake new activities, and to recognise the changing nature of these activities.

Economic analyses of BSS use tend to focus on the 'information asymmetries' resulting from the intangibility, complexity and specificity of many services, which cannot readily be demonstrated prior to production and consumption. The very unequal knowledge about just what will be delivered and how it will be produced helps explain why service sectors are often highly regulated or self-regulated, and why service firms so often seek to demonstrate their adherence to professional or quality control standards. De Bandt (1995b) noted five ways in which clients of BSS might suffer information deficits. Especially when the services in question are more specialized or knowledge-based, it may be difficult for the client to:

1. Establish the competence and experience of BSS to deal with relevant problems.
2. Accurately assess the skills required to deal with the specific problems that are confronted – and to match these to the BSS' offerings.
3. Agree with the BSS on the precise services to be rendered, and/or the criteria for assessing their quality.
4. Estimate whether this is a routine or very challenging task for the BSS, and how much effort they will have to dedicate to supply the service.
5. Determine how far the BSS is responsible for any problems arising, when the effectiveness of the service can be affected by many factors (including client responsiveness as well as unpredictable external circumstances).

An influential line of economic analysis concerns the notion of transaction costs, drawing on Williamson (1981: 552–3) who notes that the 'costs of planning, adapting, and monitoring task completion' vary according to the governing structures adopted. Internalizing functions by producing them internally is seen as the archetypal *hierarchy* option, as opposed to the *market* option of buying them from outside contractors. Decisions and the results of decisions about internalization or externalization of BSS functions will be impacted not only by the costs of production of the service, but also by these transaction costs. He discusses three transaction cost criteria:

1. *Asset specificity* – how far specialized investments are required to perform the function. The asset specificity of many business service functions – requiring investment in specialized equipment or knowledge – promotes their externalization.[3]
2. *Metering* how readily contractors' attainment of the specifications of the contract can be monitored and measured. As noted by de Bandt, this is a recurrent challenge for BS clients when the product is intangible and ill-defined.
3. *Frequency of contracting* – how often subsequent rounds of bargaining are required after a first contract has been let. The nature of many BSS also requires long-term relationships (such as investments of time in establishing trust, in understanding the client organization, and so on.).

Transaction cost analysis has provided a helpful terminology for examining the complex and diverse business relationships established between BSS and their clients. For instance, Brown and Potosk (2001) apply the framework in a statistical analysis of government decisions about service provision. But often the terminology is used much more loosely, perhaps because of the dynamic and changing nature of BSS activities, with interactive learning on the part of BSS and clients, which makes the determinants of specific choices complex and variable. The continual development of new strategies and even of new actors in the business landscape may mean that transaction cost analysis is more of a tool for examining where bottlenecks and problems have been confronted, than a guide for detailed analysis and forecasting.[4]

In addition to such attempts to understand the economic basis of decisions about the use or non-use of BSS, a series of studies have set out to examine the impacts of BSS use in terms of economic performance indicators. In Chapter 5 of this book Paul Baker examines such studies, suggesting that there are methodological flaws that make it difficult to assess the validity of their conclusions.[5] These conclusions have generally been that BSS users are rather superior performers in terms of indicators such as productivity and output growth. But the research based on input–output tables is restricted to comparison of sectors in terms of BSS use and its correlates. There is a strong possibility that the very different processes and operating conditions of different sectors mean that these sectors have inherently different requirements for service functions (and rates of change in such requirements). The factors that create these requirements plausibly contribute to the gross variations in performance. Increased use of BSS is likely to influence firm- and sector-level performance, but such influences need to be explored and explained.

2.3 Geography and the spatial dimensions of BSS

Regional and economic geographers were among the pioneers of research into business services (often labelled 'producer services' in this literature), often being concerned with the contribution of BSS to regional economies and the possibility that more peripheral regions might be disadvantaged since BSS tend to cluster around core metropolitan areas. (Thus Hansen 1994, indicates that the growth performance of the economies of US cities is related to the size of the KIBS sectors in these economies.) Many case studies of business services' role in European regional development were associated with the European Commission's FAST programme in the 1980s; in the early 1990s, the role of services in the European internal market – and the possible effects of European integration on services and their clients – attracted a great deal of attention; at the beginning of the new millennium, the question of offshoring of BS prompted another burst of activity. Bryson and Daniels' chapter in this book (Chapter 14) addresses geographical dimensions in some detail, so the present account can be fairly brief.

Geographers have been interested in the contributions of BSS to the economic performance of cities and regions, and their role in to helping to integrate the elements of such spatial units. Thus Tremblay (1998), writing about industrial districts, notes that:

> Some firms specialize in particular services, producer related services or business services: for example, there are firms specializing in the design of a product, there are firms specializing in research and development, others specialize in marketing, in exporting, and even in banking and financial services for the industrial districts. This makes it possible for these firms to benefit from advantages similar to those of large firms in terms of cost reduction through specialization. [. . .] Beyond the specialization of firms in particular activities, there obviously needs to be cooperation between them. And for this cooperation to develop there must be particular institutions in the district that coordinate all these activities. The industrial district is therefore a conglomeration or network of many different types of firms specializing in a particular stage of production, or in producer services or in business related services, which is characterized by a high degree of cooperation.

Specialization – enabling firms to supply services more efficiently, achieving greater economies of scale than in-house services – is thus seen to be a factor behind the regional agglomeration of BSS. Indeed, specialization is seen as driving the growth of BSS, as specialized services can perform operations more efficiently than in-house services, using state of the art methods and high levels of division of labour. This would be particularly the case where smaller firms are being serviced, who would be unable to support extensive in-house service support, especially when the service is required infrequently. The geographers also, as Tremblay suggests, stress the importance of cooperation and coordination. Again, BSS can benefit from such processes, as well as contributing to them.

BSS should enable their clients to benefit from economies of scale and specialization. The issue of specialization means that BSS have more opportunity and motivation to be keeping abreast of solutions to business problems that are being developed elsewhere – as well as accumulating their own experience through operations with various clients. In some cases, the BSS may be applying innovations themselves to services well before the clients would have been able to do on an in-house basis. In some cases the solutions are ones that involve the clients in undertaking or participating in innovation processes. Some technology-related services are explicitly advising clients as to technical alternatives or helping them to configure and integrate different parts of technical systems. Others may point out the utility of specific innovations in the course of less overtly technological work, such as an advertising agency drawing attention to the scope of new media for marketing, or an accountancy firm recommending the use of a software package for company accounts. Management and training innovations can be highlighted by consultancies supplying services in such fields. Thus BSS can help to diffuse innovations around their client communities.

The European Commission's KISINN project (1998) developed this line of analysis, stressing that KIBS can be sources of knowledge as to international best practice and the experiences (and markets) of other regions, and that such knowledge is extremely strategic.[6] Clients may benefit most from knowledge and the experience of technical and management standards drawn from a wider network than they are engaged in, from national and international sources, and KIBS are well placed to provide access to this. But the users of KIBS also require a 'local' presence to work closely with them. ('Local' is in large part a spatial issue, in that proximity can facilitate close and regular contact. But it may also mean familiarity with the problems of a particular sector or culture.) The problems of regional development, and those experienced by some sectors and by SMEs may be intensified by the strong polarization of access to KIBS.

In the context of this project, Wood (1998) assessed the high degree of localization of consultancy markets in the EU: more than two-thirds of users of consultancies rely on offices in their local region, for example, and more than 90 per cent employ consultancies based in their home countries. The literature stresses the important role of local KIBS (or, at least, local offices of KIBS) to SMEs in particular. Large clients search for leading-edge inputs, irrespective of location, whilst many SMEs search locally. This is not only a matter of the cost and delays that may be associated with the expert's travel. It also reflects imperfect market information that can help potential clients identify suitable BSS. Personal contacts and weak ties via friends and business acquaintances are thus used by SMEs.[7] These mainly lead to selections from the local area.

Some researchers doubt that proximity is so important, however.[8] Some of these doubters are geographers who have studied the process of agglomeration of services and their head offices in metropolitan centres (for example, Daniels *et al.* 1992). They note that proximity is not always a major factor in choosing and contracting management consultancies. We would expect the importance to vary across types of service and client, of course, and Wood is focusing on SMEs. Glückler (1999) cites a survey from the 1980s that indicated that management consultancy services tend to require considerably less proximity than other KIBS they investigated. (While it may not be surprising that engineering and recruitment tended to require more proximity, it is harder to see why this is so for advertising and data processing.)[9] Those authors who cast doubt on the continuing importance of proximity also cite studies that show that many consulting firms serve clients outside of their home regions, often over considerable distances. Wood points out that even here proximity matters: transnational KIBS strive to gain access to local expertise and 'presence', for instance, by acquiring, partnering with, or subcontracting work to, local firms.

As BSS become more strategically important, fears have been expressed that the need for proximity between client and BSS, coupled with the geographical concentration of BSS, will intensify regional disadvantages. Costs of business operations may be higher, and incentives to innovate lower, due to the lack of access to BSS, rendering more peripheral regions less competitive. It is suspected that smaller firms will be most disadvantaged by peripheral locations, lacking resources to bring in outside specialists, and being limited to less dynamic local service suppliers.

In a substantial survey of KIBS and their clients in regions of France and Germany, Müller and Zenker (2001) found substantial regional differences in the nature and performance of the SMEs and KIBS, and in their interactions. French and German firms seem to have 'national' features, some of which may reflect historically specific organizational and professional cultures, some of which may reflect broader issues of the national innovation systems. There are other studies indicative of variations in KIBS and KIBS – client relations across different countries,[10] and two implications follow. First, we need to be cautious in generalizing results from one location to other locations – perhaps even other regions of the same country, certainly across countries of the EU (even those at roughly similar levels of economic development). Second, given that we are only just coming to grips with these variations, it would be important to collate more evidence and organize more understanding rapidly, if policies are to be developed to support KIBS' role in boosting regional innovation capacities.

One study that made a start at examining relevant issues was the RETINE (REgional Typology of Innovation NEeds) project.[11] This examined regional diversity in the needs related to innovation as experienced, in particular, by

BSS and manufacturing SMEs. Drawing on the European Regional Innovation Survey database to examine ten European regions,[12] it found innovation circumstances to be very variable across different regions. Essentially, some regions confront far more difficult environments for innovative BSS (and SMEs) than do others. Regional variations could largely be depicted in terms of two main groups of variables differentiate the regions – *financial needs* ('lack of capital', ' availability of venture capital') and *access to knowledge* (research capacities, consultancy supply, regional workforce, and so on.). Generalizations about BS based on empirical evidence, and policy prescriptions for KIBS-mediated innovation, need to bear such variations in mind.

The discussion of proximity requirements for services has long featured claims that new information technologies (IT) offer opportunities for enhanced long-distance communications, reducing needs for physical propinquity. BSS have long been notable as particularly intensive users of new IT – for a recent study of the use of new technology by BSS see Empirica *et al.* (2003). One line of analysis that has received increasing attention concerns BSS, and the prospects for 'offshoring' BSS: locating service activities in low-wage regions, especially in developing countries. This includes at least three possibilities: relocating the location of specialized BS firms, sourcing BS requirements from more distant suppliers, and 'outsourcing' of service functions from within organisations to remote locations.[13]

The topic is far from a new one: as far back as 1987, Posthuma was able to review a substantial literature involving new IT and 'offshore office services'. At this point certain types of office service – notably data entry – were visibly being located in developing regions, linked by new IT to the firms they served in industrial countries. As time passed, increasingly sophisticated functions were subject to offshoring. In recent years, there has been a substantial movement of telesales and related services to developing-country locations. Software development activities have been outsourced to the Indian subcontinent (Heeks, 1996), and there is some evidence that increasingly it is the more strategic activities that are being relocated – including, for instance, R&D.

But it is the more mundane services such as back office and call centre services that have attracted most attention, especially since office data-processing services and call centres have become major employers in some regions. Call centres have not only cheapened the costs of telephone-based customer services (let alone face-to-face ones), they have also enabled clients to engage in a range of marketing and service operations that were not previously undertaken. Call centres had been used as internal services for some decades by very large organizations such as airlines and government agencies; during the 1980s, applications of computer technology rendered them more efficient, and in the 1990s more comprehensive services became possible, with extended hours of access, and the use of databases that provide detailed information on customers, products, and other topics.[14] However, many of the less routine activities are still generally maintained in-house, since call centre BSS are not always able to cope with specialized requests for information.[15]

Offshoring is a business service in its own right, as consultancies and IT service companies have moved to offer relevant training and strategic advice, as well as operational support, to firms considering offshoring and the use of shared service facilities. Employment concerns have been raised in the USA in particular, with worries that that service industries could migrate overseas on a substantial scale. Some commentators suggest that 'jobless growth' is the result – offshoring has enabled the US to grow in GDP terms while service jobs have been created at lower levels than recorded historically.[16] There are lively arguments about how far specific sorts of BSS activity require proximity, and rather less attention to the forms of organization involved in offshoring (one exception is studies of 'shared services').

2.4 BSS relationships: management studies and beyond

With the emergence of new firm strategies in the 1980s, and discussions of flexible, hollow and lean firms, there was considerable emphasis from business leaders on establishing a tight focus on core activities, contracting-out peripheral activities to others. This would enable the firm to specialize in what it does well, and to be unencumbered by personnel and plant dedicated to non-core functions. Sometimes this meant redefining what the core activity of the firm was – perhaps it was really design and integration rather than manufacturing and production, for example. These developments were studied and promoted by management researchers. They were also echoed in the public sector, where the desire to reduce government expenditure and payroll (public sector employees being strongly unionized) led to emphasis on 'contracting-out' public services as part of the new public management.

As with the economic analysis of transaction costs, management studies tend to focus on individual business units and their outsourcing, or 'make or buy' decisions – but with considerably more interest in the specific gains and losses associated with such decisions. The outsourcing of computer services has been a topic of sustained interest, with attention also apparent to such topics as call centres and even R&D services. A dominant theme in much of the management literature is essentially guidance as to good practice, and the assembly of lessons from case studies.[17] The concept of 'strategic outsourcing' was introduced to describe the processes and decisions involved in contracting-out activities: these include evaluating how strategic and critical the activities are, and how reliable, costly, and effective BSS suppliers are.

As firms become 'hollow' and outsource an increasing range of activities, they become surrounded by BSS firms performing vital functions necessary for the delivery of the core product. Sometimes the BSS are provided by ex-employees, either in 'spun-out' firms or as self-employed individuals or SMEs; ex-employees who have been made redundant and then subcontracted to carry out the same activities, typically with lower security and with less overhead for the client company.[18] The challenge for the client is to ensure that a sufficiently high quality of input is maintained. Outsourcing is associated with growing demand for certification of BSS to quality standards, as 'leaner' firms (and public authorities who are impelled to contract out some of their services) seek assurance that their suppliers will be capable of meeting their requirements.

Authors such as Davies (2001, 2003) and Lay (2002) have argued that new forms of manufacturing-service integration are emerging. Lay (2002) analyses German data on trends in the production of services that accompany manufactured products, and concludes that there are trends operating in opposite directions:

- Services without a direct relation to the industrial product are being increasingly outsourced to specialized BSS firms, as companies concentrate on their core competences.
- Services which are more directly related to the manufactured product ('product accompanying services') are growing in importance *within* manufacturing companies, and are less likely to be outsourced. For similar arguments see Davies (2003), Howells (2001), Kuusisto (2000), Mathé and Shapiro (1993).

These divergent trends render a simple diagnosis of 'outsourcing' problematic. However, we should remember the cautions above about generalizing from studies in particular countries, and perhaps also add that there could well be ebbs and flows in these trends. For instance, the 'product accompanying services' could be outsourced since past experience suggests that highly strategic activities can be conducted at least in part by BSS firms, given appropriate management.

Other lines of research focus on the service relationship. Many commentators have spoken of the importance of these relationships in affecting the success of service design, production and delivery. Shrimpton *et al.* (1998), for example, in a study of the scope for export promotion of BSS, argue that knowledge-intensive services are effectively selling the expertise of their personnel. This makes it critical for the service supplier and the client to establish a relationship of trust. These trust relationships are essentially ones between individuals, and an implication is that mobility of key staff can be a major problem for the BSS firms. Major clients may lose their points of contact with the firm and look for alternative suppliers; they may seek relationships with the new employers of the individuals with whom they have established trust.

Trust is an important quality of relationships, and traditionally implies face-to-face interaction. However, a recent study of the use of new technology by BSS by Empirica *et al.* (2003) notes that many of them are using advanced database facilities to bring together data related to contacts with clients. It is suggested that such technologies are of particular importance for those BSS firms that depend on returning customers, and whose (project-based or standardized) services are provided on an ad hoc basis; and for large firms, who have difficulty in bringing together intelligence about the numerous personal contacts there may be with their clients. Over half of the BSS firms studied exchange documents with suppliers and customers electronically (small firms appear to do so more frequently than larger ones – which may reflect the subsectors they operate in, the working relationships they establish, the greater need for collaboration among smaller firms, or the need to keep in closer touch with a small set of key employees.). Empirica also stress the use of IT for the management of relationships with business partners. The BSS may not only employ IT to assist their own relationships with the client, but also use IT for the client, to help coordinate and manage third-party relationships on their behalf. This is a core feature of some BSS: e.g. those advertising firms who go beyond designing advertising campaigns, to manage or help manage relationships along the advertising value chain – with suppliers, freelancers and contractors. Similar supply-chain relationships are managed by other BSS – for example, architectural and engineering firms manage relationships with suppliers and subcontractors, and additionally they may also deal with government agencies (for obtaining planning permission and ensuring regulatory compliance – and for seeking to influence the regulatory regime more generally).

An influential framework for describing supplier–client relationships was provided by Tordoir (1993, 1994, and 1995).[19] He distinguished between three archetypal relationships:

- *Sparring* relations, where the nature of the service to be delivered is typically negotiated between supplier and users. The latter are typically management, and their communications with the BSS are ones requiring trust and rapport, and implying rough equality in status, knowledge and competence. (The client will usually lack some expertise in the specific problem at hand, but may well be in charge of a prestigious business.) Strategic management consultancy and organizational problem solving are liable to involve such sparring relations, as can more advanced professional services (e.g. sophisticated legal support).
- *Jobbing* relations, involve less interaction, typically, and require the BSS to perform a specialist task (Tordoir focuses on technical and professional activities, but more menial BSS may be described in similar terms). The task is clearly defined by the client, who can expertly judge how well the service is being provided, and may direct the process of service provision. Some engineering and technical services, and some routine accountancy and administrative services, often take this form.
- *Sales* relations involve more standardized services, or services produced in relatively standardized ways. The service may even be developed before

the transaction (for example, some computer software, some industry intelligence reporting, etc.). Less knowledge-intensive BSS may also often be characterised in this way.

We have little evidence as to the relative distribution of these different types of relationships among different BSS and supplier–client relationships. Nählinder (2005) surveyed a thousand KIBS (excluding more routine BSS) in Sweden, and found that over 80 per cent reported that they typically have very close cooperation with clients, while over 75 per cent strongly *disagreed* that they have few contacts with clients during the course of service production. Indeed, over 40 per cent strongly agreed that they help clients 'develop products or routines' – over 23 per cent agree, and over 17 per cent agreed somewhat with this, leaving less than 20 per cent disagreeing that they play such a role.

A study using German innovation survey data from the mid-1990s (Hipp *et al.*, 2000) indicates that some BSS are far more likely to provide standardized services than others. This survey asked companies what proportions of their income were earned from '*standard services*' ('those without customer-specific changes'); from '*partially customized services*'; and from '*specialized services*' ('bespoke [custom-made] services'). *Wholesale and retail trade* tend to be the most standardized services, followed by *transport and communications, banking and insurance* and '*other business services*' (this latter category largely consists of those BS that are not KIBS). In these sectors 'standardized services' accounted for over 70 per cent of income, 'partially customized services' accounted for between 11 per cent and 27 per cent of income, and 'specialized services' for 10 per cent or less of the income (just one per cent in the *Transport and Communications* sector). *Software* services were similar, with 76 per cent of income from 'standardized services', 15 per cent from 'partially customized services' and 9 per cent from 'specialized services'. (Larger software firms are more like non-KIBS, tending to earn more from 'standardised' services, while smaller firms more like other KIBS, with 30 per cent of income coming from partially customized and 19 per cent from 'specialized' services.) As for other KIBS, *Technical Services*, and *Other Financial Services*, report earning just over half of their income from 'standardized services', whilst 25–30 per cent was due to 'partially customized services' and 16–18 per cent was due to 'specialized services' (Hipp *et al.*, 2000).

The extent of standardization is, perhaps, surprising, contrasting with Nählinder's results – though in both cases the questions used only can tell us about part of the service–client relationship. The more standardized services are presumably characterized by Tordoir's 'sales relationships' – but sparring and jobbing relationships cannot be so neatly aligned with specialized and partially customized services. Given the distribution of sources of income in *all* services, though, we might expect to find all three of Tordoir's categories within most BSS sectors. Sectoral membership is only a rough guide to what sorts of services are actually being supplied, and how BSS relate to their clients.

In a study of environmental services, Schulz (2000) suggested that BSS firms are liable to move across these categories. He began by discussing how environmental services might fall into categories based on Tordoir's framework. For example, he suggested that *sparring relations* might predominate among environmental management consultants, auditing services, eco-labelling services, R&D services, and those supporting the launch of new ecological products. Cases of *jobbing relations* included BSS engaged in air pollution control, waste water and solid waste treatment, monitoring of ground water, and environmental training and education. *Sales relations* include waste transport and disposal, the acquisition of standardized filter techniques, and remediation of specific events (for example, cleaning up after fuel spillages). But Schulz is clear that BSS firms might move from category to category. Thus a training and education service might move from a jobbing relationship to more of a sparring relation when dealing over a long period with top management in the client – or when the service is transformed towards, say, developing a training strategy for the whole enterprise. Alternatively, eco-labelling can be moved from a sparring service towards a simple sales relation, when and if it becomes a standardized act of certification. It might also be anticipated that some BS firms would adopt different types of relationship in different service transactions – even those with the same client firm.

While most of the literature on service relationships discusses KIBS, it is quite possible that other types of BSS might move across categories in the way Schulz describes, in this case away from purely sales relations to more complex ones. For instance, Djellal (2000) discusses the 'upgrading' or professionalization of French cleaning services as they extend the range of services offered (for instance, aid for injured people, reception services – and even cleaning consultancy companies, who draw up job specifications on behalf of clients).

Sparring relations, implying intensive and frequent interaction, would be expected to require proximity, which would be less necessary in the case of jobbing or sales relations. Illeris (1994) suggests that more customized services tend to require proximity since the costs of transport and communications can become significant. Highly specialized services will often require considerable face-to-face communication, but the pressure for proximity runs into another issue – the access to expert labour. Such access is harder in peripheral areas, which may discourage BSS from locating in these areas, even if some clients are based there. BSS firms are liable to be located in metropolitan centres, which will be close to their major clients and markets; the high costs of expert labour in other areas are liable to outweigh transport and communication costs.

The style of relationship between BSS and clients is liable to have substantial implications for the way in which the service is produced (for example, the extent of involvement of clients in service specification and production), and for the degree of exchange of knowledge and mutual learning between the partners. The sparring relationships are more likely to feature mutual learning and thus to induce profound change on both sides of the service relationship. (Of course, the picture can be quite complicated. For example, a 'jobbing' BSS in, say, training, is by definition engaged in increasing knowledge levels among the staff of the client in question.) KISINN (1998) concluded that KIBS are liable to have more influence on strategic and technological innovation when they attain close and co-operative working relations with client firms and their staff, with the KIBS' technical expertise complementing that of the clients' staff.

In a study of consultancy firms, Creplet *et al.* (2001) note that some provide relatively standardized services and are organized hierarchically, while others involve much more interpersonal interaction and are liable to feature more flexible organization. These researchers suggest that it makes sense to distinguish between consultants (bringing relatively standardized solutions to the clients) and experts (handling more complex or novel problems with original solutions). (There are overlaps with Tordoir's jobbing and sparring categories here, but this should not be pressed too far.) The consultant, it is suggested, provides a vector for the development and transfers of knowledge as to best practice, and may thus enhance the clients' day-to-day operation. Consultants' reputations partly reflect that of the firm for which they work, but are also underpinned by professional credentials and the practical demonstration of know-how within a community of practice. Experts, in contrast, may establish recognition through publications, conference presentations and academic credentials demonstrating their contributions to knowledge. Their services can provide strategic vision, and may effect more long-term change.

2.5 Knowledge and innovation

Until recently, innovation studies, a dynamic body of social research in the last few decades, have been focused on manufacturing innovation. Increasing attention is now being paid to services innovation, and a number of studies have examined the role of KIBS in particular in promoting innovation in client firms. KIBS are among the fastest-growing and most dynamic sectors of the economy, with many innovative users of new technologies, especially IT (Miles, 2005). KIBS can not only improve the efficiency of business processes, but can also transfer knowledge to their clients and/or participate in the generation of new knowledge. They thus may be expected to form important intermediaries and nodes in innovation systems, and this resonates with growing interest in the operation of innovation systems and networks, and the increasing emphasis on knowledge.[20]

The statistical classification of BSS with which we began effectively distinguished among KIBS in terms of their knowledge base – more science and technology (S&T) oriented, more concerned with administrative and institutional issues and regulations. The S&T-related KIBS, in particular, may play a strong role in diffusing innovations to their own clients. (In addition, some professional service firms develop strong competencies in S&T, such as lawyers who specialise in IT or patent law, financial advisors and market analysts who become expert in high-tech or consumer innovation fields.)

Recent analyses of European Community Innovation Surveys confirm that KIBS sectors, particularly technology-related ones, are among the most active innovators in the economy (Tether *et al.*, 2001). While service sectors on average lag slightly behind manufacturing (54 per cent of manufacturing enterprises, 46 per cent of services reported innovative activity), high levels of innovation are reported by computer (72 per cent) and technical services (67 per cent).[21] Though few innovating services conducted R&D in general, it was very common amongst computer and technical services. Such KIBS are more like high-tech manufacturing than they are like other services.

The S&T-based KIBS typically feature high levels of Qualified Scientists and Engineers in their workforce. Such technology-related KIBS have important roles to play in innovation processes (cf. Miles *et al.* (1995) and Bilderbeek *et al.* (1998)). There are services that actively conduct *research and development* into new technologies – R&D services, by the turn of the millennium, were accounting for 10 per cent of business R&D in the UK. Closely allied to these are services that perform *testing* of various sorts (often for conformance purposes). A rather different sort of testing is performed by *rapid prototyping* services, which construct models or full-size versions of designs so that, for example, difficulties with the production process or finished device can be identified. Some services are directly *providing technology support* for clients confronted by needs to engage with new technology – examples include as Web and Internet, software and computer services, and equivalent services emerging in the biotechnology sphere. One particular form of support includes *training* of staff to make use of new systems, while *strategic advice* may be given as to the choice and implementation of new process technologies. *Facilities management* services actively handle the task of using the new technologies for the client – managing a 'smart building', running a call centre or outsourced computer network, etc.

Increasing shares of knowledge-based services in the intermediary inputs of the total economy, and for broad sectors is clearly apparent in input–output data.[22] The term *quarternarization* has been used (for example, in the *European Competitiveness Report 2000*) to describe the steady rise of information and knowledge-based services. This differs from traditional growth in services in that these knowledge-based services can play important roles in innovation and productivity growth for the rest of the economy.[23]

Strambach (2001) is one of a number of authors influenced by the work of Nonaka and his colleagues on the production and transformation of knowledge in learning organizations, moving this work on to the arena of interorganizational relationships.[24] She depicts KIBS as developing knowledge through their interactions with clients, turning this knowledge into information and routines ('codifying' it), and then applying it to establish and implement new client relationships. KIBS integrate different types of knowledge for particular clients, and adapting the codified information to their demands and requirements. Glückler (1999) and Schulz (2000) consider the cycles of knowledge generation between KIBS (consultants) and clients, noting that KIBS learn from the businesses to which they supply knowledge. In many cases what is involved, then, is not just one-way knowledge transfer from KIBS to client, but more of a process of interorganizational learning. In the course of the service relationship, the KIBS firms have to understand the client, its processes and problems. There are two implications of this.

First, KIBS apply such knowledge in the immediate service relation, but it is also knowledge that is available to the KIBS firm for subsequent activities – including service relationships with other clients. Why then are the clients prepared to supply KIBS with strategic information, when this may be used to inform other clients? There are several things that make this a rational solution. (1) The client does stand to gain from the KIBS' application of knowledge that has been generalized out of the experiences of the sector more broadly. (2) The client needs to supply information in order to obtain the required service, and such interchange is also necessary for establishing a relationship of trust. (3) Part of the trust relationship is belief that the KIBS will behave in an ethical manner with the information that they have accumulated. It might be used to build generic knowledge for subsequent service relationships, but should not be used to provide competitors with intelligence! Contractual relationships often specify just how information can be used.

Secondly, we see that the KIBS firm depends upon several sorts of knowledge. Of course, there is knowledge about the specific service, the sorts of problems it addresses, the sorts of technical, engineering, or regulatory environment surrounding these problems, the ways of producing and delivering the service. But another critical type of knowledge will involve organizational and interorganizational knowledge. For instance, skills in extracting relevant information resources, in diagnosing the organizational practices of clients, in managing service encounters, will all be important parts of 'know-how'. Personal relationships and networks established with specific clients, and with other professionals, may well also be vital in giving a KIBS firm a competitive advantage. As already noted, this is highly dependent on the know-how of specific employees. Senior staff will have precious knowledge of, and links with, the client base. The loss of such staff can thus be a major challenge to KIBS firms.[25]

The link between knowledge and innovation in BSS–client relationships is a matter of knowledge being used to provide new solutions. Solutions may be new to the client – for example, when the KIBS firm is playing a role in diffusing a technological or organizational innovation. This may be more or less radical or incremental innovation, and one interesting line of research would be to explore under what conditions KIBS help firms move into new technological trajectories, as opposed to reinforcing established ones. The solution may be a new service altogether, in which case both parties are liable to be innovating.

In the KISINN (1998) project, case study work concluded that KIBS (especially consultancies) facilitate various types of corporate change and innovation. Among the forms of support for innovation that were noted were access to experienced and specialist personnel, knowledge of IT applications, and flexible modes of organization. In line with the knowledge-based analyses, the capabilities of KIBS to codify and adapt knowledge to diverse client needs was seen as very important, with the service firms' access to international practice also becoming increasingly critical. Sustained processes of client–consultancy interaction were often associated with innovative organisational or technical impacts.

A number of recent studies have used survey data to examine these aspects of BSS–client relationships. One particularly interesting line of analysis concerns the extent to which activities were standardized, as opposed to being customized to the requirements of specific clients. Hipp *et al.*'s (2000) analysis of German data indicated that BSS that provided partially-customised or specialized services were more likely to report undertaking innovations themselves than were Wholly Standardized service providers (controlling for features such as size). And, while one-third of the Wholly Standardized innovators claimed that their innovation(s) had an *important* impact on their users' performance and/or productivity, over 60 per cent of the Specialized and Intermediate firms thought this to be the case. Software firms were by far the most likely to claim important effects for their innovations on their users' performance and/or productivity (but, surprisingly, Technical Services had only an average propensity to make this claim). The implication is that the latter firms are adapting more of their outputs to suit specific clients; that they have a better understanding of client features and requirements; and that they build this understanding into their services in order to benefit the clients. Presumably, firms who adapt more of their outputs to suit specific clients' needs will develop superior understanding of these needs, and thus be able to act more effectively on the basis of this understanding.[26]

As noted earlier, Nählinder (2005) found a large share of her sample of Swedish KIBS to report involvement in their clients' development of products or routines. (But we do not know whether such involvement features in *all* of the relationships engaged in by these KIBS.) If her results are typical, and if the KIBS' claims are to be taken seriously, there must be a huge amount of support for innovation processes happening through these service interactions. The approach taken here would be valuably extended by analysis that link together both service suppliers and their clients, eliciting the views of each side as to the innovative contributions of the business partners.[27]

In Müller and Zenker's (2001) survey of KIBS and their clients in regions of France and Germany, data were elicited from clients, as well as the BSS firms.

As noted earlier, there were significant and intriguing differences between the two countries, but in general their results indicated higher levels of innovation and innovation-related expenditure among those manufacturing SMEs who interacted with KIBS than among those who did not (39 per cent of the former were regarded as innovative, as compared to 23 per cent of the latter). The converse was also found to apply: KIBS that engaged in such interactions were also more innovative (38 per cent of interacting KIBS as opposed to 27 per cent of noninteracting KIBS judged as innovative). Such analyses may leave questions of causality unanswered, but evidence is accumulating that interacting SMEs and KIBS are more oriented towards innovation than their non-interacting peers.

There is clearly much scope for further survey work, as well as case studies focusing on the nature of the innovation processes involved here. One task will be to explore variations among different types of BSS and across different types of service relationship. (As noted above, results may also vary from country to country, since innovation systems and corporate cultures are intimately bound up with the ways in which BSS are used.) Another topic concerns the ways in which clients make use of BSS inputs. Let us consider the literature addressing this important part of the equation.

2.6 The role of BSS clients

While there are many jokes at the expense of consultants and some other professional and technical services, and occasionally vociferous complaints about the poor quality of service received from BSS firms, the literature tends to stress the benefits that these firms provide for their clients. This may be a case where the old saying 'it takes two to tango' has resonance. Thus, den Hertog (2000) emphasizes the role of interaction between team members and employees from various organizations in the service relationship. For the client firm to be enriched by new knowledge, it will often be important for the client firm to have professionals on its staff, who can participate in dialogue with the service providers. More generally, even if there is little innovation involved, the client firms will need capacities to select among potential service suppliers, to be able to specify its problems, to manage the service contract, and to make use of whatever service inputs are being provided. This is reminiscent of the notion of 'absorption capacity' that is used to describe adopters' ability to make use of new technologies/technological knowledge. Several authors have suggested that a similar capacity affects clients' ability to benefit optimally from the use of BSS.

Glückler (1999) pointed out that it is often the stronger firms in a given sector which make most use of consultants' advice as to how to improve their products and processes. Sjøholt (2001) examined transnational consultancy firms and their clients in Norway, concluding that more sophisticated clients make better use of BSS.[28] They have already learned how to formulate problems in the course of the interaction, and to 'absorb' BSS inputs. The more sophisticated clients often sought to establish long-term sparring relations with KIBS suppliers, to maintain their competitive lead. But there were cases of unsatisfactory service relationships. While clients were often prone to blame the consultants, they did accept that some of the problems stemmed from their own lack of focus and failure to make best use of the BSS' potentials. Well-defined and controllable tasks, where learning was more systemic, were generally positively evaluated by the client, while broader and more intangible assignments (strategic consultancy), and were less likely to be seen as having provided value for money.

Sjøholt related these problems to knowledge transfer mechanisms. The teams that were commonly formed for the service–client interaction were sometimes composed in far from ideal ways. Often the difficulty was that professional teams were set up with a generalist problem approach. Some tasks can, of course, be satisfactorily handled by generalist approaches, while others may best be dealt with by specialized professional advisers (these might suit management of Tordoir's sales relations, for instance). Sjøholt suggests that teams with an explicitly transdisciplinary approach are required for handling contemporary organizational and strategic problems.

A few other studies have paid attention to client roles in the business service relationship (usually in respect of KIBS such as consultancy).[29] One line of work illustrates the influence that the client can have on the success or other of the service. Hislop (2002), for example, describes case studies of four organizations who were implementing similar technological innovations with consultancy support. The character of the consultancy relations that were established was found to be materially shaped by the clients' approach, and in turn this character was considered to have had substantial influence on the ensuing innovation process. Explaining the strategies and behaviour of different clients is an interesting avenue for future research – Hislop draws attention to the social networks and organizational cultures of staff in the client firm. This, of course, implies that we should anticipate considerable national and sectoral differences in BSS–client relations.

Another line of work is more managerial, examining the procedures that clients can adopt in relating to BSS. C. Gallouj (1997) elaborated a four-step model of how clients evaluate and select BSS (drawing on earlier work by O'Farrell and Moffat (1991) and others):

1. *Search for general information on suppliers*. This may be accomplished on the basis of past contacts, knowledge within the organization, examination of publications and conference presentations, etc. (Gallouj notes that search costs can be high, thus the firm will tend to look for a satisfactory solution, rather than making exhaustive efforts to find the 'optimal supplier'.)
2. *Evaluation of potential suppliers; the call for tender*. This may be accomplished on the basis of applying selection criteria (relevant to the nature

of the problem) to a list of potential suppliers. The client is likely to use signals of quality to help reduce uncertainty about service providers – for instance, certification (such as qualifications, membership of professional associations, etc.), reputation (for example, brand name, comments in the trade press), and various signals of quality. Formulating the call for tender is another very important task. The problem and the sort of solution required need to be spelled out, in sufficient detail to ensure that an appropriate service is obtained, but allowing for flexibility and innovation if the nature of the problem and/or solution are unclear or controversial. There may be some specification of contractual guarantees, and/or contingent contracts (payment by results) to ensure that the BSS delivers the service required.

3. *Evaluation of tenders*. This may be accomplished on the basis of the candidates' display of understanding of the problem, having proposed a valid and viable approach to solving it, and of having appropriate experience and a competent team available. Also in this step is shortlisting, to arrive at a set of (typically) two to five candidates who will be invited to present their proposals.
4. *Presentations by the selected consultancies*. This may be solely in written form, or require verbal presentations of varying degrees of intensity of interaction. The result of deliberations should be *the final choice*, which is partly based upon a more detailed application of the criteria employed in earlier steps. There is likely to be more attention to such issues as the precise methodology proposed, the control of the project and scope for delivery of results on time, the anticipated interaction between KIBS and client, etc.

The four-step model could be extended further to cover the subsequent steps in which the service relationship is managed and the service itself is delivered and used. There has been a great deal of discussion of good practice in the outsourcing of computer services, and offshoring call centre-type services,[30] but in general there has been only limited progress in mapping how clients define and implement their BS relationships. This would be valuable both from a social science perspective – helping to map and explain the nature of BSS–user relations, as a step towards better understanding the impacts of BSS use – and a more managerial one – highlighting what constitutes good practice, and how this may be achieved.

2.7 Conclusions

Business services are in many cases dynamic and rapidly growing sectors that play important roles in performance and innovation across the economy. Research on relations between BSS and their clients remains underdeveloped, and the upsurge of interest in the area suggests that we will learn a great deal about this topic in the near future. This will give us perspectives on what we can already conclude is an extremely important facet of modern economies. There will be implications for management strategy and for policy. The contribution that BSS make is liable to be affected by:

- The quality and value for money of BSS themselves.
- Access to information about the quality of BSS supplied by different providers.
- The capability of clients to make effective selection and use of BSS.

All of these elements will be in turn affected by conditions in markets more generally (for example, levels of competition and internationalization of BSS), and by features of innovation systems that influence linkages between BSS, their clients, and sources of knowledge about emerging technological and nontechnological opportunities.

We have suggested several areas where further research would be particularly useful, whether this involves case study (even ethnographic) work or survey analysis – and the usual pleas for better statistics of BSS should go without saying. While detailed policy conclusions are problematic, given the limited development of research and the likelihood that results will vary across countries, sectors and periods, there are some general points that arise. BSS-related policies could be developed, for example, to support:

- BSS clients (including public sector users) in augmenting their capabilities to effectively define service requirements and use service inputs. Some support may include training clients in use of BSS; some may involve promotion of schemes to improve market transparency, for example via quality certification.
- Types of public organizations and firms (especially SMEs), and regions, that may be disadvantaged in terms of access to, and capability to use, BSS. Equally, BSS in some regions may be supported in terms of assistance with networking and with gaining access to the sorts of tools and techniques used by their national and international competitors.
- BSS innovation, through inclusion of BSS in innovation and R&D policies, programmes to develop knowledge management and related strategies within firms and networks, orientation of the science base and technological infrastructure (e.g. telecommunications) that could be used by BSS.
- Determining and developing the Human Resources and skills that are required, on the one hand, for dynamic BSS, and on the other for effective clients. Often this will involve education and training institutions in finding ways to combine communication, interpersonal and technical skills, in creating management capabilities for dealing with multidisciplinary teams and with the demands of expert and professionalized KIBS workers.

Notes

1. Rubalcaba (1999) presents an extensive overview of European BS and relevant research.
2. The converse may also be true, in that sometimes there are no external sources of highly specialized inputs to be found.
3. We could add that the independence of a KIBS firm may be an important source of legitimacy within the client, and for other parties whose information and co-operation is required.
4. See critiques of transaction cost approaches such as Ghoshal and Moran (1996). The study of IT outsourcing by Mahnke *et al.* (2005) contrasts the transactions cost approach with approaches based more on analyses of competences and relationships, and classifies studies according to the approach taken.
5. See Drejer (2002) for an example and earlier review of such studies.
6. See the website at: http://www.tik.uio.no/Teari/eu/R4_T34_KISINN.htm. The major output from the project is Wood (2002).
7. Wood draws on Granovetter's (1985) concepts of embeddedness and weak ties, developed in the context of analysis of networks.
8. See also the Bryson and Daniels chapter in this book. It might be expected that research conducted within the framework of demonstrating the gains of the EU Single Market would tend to stress the advantages of economies of scale and traded services – for instance, access to best practice from around the world – while others might be concerned more with threats of regional disadvantage being accentuated. Here we are not able to discuss in any depth a body of analysis that has emerged concerning the functioning of the internal market with respect to services in general and (for example, CSES, 2001) BSS in particular. Suffice it to say that while some BSS are highly internationalized and feature high foreign presence, others seem to face many impediments to 'trade', for example related to professional qualifications and regulations, to need for local language, cultural knowledge, and relationships. See Kox, 2002; Miozzo and Miles, 2002, and Rubalcaba, 1999, along with the Kox, van Leeuwen and van der Wiel, chapter 11 in the present volume.
9. Glückler (1999) cites 'The efficiency of business services used by manufacturing industries', a European Commission MRB-Study from 1989.
10. For instance Grimshaw and Miozzo (2006) and Mason and Wagner (1999).
11. Available at http://www.isi.fhg.de/ir/pb_html/abgeschlossen/retine.htm
12. Alsace, Baden, Barcelona, Gironde, Lower Saxony, Saxony, South Holland, South Wales, Stockholm and Vienna.
13. Additionally, firms could choose to place their own service departments in new locations.
14. According to a press release dated 18 September 2002, from Incomes Data Services (at: http://www.incomesdata.co.uk/pressrel/pr020918.htm), a survey of 133 organizations, running over 300 UK-based call centres employing more than 100,000 people, found a third of these organizations operating their call centres 24 hours a day, seven days a week; a further third close at night but operate all days of the week. Among the services provided are: banking, betting, booking cinema tickets and driving tests, organizing holidays and obtaining health advice. This study found employment in the sector to be expanding, and dismissed fears of migration of the industry overseas; it also reported low wage levels (the average starting salary for a customer adviser was somewhat under 20,000 euros or £12,400 per year, though this was increasing at 4.6 per cent annually).

15. See, for example, the UK government's Call Centre Guidelines, 13 May 2000, available online at: http://www.e-envoy.gov.uk/assetRoot/04/00/20/44/04002044.doc
16. This has been argued by Stephen Roach of Morgan Stanley in various news articles and postings on the consultancy's Global Economic Forum website, http://www.morganstanley.com/GEFdata/digests
17. A classic review is Lacity and Hirschheim, 1993 – this is one study that is well grounded in survey and case study data.
18. For example, a publishing firm may lay off its editorial staff, and then recommission them as self-employed editors to carry out the same task.
19. This work focused mainly on professional services.
20. Cf. Andersen *et al.* (2000) for a volume that brings together services innovation and an orientation to knowledge.
21. In this survey, this group includes architectural, engineering and technical services, but surprisingly excludes R&D, technical testing and analysis (and legal, financial or management consultancy).
22. See, for example, Peneder *et al.* (2000) *European Competitiveness Report – 2000*, chapter 4.
23. See Tomlinson (2000a) and several subsequent papers in the same volume.
24. Nonaka and Takeuchi (1995), Dawson (1999).
25. The reputation of the KIBS firm is important not only for attracting clients, but also for attracting and retaining valued employees.
26. Firms that introduced more than one type of innovation – especially those introducing both service innovations and non-service innovations – were most likely to report important effects on their own and their clients' performance. This may confirm ideas about the effectiveness of combining multiple innovations, for example, much of the management literature stresses the importance of integrating technological and organizational innovation. Alternatively, it may reflect variations in strategic orientation of BSS – with more proactive firms being more effective in shaping their own and their clients' destinies. See for example Bresnahan *et al.* (2002) on the complementarity of technological innovation and firm strategy.
27. There are a few studies that combine attention to suppliers and clients. See the RISE website for one European project on this theme: http://centrim.bus.brighton.ac.uk/open/we/do/proj/rise/rise.htm, and the studies by Bolisani and Flanagan reported in Andersen *et al.* (2000) examining the fields of ecommerce and web services, for example.
28. A similar conclusion is reached by Wood (1998), among others.
29. Webb (2002) is a rare case of a detailed analysis of one specific client-BSS interaction.
30. See, for example, the material available at http://www.outsourcing.com.

3
Productivity in Business Services

Dirk Pilat

Introduction

The need for a stronger and more dynamic services sector arises primarily from the growing weight of services in OECD economies. If policy makers wish to strengthen the basis for future growth in OECD countries, the services sector will need to make a larger contribution than is currently the case. The experience of several OECD countries shows that this is feasible; in Australia, Canada, Luxembourg, the Slovak Republic and the United States, the services sector has made a large contribution to both employment and productivity growth over the past decade (Wölfl, 2005). In other countries, such as France, Italy, the Netherlands and Spain, the contribution of services to productivity growth has been low, however (OECD, 2005a).

One services industry that has been shown to be of particular interest in many OECD countries is the business-services sector. This industry has grown particularly quickly recent years and is commonly regarded as an important driver of innovation in the economy. It is also often considered as a possible source of future comparative advantage for OECD countries, as manufacturing production is increasingly moving to low-cost economies. Understanding the performance of this sector and developing policies that help strengthen its potential as a source of future growth is therefore important. This chapter contributes to this objective by examining the productivity performance of the business-services sector and the contribution of the sector to overall productivity. It first examines the level of value added per person employed of different subsectors in business services. Next, it evaluates productivity growth in business services and the contribution of this sector to overall productivity performance. Some potential influences on productivity performance are discussed in the penultimate section. A final section concludes.

3.1 The level of labour productivity in business services

Productivity performance of business services depends upon many characteristics that may vary both across the different components of the services sector and also across countries. A first question is the relative level of productivity of business services; in other words, is this sector more or less productive than other economic activities? Figure 3.1 shows that the business-services sector as a whole (ISIC 71–74) has approximately the same level of value added per person employed as the economy as a whole, with two countries (France and Germany) having relatively productive business-services sectors. At the same time, there is considerable variation within business services. Computer services (ISIC 72) typically has above-average productivity levels, whereas R&D services (ISIC 73) are about average and other business services (ISIC 74) are below average in terms of relative productivity. The fourth component of the business services sector, ISIC 71, which is the activity of renting of machinery and equipment, is very different than other business services, as it is highly capital intensive. It is therefore not shown in Figure 3.1.

The more capital-intensive business services, that is, renting of machinery and equipment, and the more technologically advanced business services, that is, computer and R&D services, thus have somewhat higher productivity levels than other business services that are often more labour-intensive. This difference between sectors becomes more visible when a more detailed breakdown of business services is used to distinguish different sectors. Such detail is typically not available from national accounts information, but can be derived from enterprise statistics. Estimates for value added per person employed

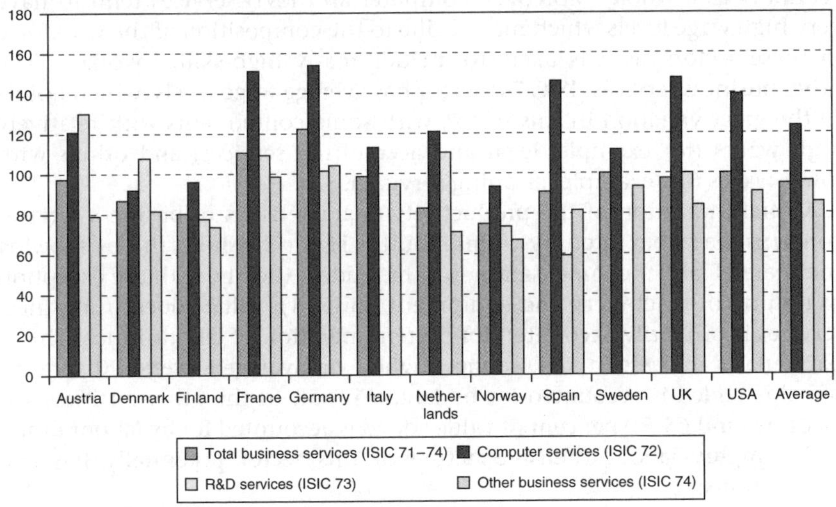

Figure 3.1 Relative level of value added per person employed, 2003[1] (total economy = 100)

Note: 1. Or most recent year available, i.e. 2001 for Spain and 2002 for France, Germany, Norway and Sweden.

Source: OECD STAN Database, December 2005.

for detailed business services, excluding renting (ISIC 71) in four EU countries are shown in Figure 3.2.

The computer services industry (ISIC 72) has some segments with relatively high productivity levels – notably software consultancy and supply (ISIC 7220) and data processing (ISIC 7230). Other industries, such as maintenance and repair (ISIC 7250), are substantially less productive, however. Cross-country differences are also considerable in this industry, with the United Kingdom having much lower productivity levels in database processing than the other countries.

The research and development industry (ISIC 73) has levels of value added per person engaged that are somewhat below the average in some countries, notably in the United Kingdom. In other business services (ISIC 74), ISIC 7410 and ISIC 7430 stand out with relatively high levels of value added per person employed; whereas business services n.e.c. (ISIC 7490) has low productivity in all of the countries in the survey. Cross-country differences are substantial for the business-services sector as a whole, with the United Kingdom having substantially less variation in productivity levels across industries than France or Italy.[1]

Another indication of these inter-industry differences can be found in relative wages by industry that can be derived from an analysis of the OECD STAN database. This suggests that business services as a whole is characterized by average wages that are slightly above average compared with the economy as a whole. Moreover, computer and R&D services tend to have very high wage levels which may be due to the composition of the workforce in these sectors, as it is likely to include many high-skilled workers. The other business services (ISIC 74) sector has average wage levels, which points to the great variation in this sector, with some components with relatively high wages (for example, legal and accounting services) and others with lower wages (for example, cleaning services).

A final indication of the productivity characteristics of business services concerns the labour intensity of this industry. Figure 3.3 shows this by showing the share of labour compensation in value added. Clearly, with the exception of renting of machinery and equipment (ISIC 71), value added in business services is primarily accounted for by remuneration of labour input. This is particularly the case in R&D services; where on average close to 90 per cent of value added is accounted for by labour input. In the other business services, around 65–70 per cent of value added is accounted for by labour input.

The highly labour-intensive nature of this sector potentially has two implications:

1. growth of output in this sector is likely to be associated with employment growth;[2]
2. labour productivity growth may be low in some business services, in particular in those industries where there is little scope to use capital and technology to enhance productivity growth (Wölfl, 2005).

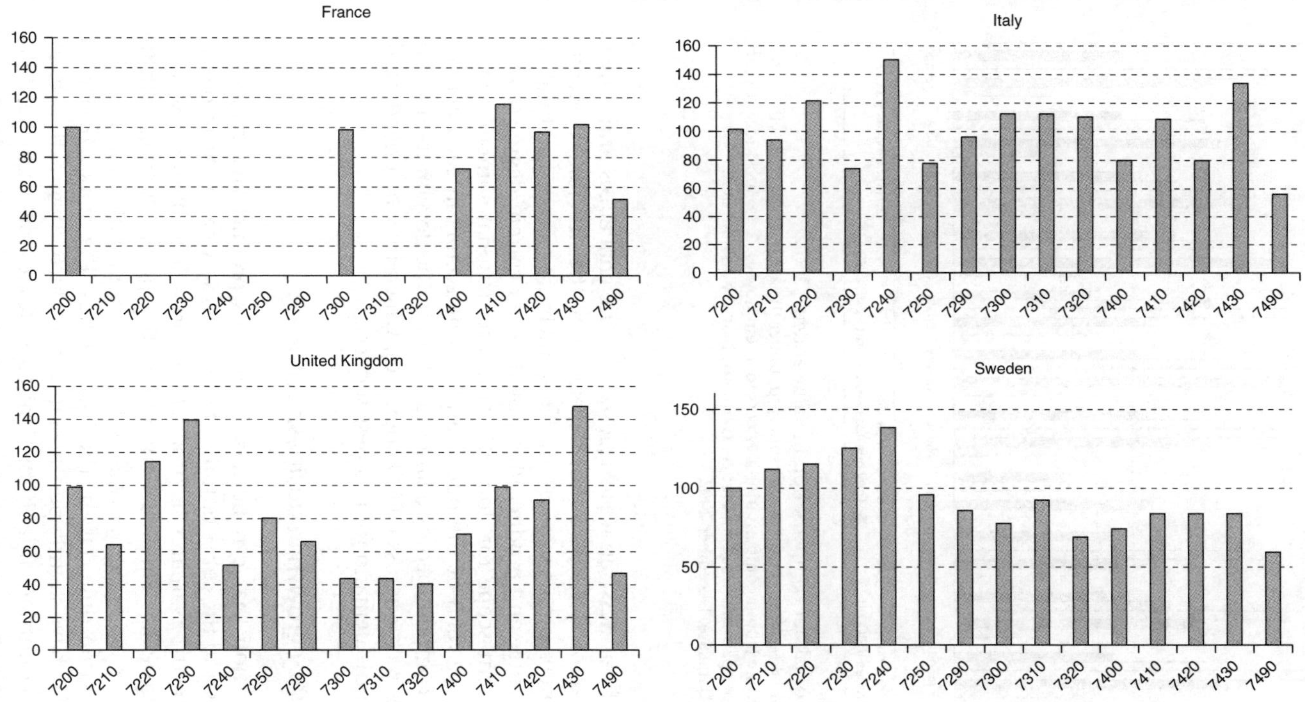

Figure 3.2 Relative level of value added per person employed, 2000 (computer services = 100)
Note: The components refer to ISIC Revision 3, with 7200 = Computer and related activities; 7210 = Hardware consultancy; 7220 = Software consultancy and supply; 7230 = Data processing; 7240 = Database activities; 7250 = Maintenance and repair of office machinery and equipment; 7290 = Other computer-related activities; 7300 = Research and development; 7310 = R&D experimentation on natural sciences & engineering; 7320 = R&D experimentation on social sciences & humanities; 7400 = Other business activities; 7410 = Legal, accounting, book-keeping, audit, tax consultancy, etc; 7420 = Architectural, engineering and other technical activities; 7430 = Advertising; 7490 = Business activities, n.e.c.
Source: OECD SSIS Database, 2003.

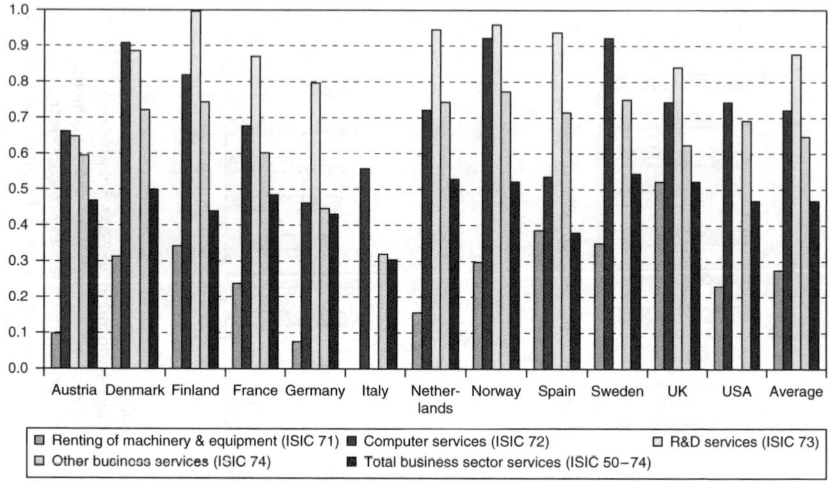

Figure 3.3 Share of labour compensation in value added,[1] 2003[2]
Notes: 1. Adjusted for labour income from self-employed, under the assumption that self-employed have the same labour compensation per person as employees. 2. Or most recent year available, i.e. 2001 for Spain and 2002 for France, Germany, Norway and Sweden.
Source: OECD STAN Database, December 2005.

This diversity of business services suggests that the challenges and growth prospects differ across activities. They depend upon the structural characteristics of different business-services markets, including their potential for technological change and productivity growth, their current degree of regulation and inherent scope for domestic and international competition, as well as the relative roles of the public and private sectors in each activity. This diversity is compounded by a large variation in the development of the business services sector across OECD countries, which may be linked partly to differences in the demand for business services.

3.2 Productivity growth in business services

The second question that can be raised concerns productivity growth in business services and the contribution that business services make to overall productivity growth. Estimates of productivity growth in business services are shown in Figure 3.4. The figure shows negative productivity growth for certain countries, such as Germany, France and Luxembourg, over long time periods. At the same time, Japan, the Netherlands, Denmark, the United Kingdom and Italy have slightly positive rates of productivity growth over the period. In some countries, notably the United States, Canada and Australia, negative rates of productivity growth in the first half of the 1990s have

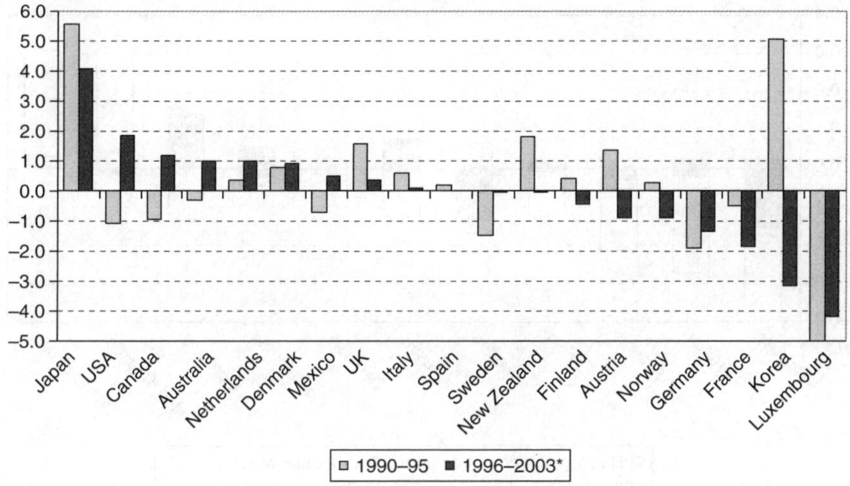

Figure 3.4 Productivity growth in business services, 1990–1995 and 1996–2003[1]
Annual average growth in value added per person employed, percentage points
Notes: 1. Or most recent year available, i.e. 1996–2002 for France, Germany, Norway and Sweden, 1996–2001 for Japan, Canada, Australia, Mexico, New Zealand, Korea and Luxembourg.
Source: OECD STAN Database, December 2005.

turned into positive rates of productivity growth in more recent years. These three countries have all experienced a broad improvement in productivity growth in services over the second half of the 1990s and the business services sector has clearly taken part in this broader improvement.

The contribution of business services to aggregate productivity can also be estimated from industry-level data, such as the data in the STAN database. Since value added is more widely available in the STAN database than production, productivity measurement is typically based on value added. The value-added based measure of labour productivity by industry (π^j) is given by the relation $\pi^j = V\hat{A}^j - \hat{L}^j$ (OECD, 2001). $V\hat{A}^j$ denotes the rate of change of real value-added in industry j and $\hat{L}^j$ the rate of change of labour input. The aggregate rate of change in value added is a share-weighted average of the industry-specific rate of change of value-added where weights reflect the current-price shares of each industry in value added:

$$V\hat{A} = \sum_j s^j_{VA} \cdot V\hat{A}^j, \text{ where } s^j_{VA} = \frac{P^j_{VA} VA^j}{P_{VA} VA}, P_{VA} VA = \sum_j P^j_{VA} VA^j$$

On the input side, aggregation of industry-level labour input is achieved by weighting the growth rates of employment (or hours worked) by industry with each industry's share in total labour compensation.[3]

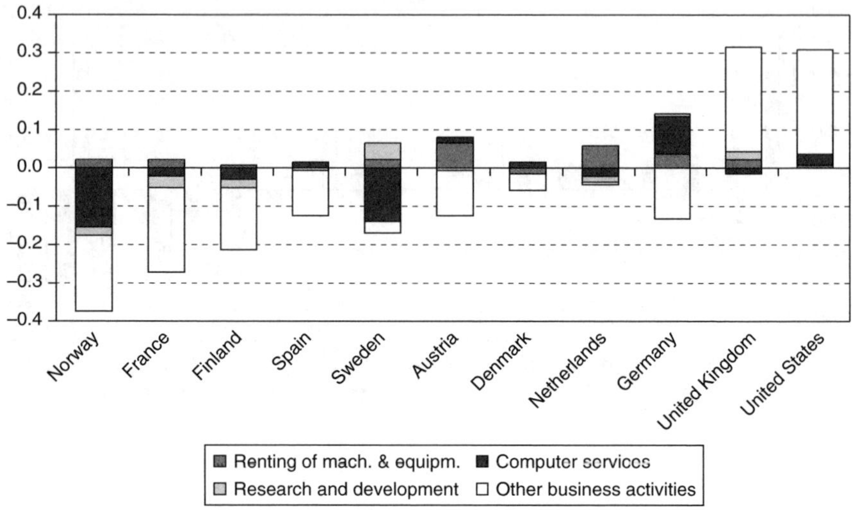

Figure 3.5 Contribution of business services to aggregate growth of value added per person employed, in percentage points, 1996–2003[1]

Notes: 1. Or most recent year available, i.e. 1996–2002 for France, Germany, Norway and Sweden and 1999-2003 for the United States. The estimates for the United States exclude R&D services.

Source: OECD STAN Database, December 2005.

$$\hat{L} = \sum_j s_L^j \cdot \hat{L}^j, \text{ where } s_L^j = \frac{w^j L^j}{wL}, \; wL = \sum_j w^j L^j$$

Aggregate labour productivity growth is defined as the difference between aggregate growth in value-added and aggregate growth in labour input:

$$\Pi = \sum_j (s_{VA}^j \hat{VA}^j - s_L^j \hat{L}^j)$$

An industry's contribution to aggregate labour productivity growth is $s_{VA}^j \hat{VA}^j - s_L^j \hat{L}^j$, or the difference between its contribution to total value-added and to total labour input. If $s_{VA}^j = s_L^j$, total labour productivity growth is a simple weighted average of industry-specific labour productivity growth.

Figure 3.5 shows that the estimated contribution of business services to aggregate productivity growth according to official national accounts measures is negative in several countries. It is positive in the United Kingdom and close to zero in Austria, Denmark, Germany and the Netherlands. This is confirmed in Table 3.1, which shows the rates of productivity growth for all business services combined, the four major components of the industry and

Table 3.1 Growth of value added per person employed, 1996–2003[1] (percentage points)

	ISIC Rev.3	*Austria 1996–2003*	*Denmark 1996–2003*	*Finland 1996–2003*	*France 1996–2002*	*Germany 1996–2002*	*Netherlands 1996–2003*	*Norway 1996–2002*	*Spain 1996–2003*	*Sweden 1996–2003*	*UK 1996–2003*	*US 1996–2003*
Total Economy	01–99	1.4	1.4	1.9	1.0	1.3	0.6	1.4	0.6	1.9	1.6	2.1
Manufacturing	15–37	3.8	3.1	4.3	3.4	1.9	1.4	1.2	1.0	6.0	0.6	0.9
Wholesale & Retail Trade, Repairs	50–52	2.1	1.3	2.0	0.8	0.5	1.7	5.1	0.2	2.2	0.2	0.4
Transport and Storage	60–63	1.1	4.2	1.2	1.2	0.9	0.3	0.7	1.4	0.8	0.1	0.1
Post and Telecommunications	64	3.9	5.0	10.9	7.5	14.1	9.1	13.8	7.7	5.7	0.2	0.2
Financial Intermediation	65–67	−1.4	5.0	5.3	−0.7	3.3	0.1	2.9	4.6	1.8	0.1	0.4
Real Estate	70	1.1	0.0	0.0	1.6	−1.4	−1.3	−4.1	−7.7	1.1	0.1	0.3
Business Services	*71–74*	*−0.9*	*0.9*	*−0.4*	*−1.8*	*−1.4*	*1.0*	*−0.9*	*0.0*	*0.0*	*0.4*	*0.3*
Renting of Machinery & Equipment	71	3.4	−3.3	1.0	−1.4	−1.5	2.5	6.0	−0.7	3.8	0.0	0.0
Computer Services	72	2.7	4.7	1.8	−0.1	3.8	0.5	−1.7	2.1	−2.3	0.0	0.0
R&D Services	73	−4.4	0.0	−1.7	−2.0	2.3	−1.9	−4.5	−1.8	–	0.0	–
Other Business Services	74	−1.8	−0.1	−1.6	−2.3	−2.6	0.6	−1.0	−0.5	0.3	0.3	0.3
Total Services	50–99	0.1	1.1	0.9	0.5	1.0	0.7	1.9	0.5	0.9	1.1	1.4
Business Sector Services	50–74	0.5	1.6	1.4	0.0	1.1	1.1	2.6	0.4	1.0	1.1	1.6
Non-agricultural Business Sector	10–67, 71–74	1.9	2.2	2.4	1.0	1.7	1.0	1.6	0.6	2.8	1.3	2.1

Note: 1. Or most recent year available, i.e. 1996–2002 for France, Germany, Norway and Sweden, 1999–2003 for the United States.
Source: OECD STAN Database, December 2005.

some other sectors of the economy. It illustrates that several business services, notably other business services, tend to have negative measures of productivity growth. Since other business services (ISIC 74) tends to account for the bulk of the business services sector, even a small negative growth rate can have a substantial impact on the aggregate for the business services sector. The United Kingdom has a small and positive growth rate of productivity in other business services. However, since this industry accounts for almost 80 per cent of total employment in total business services, this growth rate translate in a substantial positive impact on aggregate productivity growth, as shown in Figure 3.5. The United States also has a substantial positive impact of business services on aggregate productivity growth.

The official measures of productivity growth in several business-services activities seem counter-intuitive. This is particularly the case for computer services, where there is considerable evidence for rapid technological progress, which could lead to positive rates of productivity growth. The principal reason for the lack of measured productivity growth in these business services is likely to be poor measurement.[4] In most OECD countries, output measurement in services industries still leaves much to be desired and these problems also affect the business-services sector. Until recently, a common method for estimating real output changes in business services was to project output growth on the basis of employment changes, or to use wages as a proxy for the deflator (Triplett and Bosworth, 2004). In both cases, the resulting rate of labour productivity growth should be (close to) zero.

One common problem for all business services is that most business services provide some sort of knowledge, for example, in the form of legal or consultancy advice, R&D, knowledge on how to install computers (Eurostat, 2000). For statisticians, the difficulty is that the value of this knowledge cannot be quantified. An additional difficulty is that many business services are unique, which implies that statistical offices cannot easily develop price indices for such services. Moreover, the quality component of knowledge services is often quite important, which adds again to the complexity in measuring output and productivity of this sector. Despite these difficulties, statistical offices are making progress in measuring prices and outputs for some of these services, for example, certain legal, accounting and consultancy services, as well as computer services, architectural and advertising services (Varjonen, 2005).

These efforts are aimed primarily at the development of appropriate price indices for business services. For example, some legal and accounting services are somewhat standardized, which implies that actual prices of tariffs can be collected to construct a price index that can subsequently be used to deflate production. In other cases, volume measures (for example, the quantity of such services being delivered) may be available. For specialized and unique services, more complex methods can be used, such as the use of 'model' prices and hourly fees (Eurostat, 2001). Much development work along these lines is currently underway.[5]

Better measurement would most likely change the estimated productivity growth rates for business services, and could potentially lead to higher measures of productivity growth for these services (Triplett and Bosworth, 2004). It may also affect estimates of aggregate productivity growth, although much output of business services feeds into intermediate demand and therefore does not affect final demand (Wölfl, 2003).[6]

3.3 Factors affecting productivity performance

Improvements in the currently available estimates of productivity growth are also needed to improve the analysis of cross-country productivity performance for this part of the economy. While the evidence presented in this chapter points to cross-country differences in performance, it is unclear to what extent these differences are due to measurement problems or to underlying differences in the characteristics of this sector or to policies that may affect performance in this sector.

In the absence of meaningful measures, only indirect evidence on potentially important factors can be provided. One potentially important factor is the state of competition and regulation in services. Regulatory reform of many services, combined with a reduction in international barriers to trade and investment in services, have opened up service markets that were previously sheltered from competition (OECD 2005a). This has increased the incentives for firms to increase efficiency through greater use of advanced technologies, notably ICT, which has enabled innovation and productivity growth in many services, and has also forced firms to make greater efforts in introducing innovative products and processes throughout the value chain. In those countries where this process has advanced furthest, such as Australia and the United States, the resulting boost to productivity has contributed to lower prices and growing demand for service products, and to strong employment creation in certain services sectors, notably business services.

One key element in improving the business environment is better regulation. A broad range of OECD work shows that the reform of regulatory structures, for example, regulations on entry or operations, is the key to creating new opportunities in services sectors and in strengthening productivity growth. Much progress has been made over the past decade in reducing the degree of regulation in OECD services sectors. However, despite such progress, high levels of product market regulation continue to affect business services, notably in many European countries (Conway *et al.*, 2005).

Fostering entrepreneurship and the creation and growth of new firms are also important for productivity growth (Bartelsman *et al.*, 2003). Moreover, innovation and the growth of services often requires that firms can experiment in the market with new products, processes and business models. Allowing scope for experimentation may allow new ideas and innovations to appear more rapidly, benefiting growth and technology diffusion. There is much scope for action in this area; OECD estimates show that barriers to firm creation remain prevalent in many countries (Conway *et al.*, 2005).

Labour market institutions may also affect productivity growth in business services (Kongsrud and Wanner, 2005). For example, overly strict employment protection legislation may have adverse effects on labour mobility and productivity growth by reducing the capacity of firms to reorganize, experiment with new ideas or implement new technologies, such as information and communications technologies (ICT). Indeed, seizing the benefits from ICT in business services crucially depends on complementary investments in organizational change, skills and innovation (OECD, 2004a). These investments and changes, in turn, require a business environment that is sufficient flexible for firms to make the necessary changes. Many OECD countries still require further reform of product and labour markets to foster such an environment.

3.4 Conclusions

The business-services sector is a highly diversified part of the economy. It contains some highly capital-intensive industries, such as renting of machinery and equipment, some technologically advanced industries, such as software consultancy, and some labour-intensive industries, such as research and development and other business services. Its productivity performance also differs considerably across these segments. The capital-and technology-intensive segments of the sector tend to have the highest level of productivity, whereas parts of other business services have relatively low levels of productivity. A shift of resources to the more productive segments of the industry is therefore likely to have positive effects on overall productivity performance.

Much less can be said about productivity growth in business services and the contribution of this industry to overall productivity performance. Official estimates for several OECD countries point to negative rates of labour productivity growth over prolonged periods. Most likely, this is due to poor measurement and assumptions underlying the official statistics that lead to low or negative growth of labour productivity. Work is currently underway in many countries to improve the measurement of output and productivity growth in business services, which should eventually lead to a more meaningful assessment of productivity growth in this sector.

The current state of evidence on productivity performance in business services thus leaves much to be desired. That being said, further progress can also be made by using available data. For example, analysis of firm-level information on business services that is held by statistical offices could potentially provide insights in the role of reallocation for aggregate productivity performance. Moreover, firm-level analysis could potentially provide insights in the factors that contribute to productivity performance in individual firms, for example, investment in capital, innovation, organizational factors or skills.

Such work has been carried out for other services sectors, but could usefully be extended to this large and important part of the services sector.

A well-functioning business-services sector is important to the overall economic performance of OECD countries. It has the potential to be an important source of employment and productivity growth. Moreover, a more productive business-services sector also underpins better performance of other sectors, notably the manufacturing sector, as this relies increasingly on support and inputs from efficient and cost-effective business services. The evidence presented in this chapter suggests that it is, however, still difficult to assess the potential contribution of this sector to future productivity growth. While there has been in recent years a pick-up in productivity growth in business services in some countries, notably Australia and the United States, measurement problems prevent a more complete understanding of productivity developments in this sector of the economy.

Notes

1. These differences cannot be explained without a much more detailed assessment of the structural characteristics of these industries in the different countries, including the average size of firms, their specialization, and other factors.
2. The shares shown in the chapter obviously refer to averages, not to shares at the margin.
3. Estimates of hours worked per person employed are not available at the industry level for all countries. The estimates shown here therefore do not adjust for changes in average hours worked per person. This adjustment could be potentially important in certain business services, notably those characterized by a growth in part-time employment, e.g. cleaning services.
4. Another explanation that has been put forward for the computer services sector is that software companies, in particular, may have difficulties in appropriating the results of their innovative efforts, partly due to the lack of property rights for software inventions in many OECD countries.
5. The 'Voorburg Group' is an international forum of statistical offices that is aimed at the improvement of services statistics, including the development of price indices for services. Information on its annual meetings is available on the Internet.
6. Obviously, many of these problems also affect the measurement of productivity levels and the measurement of multi-factor productivity growth. The additional problems arising in this area are not further considered in this chapter.

4

The Contribution of Business Services to European Economic Growth

Henk Kox and Luis Rubalcaba

Introduction

This chapter analyses the contributions of business services to aggregate economic growth in Europe. The growth of business services represents a qualitatively new stage in the social structure of production. A major characteristic of this structural change is that firm-level scale economies with regard to knowledge and skill inputs are reduced by external deliveries of such inputs, thereby exploiting external scale economies. This combines with an increasingly complex social division of labour between economic sectors. The share of knowledge-intensive services in the intermediate inputs of the total economy has risen sharply over the past decade.

The business-services and communication sectors are in the focal point of this structural change. The direct growth contribution of the business-services industry arises from its own employment and value-added growth. The indirect growth contribution stems from the positive spillovers that business services create for other industries. The spillovers relate to the sector's role in knowledge and technology dissemination to client industries, and to its role in removing scale indivisibilities with regard to knowledge inputs.

The structure of the chapter is as follows. The first section positions the growth of the business-services industry in the context of a process of structural change in the European economy. The next two sections analyse, respectively, the direct and indirect growth contributions of business services. The relatively poor labour-productivity growth of the business-services industry in combination with its expanded share in the total European economy has raised the question of whether or not this sector contributes to growth stagnation. The fourth section briefly deals with this so-called 'Baumol disease'. The fifth section gives a brief survey of the empirical literature on the indirect growth contributions, and a final section summarises the conclusions.

4.1 Increasingly complex social division of labour

The development of business services as an industry represents a discrete step in the process of labour division. Specialized knowledge-intensive business functions that in the past were regarded as core competences of firms – and therefore not subject to outsourcing – are increasingly outsourced to specialized outside firms or are continued in close co-operation with the latter.[1] In the past 15 years, knowledge-intensive business functions have increasingly become eligible to outsourcing. One facilitating factor in this process was the substantial fall in information and communication costs due to the ICT revolution, making it easier to co-ordinate specialized and spatially separated business processes. The business-services sector has benefited from this process of structural change in a double way. Firstly, the ICT revolution partly came from within the business-services industry (software development and IT services). And, secondly, because the surge in outsourcing created new business opportunities for other branches in business services. The complexity of inter-sectoral and intra-sectoral division of labour also has an international dimension through the rise of 'offshoring', particularly since the turn of the century (Grossman and Rossi-Hansberg 2006; Baldwin 2006; Van Welsum and Vickery 2006). The specialization by some knowledge-based firms is such that even the size of most national markets is not even large enough for them. Sometimes, routinized elements within knowledge services are further split up so that parts of the process can be one in less-developed countries, benefiting from the wage-rate differences. It gives rises to new international trade flows in knowledge-intensive business services, or in brief: *KIBS* (Lesher and Nordås 2006).

The increasingly complex division of labour with regard to knowledge services allows several types of product and process innovations, more knowledge specialization, and better use of specialized inputs. Scale bottlenecks regarding knowledge-intensive specializations at the firm level become less relevant, as outsourcing makes it possible to benefit from external scale advantages in these areas. A popular way of obtaining the most from advanced business-related services is the combination of both in-house and external services. The expertise and specialist knowledge of external KIBS firms can better be absorbed and optimized if the outsourcing firm also employs highly skilled people.[2]

These structural changes may give an impetus to aggregate economic growth. This can be illustrated on the basis of macroeconomic production functions. A macroeconomic production function is a specific national production constellation, i.e. a particular relation between sectors that together form the national economy. Alternatively, we may also view this as a particular way in which the social division of labour in the economy is organized. Figure 4.1 plots two macroeconomic production functions with on the vertical axis the total value added of all industries, and on the horizontal axis

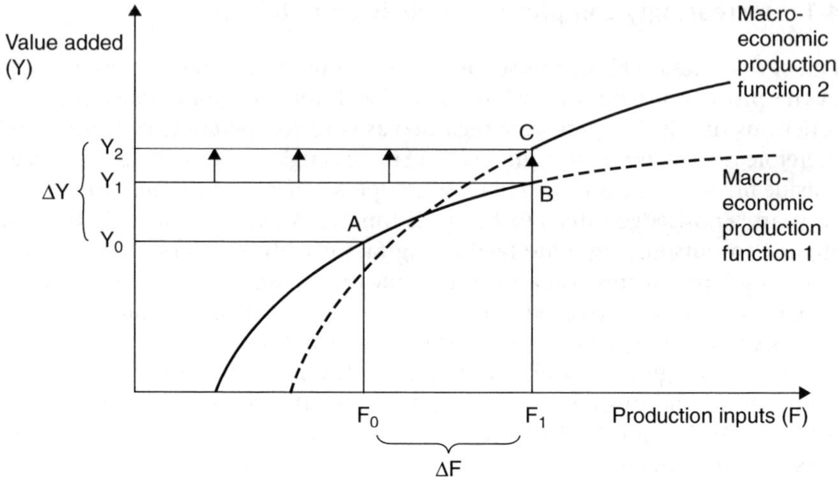

Figure 4.1 Structural change and macroeconomic growth potential

the aggregated production inputs (like labour) used to produce this value added.[3]

Initially, the relation between industries and sectors is reflected in macroeconomic production function 1. It represents all the production possibilities that are within reach by a certain state of technology and by a given social division of labour between sectors. By using production inputs F_o it yields value-added level Y_o. By increasing the amount of production inputs to F_1 value added grows to Y_1 as output shifts upwards from A to B along production function 1.

Now suppose that a technological breakthrough, such as the ICT revolution, makes possible a new arrangement of the relations between economic sectors, allowing for further division of labour, more outsourcing possibilities and more use of specialized service inputs. In Figure 4.1, the new social division of labour is represented by macroeconomic production function 2. Note that at input size F_o it is not yet profitable to switch to production function 2; it takes more scale size (amount of inputs) to bring the efficiency benefits into reach.[4] Structural change occurs when the production system switches from production function 1 to production function 2, with a 'jump' from point B to point C. With a given increase in factor inputs (ΔF), a higher level of economic growth (namely ΔY) becomes possible, thus attaining production level Y_2.

If there is indeed a positive relation between economic size and the role of the BSS sector in the inter-industry division of labour, we would expect to find a relatively larger BSS sector in the larger and more developed countries. In Figure 1.1 (Chapter 1) we indeed found the expected pattern, even within the Europe, with a clear correlation between the share of business services and GDP per capita in Europe.

Input–output analysis provides an indication that the growth of business services indeed reflects an increasingly complex social division of labour between industries, and even within industries. Total intermediate demand for business services is for an important part absorbed within the business-services sector itself (cf. Table 4.1).[5] Moreover, when the size differences between the sectors are taken into account, the business-services sector in fact appears to be the most intensive user of business-services inputs.[6] The vertical fragmentation and specialization process in the production chain translates itself into growing 'roundaboutedness' of production, that is, a higher transaction density in the trajectory between primary inputs and the final good. The term 'roundaboutedness' is derived from the neo-Austrian capital theory where it is regarded as a measure of capital intensity (Hicks 1973).[7] In our case it points more particularly to increasing human-capital intensity with KIBS firms providing the intangible assets (know-how, software, organizational skills, R&D capabilities etc.) that drive additional value creation in client firms.[8] The growth of business services since the 1990s reflects a different way of organizing social production, allowing a better spread of the advantages of knowledge specialization, more external scale economies, and a higher-level growth path. The key position of the business-services industry in this process can be expected to go along with high forward-linkage intensity: a one-unit

Table 4.1 Intermediate demand for business-service inputs: ranking of the main destination sectors, selected countries, 1994–1998

	Rank of business services as destination sector	*Five most important destination sectors of intermediate business-services inputs, ranked by importance*[1]	*Share (%) of business services in intermediate demand*
UK	1	BS - MFG - PUB - FIN - THC	**26.1**
Netherlands	1	BS - MFG - THC - PUB - FIN	**24.9**
France	2	MFG - BS - PUB - FIN - CON	**24.2**
Germany	2	MFG - BS - PUB - REA - THC	**17.1**
Italy	3	MFG - THC - BS - PUB - FIN	**14.2**
Spain	3	MFG - PUB - BS - THC - CON	**13.6**
Denmark	5	CON - THC - PUB - MFG - BS	**12.9**
Finland	4	MFG - PUB - THC - BS - REA	**8.1**
Greece	8	MFG - THC - PUB - CON - TRA	**3.1**
PM: USA	2	THC - BS - PUB - MFG - FIN	**17.7**

Note: 1. The sector codes are: MFG: manufacturing; BS: business services; FIN: financial services; PUB: public sector; THC: trade, hotels and catering; TRA: transport and storage; CON: construction; REA: real estate.

Source: The country data are based on the most recent IO table available in the OECD database over the period 1994–1998. OECD input–output tables; ECORYS-NEI (2004).

increase in final demand in the economy will necessitate the business-services industry supplying a more-than-average increase of intermediates to accommodate the economy-wide demand. Lesher and Nordås (2006) indeed find evidence for this in OECD countries.

After sketching the broader context of structural change surrounding the growth of business services, we now consider the growth contribution of business-services industry a bit closer, starting with the direct growth contributions.

4.2 The direct growth contribution of business services

The strong expansion of the business-services sector over the past decade contributes in itself to aggregate economic growth. We subsequently deal with the sector's contribution to growth in terms of employment, value added and labour productivity.

Employment growth. Table 4.2 brings out that the sector has had a most prominent role in inter-sectoral employment shifts during the last two decades. The business-services industry on its own accounted for more than half the EU's net employment growth between 1979 and 2003. This was more than the joint employment contribution of all other commercial services taken together.[9] It was even larger than employment growth in public services. Business services more than compensated the shrinking employment in manufacturing.

The largest annualised growth rate within the business services was registered by the subsector computer services. The latter started from a very small initial size in 1979, but nonetheless its employment growth accelerated to 6.6 per cent in the second half of the 1990s (OECD 2003a).[10] Over the entire period, knowledge-intensive business services (KIBS) and the rest of business services (non-KIBS) have grown at about the same pace, with the employment-growth contribution of 'non-KIBS' only being a little bit higher than the contribution of KIBS.[11]

Value-added growth. Measured in constant prices, the value-added growth between 1979 and 2003 was stronger in business services than in any other economic sector of the European economy, except for communication services (cf. Table 4.3). The share of business services in total value added doubled to 11.2 per cent over this period. Within business services, computer *services* registered the strongest growth performance, while the weakest growth occurred in *contract R&D*. The 'non-KIBS' part of business services grew slightly faster than the KIBS part.

The contribution of business services to the absolute change in total value added was much smaller than its contribution in terms of employment growth. About one-eighth of the overall EU15 change in value added was accounted for by business services. Two-thirds of this direct growth contribution stemmed

Table 4.2 The contribution of business services to EU15 employment growth, 1979–2003

	Employment in 1,000 persons, 1979	*Employment in 1,000 persons, 2003*	*Average annualized sectoral growth rate (%)*	*Contribution to aggregate growth (% point)*	*Contribution (%) to EU15 absolute employment change*[1]
Business services	***6,837***	***19,460***	***4.5***	***0.33***	***54.4***
– Equipment renting	250	563	3.4	0.01	1.4
– Computer services	571	2,450	6.3	0.05	8.1
– Contract R&D	411	632	1.8	0.01	1.0
– Professional services	2,846	7,037	3.8	0.11	18.1
– Other, n.e.c.	2,759	8,778	4.9	0.16	26.0
Total all sectors	***147,984***	***171,167***	***0.6***	***0.6***	***100.0***
– Manufacturing	53,381	42,055	−1.0	−0.30	−48.9
– Distributive trades	20,993	25,943	0.9	0.13	21.4
– Financial services	3,976	5,392	1.3	0.04	6.1
PM					
KIBS business services[2]	3,828	10,119	4.1	0.17	27.1
Non-KIBS business services[3]	3,009	9,341	4.8	0.17	27.3

Notes: 1. Each industry's absolute change in employment as percentage of the total employment change in the entire economy. 2. The group of knowledge-intensive business services (KIBS) is here taken to consist of 'Computer services', 'Contract R&D', and 'Legal, technical, accountancy, advertising'. 3. Non-KIBS business services is here taken to consist of 'Equipment renting' and 'Other, n.e.c.'.
Sources: data are from OECD National Accounts data (STAN), extended with data from GGDC.

from the KIBS, which is mainly explained from the fact that its 1979 share in value added was already larger than the 'non-KIBS' part.

Direct contribution to EU productivity growth. The direct contribution of business services to the growth of aggregate productivity is implied by the two preceding tables.[12] Productivity growth is defined as the growth of real value added per employed person, expressed in constant prices of 1995. This definition counts persons, not hours worked; it could therefore underestimate the productivity growth if the share of part-time workers grows over time.

In Table 4.4 we see that the direct contribution of business services to EU15 productivity change has been negative over the period 1979–2003. The

Table 4.3 The contribution of business services to value-added growth, 1979–2003

	Value-added level in billion euros,[4] 1979	*Value-added level in billion euros,[4] 2003*	*Average annualized sectoral growth rate (%)[5]*	*Sector contribution to aggregate growth (% point)*	*Contribution (%) to EU15 absolute value-added change[1]*
Business services	***122.9***	***1,067.4***	***4.2***	***0.28***	***12.7***
– Equipment renting	10.8	90.3	5.0	0.02	1.1
– Computer services	12.4	182.7	6.6	0.05	2.3
– Contract R&D	7.0	36.7	2.4	0.01	0.4
– Professional services	59.7	472.0	3.8	0.12	5.6
– Other, n.e.c.	33.0	285.7	3.9	0.08	3.4
Total all sectors	***2,124.0***	***9,540.1***	***2.2***	***2.2***	***100***
– Manufacturing	804.1	2515.9	2.2	0.51	23.1
– Distributive trades	218.5	936.6	2.3	0.22	9.7
– Financial services	103.7	576.4	2.5	0.14	6.4
PM					
KIBS business services[2]	79.1	691.4	4.1	0.53	8.3
Non-KIBS business services[3]	43.8	376.0	4.4	0.29	4.5

Notes: 1. Each industry's absolute change in value added as percentage of the total value-added change in the entire economy. 2. The group of knowledge-intensive business services (KIBS) is here taken to consist of 'Computer services', 'Contract R&D', and 'Legal, technical, accountancy, advertising'. 3. Non-KIBS business services is here taken to consist of 'Equipment renting' and 'Other, n.e.c.' 4. Current prices, for 1979 conversion to euro from ECU and other national currencies. 5. Based on constant 1995 prices.
Sources: data are from OECD National Accounts data (STAN), extended with data from GGDC.

reason is that the employment in business services has grown faster than did its value added. The negative productivity contribution is caused entirely by the non-KIBS part of business services, and, more particularly, by the subsector '*Other, not elsewhere classified*'. This residual category includes, *inter alia*, industrial cleaning, security services, call centres, packaging firms, and agencies for temporary labour. Branches like call centres and industrial cleaning tend to employ many part-time workers, and especially call centres form a relatively young activity. So, a growing share of part-timers could in this case lead to underestimation of real productivity growth (per hour worked).

The KIBS – though representing more than half the BSS employment – also failed to make a positive direct contribution to EU15 productivity growth over

Table 4.4 The contribution of business services to EU15 labour productivity growth, 1979–2003

	*Productivity level in euros, curr prices 1979**	*Productivity level in euros, curr. prices 2003**	*Labour productivity level 2003 based on constant 1995 prices*[1]	*Average annualized growth rate in constant prices (%)*	*Sector share (%) in EU15 growth of aggregate in productivity*[2]
Business services	17,976	54,851	16,777	−0.3	−0.023
of which:					
– Equipment renting	43,200	160,391	62,450	1.6	0.012
– Computer services	21,716	74,571	23,236	0.3	0.003
– Contract R&D	17,032	58,070	19,611	0.6	0.002
– Professional services	20,977	67,074	20,977	0.0	0.000
– Other, n.e.c.	11,961	32,547	9,504	−1.0	−0.021
Average total EU15 economy	14,353	55,736	20,961	1.6	1.600
PM: KIBS[3]	20,664	68,327	20,664	0.0	0.000
Non-KIBS business services[4]	14,556	40,253	13,280	−0.4	−0.012

Notes: 1. Using 1979 productivity levels as starting values and calculating on the base of the value-added growth rate in constant 1995 prices. 2. Employment weighted. 3. The group of knowledge-intensive business services (KIBS) is here taken to consist of 'Computer services', 'Contract R&D', and 'Legal, technical, accountancy, advertising'. 4. Non-KIBS business services is here taken to consist of 'Equipment renting' and 'Other, n.e.c.'
Sources: calculated on the basis of data in Tables 4.1 and 4.2.

the period 1979–2003. The positive exceptions in this category are *computer services* and *contract R&D*. The subsector aggregate that includes most professional services (*Legal, technical, accountancy, advertising*), and that accounts for about one-third of total BS employment, had on average a zero growth of real productivity.

Summing up, the productivity performance by business services can at best be called very poor. The same holds for this sector's direct contribution to European productivity growth, a result that was also found by the European Central Bank (ECB Task Force 2006). It gives some reason for worry. Economic growth is mainly driven by two sources, namely productivity growth and increased labour inputs (participation). In the coming decades, population ageing effects will become palpable, and increased labour participation can no longer be relied upon as a major source of economic growth in the European Union (cf. European Commission 2002b). So, productivity growth will be left as the only major source of economic growth. The weak productivity performance by the business-services industry – if carried on into the future – could become a drag on economic growth, certainly now this sector forms a major sector in the European economy. Some have even raised the question whether the 'Baumol disease' (growth stagnation due to an increasing weight of low-productivity services sectors) is lurking behind the horizon.[13] We return to this discussion in section 4.4.

First, we want to qualify some of the aforementioned conclusions on productivity growth in business services. Productivity performance in business services differs by country and by subsector, so one must be careful with generalizations (cf. Pilat in Chapter 2; O'Mahony and Van Ark 2003; Wölfl 2003). Moreover, there is international agreement nowadays that measurement issues might affect the productivity record of business services more than in many other economic sectors.[14] The high degree of product differentiation makes it difficult to distinguish between price and volume components of value added growth (cf. Triplett and Bosworth 2004; Wölfl 2003; Rubalcaba 2007a). This especially regards the KIBS, where the products are in many cases client-specific.

The theory on industry dynamics provides us with a reason for being careful about extrapolating the past productivity-growth performance of business services into the future. The business-services industry is relatively new, and some of its branches did not even exist 20 years ago. Many of its products, particularly knowledge-intensive products, are even newer. The theory on product lifecycles (Vernon 1966) states that products in an early stage of their development tend to be quite unstandardized and highly differentiated, but many of these products become more standardized over time. In the beginning, price elasticity for the output of individual firms may be quite low. Production methods still have a learning-by-doing character, and producers have a large degree of freedom in changing their inputs. Once demand for a product expands, a certain degree of standardization (commonly accepted product standards) takes place.[15] Efforts at product differentiation do not come to an end, since competitors try to avoid the full brunt of price competition. Moreover, more product variety may arise due to specialization. Over time, concern about production costs becomes more important and uncertainties diminish about how the product should best and cheapest be produced. Once standardization occurs in the product market, the price elasticity of demand for the output of individual firms increases. Firms that wish to survive, must give full attention to cost efficiency. When this happens, the productivity record in business services can be expected to improve.

4.3 The indirect growth contribution of business services

Thus far we have focussed on the growth of the business-services industry itself and how that contributes to economic growth in Europe. Two important characteristics of the sector are that its products are used as intermediate inputs, and that these inputs are often knowledge-intensive. Both characteristics affect the further role of business services in overall economic growth.

There is reason to assume that individual firms in business services are not always able (or willing) to charge the full value of their inputs to clients. An important economic explanation for this is that knowledge products are non-rival in their use. It means that once the knowledge product has been created, it is difficult for business-services firms to prevent it from being used subsequently by the client in new applications, or from being copied by other firms. It is difficult to fully appropriate the rents of new knowledge products.[16] This means that the value added of the business-services sector underestimates the sector's contribution to overall economic growth.[17] A comprehensive picture of the growth contribution by business-services industry therefore also requires that such knowledge 'externalities' or spillovers are somehow taken into account. Griliches (1979) made a distinction between knowledge spillovers and rent spillovers.

Real knowledge spillovers do not necessarily imply economic transactions between industries. Rent spillovers relate to quality improvements in intermediate inputs that are not matched by price increases. Under-pricing of products in the case of rent spillovers is the result of the market structure for the knowledge products, and not necessarily a matter of flawed statistical measuring.[18] Spillovers generated by business services firms are generally rent spillovers.

Knowledge-intensive business-services firms have an important role in national innovation systems. They contribute in three ways to modern knowledge infrastructure, through *original innovations*, through *knowledge diffusion*, and through their role in *surpassing human capital indivisibilities*. We subsequently discuss these three forms of indirect growth impacts.

Original innovations. The business-services industry has a key role in the development of original innovations. Firms in the software, engineering and contract research subsectors actively contribute to technological innovations. Other subsectors, such as accountancy, consultancy and marketing, are more active in the development of non-technological innovations. This sector's role in original innovations can be shown using the business expenditures on R&D (hereafter abbreviated as BERD) as an indicator. Figure 4.2 shows on the vertical axis that the annual growth of these expenditures over the period 1995–2004 has been very strong in most EU countries, and in several cases also higher than in the USA.

The horizontal axis of Figure 4.2 gives the annual change in the share of business services in the total economy's BERD for the period 1995–2004. We corrected for the fact that the business-services sector itself has become a larger part of the total economy. The figure therefore also allows the conclusion that the business-services sector in most of the EU15 countries became more R&D-intensive than the rest of the economy.[19] The Europe-wide *Community Innovation Survey* shows that the share of innovating firms in business

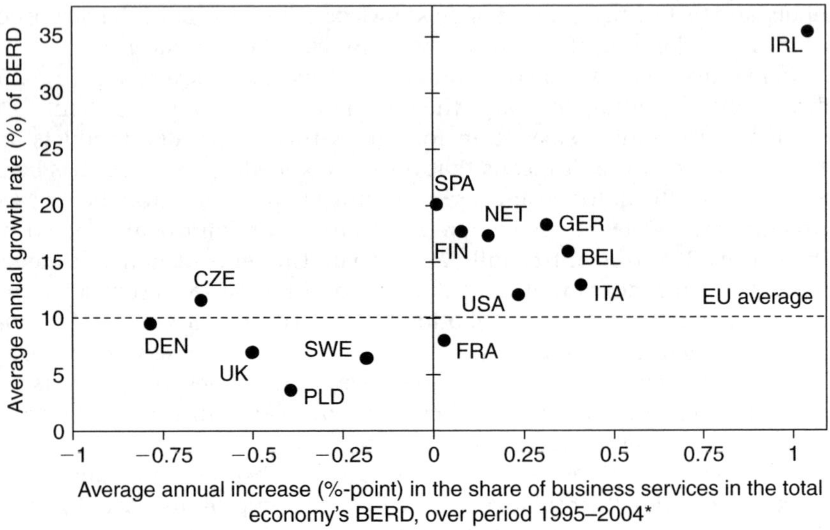

Figure 4.2 Growth of R&D expenditure by BS industry, and its changing share in the national R&D expenditures, period 1995–2004[1]
Note: 1. The share of business services is corrected for its increased share in the total economy. Business expenditures on R&D (BERD) are measured in PPP dollars.
Source: own calculations, using data from OECD ANBERD (2006) and STAN databases.

services – or, more precisely, in computer services, engineering, architecture, computer activities, contract R&D, consultancy and technical testing – is higher than in manufacturing industry (European Commission 2004b; Pain and Jaumotte 2005).

Figure 4.3 shows that there are substantial intra-EU differences in the R&D share of different subsectors. *Computer services* and *Contract research* account for a major part of the R&D expenditures in business services. Most European patent registrations in services also originate from these subsectors (European Commission 2003a; Blind *et al.* 2003). In 2000, some 16 per cent of all innovating business-services firms in the EU applied at least for one patent, only slightly less than the equivalent figure for manufacturing. In five countries (Sweden, Denmark, Germany, Spain and Portugal), the percentage of innovating firms with patents was higher in business services than in manufacturing (European Commission 2004b).

Firms in the subsector *Other Business Services* are active innovators in non-technological areas such as organizational development, firm strategy, human resources management, public relations or marketing. (Boden and Miles 2000; Rubalcaba 1999). The innovations in these sub-sectors are often of a non-technological kind, and they do not go along with formal R&D expenditure. Many of their original innovations are developed and adapted for client firms on a case-by-case basis.

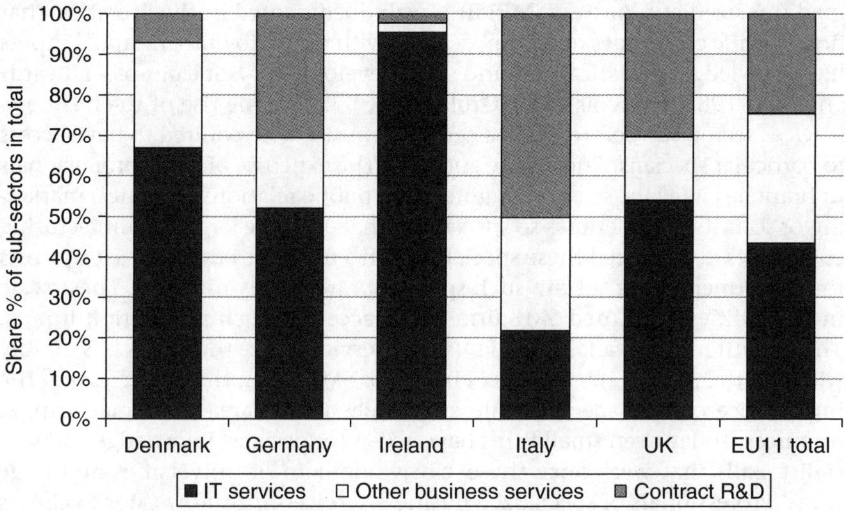

Figure 4.3 Share of subsectors in R&D expenditure in the business-services industry, 2004
Source: OECD ANBERD (2006).

Knowledge diffusion. With regard to many business competences, BSS providers lead their client firms towards the relevant efficiency frontier by spreading 'best practice' information. This is in itself an important indirect contribution to economic growth. A consistent finding from the EU *Community Innovation Survey* is that BSS firms tend to rank before universities as a source of external information for innovating companies. This pattern was found, *inter alia*, in Finland (Leiponen 2001), Netherlands (Kox 2004) and the United Kingdom (Hughes and Wood 1999). Many business-services providers are in the unique position of being able to look into the 'knowledge kitchen' of client firms. They observe localized, tacit knowledge solutions in client firms. But since their horizon is wider, they can more easily conceptualize such solutions and select 'best-practice' solutions to more common business problems. Such 'best-practice' information is subsequently introduced as input when they serve new clients. It has been demonstrated empirically that business-services firms also play a role in international knowledge dissemination. Drejer (1999) established that knowledge-intensive services have played a central role as a knowledge source for Danish firms in manufacturing as well as services. Guerrieri *et al.* (2005) have shown that international trade in business services between countries could explain bilateral knowledge spillovers as measured by patent citations.

Surpassing human capital indivisibilities. A further indirect growth contribution of business services relates to the production potential of small and medium-sized enterprises (SME). It is well documented in the literature that firm-specific economies of scale play a role with regard to human capital inputs like knowledge specializations and skills development (for example, Edwards and Starr 1987; Francois 1990; Grubel 1995). Before the rise of the business-services sector, say before 1980, a certain firm size was required to have access to particular specialist knowledge and skill. The expertise of some professionals in branches like law, science, engineering, public relations, logistics, marketing or security is sometimes so specialized that even the largest manufacturing companies do not need these specialisms on a full-time basis. The set-up costs for departments that sustain such specialists are simply too high. These scale indivisibilities prevented SME firms from access to such production inputs. The growth in the availability of business services since the 1980s has rapidly widened the potential input-mix choices of SME firms, thereby reducing the importance of firm-specific scale economies in the area of human capital resources. Today even small firms have access to specialist knowledge and specialist skills that were once the exclusive domain of universities and large firms. Professionals of specialized business-services firms now cater to clients throughout a region, country or worldwide. Their services are now accessible to small firms in more localized markets or local governments, thus widening their production and efficiency potential.

Summing up, we have good reasons to assume that the poor productivity performance of the business-services industry will, at least to some extent, be compensated by the indirect growth contributions originating from this industry. Of particular importance are three forms of spillover effects – in the form of original innovations, knowledge diffusion, and the reduction of human capital indivisibilities at firm level – that have a positive impact on productivity in other industries.

4.4 Is the 'Baumol disease' looming?

Since the business-services sector grew so fast in the preceding two decades, its own poor productivity performance may – at first sight – have had a downward impact on aggregate productivity growth. This has led some observers to conclude that the growth of this sector contributes to growth stagnation, the so-called Baumol disease. The unbalanced-growth model has been developed by Baumol (1967) and Baumol *et al.* (1989). The latter analysed how an expanding low-productivity services sector may reduce the growth rate of the entire economy, a pattern that is nowadays known as the 'Baumol disease'. The services sector in his growth model has only a limited potential for labour-saving and productivity growth. Moreover, it is characterized by a relatively price-inelastic demand, while its wages follow those of the most productive sector. In this economy, an increasing share of labour will be employed by the services sector. The imminent 'disease' is that the growth rate of the economy falls, while the relative price of services rises.

Some of these 'unbalanced-growth' characteristics also seem present in the growth of the business-services sector, in particular its vigorous employment growth and its poor productivity record, while the Baumol assumptions on wage growth and relative price inelasticity might also apply at least partially.[20]

Even apart from the likelihood that the productivity growth of the business-services sector may be downward-biased because of measurement problems, there are several further reasons why growth of the BSS industry does not necessarily contribute to stagnation of macroeconomic growth. Firstly, the Baumol model focuses on consumer services, whereas business services are intermediate inputs for other industries. Several studies have demonstrated that even low-productive intermediate industries may increase macroeconomic productivity growth if the intermediate inputs replace primary labour inputs in the client industries and if the business-services industry itself has a positive productivity growth rate[21] (Fixler and Siegel 1999; Oulton 1999; Baumol 2007). An important but implicit assumption in Oulton's model is that competition in the markets for BS products is such that all labour productivity gains (no matter how small) are passed on to its clients. This precondition may not be fulfilled.[22] The ECB has found for the euro area that gross profit margins and mark-ups in the business-services sector exceeded the mark-up in total economy and manufacturing. They infer that this might indicate lower competitive pressures in business services relative to the rest of the economy (ECB Task Force 2006). Weak competition and market opacity in business services may thus hamper the positive effects of the business-services sector on aggregate productivity. Secondly, in contrast to the service sector in the Baumol model, the business-services industry might have an unexhausted potential for labour-saving and productivity improvements (Kox 2002, 2004). Thirdly, as shown in the preceding section, the BSS industry indirectly raises the productivity of other industries by the knowledge spillovers that we dealt with in the preceding section.

In Chapter 1 (section 1.1) we find a strong and positive correlation between the employment share of business services and GDP per capita. Francois and Reinert (1995), using a cross-country sample, also find that countries with a higher share of producer services in intermediate inputs of manufacturing had a significantly higher income (GDP) per capita. Also in the future, the weak productivity growth of the business-services sector does not necessarily have a negative effect on European economic growth provided that the positive productivity and innovation spillovers to other industries are strong enough, and provided also that competition and market transparency in business services are such that productivity gains are passed on to client industries.

4.5 Measuring the contribution of business services to economic growth

If the business-services sector is indeed the source of positive spillover effects for other sectors, this must show up empirically. We surveyed a number of empirical studies that – though they use different methods and investigate different countries and periods – have in common that they try to assess the quantitative impacts of business-services use on aggregate productivity and economic growth. Table 4.5 gives a nutshell survey of empirical findings on spillovers from an important subsector of business services, namely computer-related services. The table does not claim to be comprehensive, but it is illustrative for standard findings in this area.[23] Most spillover studies focus specifically on the contributions of R&D and information technology. Crespi (2007) finds highly significant effects from the use of IT in labour productivity.

The studies in Table 4.5 focus in particular on the effects of computer-related or ICT services. With the exception of the Nordhaus study, all the surveyed studies investigate EU countries. Though the empirical evidence is incomplete and fragmentary, we may conclude that positive spillover effects from the computer (IT) services subsector have been quite strong. Other studies show positive spillover effects from business-service inputs without differentiating their sub-sector origin. A number of important results are shown in Table 4.6.

The studies for the business-services sector as a whole have met with more mixed results than those for IT services.[24] The ECORYS-NEI (2004) study, commissioned by the EU, finds statistically significant indications for the existence of positive spillovers in the EU as a whole, in France and in Germany. For the other five individual EU countries, no significantly positive effects could be established. Pilat and Lee (2001) found indications for negative impacts of non-IT business services on aggregate productivity. That effect may be caused by the poor productivity performance of the business-services sector itself. The studies by Antonelli, by Greenhalgh and Gregory, by Katsoulacos and Tsounis mostly cover the period 1980–1990, and they all found indications of the existence of positive spillover effects. Camacho and Rodriguez (2007) find positive and significant impacts of the use of knowledge-intensive services on the production and productivity of client sectors. In the second part of their study they find no significant impacts for the UK and Spain, compared to some other EU countries. In addition, they estimate impacts on innovation diffusion through product-embodied R&D: positive impacts of KIBS use prevail, but impacts differ by country and sector.

Taking these results together, we might conclude tentatively that the growth of business services during the 1980s caused overall positive productivity spillovers. The available positive evidence for the existence of technology and knowledge spillovers seems to imply that during the 1980s business-service firms were unable or unwilling to charge prices that reflect the full contribution of their services to value creation in client industries. The empirical results for the mid-1990s onwards are more mixed. IT and computer services have had an overall positive impact on aggregate productivity and growth, but for other business services, the empirical results do not allow this conclusion for all EU countries. Taken as a whole, the available empirical

Table 4.5 Survey of empirical studies with regard to the impact of computer-related services inputs on aggregate productivity change and growth

Study and main approach	*Country, coverage*	*Productivity or spillover indicator*	*Main findings*
Pilat & Lee (2001) Decomposition aggregate labour productivity growth by industry contributions	5 EU countries (DK, NL, FINL, IT, GERM), 1989–99	Aggregate labour productivity growth	Computer services contributed positively in Denmark, Germany and Italy, but negatively in Netherlands and Finland.
Nordhaus (2002) Decomposition of productivity growth (measured from income side value-added data)	USA, 1975–2000	Aggregate productivity growth	Software industry contributed 0.1% to the 1.6% productivity growth acceleration after 1995.
Crespi (2007): Cobb–Douglas-like production function, measures of IT use and proxies indicators of innovation and labour.	EU, 9 countries (GERM, F, UK, IT, SP, FL, DK), 1995–2000	Aggregate labour productivity	Highly significant fixed effects from IT use, R&D intensity and labour costs.
Van Leeuwen & Van der Wiel (2003) Growth accounting and production function model, including ICT spillovers and innovation indicators	Netherlands, market services, 1994–1998	TFP growth, labour prod. growth	Contribution of ICT spillovers to productivity growth was very strong, and even more so in innovating firms

Table 4.6 Survey of empirical studies with regard to the impact of Total Business Services (TBS) inputs on aggregate productivity change and growth

Study and main approach	*Country, coverage*	*Productivity or spillover indicator*	*Main findings*
ECORYS-NEI (2004) Cross-section production function, compares estimated coefficient for the TBS contribution to aggregate output with the actual BS cost share in intermediate inputs	7 EU countries + Australia, Canada, Japan, Norway, 1994–1998	Difference between actual cost share and estimated production contribution	(a) For France, Germany, Canada, for the EU total, and for the pooled regression: estimated contribution is 1.5 to 2.5 the actual cost share. (b) coefficient for TBS is not significant in regressions for other individual countries.
Antonelli (1999) Calculate production elasticities for TBS use in production functions for a large range of industries (cross-section and time series)	4 EU countries (IT, FRA, GERM, UK), 1988–1990	Value-added impact of TBS use	Effect of TBS use on value added of client industries: a 1% increase in BS inputs caused value added to increase by on average 2.6 to 4.2%
Greenhalgh and Gregory (2000) Growth decomposition in input–output framework: tracing key sectors that generate cost savings and product improvements	UK, 1979–1990	Labour productivity growth, R&D spillovers	TBS industry key sector for productivity growth during 1980s, causing large labour saving in other industries. TBS also important player in the forward transmission of rising product quality

Katsoulacos and Tsounis (2000) Correlation between TFP residuals of industry production functions and BS use, 75 industries	Greece, 1980–1988	TFP, TFP growth	Strong correlation between TBS use and TFP levels and TFP growth of industries
Camacho and Rodriguez (2007) Production function with KIS and KIBS as inputs. Separately: innovation diffusion by KIS/ KIBS through product-embodied R&D.	DK, GERM, SP, NL, UK, 1995–1998	Production, productivity and product embodied R&D diffused by KIS	Positive and significant impacts of KIS on production and productivity. In this second case, no clear results for the UK and Spain. Concerning diffusion on innovation, uneven results by country and sector were identified, but positive impacts dominate
Pilat and Lee (2001) Decomposition aggregate labour productivity growth by industry contributions	5 EU countries (DK, NL, FIN, IT, GERM), 1989–99	Aggregate labour productivity growth	Inputs of non-IT Business Services inputs contributed negatively except in Denmark (period 1995–1999)[1]

Note: 1 Contributions by other BS subsectors were positive in Finland and Germany during the period 1989–1994.

evidence indicates that the contribution of the business-services sector to aggregate economic growth may be positive, and that – at least during important parts of the preceding two decades – the business-services sector has created positive spillover effects for other industries.

Conclusions

The growth of business services represents a qualitatively new stage in the social structure of production. A major characteristic of this structural change is that firm-level scale economies with regard to knowledge and skill inputs are reduced by external deliveries of such inputs.

The sector has had a most prominent role in inter-sectoral employment shifts over the last two decades. On its own the business-services industry accounted for more than half the EU's net employment growth over the entire period. The direct contribution of business-services to the absolute change in total value added was much smaller than its contribution than in terms of employment growth. A consequence was that the productivity growth in the business-services industry during recent decades can at best be called poor. The poor productivity performance of the business-services industry is, at least to some extent, compensated by the indirect growth contributions originating from this industry. Of particular importance are three forms of spillover effects – in the form of original innovations, knowledge diffusion, and the reduction of human capital indivisibilities at firm level – that have a positive impact on productivity in other industries.

The empirical studies surveyed in this chapter indicate that there have been quite strong positive spillover effects from the computer (IT) services subsector. The studies for the business-services sector as a whole have met with more mixed results. The growth of business services during the 1980s caused overall positive productivity spillovers. The available positive evidence on technology and knowledge spillovers seems to imply that business-service firms during the 1980s were unable or unwilling to charge prices that reflect the full contribution of their services to value creation in client industries. The empirical results for the mid-1990s onwards are more mixed. IT and computer services persistently have an overall positive impact on aggregate productivity and growth, but for other business services, the empirical results do not allow this conclusion for all EU countries.

The weak productivity performance by the business-services industry – if carried on into the future – could be potentially become a drag on economic growth. Since the business-services sector has become a major sector in the European economy, this is some reason for concern. Some have even raised the question as to whether the 'Baumol disease' (growth stagnation due to an increasing weight of low-productivity services sectors) is lurking behind the horizon. We argue that this is not yet a big economic threat because of the sector's positive productivity and innovation spillovers to other industries.

However, improvement of market transparency in business services may be needed to ensure that productivity gains are passed on to clients industries.

Notes

1. Examples are customer relations, marketing, management information systems, quality control, logistic management, R&D functions, recruitment of top management, project management, invoicing, administrative organization, human resource management, professional training, engineering, computer services and legal affairs.
2. For evidence, see the chapters by Camacho and Rodriguez (Chapter 7), Crespi (Chapter 6) and Leiponen (Chapter 9) in this book.
3. It is assumed that diminishing returns to scale are dominant in each macroeconomic production function.
4. For example, Edwards and Starr (1987).
5. Note that this pattern would be difficult to explain if the growth of the business-services sector was purely replacement growth (cf. the discussion in Chapter 1, section 1.2).
6. This is calculated by dividing a sector's share in total intermediate demand for business services by the sector's share in total industrial output.
7. For this interpretation, see, *inter alia*, Grubel and Walker (1991), Grubel (1995) and Burda and Dluhosch (2000).
8. From an accounting point of view, expenditures on software and R&D are increasingly registered as investments rather than as current expenditures, due to their contribution to future benefits (cf. Zambon *et al.* 2003).
9. The absolute change in employment for financial services, transport, distributive trades, hotels and catering, communication together represented 46 per cent of the absolute change in European employment over the period 1979–2003. Agriculture and manufacturing made a negative contribution. Source: own calculations based on OECD STAN data and data from GGDC.
10. The OECD Science and Technology Scoreboard 2003 reports the key role of computer services. Over the period 1995–2000, OECD area employment in the sector grew by more than three million, i.e. an average annual growth rate of over 4.3 per cent a year, more than three times that of overall market-sector employment. Over the period 1995–2000, above-average growth in ICT services employment was registered in the United Kingdom (11 per cent), the Netherlands, Finland and the USA (each 10 per cent) and Spain (7 per cent).
11. The distinction between knowledge-intensive business services and other business services is not a sharp one. All sub-sectors in business services have elements of both, but the demarcation line applied in Table 4.1 is based on average human-capital inputs and the average incidence of knowledge-intensive tasks.
12. Calculated as $H_{2003} = H_{1979}\ (1 + g_{VA})^n \cdot (1 + g_{EMP})^{-n}$ in which H_{1979} is the initial labour productivity in 1979, g_{VA} and g_{EMP} are, respectively, the growth perunages for value added and employment, while n is the number of years (24 for this case). Note that g_{VA} must be measured in constant prices, so that the resulting H_{2003} does not match the current-prices value added in Table 4.2.
13. Baumol (1967) inferred that the growth of labour-intensive service industries with few opportunities for labour saving might cause an overall stagnation of economic growth.

14. Wölfl points out three different problem areas with regard to the measurement of services productivity: in the selection of inputs (mostly labour), in the selection and definition of outputs (at constant prices and quality), and, finally, in the method of aggregation over sectors.
15. It is worth noting in this context that the European Commission (DG Enterprise) is actively promoting the development of more standardized product formats for some business services.
16. From the results of the European *Community Innovation Survey* over the period 1999–2001 it appears that innovating BS firms – compared to manufacturing firms – make relatively more intense use of 'secrecy', 'design complexity' and 'lead-time advantage on competitors' to prevent copying of their innovations, and relatively less use of copyrights and trademarks (European Commission 2004b).
17. And, for that matter, it also means that the economic-growth contributions from other sectors are overestimated on the basis of the latter's value-added figures.
18. Spillovers would still exist if we knew all prices charged by individual business-services firms.
19. This did not hold for the United Kingdom, Sweden and Denmark, where the R&D expenditures of the business-services sector increased less than the share of the sector in the total economy. The same also holds for the Czech Republic and Poland who joined the Union in 2004.
20. Some evidence for this is presented in Kox (2004), where it is also shown that measurement errors with regard to business-services output are unlikely to have no effect on the measured productivity growth for the economy as a whole. If real value added created by the business sector is systematically underestimated, this implies that the value added of other sectors that use business services as intermediate inputs must be overestimated. Measurement errors with regard to business-services output do only affect the macroeconomic productivity for the small part of business-services output that is destined for final demand (consumption, export, investment).
21. This is exactly what has happened, for cost-saving reasons, in the outsourcing movement that swept across all market industries throughout the 1980s and 1990s. Privatization of government services had the same effect.
22. One problem with Oulton's paper is that he assumes full competition in business services, so that small productivity increases are also passed on to clients via lower BSS prices. We think, however, that the present situation in most EU BS branches is far from perfect competition.
23. Not included are studies by Hempell (2002), Collechia (2001), Müller and Zenker (2000), which all deal with similar research questions, though sometimes on a regional rather than national level.
24. We have only presented by studies that focus on spillover effects. Other studies like those by Windrum and Tomlinson (1999) focus on explaining production or productivity levels, using industry production functions with industry-level inputs of knowledge-intensive services (for Germany, Japan, the Netherlands, and the UK, 1970–1990). They find that input of knowledge-intensive services has a significant positive impact on gross output and productivity level of industries in all four countries.

Part II

Growth and Innovation Spillovers From Business Services

5
The Impact of Business-Services Use on Client Industries: Evidence from Input–Output Data[1]

Paul Baker

Introduction

Business services are among the fastest-growing and most dynamic sectors of the European economy. Their increasing integration into production processes means that their strategic importance is considerable, not least for the role they can play in improving the performance of client enterprises throughout the economy. At the same time, the business-services sector is a diverse one and the types of services they provide support many different business processes in many types of organizations. On the one hand they can be instrumental in helping companies to lower costs by providing services more cheaply, via economies of scale and specialization; this, after all, has been the basis for much outsourcing. On the other hand, many business services are not only innovative in their own right, but can also serve as important intermediaries and nodes in innovation systems by which they facilitate the transfer of knowledge and technology to clients and support them in their own innovation functions.

Against this background, analysis of the sector-based composition of demand for business services (BSS)[2] and levels of industrial linkages between business services and other sectors of the economy is relatively limited. Similarly, there has to date been little empirical analysis of the impact that BSS use has on the growth and productivity performance of client industries. Using harmonized input–output data this chapter seeks, first, to identify those sectors that are the most important and most intensive users of BSS. In the light of the high level of observed heterogeneity in the use of BSS, statistical cluster analysis is used to develop a typology of sectors based upon their intensity of use of BSS inputs. In turn, a comparison is made of the performance of different user groups. To complete the analysis, econometric analysis based on a production function approach is used to explore the returns to the use of business service inputs across countries.

5.1 Data issues and sources

Measurement of services output is well known to be plagued by a range of problems and statistical agencies are often required to rely on relatively crude indicators to measure output and prices of services. Data issues related to the measurement of business services are dealt with elsewhere in this book and so are not repeated here. Nonetheless, the reader is reminded that a certain degree of caution is always warranted when assessing and analysing statistical data on business services.

To try to keep the impact of differences in statistical procedures and measurement issues to a minimum, the main source of data used in this chapter is the OECD database of input–output (I–O) tables. The OECD has made a useful effort to render tables for a number of its member countries compatible. The OECD harmonised input–output tables include 40 usable sectors standardized for more than a dozen countries.[3] The country tables have been harmonized on an industry-by-industry basis; though, even here, due to data problems the tables for France and the UK remain on a product-by-product basis.[4] To the extent that the focus of this chapter is on the BSS sector (industry), and the interaction of this sector with the rest of the economy rather than on business service activities *per se* then industry-by-industry IO and industry-by-commodity (make) tables are to be preferred over commodity-by-commodity and commodity-by-industry (use) tables. In particular, it should be kept in mind that many of the productivity-increasing properties of BSS are attributed to increased specialization, both on account of the production of the BSS themselves as well as the production process in which BSS enter as an intermediate input. The literature on knowledge-intensive BSS particularly alludes to networks and pools of knowledge that are more easily accessed and exploited by specialist business service providers than by 'in-house' suppliers. Industry-by-industry IOT enable us identify these specialist providers whereas product-by-product IOT would combine both specialist and non-specialist providers.

In the analysis of composition and intensity of demand for BSS inputs, data are presented for each of the nine EU countries available in the OECD database. Moreover, an 'EU9' I–O table has been constructed as a weighted sum of the individual intermediate transaction tables of the nine member states.[5]

5.2 Sector composition and intensity of demand for intermediate BSS inputs

To a large extent the general pattern of demand for BSS inputs reflects the underlying composition of economic activity. As shown in Table 5.1, most of the output of BSS is consumed by services industries (including BSS themselves), with manufacturing generally accounting for less than a third of demand for BSS. As shown in Table 5.2, when an adjustment for sector size

Table 5.1 Consumption of business services: sector shares of total intermediate demand for business services inputs (%)

	Agriculture and mining	*Manufacturing*	*Utilities*	*Construction*	*Trade and hotels*	*Transport and storage*	*Post and telecom*	*Finance and insurance*	*Real estate*	*Business services*	*Public sector*
EU 9	**1.4**	**28.2**	**1.7**	**6.1**	**10.8**	**3.9**	**1.2**	**8.9**	**4.9**	**20.4**	**12.3**
Denmark (1997)	2.7	15.3	0.7	20.1	17.4	4.4	2.0	5.3	2.6	12.9	16.4
Finland (1995)	1.9	48.1	1.9	3.2	8.2	2.6	1.5	4.6	7.2	8.1	12.8
France (1995)	1.0	32.9	2.5	7.6	6.4	2.3	1.0	8.6	2.7	24.2	10.8
Germany (1995)	2.4	32.2	2.0	4.6	9.6	3.2	0.7	7.6	10.0	17.1	10.6
Greece (1994)	1.8	37.8	0.6	9.1	17.9	6.2	0.2	4.6	4.5	3.1	14.2
Italy (1992)	0.3	24.4	0.7	4.5	21.1	6.5	0.8	8.6	4.7	14.2	14.2
Netherlands (1998)	1.7	23.6	0.9	5.5	15.6	5.4	3.7	5.8	1.1	24.9	11.8
Spain (1995)	0.9	32.2	2.1	11.5	12.1	3.3	1.3	6.3	1.0	13.6	15.5
UK (1998)	0.8	17.8	0.9	5.3	10.4	5.6	1.9	14.1	1.8	26.1	15.2

Source: OECD IO Tables, ECORYS-NEI calculations.

is made – in this case by dividing the sector's share of demand for BSS inputs by its share in total gross output[6] – we can see that apart from the BSS sector itself, for most countries the finance and insurance sector has the highest consumption of BSS relative to sector size. At the same time, it is immediately apparent from the two tables that there are large differences in the sector composition of demand for BSS inputs across countries that do not merely reflect difference in the underlying composition of economic activity.

If we consider the intensity of use of BSS,[7] as measured by the ratio of BSS inputs to total demand for intermediate inputs, Table 5.3 again reveals the importance of BSS inputs for the finance and insurance sector. For the EU9, BSS account for over a quarter of total intermediate inputs for the finance and insurance sector, compared to around 10 per cent for the manufacturing sector. The relatively high intensity of use BSS input in finance and insurance, together with the high intensity of BSS inputs within the BSS sector, is one of

Table 5.2 Consumption of business services relative to industrial output: sector share of total intermediate demand for business services inputs divided by sector share of industrial output

	Agriculture and mining	*Manufacturing*	*Utilities*	*Construction*	*Trade and hotels*	*Transport and storage*	*Post and telecom*	*Finance and insurance*	*Real estate*	*Business services*	*Public sector*
EU 9	**0.44**	**0.91**	**0.71**	**0.84**	**0.88**	**0.86**	**0.73**	**1.78**	**0.73**	**2.52**	**0.69**
Denmark 1997)	0.58	0.62	0.33	2.77	1.27	0.57	1.06	1.33	0.36	2.02	0.82
Finland (1995)	0.50	1.27	0.64	0.50	0.82	0.49	0.97	1.67	0.86	1.86	0.76
France (1995)	0.26	1.06	1.04	1.15	0.59	0.58	0.60	1.76	0.36	2.41	0.62
Germany (1995)	1.17	1.01	0.95	0.62	0.91	0.80	0.43	1.64	1.29	2.09	0.54
Greece (1994)	0.20	1.57	0.30	1.06	0.86	1.66	0.14	1.52	0.50	1.22	0.90
Italy (1992)	0.10	0.70	0.30	0.62	1.49	1.28	0.63	1.73	0.83	2.37	0.92
Netherlands (1998)	0.35	0.85	0.35	0.71	1.20	1.04	1.85	1.15	0.21	2.60	0.69
Spain (1995)	0.20	0.99	0.84	1.16	0.76	0.68	0.80	1.52	0.20	3.10	1.09
UK (1998)	0.30	0.71	0.32	0.83	0.80	1.02	0.77	1.93	0.34	2.60	0.79

Source: OECD IO Tables, ECORYS-NEI calculations.

relatively few consistent patterns across all countries. In fact the BSS sector is by and large the most intensive user of BSS inputs; for example, for France, Germany the Netherlands and the United Kingdom, BSS inputs account for over 40 per cent of intermediate inputs used by the BSS sector itself.

Elsewhere the picture is more mixed and sectors that appear to be relatively intensive users of BSS in one country may reveal lower-intensity use in another country or vice versa and there are clear exceptions to general patterns. For example, agriculture and mining is shown to have low intensity of use of BSS in all countries except Germany and, similarly, construction shows typically low intensity of use of BSS, but in Denmark the share of BSS inputs in total intermediate inputs of the construction sector is nearly twice the average for all sectors. In fact, the heterogeneity of industrial linkages of the business services sectors across countries is perhaps the most outstanding observation from the analysis.

Table 5.3 Intensity of use of business services: business service inputs as a share of total intermediate inputs (%)

	Agriculture and mining	*Manufacturing*	*Utilities*	*Construction*	*Trade and hotels*	*Transport and storage*	*Post and telecom*	*Finance and insurance*	*Real estate*	*Business services*	*Public sector*	*All sectors*
EU 9	**6.6**	**9.9**	**10.3**	**10.3**	**15.3**	**11.6**	**17.1**	**27.6**	**24.1**	**44.8**	**12.9**	**14.5**
Denmark (1997)	6.0	5.0	4.4	21.4	15.4	4.8	15.7	18.8	9.9	25.8	15.7	**11.2**
Finland (1995)	4.4	6.6	4.1	3.1	6.6	4.4	11.1	19.3	8.0	14.4	8.7	**7.0**
France (1995)	4.6	13.9	19.8	17.7	14.9	10.7	19.8	34.8	19.9	49.5	18.5	**18.9**
Germany (1995)	15.4	10.8	14.4	7.8	14.9	10.0	13.7	24.0	35.0	43.1	8.7	**14.1**
Greece (1994)	1.5	5.4	2.0	5.1	5.1	8.9	4.5	16.3	10.9	7.2	8.1	**5.7**
Italy (1992)	1.3	5.9	4.1	6.0	19.5	12.1	12.1	26.9	21.7	32.9	13.6	**11.2**
Netherlands (1998)	6.5	9.8	4.3	8.8	23.0	17.3	36.3	23.5	8.1	49.7	17.1	**16.2**
Spain (1995)	1.5	4.9	6.8	6.7	6.9	6.0	12.0	17.1	3.5	27.4	14.0	**7.2**
UK (1998)	6.2	10.7	4.6	12.5	16.6	17.4	15.7	29.8	16.1	52.9	15.9	**18.1**

Source: OECD IO Tables, ECORYS-NEI calculations.

Some country differences can obviously be attributed to somewhat heterogeneous activities that may be still be grouped together under the different sectors of activity. However, from Table 5.4, which shows a more detailed sector breakdown, we can still see considerable variation across countries. Table 5.4 shows both the direct (technical) coefficients and estimates of total demand for BSS that make use of the total (or inverse) requirements matrix to estimate the level of BSS incorporated within intermediate inputs purchased from other sectors[8] (that is, direct plus indirect demand for BSS). These latter total demand estimates are interpreted as the total increase in output of BSS resulting from the production of one additional unit of final output; for example, a one euro increase in final demand (output) of the agriculture and fishing sector in Denmark would result in increased output of BSS of around 9.1 cents, which may be compared to the increased direct demand of only 3.4 cents.

Table 5.4 allows, in particular, for a more detailed breakdown of BSS demand for manufacturing sectors. Looking across sectors, there are a number of sectors

Table 5.4 Intensity of use of business services: direct and total (direct plus indirect) requirements for BSS as a share of total output (%)

	Denmark (1997)		*Finland (1995)*		*France (1995)*		*Germany (1995)*		*Greece (1994)*		*Italy (1992)*		*Netherlands (1998)*		*Spain (1995)*		*UK (1998)*	
	Direct	*Total*	*Direct*	*Total*	*Direct*	*Total*	*Direct*	*Total*	*Direct*	*Total*	*Direct*	*Total*	*Direct*	*Total*	*Direct*	*Total*	*Direct*	*Total*
Agriculture & Fishing	3.4	9.1	0.4	3.6	2.4	13.7	6.9	15.6	0.1	1.3	0.2	3.8	2.5	11.6	0.4	3.8	4.5	17.8
Mining & Quarrying	1.2	3.0	13.3	19.1	2.4	16.3	10.3	19.5	5.5	7.5	3.1	7.3	3.6	8.3	2.8	6.2	1.3	7.4
Food & Tobacco	3.3	10.6	4.1	10.0	9.4	24.7	7.4	19.6	2.7	4.9	2.7	8.9	6.5	20.1	2.8	7.9	8.0	24.0
Textiles, Leather & Footwear	2.0	7.9	5.9	12.1	7.8	24.8	4.2	15.3	5.0	8.5	3.3	11.0	5.5	20.0	2.9	9.1	6.1	19.6
Wood & Cork	1.1	6.2	2.6	6.7	1.4	11.7	6.9	17.7	2.3	5.5	2.9	9.6	5.6	18.6	2.0	6.6	3.8	16.3
Pulp, Paper, Printing & Publishing	3.7	9.3	3.4	9.0	6.7	20.9	8.2	18.8	5.9	10.7	5.0	13.5	8.3	21.6	2.7	8.0	6.1	19.0
Coke, ref. Petr. & Nucl. Fuel	2.2	6.3	2.4	16.2	10.1	28.0	6.2	23.7	1.5	7.1	0.3	3.4	4.7	15.0	2.9	8.1	6.1	17.8
Chemicals (inc. Pharm).	7.2	13.8	3.8	10.3	12.0	31.1	10.8	22.5	8.5	14.8	5.6	14.9	7.7	22.9	5.9	12.6	9.9	26.5
Rubber & Plastic	2.4	8.0	4.6	10.6	11.4	29.4	6.6	18.0	5.1	11.7	3.1	11.6	7.5	21.8	2.4	8.7	6.1	20.7
Other Non-Metallic Mineral	1.7	6.2	4.1	10.2	7.4	20.8	9.4	19.4	2.9	6.4	4.1	11.1	6.9	18.5	4.4	9.1	4.6	16.1
Iron & Steel, Non-Ferrous Metals	0.9	6.4	2.7	11.6	3.4	18.1	3.9	15.4	2.5	7.1	4.8	14.3	4.5	17.1	3.6	9.8	2.9	16.9

Fabricated Metal Products	2.2	6.7	9.1	16.6	4.7	16.7	4.9	14.1	2.7	6.8	4.6	12.6	5.5	18.2	3.0	8.8	4.9	16.6
Machinery & Equipment, n.e.c.	2.7	7.4	7.0	14.8	14.9	31.7	5.9	15.5	4.2	8.3	4.4	13.2	7.0	21.3	4.1	9.9	6.3	19.6
Elec., Electronic & Prec. Equip.	3.1	8.0	5.3	13.9	15.0	35.0	8.9	19.5	4.7	9.2	6.7	15.3	11.3	28.6	6.4	13.3	6.8	22.1
Elec. Machinery & Equip. n.e.c.	2.7	8.5	4.1	11.3	10.0	25.5	8.8	19.3	2.8	7.6	4.3	12.8	8.1	23.2	4.2	10.3	6.3	19.6
Motor Vehicles & Trailers	1.8	6.8	3.1	10.3	10.4	32.6	4.3	15.1	1.6	6.4	4.1	14.2	5.6	22.7	3.0	10.6	5.6	21.7
Other Transport Equipment	1.8	7.6	11.9	20.6	10.5	32.7	6.2	17.6	0.8	2.1	4.8	14.4	5.6	21.8	3.2	9.0	11.9	29.5
Manufacturing n.e.c.; Recycling	3.6	9.1	4.2	9.6	8.3	21.6	8.0	18.3	3.4	5.8	3.6	11.8	4.6	14.4	3.7	9.2	5.7	18.6
Electricity, Gas & Water Supply	1.7	4.8	2.3	8.2	9.4	21.2	6.5	14.1	0.7	2.9	1.6	5.0	2.8	10.4	3.0	6.3	3.1	13.3
Construction	14.3	20.6	1.8	7.6	10.4	24.9	4.2	13.3	2.5	5.7	3.4	10.2	5.8	19.0	4.1	9.6	7.9	22.2
Wholesale & Retail Trade	7.1	10.7	2.5	5.8	5.9	13.1	6.9	12.9	2.4	4.2	9.5	14.8	10.2	19.0	3.5	6.2	7.9	19.7
Hotels & Restaurants	3.3	7.9	4.6	9.6	3.6	13.9	3.1	12.9	1.2	3.0	3.2	8.1	7.8	17.7	1.6	4.8	6.8	17.1
Transport & Storage	2.9	5.6	1.7	5.2	5.3	16.0	5.5	14.0	3.8	5.9	7.0	14.1	8.5	18.3	2.4	5.3	9.8	24.6
Post & Telecommunications	5.5	9.6	3.5	6.1	5.5	11.8	3.0	6.1	0.3	0.6	3.5	7.1	15.1	25.7	2.8	4.7	7.4	18.8
Finance, Insurance	6.9	10.9	6.0	8.6	15.9	28.3	11.3	20.1	3.5	4.5	9.5	14.5	9.4	18.1	5.3	7.9	18.5	36.4
Real Estate Activities	1.8	4.8	3.1	6.0	3.3	6.6	8.8	13.0	1.2	1.7	4.6	7.4	1.7	5.8	0.7	2.6	3.3	9.0
Business Services	10.4	14.7	6.7	10.5	21.8	33.8	14.3	19.9	2.8	4.2	13.0	18.3	21.2	31.9	10.9	14.5	24.9	40.1
Public Admin. & Defence	4.7	7.4	4.4	7.7	8.1	15.3	3.2	10.0	3.1	4.7	5.8	9.5	6.3	12.8	4.8	6.9	6.5	17.7
Education	2.7	4.9	1.0	3.3	2.3	6.6	2.4	5.4	1.6	2.1	1.5	3.5	4.6	8.6	1.4	2.7	7.1	14.9
Health And Social Work	2.6	4.9	2.5	4.5	3.2	11.0	3.7	8.9	1.7	3.4	5.0	12.2	3.0	7.9	3.6	6.5	5.0	17.7
Other Services	8.2	12.5	2.9	6.0	7.4	16.8	5.7	10.8	1.0	2.0	6.8	11.5	8.3	18.6	4.2	7.0	13.6	26.1

Source: OECD IO Tables, ECORYS-NEI calculations.

that tend to stand out for their high intensity of use of BSS irrespective of whether direct or total requirements are examined; notably (i) chemicals;[9] (ii) electrical, electronic and precision equipment;[10] (iii) electrical machinery and equipment n.e.c.; and (iv) finance and insurance. Beyond these, there are a number of sectors which display only relatively high intensity of use of BSS when account is taken of indirect inputs of BSS via other intermediate inputs – for example, motor vehicles, other transport equipment, and rubber and plastics. More generally, differences between direct and total requirements coefficients tend to be more important for manufacturing than for service sectors, indicating that even where these industries appear to consume few BSS directly they can still indirectly induce relatively high levels of demand for BSS inputs.

Overall, although a number of manufacturing sectors are revealed to be among the most intensive business services we can still observe considerable variation in the BSS intensity of the same industries across countries, even allowing for differences in the overall country level of use of BSS. More generally, looking across all sectors it appears that there is considerable cross country heterogeneity in the patterns and intensity of linkages of BSS to other sectors of economic activity.

5.3 Statistical cluster analysis-based typology of business services use

The previous section illustrates the difficulty of identifying clearly discernible patterns in the use of BSS. Moreover, any attempt to break down BSS into its four main statistical sub-groups further exacerbates the problem. To try to get around this problem, statistical cluster analysis has been used to try to develop a typology of industry sectors based on the intensity of use of different BSS categories. The cluster analysis was applied to an extended pooled database of national input–output tables for 13 countries and a sector classification based on 57 sectors.[11] The cluster analysis used a two-stage clustering process[12] applied to direct requirement coefficients for each of the four BSS categories expressed as a share of total output; the values were standardized to reduce the impact of different statistical methodologies and potential dominance by countries with high overall levels of BS inputs.

For the purposes of this chapter it is not necessary to enter into a detailed explanation of the clustering process. Nonetheless, the resulting taxonomy that is described below was validated by further statistical analyses that showed the classification to be robust to country specific difference in overall use of BSS.

The cluster analysis identified six distinct categories of BSS users:[13] four groups of users that are particularly intensive in one of the four BSS classes, one group that appears an average user of BSS, and one group that uses only very little BSS:

High 71 – intensive users of NACE 71 (Renting)
High 72 – intensive users of NACE 72 (Computing)

High 73 – intensive users of NACE 73 (R&D)
High 74 – intensive users of NACE 74 ('Other' BSS)
Intermediate – average users of all BSS
Low – low users of all BSS

Overall, the outcome of the clustering exercise appears to lead to intuitively reasonable results:

- Intensive users of BSS related to the renting of machinery and equipment (High 71) consists largely of transport services, mining and construction, which are all activities where the use of rented and leased machinery and equipment is widespread.
- Intensive users of computing and related services (High 72) incorporate all the sub-activities of financial services, together with telecommunications, and logistics and travel services.
- Intensive R&D service users (High 73), is a somewhat diverse category, including pharmaceuticals – well known for the importance of R&D – and public administrations, including defence. It also includes water distribution and sanitation services, which may relate to expenditures on environmental R&D, for example. Finally, the consumer electronics and communication equipment sector and rail transport equipment are identified as intensive users of R&D services inputs.
- The final category of intensive BSS services users relates to the residual 'other' BSS category (High 74), which itself covers a diverse range of services that are quite varied in their main characteristics. On the one hand, 'other' BSS includes high-skilled knowledge-intensive professional, technical, and marketing services. On the other hand, it includes more operational and support services, such as security, industrial cleaning and labour recruitment. Intensive users of 'other' BSS include the retail and wholesale distribution sectors, chemicals (excluding pharmaceuticals), tobacco, recycling, and some social and cultural services.
- On the whole, the category of 'Low' BSS users tends to cover sectors that are involved in primary production and the production of intermediate goods. Whereas, the 'Intermediate' category tends to cover manufacturing sectors that are typically involved in the production of final goods, together with a range of service sectors orientated towards private 'consumers' (households and private individuals) as opposed to services for the business sector.

5.4 Performance analysis of cluster groups

Having arrived at a typology of sectors according to their intensity of BSS use, the question arises as to whether there is any observable difference in the economic performance of the identified industry clusters.

Table 5.5 Average annual growth rates by BSS client categories (percentage)

	Value added			*Employment*			*Labour productivity*			*Share of total in 1995 (%)*	
	1990–1995	*1995–2000*	*1990–2000*	*1990–1995*	*1995–2000*	*1990–2000*	*1990–1995*	*1995–2000*	*1990–2000*	*VA*	*Emp.*
BSS	3.16	7.22	5.21	2.17	6.79	4.41	0.88	0.84	0.75	*8*	*8*
BSS client categories:											
High71 (renting)	0.61	2.50	1.45	−1.40	1.80	−0.07	2.18	0.65	1.58	11	11
High72 (computer)	1.32	4.70	3.13	−1.54	0.22	−0.64	3.00	4.46	4.00	11	7
High73 (R&D)	2.22	2.28	2.28	0.44	1.00	0.77	1.80	1.27	1.67	12	16
High74 (other)	1.00	3.38	2.19	−0.60	1.68	0.47	1.66	1.69	1.79	13	16
Intermediate	1.22	1.72	1.41	−0.25	0.98	0.42	1.51	0.78	1.05	24	32
Low	1.61	1.88	1.77	−3.41	−0.62	−2.15	5.28	2.51	4.07	21	11
All Sectors	1.35	3.01	2.21	−0.66	1.66	0.40	2.06	1.72	1.80	100	100

Source: ECORYS-NEI.

Table 5.5 shows average growth rates of value-added, employment and labour productivity for a sample of nine EU countries[14] for each of the six categories identified in the cluster analysis described above, together with BSS themselves. The data on value added and employment by sector were obtained from the OECD STAN database for industrial analysis;[15] growth rates were calculated separately for each country and the table shows a simple average of the individual country estimates.

The impressive performance of the BSS sector itself stands out, and its growth performance ranks highest in both value added and employment terms, although growth in labour productivity has been relatively low. In terms of growth in value added, we see that for the 1990s as a whole, and particularly in the second half of the decade, sectors identified from the cluster analysis as intensive (high) users of BSS typically had higher average growth rates than intermediate and low users. The picture in terms of employment performance is more mixed, but this in itself is not surprising when one considers the factors that may be at work here. If BSS inputs have a positive effect on performance then we may expect high-user sectors to have a stronger employment growth than low-user sectors. At the same time, where BSS use is associated with a substitution of (actual or potential) employment in the user sector by employment in BSS then this would lower employment growth in high BSS user sectors.

One feature that stands out from the average growth in productivity is the strong performance of those sectors identified as intensive users of computer services inputs (High 72). Moreover, in the second half of the 1990s this productivity growth was achieved alongside an increase in employment. This situation may be contrasted with the performance of the category of 'Low' BSS users, which also achieved very strong productivity growth, particularly in the early 1990s. For this category, which includes sectors such as agriculture, textiles and clothing, metals and transport equipment, these productivity gains were accompanied by major reductions in employment. Here the story appears to be much more about the impact of industrial restructuring brought about in response to global competitive pressures rather than the impact of use of BSS.

5.5 Econometric analysis of BSS impact on economic performance

In Chapter 7 Camacho and Rodriguez provide an overview of the main approaches and empirical findings from a number of studies have attempted to use I–O data to analyse the relationship between BSS (or knowledge-intensive services – KIS) as a production input and total production output or value added. They identify two main approaches: the first introduces BSS as an additional input in a traditional production function (for example, Antonelli 1998, 2000; Drejer 2002), while the second assumes the hypothesis that output is produced by the interaction of labour on material and non-material

(BSS) inputs (for example, Tomlinson, 2000a). Whereas Camacho and Rodriguez adopt the second of these approaches[16] in the following empirical analysis a traditional production function approach is retained.

The model used to estimate the effect of BSS on production assumes a (Cobb–Douglas) production function in which BSS enters as an additional input in the production function. The model can be used to examine two hypotheses. Firstly, whether BSS has a positive (and significant) effect on production and, secondly, whether there is a return (quasi-rent) on the use of BSS inputs. Under this second hypothesis, not only should BSS inputs have a positive effect on the level of production (output) of client industries, but also the magnitude of this effect should exceed the cost share of BSS inputs in total primary production inputs. To establish the presence of quasi-rents, however, requires that the estimated model should contain a complete range of input factors so as to avoid bias induced by omitted variables that may tend to increase the size of the estimated parameter on BSS.[17] With this in mind, the model incorporates measures of capital, labour, business services inputs, together with other material and non-material inputs. This results in a model with the following specification:

$$\log Q_i = \alpha + \beta \log K_i + \gamma \log L_i + \delta \log BS_i + \varepsilon \log MNF_i + \phi \log OS_i$$

Where Q is total output, K represents consumption of fixed capital, L is the wage bill, BS constitutes the value of *BSS* (NACE codes 71 to 74) inputs, *MNF* captures material inputs including utilities (NACE codes 01 up to and including 41), and *OS* captures other services inputs (NACE codes 45 to 70 and 75 to 99). In other words, total output is estimated as a function of its primary production inputs, capital and labour, and total intermediate inputs; the latter being separated into three categories: material inputs, business services inputs and 'other' service inputs. α, β, γ, δ, ε, and ϕ are parameters to be estimated, and i is a sector index.[18]

With the exception of the consumption of fixed capital, all of the data used in the estimations are taken from the OECD harmonized I–O database that has already been described. For the purposes of the empirical analysis, where it is available the OECD measures of consumption of fixed capital from the OECD STAN databases is used in the regressions, otherwise capital stock estimates have been made using data on new capital formation and capital stock deflators from the same data source and using a Perpetual Inventory Method (PIM) and assuming linear depreciation (of all new capital investments) over five years.[19] Even so, for any single country, capital data is available for generally less than 30 sectors.[20]

The model has been estimated separately for each country and, additionally, using pooled data and a fixed effects specification (EU pooled) with the results shown in Table 5.6. The small numbers of observations reflect the fact that sectors have been dropped because of the lack of data on capital

Table 5.6 Regression results: individual country estimations and pooled fixed effects estimations

	Denmark	*Finland*	*France*[1]	*Germany*	*Greece*	*Italy*	*Netherlands*	*EU Pooled*
L	0.163	0.321	0.248	0.242	0.256	0.162	0.103	0.174
	(2.52)*	(4.24)**	(2.98)*	(3.04)**	(3.79)**	(1.35)	(1.36)	(5.89)**
K	0.288	0.152	0.143	0.226	0.182	0.200	0.315	0.244
	(5.06)**	(3.69)**	(2.46)*	(4.12)**	(3.41)**	(2.11)	(7.26)**	(11.94)**
BS	0.006	0.057	0.122	0.301	−0.098	0.042	0.089	0.107
	(0.12)	(1.21)	(1.75)	(4.86)**	(1.43)	(0.72)	(0.85)	(4.82)**
MNF	0.188	0.302	0.261	0.138	0.241	0.146	0.213	0.207
	(7.03)**	(9.32)**	(5.62)**	(4.00)**	(6.27)**	(3.73)**	(4.80)**	(14.45)**
OS	0.384	0.179	0.231	0.177	0.450	0.450	0.292	0.286
	(3.34)**	(2.39)*	(2.69)*	(2.15)*	(5.75)**	(4.51)**	(2.60)*	(8.51)**
Constant	1.664	1.959	1.927	1.428	3.52	2.128	2.285	2.327
	(5.45)**	(6.73)*	(2.78)*	(3.55)**	(5.41)**	(5.05)**	(5.65)**	(17.54)**
Observations	*24*	*28*	*18*	*30*	*30*	*18*	*18*	*166*
R-squared	*0.99*	*0.98*	*0.96*	*0.97*	*0.99*	*0.98*	*0.98*	*0.97*

Notes: Absolute value of t statistics in parentheses; *significant at 5%; **significant at 1%
For France consumption of fixed capital (K) is estimated using a PIM procedure with a linear depreciation over 5 years.
Source: ECORYS-NEI.

consumption.[21] This does not affect the consistency of the estimates, but it does reduce their accuracy and therefore leads to relatively high standard errors. For the individual country regressions, with the exception of Greece the estimated coefficients on BSS inputs are all positive, although only in the case of Germany is the estimated coefficient significant at the 5 per cent error level. By contrast, the estimated coefficients on all variables are highly significant for the pooled regression, which points to the fact that the low number of observations may explain the lack of significant estimates of the coefficient of the BSS parameter for individual country estimates.

Table 5.7 compares the estimated coefficients with the actual cost shares of the intermediate inputs.[22] By dividing the two, we obtain a measure of the return associated with a unit increase in the use of the intermediate inputs. Regarding BSS, the coefficient for Greece indicates that there is actually a negative relationship between BSS inputs and output, while for Italy and Denmark the estimations indicate that on average the value of 'additional' output generated by an increase in BSS inputs is less than their cost. For the other countries, however, the 'additional' output generated by an increase in BSS inputs is greater that the cost of the additional BSS inputs. In fact, comparing across the individual country estimates there is a tendency for returns to be higher the more developed is the BSS sector. The pooled regression results for the seven EU countries indicate a nominal return of 1.67. Thus, each euro worth of input of BSS increases the value of total output by around

Table 5.7 Comparison of estimated coefficients, cost shares of intermediate inputs and calculated nominal return

	Denmark	*Finland*	*France*	*Germany*	*Greece*	*Italy*	*Netherlands*	*EU Pooled*
1. Estimated Coefficients								
BS	0.006	0.057	0.122	0.301	−0.098	0.042	0.089	0.107
MNF	0.188	0.302	0.261	0.138	0.241	0.146	0.213	0.207
OS	0.384	0.179	0.231	0.177	0.450	0.450	0.292	0.286
2. Actual cost shares								
BS	0.05	0.05	0.08	0.08	0.03	0.04	0.06	0.06
MNF	0.23	0.36	0.29	0.27	0.30	0.32	0.30	0.29
OS	0.18	0.21	0.15	0.18	0.15	0.16	0.18	0.16
3. Nominal return (=1/2)								
BS	0.12	1.19	1.54	3.76	−3.30	0.97	1.43	1.67
MNF	0.82	0.84	0.89	0.52	0.80	0.46	0.72	0.71
OS	2.12	0.84	1.58	1.00	3.09	2.77	1.64	1.74

Source: ECORYS-NEI.

1.67 euros. Overall, a fairly consistent picture emerges in which the use of BSS appears to create rents that are captured by the client industry.

It is interesting to observe that from the pooled estimates the nominal return to other services inputs is of roughly the same magnitude as the return to BSS inputs, while the return to manufacturing inputs is actually below one. In this sense, the use of business services does not necessarily appear to have any different impact compared to 'other' services. However, for both categories the conclusion from the empirical estimates is that the value of 'additional' output generated by an increase in services input is greater than their cost. In other words, this points to evidence of positive returns from the use of business services (and other services).

5.5 Conclusions

Demand for business services is not, as is sometimes argued, predominantly a mere reflection of the externalization (outsourcing) of activities from manufacturing and the migration of jobs from manufacturing to services activities. Externalization may well be an important explanatory factor behind the growth of demand for BSS but, if this is the case, then it encompasses a far broader range of sectors than just manufacturing. Although data from input–output tables indicate that manufacturing accounts for around 30 per cent of demand for BSS, nearly double this amount is consumed by services sectors and over 10 per cent goes to the public sector. Service sectors are also more intensive users of BSS, with BSS accounting for a quarter of intermediate inputs used by business-related services[23] and over 15 per cent for the public sector, but only about ten per cent of intermediate inputs for manufacturing industries.

The widespread and increasing use of BSS implies that their impact on the performance of client sectors is of immense importance. Using a typology of sectors derived from statistical cluster analysis to categorize sectors according to their use of BSS, those sectors identified as 'high' users of BSS appear to have enjoyed higher average growth rates in value added than 'low' or 'intermediate' users, particularly during the second half of the 1990s. The picture with regard to relative employment and productivity performance across the various categories of BSS users is somewhat mixed. In general, the productivity performance of intensive users of BSS was greater than that of 'intermediate' users and of the BSS sector, itself. At the same time, the highest growth of productivity was recorded in those sectors found to be 'low' users of BSS but, at the same time, these sectors were on average marked by rapidly falling employment levels. One striking feature is the particularly strong performance both in terms of (partial) labour productivity and value-added growth of those sectors characterized as being high users of computer services.

The findings from the econometric estimation of a model that incorporates BSS as an additional input into the production function generally support the proposition that BSS use has a positive impact on production and productivity. Absence of data on capital is an important limiting factor on the number of observations that may be included in estimation and individual country regressions, though indicating a positive effect, do not generally yield a statistically significant coefficient on BSS use. Estimates from a pooled sample, however, do provide a positive and statistically significant coefficient on BSS use. Moreover, the estimates indicate that the overall economic return to the use of BSS far exceeds their value of market transactions; in other words, the contribution of BSS to the value of final output of user sectors considerably exceeds their cost as inputs into production, which indicates that BSS use generates economic rents that are captured by user industries.

Although the findings from the analysis presented in this chapter are supportive of proposition that BSS use makes a positive contribution to economic performance, it is important to recognise the very strong heterogeneity in the use of BSS across both sectors and countries. Although within a country, the variation across sectors in BSS use may result from different optimal production structures for different industries, the variation across countries for the same sector cannot be dismissed as mere statistical discrepancies (that is, country fixed effects). Moreover, when combined with the observation of very large differences in the relative productivity levels of BSS between countries, these differences may provide a sign that European markets remain highly fragmented and that Europe is a long way from achieving an integrated

Internal Market for BSS. Though the causes of this fragmentation have not been analysed in this chapter,[24] given the high growth potential of BSS and their potential contribution to productivity growth in user sectors, the continued fragmented nature of the market for BSS could impose significant costs on the European economy as a whole.

Notes

1. This chapter is based on the findings of a study of the 'Contribution of Business Services to Growth and Productivity in the European Union' funded by the European Commission under the contract FIF 20020652 (ref: ENTR/02.03). The analysis was undertaken by a team of researchers from ECORYS-NEI (Netherlands); the ESRC Centre for Research on Innovation and Competition (CRIC), Manchester University (United Kingdom); and WIFO – Austrian Institute of Economic Research (Austria). The individual authors of the Final Report of this study are Paul Baker, Vincent de Boer, Ian Miles and Michael Peneder.
2. Business services are narrowly defined so as to include only renting of machinery and equipment without operator and of personal and household goods (Industry 33 of the OECD classification of industries; NACE 71), computer and related activities (OECD 34; NACE 72), research and development (OECD 35; NACE 73), and other business activities (OECD 36; NACE 74).
3. For each country, three tables are provided, concerning total use, domestic use and imported use; the analysis provided in this chapter focuses on the total-use tables only.
4. This difference for France and the UK should be kept in mind when analysing cross-country differences in the level and intensity of BSS use. In particular, product-by-product data will tend to increase the overall level of recorded intermediate inputs of BSS, and this may explain why overall recorded BSS use is found to be highest in these two countries.
5. The 'EU9' IO Table is constructed as the weighted sum of the individual intermediate transactions tables. The weights are determined by (i) the overall sum of all entries in the individual intermediate transactions tables and (ii) the countries' size of GDP in 1995. For the second step, the purpose was to provide an adjustment for aggregating across countries in order to obtain a common base year (1995). It would have been preferable, for this second step, to use data on the total intermediate demand for a common year rather than GDP, as the latter measures final demand rather than total intermediate demand. To the extent that the relative size (weight) of countries differ in terms of total intermediate consumption as opposed to GDP, and changes in GDP between the data period and the common base year differ from changes in total intermediate demand over this period, then the use of GDP weights will reduce the reliability of the weighting procedure. In the absence, however, of available and easily comparable data across all countries of total intermediate demand, GDP-based weights were used to provide a simple approximation of the weight of each country's contribution to the aggregate 'EU9' IO Table.
6. A value of 1 indicates that the use of BSS inputs corresponds to a sector's weight in total output, if the indicator is greater than one then this implies the sector uses proportionately more BSS inputs than its weight in total output would indicate.

7. There are two commonly used measures of BSS intensity based on the ratio of BSS inputs to either total demand for intermediary inputs or to total output. The analytical difference between these two measures depends on the fraction of value added and taxes contained in the total value of output of each sector. Here, only analysis based on the ratio of BSS inputs to total demand for intermediary inputs is presented, but analysis with respect to the total output is provided in ECORYS-NEI (2004).
8. The direct (technical) coefficient or direct requirements matrix shows the value of intermediate and primary inputs required in the production of one unit of output in the sector, while the total (or inverse) requirements matrix shows the production required, both directly and indirectly, per unit delivery to final demand.
9. This can be explained by high demand for R&D services in the pharmaceuticals subsector of chemicals.
10. This is an aggregate of office, accounting and computing machinery; radio, television and communications equipment; and medical, precision and optical instruments.
11. Data obtained from the national statistical agencies are used for Germany (2000), Great Britain (2000) and the Netherlands (2001); the OECD input–output database is used for Denmark (1997), France (1995), Greece (1994), Japan (1997), Norway (1997), Spain (1995), and the USA (1995); Eurostat data are used for Finland (1995), Belgium (1995) and Austria (1995). Due to differences across data sources the final database contains data on 71 partly overlapping sectors. Although ideally the cluster analysis should be performed on a on a set of fully harmonised data for the same year, cluster analysis can to some extent accommodate differences in sector breakdown among countries as long as these differences do not affect the conditioning variables (i.e. the BSS sectors). Moreover, since we are looking at industrial linkages and not year-to-year growth rates, the use data from different points in time is acceptable.
12. The two-stage clustering process combines *k*-means in the first and agglomerative hierarchical methods in the second step of the analysis. The *k*-means method produces a first partition, which reduces the large initial dataset for better use in the second step of hierarchical clustering. The second stage results in the final identification of all observations into a set of mutually exclusive classes.
13. The NACE codes covered by each category are as follows: 'High 71': 10, 14, 353, 45, 60, 61, 62; 'High 72': 63, 64, 65, 66, 67; 'High 73': 2423, 32, 352, 359, 41, 75, 90, 91; 'High 74': 16, 24 (excluding 2423), 37, 50, 51, 52, 92, 93; 'Intermediate': 13, 15, 22, 23, 25, 26, 29, 30, 31, 33, 351, 36, 55, 80, 85; 'Low': 01, 02, 05, 11, 17, 18, 19, 20, 21, 27, 28, 34, 35, 40, 70. In most cases sectors are defined at a two-digit NACE level, though there are a few exceptions which arise where data from sub-categories of a two-digit NACE sector where allocated to different cluster categories. Specifically this arises in the case of Chemicals (NACE 24), for which the clustering procedure placed the sector as a whole in the category 'High 73', as was the subsector Pharmaceuticals (NACE 2423) but the subsector Chemicals excluding Pharmaceuticals (NACE 24 excl. 2423) was classified as 'High 74'. Similarly, Other Transport equipment (NACE 35) was placed by the clustering procedure in the category 'Low', but 3 subsectors were placed in different categories: (i) Building and repair of ships and boats (NACE 351) in 'Intermediate'; (ii) Railroad equipment and transport equipment n.e.c. (NACE 352 plus 359) in 'High 73'; (iii) Aircraft and spacecraft (NACE 353) in 'High 71'.

14. Austria, Denmark, Finland, France, Germany, Italy, the Netherlands, Spain and the UK. Individual country growth rates are shown in ECORYS-NEI (2004).
15. For some countries the available data only covered the period up to 1999 and for these the period of analysis was adjusted accordingly.
16. The reader should note that in their chapter Camacho and Rodriguez focus on the effect on knowledge-intensive service (KIS) inputs, which they define as the three following industries: post and telecommunications, computer and related activities, and research and development. Additionally, they estimate a model that replaces KIS with KIBS, defined as the aforementioned three sectors together with 'other' business activities. In the model presented in this chapter, the focus is on business services *per se* (i.e. renting of machinery and equipment, computer and related activities, research and development, and 'other' business activities). Both papers use the same primary data source (i.e. the OECD input–output database), although in this chapter a number of 'outlier' industries are excluded from the regression analysis together with sectors for which data on capital measures are unavailable. Notwithstanding these differences, both papers point to a positive impact of BS/KIS on production.
17. In the case where some input factors (for example, capital) are omitted from the empirical specification of the production function then the cost shares of the included variables will not sum to one. If, in fact, the production function exhibits constant returns to scale with respect to all production factors, then the sum of estimated of the estimated coefficients will tend to sum to one, even where their combined cost share is less. The coefficients on the included variables will partly pick up the effect of the omitted variable(s). This means that that in the current context, if the estimated coefficient on business services exceeds the cost share of BS this cannot be directly interpreted as an indicator of quasi-rents for the use of BS.
18. Following Tomlinson, a 'productivity' version of the model may also be estimated; Camacho and Rodriguez, also reported in Chapter 7 of this book, estimate just such a productivity version of their model. It may be shown, however, that to the extent that the estimated coefficients on the production version of the model sum to one then both the production and productivity versions will yield identical results. As this is the case for the empirical estimates for the production model described in this section, separate 'productivity' version estimates are not reported. This can also explain why the estimates presented by Camacho and Rodriguez show little difference across the production and productivity versions of their model for the estimated coefficients on material inputs (their M) and KIS/KIBS inputs (their B).
19. Where possible, we compared estimations using the OECD estimate on consumption of fixed capital, and our constructed capital stock measure using alternatively a five-year and a ten-year depreciation period. In most cases, the empirical results are very similar if not almost identical.
20. Sectors for which capital data are missing for all countries are Chemicals; Pharmaceuticals; Aircraft and Spacecraft; Railroad and Transport equipment; Iron and Steel; and Non-ferrous metals. For all other sectors data are available for more than one country, but the number of times each sector is included inevitably varies.
21. In addition, three 'outlier' sectors were removed from the data sample as they had disproportionate impact on the estimated coefficients. The removed sectors are: (i) Coke, Refined Petroleum Products and Nuclear Fuels (NACE 23), (ii) Real Estate Activities (NACE 70), and (iii) Education (NACE 80).

22. The cost shares of the business services may deviate from the direct requirement coefficients reported elsewhere in this report as for this table only those sectors are considered that are included in the regression analysis, i.e. for which capital data are available.
23. Business-related services is defined to include utilities, wholesale and retail trade, transport and storage, post and telecommunication, finance and insurance, business services.
24. For a discussion of the fragmentation of the BS market in the EU, see Kox and Lejour (2004).

6
IT Services and Productivity in European Industries

Francesco Crespi[1]

Introduction

The aim of this study is to verify the hypothesis of a potential positive impact of IT services, namely computer and related services, on productivity which operates indirectly via enhancing efficiency in those industries that use them. This hypothesis is tested through an econometric analysis conducted on a panel of European manufacturing and service industries for the period 1995–2000. The results are statistically robust and they show that the use of IT services is a crucial factor in explaining productivity differentials across European industries. Moreover, the analysis provides evidence that the complementarities between the quality of human capital, deliberate activities carried out to develop and effectively absorb new technological knowledge and the productive use of IT services identify a relevant mechanism to obtain productivity gains.

Since the mid-1990s, the rapid growth of the US economy and the large-scale introduction of ICTs have renewed interest in the evolution and the sources of productivity dynamics. There is broad consensus in the literature that the use of new information and communication technologies explains a great part of the striking acceleration of US productivity growth (Jorgenson and Stiroh, 2000; Oliner and Sichel, 2000; Jorgenson *et al.*, 2005).

ICTs share all the features of General Purpose Technologies. The wide scope for improvement and elaboration, the applicability across a broad range of uses, the potential for use in a large variety of processes and products and the complementarities with existing and emerging technologies of ICTs determined their pervasive diffusion throughout almost all sectors of economic activity, causing what many economists termed the ICT revolution (David, 1990; Bresnahan and Trajtenberg, 1995). However, while the effects of the growing importance of ICT on productivity dynamics and economic growth in the USA appear to be evident, the picture in Europe is not that clear. Significant differences emerge between the two areas (Timmer and van Ark, 2005; Inklaar *et al.*, 2005). First of all, there is still a disparity in the dimension of ICT investments even if, over the last decade, there has also been a substantial expansion of ICT-capital deepening in European countries. Second, the increase of ICT investments in Europe has not always been translated into an equivalent acceleration in productivity growth; third, the contribution of information technologies to economic growth differed across European countries (Schreyer, 2000; Daveri, 2002; van Ark, 2005).

New information at the sectoral level shows that the service sector, and in particular those services that make more intensive use of the new information and communication technologies, accounts for much of the productivity slowdown in the European economy. This result raises the question of whether or not Europe has been affected by the consequences of the well-known Baumol's disease. The latter implies that the growing importance of a sector (services) with stagnating productivity hampers the growth of productivity across the whole economy. In this paper we find that this negative influence of services on productivity at least can not be generalized, in particular when services producing intermediate inputs are considered. Since the study is carried out at the industry level, it is possible to consider the specificities of individual (manufacturing and service) industries, and account for a variety of structural factors that constrain or support the operation of firms.

The remainder of the chapter is organized as follows. Section 6.1 provides an overview of the literature on the determinants of productivity growth. Section 6.2 analyses the relationships between IT services and productivity. Section 6.3 and 6.4, present the model, the methodology and the data used for the analysis while section 6.5 discusses the results of econometric estimates. Finally, section 6.6 draws the main conclusions and policy implications.

6.1 On the sources of productivity gains

This paragraph provides an overview of the main streams of research on the leading sources of productivity growth, in particular from a technology-supply perspective. Much effort has been devoted to quantifying the contribution of technological change to productivity growth. The growth-accounting literature, moving from the pioneering work by Solow (1957), focused the analysis on assessing the statistical relevance of the 'unexplained' productivity once the growth of capital and labour is accounted for. This 'residual' is supposed to reflect the importance of technological change (Denison, 1967; Jorgenson and Griliches, 1967). A second stream of literature with seminal contributions by Mansfield (1965) and Griliches (1979) explicitly considered measures of technological change (typically measures of R&D expenditures) in models on the determinants of productivity growth. The main results from this framework of analysis are as follows. First, there is strong evidence in favour of the hypothesis of a positive effect of R&D on productivity dynamics from studies using cross-sectional data. Secondly, the results from time-series estimates of productivity models appear to be less conclusive (Mairesse and Sassenou, 1991). Thirdly, industries are found to differ in terms of returns from R&D investments, reflecting the existence of different scientific and technological opportunities peculiar to each industry, and the presence of R&D spillovers, which differ across industries as emphasized by the literature on technological regimes and sectoral systems of innovation (Malerba, 2004). The impact of innovation on productivity has been further explored by studies using innovation-surveys data. The latter have confirmed the importance of innovation in sustaining productivity, alongside the role played by structural factors, with strong cross-sector and cross-country differences (Crépon, Duguet and Mairesse, 1998; Mohnen, Mairesse and Dagenais, 2006). Among structural factors capable of generating differences in productivity performance across sectors, attention should be devoted to the size distribution of firms. Recent evidence found a positive correlation between average size and productivity due to the presence of scale economies in particular in R&D activities (Pagano and Schivardi, 2003).

Recently, much effort has been devoted to evaluating the impact of the emergence of a new technological paradigm based on the ICTs on productivity growth. Researchers have identified three main transmission channels through which the diffusion of these new technologies can positively affect production efficiency. First, the high pace of technological change in ICT-producing industries determines a rapid growth of productivity in the same industries. Secondly, the fall in prices of ICT goods spurs ICT investments in ICT-using industries making them more productive. Thirdly, the strong complementarities of ICTs with existing and newly emerging technologies facilitates the development of innovations and more efficient new organizational forms within firms.

Studies conducted in the US largely support the hypothesis that the US growth performance is to a large extent explained by a long-term rise in the total factor productivity, especially in ICT sectors (Jorgenson and Stiroh, 2000). Initially, the Gordon hypothesis suggested that the computer industry bears the major responsibility for the acceleration of US productivity and this intuition has been confirmed by Oliner and Sichel (2000) and Nordhaus (2002). Moreover, recent analysis found that ICT's technological complementarities determined strong TFP growth in ICT-using industries (Triplett and Bosworth, 2004; Jorgenson *et al.*, 2005).

In parallel, many firm-level studies have emphasized the role of ICTs in supporting productivity growth at the micro level (Brynjolfsson and Hitt, 2000). In particular, it has been argued that information technologies are capable of enabling complementary organizational changes within firms and of spurring productivity gains through cost savings and increasing output quality. In this framework, the complementarity between the adoption of ICTs and labour skills emerges as crucial (Bresnahan, Brynjolfsson and Hitt, 2002; Chun, 2003). This adds new evidence to the ample literature on the contribution of human capital to productivity (e.g. Jorgenson, Gollup and Fraumeni, 1987).

The evidence from studies for Europe indicates that the contribution of ICT-capital deepening to labour productivity has been much lower (about half the rate observed in the USA). So, despite the speeding up of ICT diffusion in Europe, the growth's rate of labour productivity in EU15 declined from 2.2 per cent during the period 1987–95 to 1.5 per cent during the period 1995–2004 with an opposite pattern with respect to the USA which accelerated over the same subperiods, from 1.1 per cent to 2.5 per cent (van Ark and Inklaar, 2005).

The smaller contribution of ICT capital deepening, associated with the persisting difference between the USA and Europe in the size of the ICT-goods-producing sector, explains much of the difference in labour productivity growth between the two economic areas since 1995 (Timmer and van Ark, 2005). However, differences in the dynamics of labour productivity across European countries can be attributed in particular to a wide variance in non-ICT capital contributions, and to the variance in TFP growth in non-ICT-producing sectors. A major difference between the EU and the USA appears to be caused by the relatively poor performance in terms of TFP growth of European market services compared to those of the USA.

A possible explanation for the inability of European services with an intensive ICT-use to generate a pronounced acceleration in TFP growth may be grounded in the EU's institutional framework. The OECD 'growth project' has tried to explain productivity growth with ICT production and use, R&D expenditure, labour skills, product market competition, but also with a number of institutional factors, in order to account for cross country differences and in particular the contrasting performances of the US and Europe (OECD 2003b).

6.2 The impact of IT services on productivity

Services have for a long time been considered the 'sick' industries in terms of efficiency gains. The seminal contribution by Baumol (1967) highlighted that the inherent nature of services limits their potential for productivity growth. The bad productivity-growth performance of the service sector, associated with its expansion and the consequent wide process of structural change within advanced economies, may hamper the growth potential of the economy as a whole.

However, in recent years this interpretation has been questioned on both theoretical and empirical grounds, in particular when the distinction between consumer services and business services is introduced (Kox, 2004). The latter in fact represents intermediary inputs for user industries. Oulton's theorem (Oulton, 2001) shows that, in the model of cost-disease, if the stagnant sector, in terms of productivity dynamics, supplies only final goods and increases its share in the economy, it can be expected that a pattern of the progressive reduction of productivity-growth rates will be realized in the entire economic system. On the contrary, if the sector characterized by stagnant

Table 6.1 Average annual growth of GDP per hour worked and contribution to aggregate productivity of ICT-producing services, EU 15 and USA, 1995–2002 (percentages)

	1995–2002	
	EU 15	*USA*
Average annual growth of GDP per hour worked		
Total economy	1.8	2.5
ICT-producing services	5.9	2.7
ICT-using industries	1.7	5.3
Contribution to aggregate productivity of ICT-producing services		
Communications	13.0	8.0
Computer and related activities	9.0	4.0

Source: van Ark, 2005.

productivity growth produces intermediate goods or services, its expansion may, under certain conditions, actually enhance productivity gains in the economy.

From an empirical point of view, recent evidence from the USA showed that labour productivity in services has grown, after 1995, at comparable rates with respect to the rest of the economy and experienced a strong rise in total factor productivity (Triplett and Bosworth, 2004; Jorgenson *et al.*, 2005). The same trend cannot be found in Europe. However, the ICT-producing service sectors realized high growth rates in the EU, even greater than that of US and represent the major contributors in terms of productivity growth in EU (See Table 6.1).

The focus of this chapter is on the effects on productivity of the use of a particular type of business services that is computer and related services. It consists of hardware and software consultancy and supply activities, data processing and database activities, and other computer-related activities. In this way we can assess the indirect contribution of IT services on the productivity of other industries. We expect this impact to be positive and significant for the following reasons. IT support services are a crucial driver in the diffusion and the effective use of the new information technologies among firms. Moreover, the production of IT services is often the outcome of the continuous interaction between service provider and client. Indeed, the quality and intensity of such joint efforts may crucially affect the value of the produced service. IT-services companies, when providing their services interact with their clients in a co-production process of customized solutions to problems and challenges. Learning processes are activated both within the client firm which changes its knowledge base and in the service provider that acquires new knowledge that is useful for differentiating the offered services and for increasing efficiency. IT services, through a closer interaction between user firms, may observe tacit and localized knowledge and creatively adapt generic information to the specific needs of client firms. In this way they play a major role in transferring, creating and combining knowledge and, consequently, in increasing productivity in the economy (Miles *et al.*, 1995; den Hertog, 2000; Pilat and Lee, 2001; Antonelli, 2006). The model proposed in the next section aims at verifying the existence and the strength of such 'spillover effects' deriving from the use of IT services throughout the European economy.

6.3 Model description

The estimated model used to test how the use-intensity of IT services affects labour productivity in European industries is derived from an augmented Cobb–Douglas production function as in equation (6.1)[2].

$$Y_{ijt} = A\, L_{ijt}^{\alpha}\, K_{ijt}^{\beta}\, IT_{ijt}^{\gamma} \tag{6.1}$$

where Y represents the output (in this case value added) of sector i and country j at time t, K and L represent, respectively, capital and labour inputs, and IT the expenditures for the use of IT services. Dividing all terms by L and taking logarithms, equation (6.1) becomes:

$$y_{ijt} - l_{ijt} = a + \beta(k_{ijt} - l_{ijt}) + \gamma(it_{ijt} - l_{ijt}) + \eta l_{ijt} \tag{6.2}$$

where η represents the returns-to-scale parameter ($\eta = \alpha + \beta + \gamma - 1$).

We now expand equation (6.2) to include a set of key control variables that influence labour productivity so that the equation to be estimated becomes the following:

$$\begin{aligned} y_{ijt} - l_{ijt} &= a + \beta(k_{ijt} - l_{ijt}) + \gamma(it_{ijt} - l_{ijt}) + \eta l_{ijt} \\ &\quad + \sum_{m=1}^{M} \vartheta_m X_{mijt} + \lambda IE_{ij} + \mu YR_t + \varepsilon_{ijt} \end{aligned} \tag{6.3}$$

where X is the set of M (log-transformed) control variables, IE is the individual unobserved effect, YR is a set of time dummies and ε_{ijt} the error term.

Relevant control variables have been identified mainly by considering the literature reviewed in previous paragraphs. In particular, our main interest is to assess the influence of the complementarities between the use of IT services, innovative efforts and the quality of human capital on productivity differentials across European industries. We use R&D per unit of labour and labour costs per unit of labour as proxies, respectively, for the intensity of innovative activities and for the quality of human capital. For the reasons outlined before in the text we expect that each of these variables plays a significant positive role in our analysis. Potential endogeneity issues related to the use of these variables are discussed later on.

Another factor that is also likely to play a role in determining productivity differentials is the average firm size, here measured by the average number of employee per firm. In addition for this variable we expect to find a positive and significant impact on productivity because of the effects of size on R&D investments and scale economies. For the same reasons, when we enter this variable in the regression, the R&D intensity covariate is omitted.

In this chapter we focus on the effects of different patterns of the use of IT services and complementary activities, and we are less concerned with differences in capital intensities and their impact on productivity. Moreover, data on capital stock of industries derived from the OECD STAN database were available only for a sub-sample of sectors and countries. However, using this sub-sample we will show that sectoral differences in capital intensities (measured by net capital stock per labour unit) can be effectively treated as unobserved industry characteristics. Therefore, for those cases where the variable on capital intensity is omitted the tested equation becomes:

$$\begin{aligned} y_{ijt} - l_{ijt} &= a + \gamma(it_{ijt} - l_{ijt}) + \nu l_{ijt} \\ &\quad + \sum_{m=1}^{M} \vartheta_m X_{mijt} + \lambda IE_{ij} + \mu YR_t + \varepsilon_{ijt} \end{aligned} \tag{6.4}$$

6.4 Methodology and data sources

The database used for the analysis considers 20 manufacturing sectors and nine service sectors for the period 1995–2000 and is the result of the matching of different sets of data. The countries considered in the analysis are: France, Germany, the UK, the Netherlands, Italy, Spain, Sweden, Finland and Denmark. Following the OECD Productivity Manual (2001), we choose to measure sectoral labour productivity as value added per hour worked in order to take into account changes in the average work time per employee. While data on value added are directly available from the OECD STAN database, complete series for total hours worked have been derived from the 60 industries database of the Groningen Growth and Development Centre. Our key variable for the analysis has been obtained by using the expenditures for computer and related services that can be extracted from the EUROSTAT Input–Output tables.[3] Figures on R&D activities and labour compensation have been derived respectively from the OECD ANBERD and STAN databases. Data on the number of firms at sectoral level have been obtained from the EUROSTAT New-Cronos Database. All monetary variables included in the database are converted in euros[4] and reported at constant prices (1995 base year). In particular, the deflation procedure used to obtain value added and the expenditures for computer and related services at constant price had to be industry specific. The intensity of use of IT services has then been computed by dividing the expenditure for computers and related services of each sector (deflated with the deflator of value added of the IT services industry) for the value added of each sector (deflated with its specific deflator of value added). Sectoral deflators have been derived from the OECD STAN database.

An important issue emerges from the specific structure of the database and the information available. In fact, the Input–Output tables are missing from some years in a number of countries. As an example, data for France in the years 1996 and 1998 or for Germany 1996 are not available. Thus, we choose to estimate the baseline model in levels instead of in growth terms as usually done in the literature. Considering variations in productivity, in fact, would mean losing much of the variability through time for particularly important countries. However, separate estimates of equation (6.4) using the First Difference Estimator are also provided to prove that our choice does not affect the core of our results. Different specifications of the model are tested in order to check the robustness of our results. As reported in the model equations (6.3) and (6.4) country and industry individual effects are included in the analysis in order to account for the importance of national macroeconomic contexts and for the relevance of country and sectoral specificities.

Preliminary analyses on the correlations between variables have led us to exclude the presence of multicollinearity problems. Issues related to the presence of heteroskedasticity and endogeneity among regressors are addressed by means of two robustness checks using FEGLS and Instrumental Variable estimators.

6.5 Results discussion

Table 6.2 reports the outcomes of different specifications of the baseline model proposed in the previous section. The results provided in the first two columns refer to the sub-sample of industries for which data on capital stock were available. They show that it is important for the analysis to take into account individual effects and that differences in capital intensities can be treated as unobserved industry characteristics. In fact, by comparing the Fixed Effects (FE) and the Random Effects (RE) estimators by means of the Hausman test, it turns out that the FE is the most appropriate model for the analysis of our data and that, when we control for individual effects, the statistical significance of the capital intensity variable disappears completely.

Columns 3–6 contain the results of estimates carried out on the full sample, taking into account fixed effects per industries and countries. Column 3 shows the intensity of use of IT services, along with the innovative efforts carried out by firms and the quality of human capital employed. These variables significantly explain differences in productivity levels across European industries. This confirms the hypothesis that strong spillover effects from the computer and related services sector have been generated in the economy. The coefficient reflecting returns to scale is also positive and (weakly) significant providing evidence for the presence of increasing returns to scale.

Column 4 reports the results obtained by using the Least Squares Dummy Variable estimator, which allows us to differentiate also between manufacturing

Table 6.2 The influence of IT adoption on productivity in European manufacturing and service industries

Dependent variable: Labour Productivity (value added per worked hour), 1995–2000, selected EU countries[1]

	1	*2*	*3*	*4*	*5*	*6*
	Fixed effect estimator	*Random effect estimator*	*Fixed effect estimator*	*LSDV*	*Fixed effect estimator*	*First difference estimator*
Intensity of use of IT services	1.22*	1.73***	1.56***	1.56***	0.82*	1.10***
	(1.87)	(2.91)	(3.87)	(3.87)	(1.62)	(2.64)
R&D intensity	2.86***	2.37***	0.69***	0.69***		0.41**
	(6.82)	(7.50)	(3.98)	(3.98)		(2.29)
Labour costs per worked hour	1.76***	1.50***	1.46***	1.46***	1.60***	1.86***
	(4.53)	(6.85)	(6.69)	(6.69)	(7.31)	(10.33)
Average Firm Size					0.03***	
					(23.63)	
Capital Intensity	−0.03	0.12***				
	(−0.55)	(6.19)				
Total hours worked	0.005	0.003***	0.005*	0.005*	−0.007***	0.008***
	(1.56)	(3.71)	(1.80)	(1.80)	(−3.12)	(2.88)
Constant	−0.06	−0.04***	−0.05	−0.06	0.06**	0.0004*
	(−1.47)	(−3.62)	(−1.62)	(−1.59)	(2.01)	(1.89)
Manufacturing/ Services				0.03*		
				(1.88)		
Years Dummies	Yes	Yes	Yes	Yes	Yes	Yes
Individual Effects	Yes	No	Yes	Yes	Yes	Yes
Hausman Test	19.53					
p-value	0.03					
R-sq	0.35	0.32	0.20	0.89	0.48	0.13
Number of Observations	353	353	1154	1154	1248	859

Notes: [1] Asterisks demarcate significance levels: *significant at the 90% level; **significant at 95%; ***significant at 99%. Figures in parentheses are t-statistics and z-statistics. Countries in the sample include: Germany, France, Italy, the Netherlands, the United Kingdom, Spain, Sweden, Denmark and Finland.

and service industries. The coefficient associated to the dummy for manufacturing and services turns out to be positive and (weakly) significant, suggesting the presence of some productivity positive differential for manufacturing industries.

A further specification of our baseline model has been carried out by including the variable reflecting average firm size, which captures both the scale effects in labour productivity and the impact of size on R&D investments. Interestingly, this variable enters with a positive and significant sign in the analysis confirming recent evidence on the issue (cf. section 6.1). Consistently, once the returns to scale effects are controlled for, the labour input coefficient becomes significantly negative. Finally, equation (6.4) has been estimated using the First Difference Estimator, though losing much information. Column 6 reports the outcomes of this regression. They do not differ from previous results. This supports our choice for estimating the baseline model in levels in order to use more information does not affect the robustness of the results. It shows that the relationships identified among the variables are stable.

Two robustness checks have been performed in order to address the problems of heteroskedasticity and potential endogeneity of some regressors. Results are reported in Table 6.3. In order to verify if potential problems of

Table 6.3 The influence of IT adoption on productivity in European manufacturing and service industries – Robustness Checks (FEGLS, FDIV estimators)

Dependent variable: labour productivity (value added per worked hour), 1995–2000, selected EU countries[1]

	1	*2*
	Fixed effects GLS Estimator	*FD Instrumental variable estimator*
Intensity of use of IT services	1.41***	3.99***
	(7.77)	(1.54)
R&D intensity	0.54***	2.79***
	(5.32)	(4.25)
Labour costs per worked hour	1.41***	1.86***
	(27.50)	(6.96)
Total hours worked	−0.0001	0.009***
	(−0.07)	(2.65)
Constant	0.06***	−0.0004
	(2.76)	(−0.90)
Years Dummies	Yes	Yes
Individual Effects	Yes	Yes
Wald chi2	139,326	
p-value	0.00	
F-statistic		15.58
p-value		0.00
Number of observations	1,154	652

Notes: [1] Significance levels: *significant at the 90% level; **significant at 95%; ***significant at 99%. Figures in parentheses are t-statistics and z-statistics. Countries in the sample include: Germany, France, Italy, the Netherlands, the United Kingdom, Spain, Sweden, Denmark and Finland.

heteroskedasticity affect our results, we have relaxed the assumption of time-invariant variance in the idiosyncratic errors by applying the FEGLS estimator. Column 1 contains the results of these robust estimates. Since differences in the magnitude and the significance of these coefficients are modest with respect to the FE estimator, it is possible to conclude that heteroskedasticity has not seriously biased previous figures.

Finally, our baseline model poses a further problem because of the potential endogeneity of the variables relative to the intensity of use of IT services, the intensity of R&D investments and of our proxy for the quality of human capital. Simultaneity in fact would arise where these explanatory variables are determined simultaneously with the dependent variable. In this case there would exist correlation between the error term and simultaneous covariates and our FE estimates would be inconsistent. The strategy adopted here to deal with this issue is to carry out separate estimates using appropriate instruments for these three variables which are suspect to be endogenous and then comparing the obtained results with those deriving from the FE estimator. If the sign and the significance of the coefficients obtained with the two methods do not differ it will mean that the potential bias due to endogeneity has not affected the goodness and reliability of our results.

A general approach to deal with panel data models when the strict exogeneity assumption fails is to remove the unobserved individual effects by means of a transformation and then to find appropriate instruments for the endogenous regressors. However, with the FE transformation it is necessary to have strictly exogenous instruments. On the contrary, the use of a FD transformation allows the removal of the unobserved individual effects and lagged levels (two periods back) of the endogenous covariates can be employed as valid instruments. The results obtained by applying this technique are shown in the second column of Table 6.3. Since the results obtained with the use of appropriate instruments are consistent with those obtained before, we can conclude that the potential bias in previous estimates does not alter the significance of the relationships identified between our variables. This confirms our considerations about the role of IT services in enhancing productivity in European industries along with the importance of complementarities with innovative efforts and the quality of human capital.

6.6 Conclusions

This study finds that the diffusion of IT services has had a strong and positive role in shaping productivity in European industries in the period 1995–2000. The contribution of this sector to aggregate productivity, then, is not limited to its own positive productivity growth; it also extends to positive and statistically significant spillover effects that are generated in IT-using industries. The use of IT services plays a key role in enhancing the effective and productive use of the new information technologies, and in transferring, creating and combining knowledge among firms. IT thus emerges as a crucial factor in explaining productivity differences in European industries. In the context of the literature on the 'Baumol disease', our finding adds some evidence that business services like IT services can, as providers of intermediate inputs, positively contribute to increasing the efficiency of an economy.

The innovative efforts carried out by firms and the availability of skilled human capital are also positively associated to productivity performance of European industries. We find complementarities between the activities oriented to the development and the absorption of new technological knowledge, the quality of human capital and the productive use of IT services. These complementarities represent a crucial mechanism through which productivity gains may be achieved. Moreover, a positive relationship between firm size and productivity has been identified.

These appear to be important results with relevant policy implications. Policies oriented to supporting firms in grasping the potential deriving from the use of IT services and effectively exploiting the benefits deriving from ICT investment can be particularly relevant. Policy instruments that enhance the development and the absorption of new technological knowledge, and policies that strengthen the level of human capital (for example, by creating a strong higher education system), can effectively increase the productivity performance of the European economy.

Notes

1. The author would like to thank Cristiano Antonelli, Mario Denni and the Editors of this book for comments and suggestions on earlier drafts of this work. I also acknowledge the funding provided by the CSI Piemonte within the context of the research project "Analisi economica dell'innovazione nei servizi di rete nel caso piemontese", in progress at the Laboratorio di Economia dell'Innovazione of the Dipartimento di Economia Cognetti de Martiis, coordinated by Professor Cristiano Antonelli. The usual caveats of course apply.
2. Despite the well-known problems related to such an approach this is a convenient starting point, common to much of the literature on the determinants of productivity, for the limited purposes of our analysis.
3. Information on the Eurostat Input–Output tables can be directly obtained from the EUROSTAT-New Cronos database: http://epp.eurostat.cec.eu.int.
4. The availability of sectoral PPPs is limited to manufacturing industries. Therefore, in order to have comparable data we converted all monetary variables into eUROs. In particular, for eURO zone countries variables are originally expressed in Euro-Fixed series. For non-eURO zone countries national currencies are converted into eUROS, using the official exchange fixed on 28 December, 2000.

7

Integration and Diffusion of KIS for Industry Performance

José A. Camacho and Mercedes Rodriguez

Introduction

The relative importance of business services is growing intensively, in terms of both production and employment. The main explanation for this trend is based on the changes brought about by the so-called 'Knowledge-based economy' (Archibugi and Lundvall, 2001; Rodrigues, 2002): economic agents and especially firms are involved in an environment that is increasingly changing and where knowledge has become the 'key asset'. Within this context, business services, and more concretely knowledge-intensive services (KIS), play a critical role.

The aim of this chapter is to conduct an econometric analysis of the impact of KIS on the performance of other industries. In particular, we examine whether the use of KIS has a positive effect on production, productivity and innovation. To measure the impact of the use of KIS on production and productivity we estimate production and productivity functions that incorporate KIS. In terms of the role played by KIS in the domain of innovation, we apply a new methodology to asses the diffusion of product-embodied R&D. The structure of the chapter is as follows. In the second section, we offer a brief review of different theories regarding the role played by KIS in the diffusion of knowledge. In the third section we employ a 'production function approach' to calculate the effects that the use of KIS has on production and productivity. We also compare these results with those obtained by previous works. The next section applies an input–output model to measure the diffusion of product-embodied R&D that takes place by means of the acquisition of KIS. Finally, we draw some conclusions about the future prospects of the use of KIS by industries.

7.1 Knowledge-intensive services: more than intermediate inputs

It is commonly agreed that the interest in the study of innovation activities in services emerged quite late (i.e. the 1990s). Nevertheless, the works underlining the potential role of services as knowledge diffusers appeared earlier. In the 1960s, economists such as Machlup (1962) or Greenfield (1966) pointed out the role of some services, specifically business services, as creators and diffusers of knowledge. More recently, the considerable increase in the number of studies on service innovation (Gadrey *et al.*, 1995; Gallouj and Gallouj, 1996; Gallouj and Weinstein, 1997; Miles *et al.* 1995; Miles, 1996, among others) confirms that the role played by services in the innovation scope, and particularly the role played by those called knowledge-intensive services (KIS), are now a central focus of attention for many innovation scholars.[1]

It is clearly their special relationship to knowledge that differentiates KIS from other activities. They are innovative in their own right, but unlike high-innovative manufacturing activities, one of their main functions is to provide knowledge to other industries. Antonelli (2000: 171) describes the way they operate as follows: 'they function as holders of proprietary "quasi-generic" knowledge, from interactions with customers and the scientific community, and operate as an interface between such knowledge and its tacit counterpart, located within the daily practices of the firm'. That is to say, they act as 'bridges' for knowledge (Czarnitzki and Spielkamp, 2000) or, as den Hertog and Bilderbeek (1998) put it, 'as a second knowledge infrastructure', even substituting for functions traditionally attributed to the public sector. Hauknes (2000) calls this diffuser role of KIS 'induced innovation', which indicates a new type of innovation that has to be added to the five Schumpeterian types of innovation.

In other words, a highly educated workforce, in combination with strong efforts in innovation (not only in terms of R&D expenditures, but also in training and acquisition of new technologies), allows these service industries to improve their clients' knowledge bases, and, at the same time, their own knowledge bases. For example, the study carried out by Windrum and Tomlinson (1999) for the United Kingdom, the Netherlands, Germany and Japan demonstrates that those countries where there are strong links between KIS and other industries obtain higher spillovers from service innovation.

Starting from these premises, in the remainder of this chapter we try to measure econometrically the 'bridge' role of KIS for industries, by employing two techniques – the estimation of production and productivity equations and the application of an input–output model. The selection of countries and years has been based primarily on the availability of R&D data. For instance, concerning the countries, despite the existence of detailed input–output tables, some of them do not show R&D data for any of the KIS industries (Finland) or have data for only one of the three KIS industries (France). Greece is not even included in the ANBERD database. So, our analysis concerns the following countries: Denmark, Germany, the Netherlands, Spain and the United Kingdom in 1995 and 1999.

In reference to the service industries included within the group of KIS, although commonly used classifications, such as that elaborated by Eurostat and the OECD, encompass a greater number of industries under the name of 'knowledge-intensive services', we consider these groupings too broad to permit accurate interpretation of the results obtained.[2] This is why we have preferred to analyse those service branches called 'knowledge-intensive high-tech services' by the Eurostat classification, that is to say, post and telecommunications, computer and related activities and research and development.

7.2 Knowledge-intensive services, production and productivity: a production function approach

The changes in the production strategies implemented by firms, in combination with the increasing need for specialized knowledge, have resulted in a considerable rise in the use of KIS as intermediate inputs. In Table 7.1 we report the participation of KIS in total intermediate consumptions. The data refer to 1995, except for Denmark (1997) and the United Kingdom (1998).

As can be seen from the table, there are considerable differences among countries. For instance, the greatest average use of KIS is to be found in the United Kingdom, with a participation of KIS in total intermediate consumptions of 7 per cent. Germany and Spain show shares above 4 per cent and Denmark above 3 per cent. The Netherlands is the country with the lowest participation – 2.32 per cent.

Concerning industries, if we exclude the self-consumption of KIS branches, we observe a high participation of KIS in the intermediate consumptions of other service industries, such as finance and insurance, other business services, public administration or education. The industry of finance and insurance stands out in all countries (except Germany), with shares of KIS that range from 9.9 in Spain to 21.3 in the United Kingdom.

Nevertheless, KIS also have an important role in the intermediate consumptions of manufacturing industries, and in particular in high- and medium-tech industries. This is the case of the renting of machinery and equipment; office, accounting and computing machinery; pulp, paper and paper products or pharmaceuticals. Hence, the high- and medium-tech nature of these manufacturing industries seems to confirm the hypothesis that KIS act as 'bridges' for knowledge.

It was mentioned above that the 'knowledge intensity' of KIS has a direct effect on the growth and productivity of their user industries. Although the analyses that evaluate this type of result start from a production function, we can distinguish two approaches. The first one (Katsoulacos and Tsounis, 2000; Antonelli, 1998, 2000; Drejer, 2002) introduces KIS as an additional input in a traditional production function. The second one, which is slightly different (Windrum and Tomlinson, 1999; Tomlinson, 2000a, b), assumes the hypothesis that output is produced by means of labour that acts on material inputs and/or KIS. Therefore, a distinction is made between 'immaterial' inputs (KIS) and 'material' inputs (the remainder of intermediate

Table 7.1 Participation of KIS in total intermediate consumptions by industry

	Denmark (1997)	*Germany (1995)*	*Netherlands (1995)*	*Spain (1995)*	*United Kingdom (1998)*
Agriculture, hunting, forestry and fishing	0.91	0.79	0.90	0.43	2.24
Mining and quarrying	1.33	1.76	3.68	1.42	0.63
Food, beverages and tobacco	0.73	0.60	0.74	0.71	1.90
Textiles, leather and footwear	1.09	0.80	1.40	1.02	2.15
Wood, products wood	1.00	0.81	1.08	1.13	1.33
Pulp, paper, printing and publishing	8.39	4.56	4.36	2.04	2.44
Coke, refined petroleum products	1.20	1.15	0.71	0.80	1.62
Chemicals exc. Pharmaceuticals	1.89	3.79	1.80	1.74	3.13
Pharmaceuticals	3.90	n.a.	n.a.	1.74	5.15
Rubber and plastics products	0.95	1.93	1.70	0.89	2.08
Other non-metallic mineral products	1.22	1.82	1.85	1.28	2.29
Iron & steel	1.07	0.90	0.98	1.36	1.50
Non-ferrous metals	0.77	n.a.	n.a.	n.a.	0.81
Fabricated metal products	1.47	2.00	1.33	1.12	1.88
Machinery and equipment, n.e.c.	1.47	1.90	1.69	1.77	2.17
Office, accounting machinery	1.88	9.82	1.13	3.92	2.07
Electrical machinery and apparatus	1.06	1.77	1.84	1.43	2.60
Radio, television and com. equipment	1.27	1.87	2.31	2.42	2.44
Medical, precision and opt. instruments	2.31	2.08	2.08	2.35	3.94
Motor vehicles, trailers and semi-trailers	1.19	0.98	0.73	0.67	1.79
Building and repairing of boats and ships	0.77	1.29	1.53	2.50	1.24
Aircraft and spacecraft	n.a.	n.a.	0.99	2.50	6.72
Railroad equipment	1.11	n.a.	1.57	2.50	1.26
Manufacturing n.e.c.; recycling	1.43	1.15	2.09	1.20	1.79
Electricity, gas and water supply	1.76	2.04	0.87	2.19	2.36
Construction	2.00	0.86	0.80	1.06	1.68

(Continued)

Table 7.1 (Continued)

	Denmark (1997)	*Germany (1995)*	*Netherlands (1995)*	*Spain (1995)*	*United Kingdom (1998)*
Wholesale and retail trade; repairs	4.99	5.78	5.91	2.84	7.05
Hotels and restaurants	2.70	3.08	2.20	1.13	8.77
Transport and storage	3.38	3.79	3.68	1.70	7.66
Post and telecommunications	23.65	31.70	16.98	15.44	32.97
Finance, insurance	14.27	4.51	15.94	9.90	21.27
Real estate activities	3.00	1.24	4.66	1.90	5.64
Renting of machinery and equipment	15.39	3.67	2.08	5.77	5.96
Computer and related activities	18.40	39.83	31.59	15.59	13.19
Research and development	14.03	17.57	70.50	4.91	17.40
Other business activities	14.10	4.23	4.45	7.39	12.06
Public admin. and defence	13.63	3.45	11.13	11.61	8.86
Education	8.94	7.54	5.15	5.14	14.56
Health and social work	8.26	3.19	4.74	4.12	3.84
Average	**3.22**	**4.76**	**2.32**	**4.05**	**7.17**

Source: OECD input–output database 2002.

inputs). In this section, we employ this latter approach.[3] An application of the first approach, using the same input–output tables as here, can be found in the chapter by Paul Baker (Chapter 5) in this book.

Thus, Q (gross output) is considered a function of M, B and L, where M is the amount of material inputs, B is the amount of KIS and L is the employment:

$$Q = A(ML)^a(BL)^b \tag{7.1}$$

Taking logarithms, we obtain the following equation to estimate:

$$\log Q = \log A + a \log M + b \log B + (a + b) \log L \tag{7.2}$$

where A is a constant and a and b are the parameters to estimate.

Starting from equation (7.1) we can also obtain an equation for productivity if we divide each term by the amount of labour employed (L).

$$Q/L = A(M/L)^a(B/L)^b \tag{7.3}$$

taking logarithms:

$$\log Q/L = \log A + a \log M/L + b \log B/L \tag{7.4}$$

Table 7.2 shows the results of the estimation of equation (7.2) in our four countries examined.[4]

We observe that, in general, KIS have a positive (and significant) impact on production. Moreover, the estimation obtained for the parameter b is quite similar among countries.[5] The exception is the United Kingdom, which shows the lowest estimation for the impact of KIS. Nevertheless, this estimation is non-significant at the 10 per cent level. With reference to the estimations obtained for the constant (which can be interpreted as an indicator of total factor productivity), they are very similar among the different countries with the exception of Spain which shows a much lower value, approximately one half of the values obtained for the rest of the countries. This could indicate that less efficient production methods are employed in this country.

In Table 7.3 we report the estimations obtained for equation (7.4). As happens with the abovementioned effect on production, the use of KIS has a positive and similar impact on productivity in the countries examined. The exceptions are the United Kingdom again, and Spain. These countries have the lowest estimations for the parameter b. We have to note that in the case of Spain, the estimation is non-significant at the 5 per cent level and in the United Kingdom the model shows the lowest goodness of fit (an adjusted R^2 of 0.61).

In order to compare the results obtained with those of the abovementioned works that employed the same methodology we estimate the same equations including the industry of 'other business services' within our group of KIS. The values obtained are shown under the heading 'KIBS' in Tables 7.2 and 7.3.

With reference to the changes in the estimated values, as can be expected, the inclusion of quite a large industry such as 'other business services' within

Table 7.2 Estimation of the impact of KIS and KIBS on production

	Denmark (N = 39)	*Germany (N = 36)*	*Netherlands (N = 38)*	*Spain (N = 39)*	*United Kingdom (N = 40)*
			KIS		
constant	1.56**	1.41**	1.38**	0.73	1.49**
	(0.44)	(0.61)	(0.41)	(0.49)	(0.56)
M	0.66**	0.66**	0.65**	0.62**	0.63**
	(0.07)	(0.08)	(0.07)	(0.05)	(0.10)
B	0.18**	0.20**	0.23**	0.19**	0.10
	(0.06)	(0.06)	(0.06)	(0.08)	(0.07)
L	0.16*	0.15*	0.15*	0.26**	0.25**
	(0.08)	(0.09)	(0.08)	(0.08)	(0.11)
Adj. R^2	0.94	0.89	0.94	0.96	0.93
F-statistic	214.22**	98.04**	182.31**	288.81**	163.96**
			KIBS		
constant	1.81**	1.44**	1.24**	0.67	1.75**
	(0.45)	(0.56)	(0.44)	(0.52)	(0.48)
M	0.56**	0.43**	0.55**	0.57**	0.51**
	(0.07)	(0.08)	(0.07)	(0.06)	(0.08)
B	0.23**	0.40**	0.29**	0.12	0.19**
	(0.06)	(0.08)	(0.10)	(0.09)	(0.07)
L	0.18**	0.19**	0.19*	0.36**	0.27**
	(0.07)	(0.07)	(0.10)	(0.08)	(0.11)
Adj. R^2	0.94	0.91	0.91	0.95	0.92
F-statistic	216.35**	116.70**	151.48**	251.69**	152.25**

Notes:**Significant at 5%. *Significant at 10%. Standard errors in brackets.
Source: OECD input–output database 2002.

'immaterial inputs' causes higher estimated values for the parameter *b* and lower estimated values for the parameter *a* in the equations for both production and productivity. The exception is Spain, where the estimations obtained for the parameter *b* are non-significant. Nevertheless, an increase in the goodness of fit is not observed: the adjusted R^2 only increases in the case of Germany.

Concerning the results of previous analyses, we can differentiate between those that estimate a traditional production function (Antonelli, 2000; Katsoulacos and Tsounis, 2000; Drejer, 2002) and those that employ the same methodology as here (Tomlinson, 2000a, 2000b; Windrum and Tomlinson, 1999).

We begin with those studies that estimate a traditional production function. Antonelli (2000) and Katsoulacos and Tsounis (2000) analyse two aspects: the co-evolution of communication services and business services and the effects of the use of these two types of services on productivity in several countries – Antonelli for four countries, France, Germany, Italy and

Table 7.3 Estimation of the impact of KIS and KIBS on productivity

	Denmark (N = 39)	*Germany (N = 36)*	*Netherlands (N = 38)*	*Spain (N = 39)*	*United Kingdom (N = 40)*
			KIS		
constant	1.50**	1.54**	1.61**	1.47**	1.18**
	(0.17)	(0.19)	(0.17)	(0.26)	(0.17)
M/L	0.67**	0.65**	0.63**	0.60**	0.66**
	(0.06)	(0.07)	(0.05)	(0.05)	(0.08)
B/L	0.18**	0.20**	0.22**	0.15*	0.08**
	(0.06)	(0.06)	(0.06)	(0.08)	(0.06)
Adj. R^2	0.80	0.76	0.80	0.79	0.61
F-statistic	76.84**	57.66**	75.18**	70.56**	31.58**
			KIBS		
constant	1.49**	1.69**	1.50**	1.27**	1.37**
	(0.13)	(0.13)	(0.15)	(0.18)	(0.11)
M/L	0.59**	0.42**	0.52**	0.55**	0.54**
	(0.06)	(0.07)	(0.06)	(0.06)	(0.07)
B/L	0.22**	0.39**	0.28**	0.10	0.18**
	(0.06)	(0.07)	(0.10)	(0.09)	(0.02)
Adj. R^2	0.80	0.80	0.76	0.77	0.58
F-statistic	76.26**	69.96**	60.38**	62.97**	27.80**

Notes: **Significant at 5%. * Significant at 10%. Standard errors in brackets.
Source: OECD input–output database 2002.

the United Kingdom and Katsoulacos and Tsounis for Greece. The impact on productivity is examined using data for 1990, except in Italy and Greece where the input–output tables employed are for 1988. In both cases, the effects on productivity of what they define as KIBS (communication services and business services) are positive and significant, ranging from 0.173 in Greece to 0.327 in the United Kingdom. The paper by Drejer (2002) tries to extend the analysis by introducing a sectoral dimension and examining a longer period of time. Thus, she estimates a production function using data for 52 industries during the period 1970–95. The results show the existence of considerable sectoral differences in the importance of the use of business services.

In the case of those studies that estimate the same equations, we can directly compare our estimations for the impact of KIBS with those obtained by Windrum and Tomlinson (1999) and Tomlinson (2000a).[6] In Windrum and Tomlinson (1999), KIBS are defined as post and telecommunications and most of the industries included under 'business services'.[7] They estimate equations for four countries for the years indicated in parenthesis: Germany (1993), Japan (1990), the Netherlands (1994) and the United Kingdom (1990). The values they obtain for the effects of KIBS on production and productivity are very similar to those estimated here in the case of the Netherlands and exactly the same in the case of the United Kingdom. Only in the instance of Germany are there differences: we obtain higher estimated values (0.40 in production and 0.39 for productivity) than they do (0.29 for production and productivity).

Tomlinson (2000a) compares the situation of Japan and the United Kingdom in the years 1970 and 1990. He defines KIBS as communications and business services Again, the values that he estimates for the impact of KIBS on production and productivity using the United Kingdom input–output table for 1990 are exactly the same as those we obtain: 0.19 for production and 0.18 for productivity. This fact confirms that the significance of KIBS has not diminished in recent years. The opposite trend is observed in the case of labour: its importance has lessened in favour of 'material inputs' (the estimation of the effect on production decreased from 0.40 in Tomlinson's work to 0.27 here). As a consequence, the estimated value for the impact of material inputs on productivity is considerably higher in our results (0.54 compared to 0.40 in Tomlinson's work).

Therefore, we can conclude that, in line with the conclusions reached by previous studies, the use of KIS as intermediate inputs has a positive impact both in terms of production and in terms of productivity. In the following section, we try to take the next step and analyse the role of KIS in the innovation domain.

7.3 Can knowledge-intensive services contribute to innovation?

The methodology employed in this part is a modified version of that introduced in the work of Papaconstantinou *et al.* (1998) and applied to service activities by Amable and Palombarini (1998). However, in our chapter we adopt a 'supply-side' vision (Rodriguez, 2003). That is to say, instead of assessing which industries incorporate more product-embodied R&D through the acquisition of intermediate inputs, we appraise which industries 'diffuse' more product-embodied R&D through intermediate sales. Due to the limited information available on services, we restrict our analysis to domestic embodied R&D flows.

We define the R&D intensity in industry i as R&D expenditures per value added:[8]

$$r_i = \frac{R_i}{W_i} \qquad (i = 1, 2, \ldots, N) \tag{7.5}$$

We choose to compute R&D intensities with respect to output instead of employment because, as Amable and Palombarini (1998) point out in their paper, the use of employment entails two problems when comparing the growth of R&D intensities among countries: firstly, differences can hide variations in capital and labour ratios, and, secondly, increases in R&D intensities can be explained by labour productivity gains. In reference to the output indicator, we consider value added to be a better measure of output than production or turnover. Since production includes intermediates, any output of intermediate goods consumed within the same sector is also recorded as output. As a result, the impact of such intra-sector flows depends on the coverage of the sector. For its part, turnover refers to the actual sales in the year and can be greater than production in a given year if all products are sold together with stock from previous years. Consequently, the turnover can be higher or lower in an industry, depending on how perishable the stock is.

Given the output inverse matrix, introduced by Ghosh (1958), the equilibrium equation in the domestic supply model is:

$$X = W(I - B)^{-1} \tag{7.6}$$

where X is the vector of domestic gross outputs, W is the vector of value added and $(I - B)^{-1}$ is the domestic output inverse (Ghosh) matrix. We can define the matrix of domestic product-embodied R&D diffusion, D, by introducing the diagonalized matrix of R&D intensities in equation (7.6) as follows:

$$D = W\hat{r}\Lambda(I - B)^{-1} \tag{7.7}$$

where *r hat* ($\hat{r}$) indicates a diagonal matrix whose elements are those of vector r. Given the fact that firms need to carry out their own R&D activities in order to be able to absorb knowledge (and in this case R&D) from other firms, we introduce a weighting diagonal matrix, Λ, whose elements, λ_j, are based on the R&D expenditures of the different client industries:

$$\lambda_j = \frac{r_j}{\frac{1}{N}\sum_{j=1}^{N} r_j} \qquad (j = 1, 2, \ldots, N) \tag{7.8}$$

Equation (7.7) relates domestic product-embodied R&D diffusion to the value-added components (compensation of the employees and gross operating surplus). Thus, the domestic product-embodied R&D diffusion per unit of value added of industry i, UD_i, can be defined as the sum of the ith row of matrix $\hat{r}\Lambda(I - B)^{-1}$:

$$UD_i = \sum_{j=1}^{N} r_i \lambda_j q_{ij} \quad (i = 1, 2, \ldots, N) \tag{7.9}$$

where q_{ij} are the elements of the Ghosh inverse. Since the ith row of the Ghosh inverse measures the impact on domestic production when the value added of the ith industry varies by one unit, equation (7.8) provides the amount of domestic product-embodied R&D diffused per unit of value added of industry i. We can obtain the total domestic product-embodied

R&D flows diffused through the intermediate sales, *TD*, by pre-multiplying equation (7.8) by the value added (where w_i is the value added of industry i):

$$TD_i = w_i \sum_{j=1}^{N} r_i \lambda_j q_{ij} \qquad (7.10)$$

The calculation of the flows per unit of value added is a way of approximating the relevance of services as transmitters of their own R&D efforts. In a complementary way, the computation of the total flows allows us to simultaneously evaluate the processes of structural change (growth in the contribution to value added) and of intensification of R&D efforts (growth in R&D intensities).

Table 7.4 reports the domestic product-embodied R&D diffused by KIS in 1999, both per unit of value added and in total.

Entering into the product-embodied R&D diffused per unit of value added, within the three industries called KIS examined in this chapter, we can clearly differentiate between the industry of research and development and the two

Table 7.4 Product-embodied R&D diffused by KIS, 1999

	Flows per unit of value added									
	Denmark		*Germany*		*Netherlands*		*Spain*		*UK*	
	Value	*Rank*	*Value*	*Rank*	*Value*	*Rank*	*Value*	*Rank*	*Value*	*Rank*
Post and telecom	n.a.	n.a.	0.0004*	19	0.0025	14	0.0139	14	0.0190	15
Computer and related activities	0.2712	5	0.0293	10	0.0048	13	0.0146	13	0.0477	13
Research and development	2.3448	1	0.4287	6	0.0052	12	0.7564	3	0.4596	4
	Total flows (millions of national currency)									
	Denmark		*Germany*		*Netherlands*		*Spain*		*UK*	
	Value	*Rank*	*Value*	*Rank*	*Value*	*Rank*	*Value*	*Rank*	*Value*	*Rank*
Post and telecom	n.a.	n.a.	48.37*	17	19.98	10	191.83	7	459.53	12
Computer and related activities	3984.85	3	844.28	10	30.72	9	68.87	13	926.37	7
Research and development	7780.12	2	2589.23	8	7.75	17	130.86	10	1708.20	5
Number of industries	17	27	29	30	27					

* Includes Transport and Storage.
Source: STAN, ANBERD and input-output databases.

other industries: post and telecommunications and computer and related activities. In the case of research and development, because of the type of services it provides, this industry shows a R&D intensity superior to any other service industry in all countries under study, excluding the Netherlands. This aspect contributes to explaining why its position is considerably better than any other service industry in terms of product-embodied R&D diffused per unit of value added. It is the leading industry in Denmark and holds the third and fourth position in Spain and the United Kingdom, respectively. Nevertheless, a greater or lesser integration with the rest of the production system is also an important factor, which translates into a higher or lower quantity of product-embodied R&D diffused per unit of value added. For example, in spite of having a higher R&D intensity in Germany than in the United Kingdom, the industry of research and development diffuses more R&D per unit of value added in this latter country (0.4596) than in Germany (0.4287).

In the cases of the other two industries, the first thing that captures our attention is the relatively high position that these two industries show, given their relatively low R&D intensities in comparison with the manufacturing average. Moreover, the positions held by the industries in the different countries are quite similar (excluding Denmark, where the total number of industries is much lower: 17). The industry of computer and related activities ranges from the fifth position in Denmark, to tenth in Germany and thirteenth in the Netherlands, Spain and the United Kingdom. The industry of post and telecommunications ranks fourteenth in the Netherlands and Spain, fifteenth in the United Kingdom and nineteenth in Germany.[9]

The total domestic product-embodied R&D flows diffused takes into account, along with the innovation efforts, the contribution of each industry to value added. In general, we observe a higher ranking in KIS industries. Post and telecommunications ranks among the top ten product-embodied R&D diffusers in the Netherlands and Spain. Computer and related activities holds the third position in Denmark and the seventh in the United Kingdom. The only exception to this trend is found in the industry of research and development, because of its lower contribution to value added.

Two works have employed a similar methodology to evaluate the product-embodied R&D by industries: Papaconstantinou *et al.* (1998) and Amable and Palombarini (1998).

All of the countries analysed in this chapter, with the exception of Spain, are included in the work by Papaconstantinou *et al.* (1998). In their paper they identify the five top R&D performers and the five biggest technology-using industries in every country, considering both direct R&D efforts (business expenditures on R&D) and indirect R&D efforts (R&D incorporated through intermediate consumptions and investment goods, both domestic and imported). Using their classification we can evaluate whether, as should be expected, those industries classified as the 'five top R&D performers' at the beginning of the nineties, that is to say, the five top industries in terms of

R&D efforts (both direct and acquired),[10] also act as the top embodied R&D diffusers at the end of the 1990s, namely, as the main industries in terms of diffusion of product-embodied R&D through intermediate sales. In general, we observe that the industries named as the five top R&D performers are also the five biggest product-embodied R&D diffusers.[11] This is the case for pharmaceuticals and machinery and equipment in Denmark, chemicals and motor vehicles in Germany, chemicals in the Netherlands and pharmaceuticals in the United Kingdom. Our attention is drawn to the relevant position of KIS industries in most of the countries. We can affirm, therefore, that KIS could be classified as a 'new technological cluster', which indirectly provides product-embodied R&D through intermediate sales, along with the three 'classical' technological sources: the chemical industry, the industry of machinery and equipment and the industry of transport equipment.

The second paper referred to is that of Amable and Palombarini (1998). Although it applies the same methodology developed by Papaconstantinou *et al.* (1998), it focuses, for the first time, on service industries. In particular, five service industries (transportation services, communication services, financial services, trade and hotels and social and governmental services) are examined in eight countries (Canada, Denmark, France, Germany, Japan, the Netherlands, the United Kingdom and the United States). The results obtained confirm the existence of similarities in R&D intensities in the communication industry, as we observe in our work. Nevertheless, Denmark stands out with a low R&D intensity in the service sector, a trend that contrasts with the picture portrayed by our results. Currently, Denmark is a country where services, and in particular KIS, are playing a key role both in terms of R&D expenditures and in terms of diffusion of product-embodied R&D.

In conclusion, we can state that KIS industries carry out an important task in the process of product-embodied R&D diffusion. Although this role is quite new (see, for example, the great differences in the role of services in Denmark at the beginning and the end of the 1990), it is becoming a common feature in the countries analysed, even in traditionally manufacturing-oriented countries, like Germany.

7.4 Conclusions

It is undeniable that services and manufacturing are becoming ever more closely intertwined. The changes in the economic environment, in combination with an increasing demand for specialized knowledge, have caused KIS to become key intermediate inputs within production systems. Nevertheless, as indicated in the second section, today KIS are much more than mere intermediate inputs. By creating and diffusing knowledge, they are real drivers for innovation in many industries.

In this chapter we have attempted to econometrically assess, from a double perspective, the impact that the use of KIS can have on the performance of other industries, the effects on production and productivity and the role played in the diffusion of product-embodied R&D. KIS are defined as the three following industries: post and telecommunications, computer and related activities and research and development. We have taken five European countries as the scope of our analysis: Denmark, Germany, Spain, the Netherlands and the United Kingdom.

First of all, we estimated the effects that the use of KIS generates on production and productivity. In line with previous analyses, the results obtained corroborate the existence of a positive impact on production and productivity. Furthermore, the estimations obtained for the different countries are very similar, except in the United Kingdom and also in Spain in the case of the parameter estimated to measure the effect on productivity. When we put these cases aside, the values obtained range from 0.18 in Denmark to 0.23 in the Netherlands, in relation to production, and from 0.18 in Denmark to 0.22 in the Netherlands, in relation to productivity.

Secondly, we calculated the domestic product-embodied R&D diffused in total, as well as per unit of value added.

Concerning the flows per unit of value added, the research and development industry is shown to be the leading industry in Denmark and holds the third and fourth positions in Spain and the United Kingdom, respectively. The industry of computer and related activities ranks fifth in Denmark, tenth in Germany and thirteenth in the Netherlands, Spain and the United Kingdom. The industry of post and telecommunications ranks fourteenth in the Netherlands and Spain, fifteenth in the United Kingdom and nineteenth in Germany.

With reference to the total flows, a higher ranking in KIS industries is observed. Post and telecommunications ranks among the top ten product-embodied R&D diffusers in the Netherlands and Spain. Computer and related activities holds the third position in Denmark and the seventh in the United Kingdom. The only exception is found in the industry of research and development, because of its lower contribution to value added.

Therefore, the results obtained in this empirical assessment of the impact of KIS on the production systems reveal that they exert a highly positive influence on the performance of other industries. Furthermore, the growing importance of KIS activities, in terms of production and employment, highlights the dawning realization of their increasing relevance in years to come.

Notes

1. For more information on the definition and functions of KIS, consult Chapter 2 by Miles and Chapter 4 by Kox and Rubalcaba in this book.
2. Eurostat (together with the OECD) defines Knowledge-intensive services (KIS) according to technological intensity and based on the NACE Rev. 1.1 classification at a 3-digit level as follows: Water transport (61); Air transport (62); Post and Telecommunications (64); Financial intermediation, except insurance and pension

funding (65); Insurance and pension funding, except compulsory social security (66); Activities auxiliary to financial intermediation (67); Real estate activities (70); Renting of machinery and equipment without an operator, and of personal and household goods (71); Computer and related activities (72); Research and development (73); Other business activities (74); Education (80); Health and social work (85); and Recreational, cultural and sporting activities (92).

The Total Knowledge-intensive services (KIS) are classified into five groups: Knowledge-intensive high-tech services: Post and Telecommunications (64); Computer and related activities (72); Research and development (73); Knowledge-intensive market services (excl. financial intermediation and high-tech services): Water transport (61); Air transport (62); Real estate activities (70); Renting of machinery and equipment without operator, and of personal and household goods (71); Other business activities (74). Knowledge-intensive financial services: Financial intermediation, except insurance and pension funding (65); Insurance and pension funding, except compulsory social security (66); Activities auxiliary to financial intermediation (67); Other knowledge-intensive services: Education (80); Health and social work (85); Recreational, cultural and sporting activities (92).

3. One of the main reasons for the selection of this second approach is the absence of detailed capital series at the desegregation level employed in the input–output tables, as Paul Baker notices in Chapter 5 of this volume. Moreover, the option of estimating a traditional production function that includes capital inputs and distinguishes between business services and other business services has additional problems such as the potential multicollinearity that arise (especially in some countries) from the high correlation between the use of business services and the use of other services.
4. Non-autocorrelation tests were carried out for the different countries. The Durbin–Watson test accepts the null hypothesis of non-autocorrelation in Denmark and the United Kingdom. In the rest of the cases the test is non-conclusive. This is why we calculated the Breusch–Godfrey statistic, which accepts the null hypothesis of non-autocorrelation (of first order), at the five percent level in all of the cases.
5. We have to note that, in contrast to the theoretical model, the parameter of labour is not equal to the sum of the parameters a and b.
6. Tomlinson (2000b) again examined the case of the United Kingdom starting from the 1990 input–output table using the same definition of KIBS as Windrum and Tomlinson (1999). The novelty is the estimation of separate equations for each industry included within the group of KIBS.
7. The group of KIBS comprise the following industries. In Germany: post and telecoms, banking and financial services, insurance, real estate agencies, science and culture and publishing business services and other business services. In Japan: communication services, financial and insurance services, real estate agencies and business services. In the Netherlands: post and telecoms, banking, financial services, insurance, real estate agencies, letting services, legal, accounting and business services, computing services, advertising agencies, general business services and employment agencies and recruitment services. In the United Kingdom: postal services, telecoms, banking and finance, auxiliary finance, insurance, real estate agents, legal services, accounting, other professional services, advertising, computer services and other business services.
8. R&D expenditures are obtained from the ANBERD database. Value-added data come from the STAN database. The number of industries under analysis were

reduced to 31, of which seven were services, in order to homogenise the ANBERD, STAN and input-output classifications.

9. We have to take into account that in Germany, as indicated in Table 7.4, the industry of post and telecommunications also includes the transport and storage industry.
10. They calculate the total R&D efforts by taking into account the R&D expenditures and the product-embodied R&D acquired through intermediate consumptions and through acquisition of machinery and equipment (both domestic and imported).
11. Detailed tables are available on request.

8

Innovation in Business Services: From Technological Adoption to Multiple, Complementary, Concurrent Changes

Jeremy Howells, Bruce S. Tether and Elvira Uyarra

Introduction

Services not only comprise a large part of the economy, but also represent the main sector of growth within advanced industrial economies (see Chapters 1 and 4). Despite this, relatively little is known about the underlying dynamics and nature of the service sector, as compared with other sectors – particularly manufacturing. In particular, little is known about the role of innovation in this process of dynamic change. Innovation in services is less well understood than innovation in manufacturing (OECD, 2005b). This study highlights the partial view that most studies have adopted in relation to understanding innovation, particularly in the services sector. Innovation studies have tended to overlook the fact that at any one time firms and organizations are typically generating, adopting and implementing multiple forms of innovation. This chapter therefore addresses these issues by exploring innovation processes using data from a survey which covered firms located across Europe and which were active in three business service sectors: road transport, information processing and design and related activities. The chapter also explores some of the behavioural aspects associated with innovation, such as how firms compete and their growth objectives.

8.1 The limited technological vision of innovation

Services have long been perceived as being either non-innovative or technologically backward. Until the 1990s, they were perceived largely as passive adopters of technologies developed by manufacturers. Thus, Pavitt's (1984) famous taxonomy of sectors by technology profile conceptualized services as being simply 'supplier dominated'. Throughout the 1990s and into the twenty-first century, it has become increasingly clear that this view is, at best, an oversimplification (Howells, 2001). Services are certainly major users of technologies, not least information and communication technologies (ICTs), and they often use these in creative rather than standard ways. However, services are not just innovators through the use of acquired technologies. For example, 'knowledge-intensive business services' (KIBS), such as those involved in market research, design, engineering and technical services, are particularly important economic actors which are becoming increasingly proactive, generators of innovations that are taken up and implemented by manufacturers and other service providers (Miles *et al.*, 1995; Hargadon and Sutton, 1997). In Europe, an increasing proportion of business R&D is being performed in the services sector (up from 11.5 per cent in 1997 to 15.1 per cent in 2002; European Commission 2005). Furthermore, studies using Community Innovation Survey (CIS) data have also shown that services are generating more innovations. Thus, no longer can *all* service firms be dismissed as passive consumers of technology, whereas manufacturers are seen as the 'real innovators'.

The analysis in this chapter has three basic aims, namely: (i) to investigate innovation in services through a broader conceptual framework, including both technological and non-technological forms of innovation (section 8.3); (ii) to highlight that innovation in services is often a much more complex, interactive and complementary process than has hitherto been appreciated (also in section 8.3); and (iii) to explore innovation in a wider context of service firms' 'task environments' (section 8.4).

In the context of the first issue, it is evident that service innovations are often tacit and intangible in nature, as they are associated with personal knowledge, training and informal interaction, and are therefore typically disembodied and non-technological. Other issues, such as service automation and the significance of self-service, are important aspects of the innovation process within service activities, but remain largely uncharted for the purposes of providing an adequate mapping and measuring of the new service economy. This is largely because innovation surveys, such as the European CIS, still concentrate on more traditional forms of technological innovation. In part, this stems from conceptual gaps in our understanding of innovation processes within services, but there have also been problems with measuring innovation in services. Service innovations are difficult to capture with existing measurement tools because of their often-tacit and disembodied nature, as noted above. Underlying this there are intrinsic, dynamic qualities of services, such as their emphasis on customization, variation and continuous change (rather than punctuated change), which make them difficult to study (Tether 2005). This also relates to factors such as the 'servicization' of manufacturing, and the blurring of the division between these two great 'sectors'. However, this neglect of non-technological, organizational innovations, which are both harder to define and harder to measure, is not just an academic regret, it has enormous potential significance both to individual companies and to economies as a whole. Organizational and administrative innovation resulting in new structural forms is probably as significant a mode of innovation as major technological innovations because it is essential to both effective organizational performance and institutional problem solving (Schulman 1969; Teece 1980; Tether and Metcalfe 2003).

We should be wary, however, of conceptualizing different forms of innovation as being mutually exclusive. Rather, technological and organizational innovations should be seen as often being complementary, such that the full benefits of a technological innovation cannot be fully realized without accompanying organizational change and vice versa. This brings us to the second and third issues, and our belief that the study of innovation, particularly within empirical studies, has tended to focus on narrow, one-dimensional, 'single-issue' aspects, that have tended to highlight certain types of innovation, such as product innovation or process innovation, in isolation, such that these different types of innovation are typically viewed as being independent of one another (Damanpour and Evan 1984: 406). Even when innovations are treated together this tends to be confined to the firm or organization, rarely in relation to inter-organizational types of innovation. By contrast, we consider that, perhaps especially in the case of services, different types of innovation often interact with each other in complex, interdependent and complementary ways. It follows that one of our objectives is to move towards are more holistic, interdependent view of innovation than has prevailed hitherto.

8.2 Methodology and survey

As noted above, all sectors have innovative activities, which include not only technological, but also organizational and relational forms of change. The aim of the survey which we analyse in this chapter was to explore some of the basic characteristics concerning the pattern of innovation within a variety of service activities. The survey was undertaken as part of a wider study funded by the European Commission. Given space restrictions, details and further particulars (such as questionnaire design and sampling methodology) can be found in the main report of the study (Howells and Tether 2004).

A number of issues are worth highlighting, however. Innovation is, by its very nature, highly diversified and a large-scale survey of innovative behaviour is necessarily reductive. In this chapter we use the survey results for firms active in three sectors (road transport, call centres and information processing, and design and related activities). We selected these three activities to reflect some of the diversity within the broad 'services sector'. The three activities can be considered to be engaged in different types of transformations: road transport involves physical transformations, handling and moving goods from place to place; call centres and information processing involve transforming information; whilst design and related activities involve transforming knowledge. A total number of 799 firms responded to the survey in these three sectors: 261 in road transport; 241 in call centres and information processing; and 297 in design and related activities. Firms were surveyed in all the EU15 member states of the European Union. Of the 799 respondents, 191 were based in Germany,

148 in the UK, 141 in France, 104 in Italy, 102 in Spain, and 113 in the other, smaller, European countries.[1]

The aim of the survey was to be exploratory in nature, rather than a strictly scientific survey. On this basis, it was decided to over-sample (relative to the population) amongst the larger and 'more likely to be interesting' businesses in each sector.[2] In the analysis that follows, a third of the responding firms have fewer than ten employees, and only 15 per cent had more than 250 employees. Three-quarters are independent companies or partnerships, with the remainder being subsidiaries or divisions of larger company groups (see Howells and Tether 2004 for further details).

It is also important to note that there were several novel (or innovative) aspects to the survey. Firstly, the language and phrasing of the survey was kept simple, partly to reduce the problems inherent in translating the concepts from one language to another, but in particular the term 'innovation' was avoided in the early part of the questionnaire. Instead, the respondents were asked about the extent to which various aspects of their business had 'changed'. The term 'innovation' was avoided in the early part of the survey because it has become arguably a very loaded concept, which would have required a definition (which creates as many problems as it solves) and also because innovations tend to be associated with discrete events, which may be harder to identify in services where change tends to be more continuous. Although the relationship between 'change' and 'innovation' is contentious (because services or processes may change for reasons other than innovation), it was felt that the advantages of avoiding the term innovation outweighed the disadvantages. Secondly, the survey sought to extend the investigation of innovation beyond the narrow confines of 'product', 'process' and 'delivery' innovations, by exploring changes to the technologies and skills of the organization, as well as changes in its organizational structure and its inter-relations with customers and other businesses. Lastly, the survey also included questions about the nature of the services provided and how the firms compete. These aspects were included because we were interested in trying to understand innovation (or 'change') in its wider context, rather than 'counting innovations' and comparing rates of innovation.

8.3 A more holistic approach: innovation as multiple, complementary, concurrent changes

This section explores the pattern of 'change' in the firms that responded to the survey across the three service sectors. As indicated in section 8.1, it seeks to highlight the fact that by concentrating our attention on product, process and technological indicators of innovation we restrict and narrow our view of innovation. Figure 8.1 includes all the dimensions of 'change' about which the businesses were questioned. In each case firms were asked to indicate the extent to which these had changed, over the last three years, from 'changed

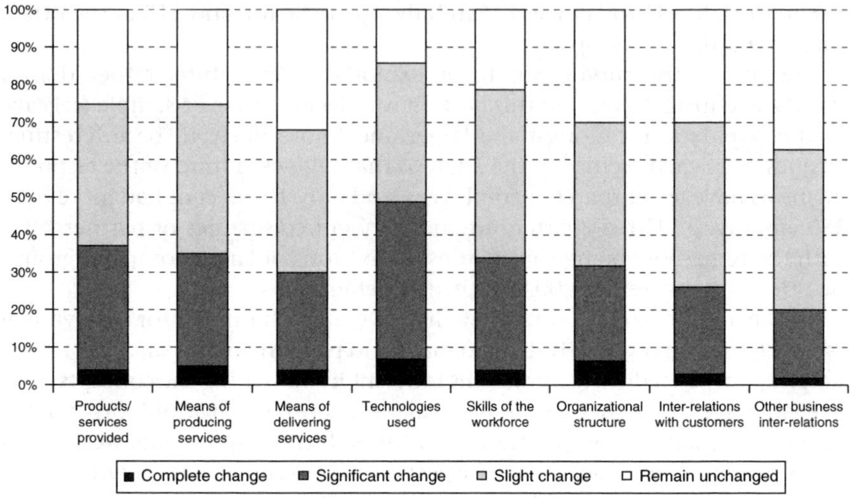

Figure 8.1 The extent of change reported across eight dimensions

completely', through 'changed to a significant extent', and 'changed but only slightly', to 'remain unchanged'. The first four dimensions of change cover what might be termed 'technological innovation':

- changes to the products or services provided;
- changes to the means of producing services;
- changes to the means of delivering services; and,
- changes to the technologies used to produce or deliver services.

Of these, the most widespread change was found in the technologies used to produce or deliver services, with almost half the firms reporting significant or complete changes, and only 14 per cent claiming that their technologies had remained unchanged. Around a third of the businesses claimed that their products or services had changed either completely or significantly, with a quarter claiming they had remained unchanged. A very similar pattern was found for changes to the means of producing services, whilst slightly fewer firms reported extensive change to their means of delivering services.

Turning to other types of change, which we consider 'soft/organizational innovation', the following were considered:

- change to the skills of the workforce used to produce or deliver services;
- changes to the organizational structure of the business;
- changes to customer inter-relations; and,
- changes to other business inter-relations.

The extent of 'change' reported to the skills used to produce and deliver services was similar to the extent of change to the firms' services and their means of producing and delivering services, with a third of the businesses claiming the skills they used had changed completely or significantly in the last three years.[3] Meanwhile, the extent of change to firms' organizational structures, and to their inter-relations with other businesses (including customers) tended to be less, but still substantial with at least a fifth claiming complete or significant changes to these in the last three years.

It is notable that almost as many firms recorded significant or complete change to at least one of these 'soft/organizational' dimensions as recorded significant or complete change to one or more of the technological forms of change. If we aggregate these into two sets of change, where the greatest extent of change reported to the first four dimensions is used as an indicator of technological change, whilst the greatest extent of change to the last four dimensions is taken as an indicator of soft/organizational change we find the following: 11 per cent of businesses reported complete change to one or more of the technological dimensions. Excluding these, 57 per cent reported significant change to one or more of the technological dimensions, 37 per cent recorded only at most slight change, and 6 per cent reported no change at all. Of the soft/organizational dimensions, 11 per cent reported complete change to one or more of these, with a further 50 per cent reporting some significant change, a third recording at most slight change, and the remaining 7 per cent no changes. These levels of change are strikingly high, and are unlikely to be representative, but here we are more interested in the interconnections between forms of change than in their levels.

To explore further the extent of connections between the various dimensions of change, we calculated the conditional probabilities that a firm would have changed (significantly or completely) in one dimension given that it had also changed (significantly or completely) in another dimension. Although this analysis does not tell us anything about the direction of causation, it can be used as a test of complementarities. If a firm is more likely than not to do a second activity given that it has done a first activity, the two activities can be considered to be complementary. Note, however, that complementarity scores are not necessarily symmetrical – the probability of doing B given that A has been done is not necessarily the same as the probability of doing A given that B has been done.

The results are shown in Table 8.1, which shows the conditional probability that the firm changed significantly or completely the dimension identified in the column given that it had changed significantly or completely the dimension identified in the row. For example, of the firms that changed their services, 59 per cent also changed their production processes. Cells in which the probabilities equal or exceed 50 per cent indicate complementarities – firms that changed in the row dimension are more likely than not to also change in the column dimension. What is striking is that the scores in a large number (24) of cells equal or exceed 50 per cent, whilst the scores in another 13 cells are between 45 per cent and 49 per cent, indicating firms that changed in the row dimension are almost as likely as not to also change in the column dimension. In only 14 cells are the scores below 40 per cent, with the lowest score being 24 per cent – i.e., only a quarter of the firms that changed their technologies also changed their inter-relations with other businesses. Interestingly, if they made any other significant or complete change the firms were more likely than not to also change their technologies (significantly or completely). The dimensions of change that showed the least connection to the others were changes to customer and other business inter-relations, and changes to the firms' organizational structure. In fact, fewer than half of the firms that changed substantially or completely in any other dimension also claimed to have changed their organizational structure. This implies organizational structure is rather more 'sticky' than technologies.

Overall, the analysis in Table 8.1 suggests that firms that engaged in one form of change are also more likely to be engaged in other forms of change. Indeed, Figure 8.2 shows the observed distribution of firms by the count of the dimensions for which they reported significant or complete change, against the expected count distribution which would arise if the various dimensions were independent of one another (that is, if the probability of each change was independent of any of the others). This shows that firms were both much more likely to report no significant or complete changes, and to report change to several dimensions (that is, five or more) than would be

Table 8.1 Complementarities between the dimensions of change (percentages)

	Ser.	*Prod.*	*Deliv.*	*Tech.*	*Skill*	*Org.*	*IRC*	*OBI*
Services (Ser.)	**100**	59	47	60	51	49	39	30
Production Processes (Prod.)	62	**100**	56	73	52	42	40	27
Distribution Processes (Deliv.)	57	65	**100**	70	48	39	38	27
Technologies (Tech.)	46	52	44	**100**	47	36	33	24
Skills (Skill)	56	54	44	69	**100**	47	39	27
Organizational Structure (Org.)	57	46	37	56	49	**100**	39	31
Customers Interrelations (IRC)	56	53	45	60	50	47	**100**	51
Other Interrelations (OBI)	55	45	41	57	45	48	66	**100**

Note: Cells show the conditional probability that a firm has changed (significantly or completely) the dimension in the column given that it has changed (significantly or completely) the dimension in the row. For example, 59 per cent of firms that changed their services also changed their production processes.

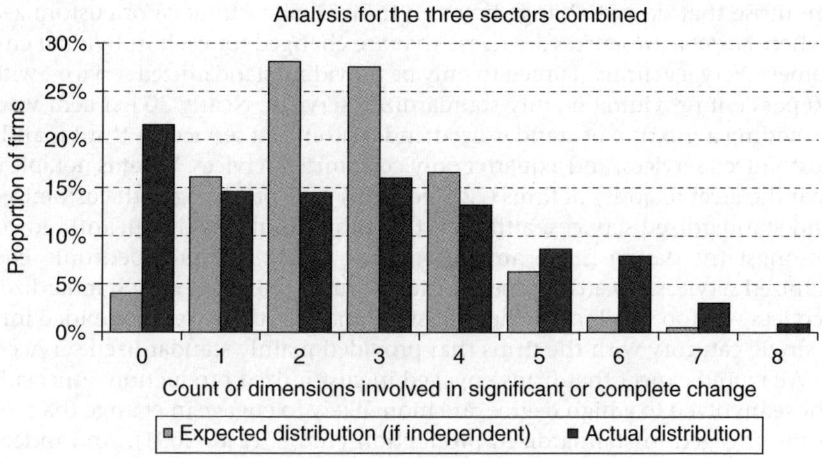

Figure 8.2 The inter-related nature of innovation in services

expected if the dimensions of change were statistically independent. It is also notable that fewer firms reported significant or complete change to two or three dimensions than would be expected if these dimensions of change were statistically independent of one another. Unfortunately, we cannot prove that the changes the firms made were actually interrelated, rather than just coincidental or concurrent, but it does seem likely that innovation in services often involves inter-related changes along multiple dimensions.

8.4 Contextualizing the innovation process

8.4.1 Introduction

In this section, we attempt to contextualize the changes reported by the firms. We do this in relation to three factors: the extent to which the firms provided standardized or customized services; the competitive orientation of the firms; and their growth intentions. We will first explore briefly simple bivariate relationships between these factors and the extent of change reported by the firms, after which we will explore the interrelationships between these factors and the extent of change in a multivariate framework. We do not claim that these three factors are the only drivers of change, instead our intention is to explore the relationship between other behavioural characteristics of the firms and the extent to which they report change across the various dimensions we have already discussed.

8.4.2 Customization

The first factor we examine is the nature of the services the firms provided according to the extent to which they are standardized (where *standard services* are those that do not change between individual customers) or customized (where *customized services* are those that are changed for each individual customer). Very few firms claimed to only be providing standardized services, with 10 per cent providing mainly standardized services. Nearly 30 per cent were providing a mixture of standardized and customized services, a third mainly customized services, and a quarter only customized services. What is notable is that the great majority of firms (72.5 per cent) were providing both customized and standardized services, although this proportion was significantly lower amongst the design firms, amongst which nearly half provided only customized services. Because the proportion of firms providing only standardized services was too small for further statistical analysis, these were combined into a single category with the firms that provided mainly standardized services.

We would expect that firms engaged in customized production, especially those involved to a high degree, are more likely to engage in change than are firms engaged in standardized production (Tether *et al.* 2001). And indeed simple cross-tabulations find some association between the number of significant or complete changes (across the various dimensions) reported by the firms and their extent of customization. Wholly and mainly standardized service providers are less likely to engage in any change, and none of these firms reported significant or complete changes to seven or eight of the dimensions. On average, firms that provided wholly or mainly standardized services reported significant or complete changes to two of the eight dimensions, whilst those providing largely or wholly customized services reported (on average) three significant or complete changes. When disaggregated between technological and soft/organizational forms of change, it is apparent that the association between the extent of customization and the extent of reported change is stronger and more linear for the technological forms of change than for the soft/organizational forms of change.

8.4.3 Competitive strategy

The second factor we examine concerns the firms' competitive orientation. The firms were asked to rank on a four-level scale, from 'not important' through to 'of high importance', 15 aspects that might relate to the success of their business. These aspects and the simple distribution of responses are shown in Figure 8.3, which ranks the aspects from highest to lowest in terms of the proportion of firms that considered this of high importance. Top of the list was the quality of services provided, whilst interestingly the introduction of new services was third from last, and using new or advanced technologies was a middle-ranking aspect.

To simplify the response to this question, we undertook a principal components analysis (using varimax rotation). This found five principal components (PC) with eigenvalues greater than one. These explained 55 per cent of the variance in the data.[4] The results are shown in Table 8.2. The first PC clearly relates to competing through *service products*, including the provision of a broad

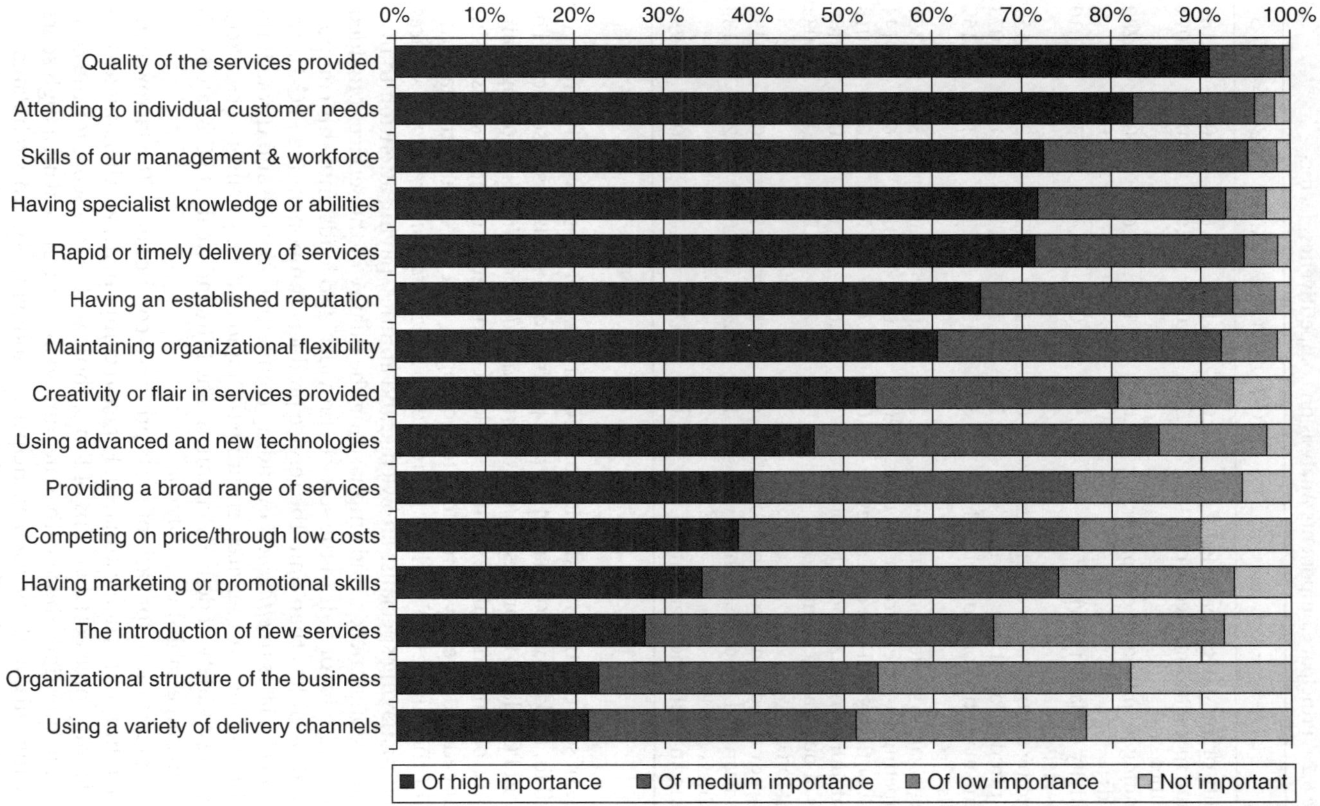

Figure 8.3 Importance of various factors in the firms' competitiveness

Table 8.2 Principal Components Analysis on competitiveness factors

	PC-1	*PC-2*	*PC-3*	*PC-4*	*PC-5*
Quality of the services provided	−0.037	0.174	**0.621**	0.068	−0.184
Having specialist knowledge or abilities	0.249	0.062	**0.691**	−0.058	0.021
Attending to individual customer needs	0.049	0.119	**0.630**	0.069	0.280
Creativity or flair in services provided	**0.560**	−0.051	0.426	−0.388	−0.010
Providing a broad range of services	**0.619**	0.123	0.216	0.272	0.159
The introduction of new services	**0.753**	0.152	0.120	0.131	−0.073
Having marketing or promotional skills	**0.590**	0.281	−0.104	−0.169	0.159
Using a variety of delivery channels	0.439	0.078	−0.033	**0.529**	0.351
Competing on price/through low costs	−0.031	0.042	−0.125	**0.639**	−0.144
Rapid or timely delivery of services	0.060	0.111	0.263	**0.687**	0.018
Maintaining organizational flexibility	0.127	**0.688**	0.157	0.064	0.139
Skills of our management and workforce	0.045	**0.735**	0.270	−0.024	0.034
Using advanced and new technologies	0.398	**0.515**	0.136	0.052	−0.438
Organizational structure of the business	0.189	**0.578**	−0.077	0.212	0.138
Having an established reputation	0.141	0.249	0.075	−0.071	**0.752**

range of services, the introduction of new services, services involving creativity and flair, and the use of marketing and promotional skills to sell services. The second PC relates to processes and *organizational capabilities*, including maintaining organizational flexibility, workforce and management skills, using advanced and recently introduced technologies, and the organizational structure of the business. The third PC relates to *specialization & relational services*, including having specialist knowledge and abilities, paying attention to individual customer needs, and emphasizing the quality of the services provided. Using creativity or flair in the services provided also loads onto this component, although less than onto the service products component (i.e., PC-1). The fourth PC relates to *efficiency*, including competing on price and through the provision of low-cost services, ensuring the rapid or timely delivery of services, and using a variety of delivery channels. The fifth and weakest PC related only to having an established *reputation*.

Using regression, for each of these principal components, the factor scores for each firm were then estimated. For each component, we then divided the sample into three equal groups of firms: those with a low score for the component in question, those with a medium score, and those with a high score. Following this, and for each principal component, we cross-tabulated the low–medium–high classifications of firms against the extent of change reported

Table 8.3 Relationship between change dimensions and principal components

Dimension	*PC-1*	*PC-2*	*PC-3*	*PC-4*	*PC-5*
Services	⬆	—	—	—	n
Production Processes	⬆	—	—	↓	n
Delivery Processes	⬆	—	—	—	—
Technologies	⬆	↑	—	—	⬇
Skills	⬆	⬆	—	—	n
Organizational Structure	⬆	⬆	—	—	—
Inter-Relations with Clients	⬆	↑	—	—	—
Inter-Relations with Other Businesses	↑	↑	—	—	—

Notes: — = no significant relationship; ⬆ = significant (at <1%) and positive relationship ↑ if significant at 1%–10%; ⬇ = significant (at <1%) and negative relationship ↓ if significant at 1%–10%; n = Inverted U-shaped relationship (significant at <10%).

across the various dimensions, where the extent of change was categorized as: none; slight change; and a combined category of significant or complete change. This generated 40 cross-tabulations (five PCs × eight dimensions of change). The findings are summarized in Table 8.3, which shows whether or not a significant association existed between the classification of firms by their competitive orientation and the extent of change they reported.

The results show significant and positive associations between all of the change dimensions and the first (and strongest) principal component – i.e., that relating to competitiveness through *service products*. In short, firms that scored highly on this component were more likely than other firms to report change in all of the eight dimensions of change. Beyond this, there were significant and positive associations between changes to technologies and all of the soft/organizational dimensions of change and the second principal component; that relating to competing through *organizational capabilities*. Firms that scored highly on this component were not, however, more likely to report changes to their service products, or means of production or delivery. There were no significant relationships between any of the dimensions of change and the third principal component – competitiveness through *specialization & relational services*. For the fourth principal component – that concerned with competitiveness through *efficiency* – the only significant relationship with a change dimension was a negative relationship with changes to the means of producing services: in other words, firms that scored highly on this component were less likely to report extensive change to their production processes than were other firms. Finally, the fifth (and weakest) principal component, competitiveness through *reputation*, had some significant relations with the change variables, although with the exception of changes to technologies (significant and negative) these tended not to be linear. Instead, the firms that scored highly on this component were more likely to report slight changes (and less likely to report either no changes, or significant or complete changes) to their service products, production processes and skills. This makes sense. If these firms are highly reliant on their reputation they will not want to damage this by engaging in radical change, and will instead prefer steady, incremental change. The finding that these firms are less likely to report technological change may also indicate that they may perceive extensive technological change as damaging their reputation, and hence competitiveness.

The contrast between the presence of a full set of significant positive relationships between the 'change' variables and the first *service products* principal component, and no significant relationships between the 'change' variables and the third *specialization & relational services* principal component is particularly striking. This might make us question whether a high degree of change is necessarily a 'good thing' (particularly in the absence of further information concerning the levels of performance). Possibly, those firms that scored highly on the *specialization & relational services* principal component have found a niche, in which they perform strongly, and whilst they are not less likely to engage in change than other firms, they are not – unlike the firms that scored highly on the *service products* component – highly dynamic across multiple dimensions of change. Perhaps instead, these firms tend to have a more measured, incremental approach to change.

This difficulty in assessing change in the absence of information on performance is also pertinent to the (weak) negative relationship between changing the methods of producing services and scoring highly on the competing through *efficiency* component. Although initially this seems counter-intuitive, it may signal that those firms that emphasize *efficiency* tend to have achieved relatively stable process arrangements that allow them to achieve high levels of efficiency, whereas other firms are still seeking to improve upon their productive efficiency.

8.4.4 Growth

The third factor we consider in relation to various types of change reported by the firms is their intentions in relation to growth. Few firms expressed the desire to become smaller (3 per cent), some wanted to remain the same size (16 per cent), whilst most sought to grow moderately (59 per cent), and one in five (22 per cent) sought to grow substantially. Because of the small number of firms seeking to become smaller, this group was combined with those that sought to remain the same size into a 'no growth' category (19 per cent). Cross-tabulating these intentions concerning growth against the extent of change reported by the firms, we found a strong and linear relationship: the greater the growth ambitions of the firm, the more likely it was to have changed, and to have changed across several dimensions. In summary, on average the firms that did not seek to grow reported significant or complete change in 1.6 of the eight dimensions, compared to an average of 2.7 for the firms that sought to grow moderately, and 3.4 for the firms that sought substantial growth. This pattern was also observed when the dimensions of change were subdivided between the technological forms of change, and the soft/organizational forms of change.

8.4.5 Multivariate analysis

This section brings together the analysis through multivariate (binary and ordinal) logistic regressions. For each of the eight dimensions of change we estimate a binary logistic regression for firms reporting significant or complete change (coded 1) against those reporting at most slight change (coded 0), whilst we also estimate two ordinal logistic regressions (where the dependent variable is the count of significant or complete changes reported, which can vary from 0 to 4), one for each of the two sets of technological and soft/organizational forms of change. In each model, the variables of most interest are the following:

Standardized: 1 if the firms produced mainly or wholly standardized services.
Mainly Cust.: 1 if the firms produced mainly customized services
Wholly Cust.: 1 if the firms produced wholly customized services
(The reference category here is firms that produced a mixture of standardised and customized services.)
PC1 – High: Which is 1 if the firm was classified as having a high (top third) score on the first principal component concerning the firm's success.
PC2 – High: Which is 1 if the firm was classified as having a high (top third) score on the second principal component concerning the firm's success.
PC3 – High: Which is 1 if the firm was classified as having a high (top third) score on the third principal component concerning the firm's success.
PC4 – High: Which is 1 if the firm was classified as having a high (top third) score on the fourth principal component concerning the firm's success.
PC5 – High: Which is 1 if the firm was classified as having a high (top third) score on the fifth principal component concerning the firm's success.

No Growth: 1 if the firm intended to become smaller or remain the same size
Substantial: 1 if the firm intended to grow substantially.
(The reference category here is firms that sought to grow moderately)

Beyond these, in each model we also included the size of the firm (as the natural log of the number of employees in the firm), a dummy variable for new firms (which is 1 if the firm was established in 1998 or 1999; else 0), a dummy variable (InfoProc) for firms in the information processing sector and a dummy variable (Design) for firms in the design and related activities sector: road transport was the reference sector. Although we will not report the coefficients of these variables in the tables below, we also included country dummies for all countries except Germany.

The models were first estimated with all the variables, after which (using the general to specific approach) insignificant variables were deleted until only

Table 8.4 Binary and ordinal logistic regressions on changes

	Services	*Production processes*	*Delivery processes*	*Technologies*	*Count of these (0–4)*
Constant	−1.723***	−1.338***	−1.777***	−1.171***	See Note
Standardized		−0.715**	−0.853**	−0.768***	−0.611**
Mainly Cust	0.288#		0.345*		0.271#
Wholly Cust	0.529**	0.620***		0.237n.s.	0.497**
PC1 – High	0.694***	0.324*	0.453**	0.343*	0.507***
PC2 – High				0.226n.s.	
PC3 – High	0.195n.s.				
PC4 – High		−0.233n.s.		0.195n.s.	
PC5 – High	−0.265#			−0.383**	−0.309**
No Growth	−0.617**	−0.768***	−0.806***	−0.634***	−0.850***
Substantial G	0.578***			0.443**	0.393**
New Firm			−0.636*	−1.392***	−0.574**
Size	0.148***	0.086#		0.147***	0.144***
InfoProc		0.494**		0.854***	0.531***
Design	0.304#	0.436*	0.603***	0.583**	0.690***
N.	694	694	694	695	694
−2 LL	848.1	838.9	775.4	870.7	1988.2
Model χ^2	65.7***	59.9***	77.1***	92.6***	121.3***
Pseudo R-sq	0.123	0.114	0.149	0.166	0.168

Notes: Threshold values for Count Model: **0–1**: 0.456; **1–2**: 1.471; **2–3**: 2.511; **3–4**: 3.782; Asterisks indicate significance: *** = at 1%; ** = at 5%; * = at 10%; # = significant at 20%; n.s. = not significant. Country dummies entered but not reported.

	Skills	*Structure of organization*	*Customer relations*	*Other Interrelations*	*Count of these*
Constant	−1.357***	−2.483***	−1.087***	−1.470***	See Note
Standardized			−0.493#		
Mainly Cust	0.428**	0.308*	0.445**	0.472**	0.557***
Wholly Cust	0.637***				0.414**
PC1 – High	0.635***		0.436**		0.431***
PC2 – High				0.280#	
PC3 – High	0.279#				0.228#
PC4 – High	0.271#	−0.288#			
PC5 – High					
No Growth	−1.010***	−0.577**	−1.251***	−0.876***	−1.163***
Substantial G	0.269#	0.555***		0.349#	0.415**
New Firm	−0.544*				
Size		0.296***			0.112***
InfoProc		0.532**	−0.472**		
Design		0.555**	−0.358*		

(Continued)

Table 8.4 (Continued)

	Skills	*Structure of organization*	*Customer relations*	*Other Interrelations*	*Count of these*
N.	694	695	649	695	694
−2 LL	828.7	797.2	742.9	673.4	1,747.9
Model χ^2	55.7***	73.6***	55.8***	30.4	101.2***
Pseudo R-sq	0.107	0.141	0.113	0.067	0.145

Notes: Threshold values for Count Model: 0–1: 0.423; 1–2: 1.740; 2–3: 2.938; 3–4: 4.280. Asterisks denote significance level: *** = at 1%; ** = at 5%;* = at 10%;# = at 20%; n.s. = not significant. Country dummies entered but not reported

significant variables remained. In some cases insignificant variables were retained where their deletion caused problems with goodness of fit. Space restrictions mean these models cannot be commented upon in detail, but it is notable that all three of the factors we have discussed above have some relationship with the extent of change reported by the firms.

The strongest and most consistent relationship is found between growth orientation and change. Across all eight dimensions of change, those firms that reported they intended to remain the same size or become smaller were (as expected) less likely to report significant or complete change than those firms that sought moderate growth (the reference group), whilst for five out of the eight dimensions (including service products, technologies, organizational structure, and – less powerfully – skills and interrelations with other businesses) those firms seeking substantial growth were more likely to report significant or complete changes. This is understandable, and shows that firms' ambitions with respect to growth are associated with differences in their innovation behaviour.

Firms that scored highly on the principal component relating to competing through service products (that is, PC-1) also had a consistent and positive relationship with the technological dimensions of change. These firms were also significantly more likely to change their skills and customer relations. All this is understandable given that these firms are the most obviously aggressive in terms of their strategy.

By contrast, the models show that the significant positive relationships between scoring highly on the organizational capabilities principal component (i.e., PC-2) and the soft/organizational forms of change that were found in the earlier bivariate analysis are not maintained (with the exception of a weak positive relationship with change to other business relationship) once other variables are taken into account.

The firms that scored highly on the specialization and relational services principal component (i.e., PC-3) were slightly more likely to claim to have changed their skills, than were the firms that scored highly on the efficiency principal component (i.e., PC-4). The firms that emphasized efficiency were also slightly less likely to claim they had changed their organizational structures, which may indicate they require a more stable organizational basis for highly efficient production. Finally, the firms that scored highly on the reputation principal component were slightly less likely to change their services (significantly or completely), which is also understandable. These firms were also significantly less likely to change their technologies (significantly or completely), perhaps fearing that such change could damage their hard-won reputation. This does not mean, of course, that they did not engage in some more incremental forms of change.

The extent of standardization or customization also appears to have some relationship to the extent of change reported by the firms. As anticipated, those firms that provided wholly customized services were more likely (than the reference group of firms providing a mixture of standardized and customized services) to report significant or complete changes to their service products, means of production, and skills, whilst those providing mainly customized services were more likely to change their delivery processes, their skills, their organizational structure, their customer inter-relations and their inter-relations with other businesses. Indeed, it is notable that firms that provided mainly customized services were more likely to report changes to their organizational structure and relations with other businesses, including customers, than were those firms providing wholly customized services. Meanwhile, those firms that claimed to be providing only or mainly standardized services were less likely (than the reference category of firms providing a mixture of standardized and customized services) to report changes to their means of producing or delivering services, their technologies or (to a lesser extent) their customer relations. All of this makes a great deal of sense, and shows that the nature of the services provided (in terms of customization or standardization) is likely to impact on the extent of innovation (or change) reported by the firms (Tether *et al.*, 2001).

Lastly, we discuss the three control variables of size, age and sector. Larger firms are found to be more likely to have changed their services, technologies and organizational structure, and there is also a weak positive relationship with changes to production processes. Larger firms are not more or less likely than smaller firms to have changed their delivery processes, skills or customer and other business relationships. New firms were found to be less likely to have changed their delivery processes, technologies or skills than were longer-established businesses, with no other significant differences. With regard to sector, information processing and design firms were both more likely than road transport firms (the reference sector) to have changed their technologies and production processes, as well as the structure of their organizations. They were less likely, however, to have changed their customer relations. Meanwhile, design firms were also more likely to have changed their delivery processes and (to a lesser extent) the services they provide. This pattern of results probably reflects the faster pace of technological and other change in information processing and design activities than in road transportation.

8.5 Conclusions

This chapter began by highlighting the partial view that most innovation studies have adopted in relation to understanding the innovation process, particularly with reference to services. Moreover, and particularly in quantitative empirical work, innovation studies have tended to overlook the fact that most firms are generating, adopting and implementing multiple forms of innovation at any one time. Our analysis suggests that innovation in services is often more complex, interactive and interdependent, involving complementary changes across a number of dimensions. In particular, we have highlighted the existence of (at very least) coincidences between technological and soft/organizational forms of change. The existence of these coincidences should not be surprising given one would expect that changes to services (or service products) and means of production and delivery are often accompanied by complementary changes in organizational and work practice design, even in manufacturing industries (Kraft 1990: 1030), but arguably, most studies[5] have tended to focus on very specific types and attributes of the innovation process, and have not explored the interaction and interdependence between different types of innovation and change processes (Meyer and Goes 1988). Consequently, the interactions and complementarities in innovation processes (including here related investments, adjustments and displacement of activities required with the innovation process) have been neglected.[6]

In the wider organizational literature, the issue of complementarities has been raised in the context of organizational[7] and strategic 'fit' (see Lawrence and Lorsch 1967; Itami and Roehl 1987; Milgrom and Roberts, 1990; Porter 1996; Rivkin 2000; Siggelkow 2002). These studies highlight the importance of mutual reinforcement, interaction and optimization of effort both amongst and across activities (as well as the maintenance of consistency between each activity and overall strategy). In short, the value of one element is enhanced by the presence of other elements. Complementarity, in turn, involves the issue of additionality and effects on performance. Thus, for example, Carmeli and Tishler (2004: 1267) found that intangible organizational elements (managerial capabilities, human capital competences, internal auditing systems, labour relations, organizational culture and perceived organizational reputation) and their interaction had a positive effect on organizational performance.

Overall, it is clear from the evidence presented in this chapter that innovation in services is far from the simple (and passive) adoption of technologies that the nomenclature 'supplier dominated' would imply. Instead, our analysis points to innovation in services tending to involve complex, interdependent and complementary dimensions of change, in which changes to skills and organizational structure are as significant as changes to technologies, and in which changes to the relational aspects of services are significant alongside the more traditional technological (product/process) dimensions. Beyond this, such innovative change is also linked to the growth possibilities, strategy, and other behavioural dimensions (fox example, the extent to which firms provided customized or standardized outputs) of the firms themselves, as we have shown in this chapter.

Notes

1. The original survey also included a fourth sector of activity – elderly care services. We have omitted this sector from the analysis in this chapter because elderly care services are not business services, which is the focus of this book. The original survey also included responses from the United States for firms in the three sectors of road transport, information processing and design and related activities. To simplify matters we have confined our analysis in this chapter to European firms. The surveying of European firms was undertaken by ourselves and our partners in the project. The project partners included: Faiz Gallouj, Faridah Djellal and Camal Gallouj from IFRESI, University of Lille, France; Knut Blind and Jacob Edler from the Fraunhofer Institute for Systems and Innovation Research (ISI), Karlsruhe and Christiane Hipp from the University of Hamburg-Harburg, Germany; Fabio Montobbio and Nicoletta Corrocher from CESPRI, Bocconi University, Milan, Italy.
2. A 'strictly scientific' approach might seek to focus on a 'representative sample' of businesses in each sector, but in sectors like road transport we considered that this would probably give rise to uninteresting samples, as small independent trucking firms are arguably the representative firms in that sector. In any case, it is very difficult to achieve a 'representative sample' with a voluntary survey. Businesses have to be persuaded to participate, and participation is very likely to be biased towards more innovative businesses, as these are more likely to want to discuss their innovation efforts.
3. This proportion is certainly high, and is unlikely to be representative of all businesses in these sectors. As mentioned earlier, we expect there is a bias in our results towards more dynamic or innovative firms.
4. After rotation, PC1 explained 14.0 per cent, PC2 12.4 per cent, PC3 11.5 per cent, PC 4 10.0 per cent and PC5 7.4 per cent of the variance in the data.
5. There has, however, been much discussion about the co-relationship between product and process innovations within services. Some see that product innovations can be introduced without accompanying process innovations, although others view this is as unlikely (Tether and Hipp 2002).
6. Exceptions to this can be found in the diffusion literature (Rogers 1983; Alange *et al.* 1998) and works covering process innovations (Kraft 1990), as well as studies of complex innovation processes and systems integration (Prencipe *et al.* 2003).
7. This in turn includes the ongoing 'organization–environment' fit debate, in otherwords, that for effective firm performance the organizational structure should fit its overall environmental contingencies. Most 'fit' debates are, however, very static in nature.

9

The Impact of Contractual Arrangements on Innovation in Knowledge-Intensive Business Services

Aija Leiponen

Introduction

Knowledge-intensive business services (KIBS) have become a very important source of new knowledge in the economy. For example, according to recent British estimates, 25 per cent of intermediate inputs in the UK economy derive from knowledge services (Tomlinson 2000a). However, we know relatively little about how knowledge is actually transferred through service processes. In particular, in many KIBS industries, the knowledge to be transferred is partly tacit and collective, which makes it especially difficult to share. On the other hand, knowledge being an immaterial asset, it can also be difficult to control and prevent from being circulated. This chapter explores the role of contractual arrangements in structuring knowledge creation and transfer activities. Understanding the incentives and processes of knowledge creation and transfer is critical in the assessment of knowledge-intensive services in economic growth.

Services have recently been recognized as important sources of knowledge for the economy (for example, Miles *et al.* 1995), and, subsequently, there has emerged a literature examining whether innovation in service industries differs from that in manufacturing industries. Earlier research (Sundbo 1997; F. Gallouj 1997) emphasized the ad hoc nature of service innovation projects, while statistical analyses of survey datasets suggest that there may be more variation within the manufacturing and service sectors than across the sectors (see Evangelista 2000; Hollenstein 2002; Leiponen and Drejer forthcoming). Most recent research has looked into the nature of business-service innovation processes in more detail (Leiponen 2005, 2006). These studies suggest that innovation in KIBS firms depends upon skills obtained in higher education, ability to learn on the job, and investments in service development activities. On the other hand, over-reliance on tacit knowledge based on individual experts may be detrimental to innovation activities; organizational procedures that render knowledge collective or explicit (see Leiponen 2006; also Nonaka 1994) may facilitate business service innovation.

Organization of innovation has become a substantial field within the economics of innovation (see, for example, Teece 1986, 1992; Kamien, Muller, and Zang 1992; Veugelers 1997; and Veugelers and Cassiman 1999). In particular, this literature has focused on the question of whether and when firms should cooperate in their innovation activities. This focus follows directly from the Williamsonian transaction cost economics where the main question is whether to produce an input internally or outsource it – make or buy (Oxley 1997; Pisano 1991). However, there are many other interesting questions related to how innovation activities should be organized. A few recent studies have examined the role of decentralization of R&D activities (see, for example, Argyres and Silverman 2004; Siggelkow and Levinthal 2003) and control right allocation in strategic alliances (Elfenbein and Lerner 2003; Lerner and Merges 1998).

The focus of the current chapter is on contractual arrangements between business-service firms and their clients and employees. Within a cross-sectional dataset of 167 business-service firms, we examine the relationships between firms' client and employee contracts and their innovation activities. The data were collected through a mail survey over the autumn of 2000 by the Research Institute of the Finnish Economy. These cross-sectional data enable exploratory research concerning the relationships between contractual specifications and innovation activity outcomes. However, causality is impossible to establish as the results may be affected by simultaneity and endogeneity. The results reported here should thus be interpreted with caution. Nevertheless, the focus of the study is not on the institutional specificities of the Finnish economy, but on more fundamental aspects of economic behaviour. Hence, it is argued that the results are very likely to be generalizable to other European business environments.

Bearing in mind the aforementioned limitations of the study, the statistical results obtained here suggest that internal incentive schemes for employees and external control right and pricing arrangements with clients are significantly associated with business service innovation. More specifically, non-financial incentives for KIBS employees are better aligned with innovation than are financial incentives; control rights to intellectual assets are positively associated with innovation activity; and performance pricing that emphasizes speed may be negatively related to innovation.

These results generate management implications for both suppliers and buyers of business services. Where innovation is an important strategic goal, firms might benefit from setting up qualitative non-financial incentives for key employees, from retaining control rights to intellectual output, and from rejecting performance incentives based on time to project completion. For policy makers, the results relay that in a knowledge-based economy, contractual and ownership arrangements have implications for the incentives to learn and create new knowledge. This aspect has largely been ignored in the economics of innovation literature. While policy makers are likely to have limited influence on contracts between private parties, they can perhaps have an impact on the terms used in public procurement contracts and in publicly supported R&D projects and alliances. More generally, actors in the innovation system should be aware that the characteristics of contractual arrangements they enter may generate important incentives – or disincentives – for innovation.

9.1 Theoretical framework and hypotheses

The empirical study to be reported in the following sections builds on extant frameworks in the theory of the firm. However, instead of profits, the main dependent variable here is whether firms introduced new or significantly improved services in the preceding three years. It can be argued that firms are profit-maximizing, rather than innovation-maximizing organizations. Therefore, the results here should not be interpreted to mean that firms are organized suboptimally if they employ arrangements that are in a negative relationship with innovation – their strategy simply might not be focused on innovation activities. Depending on the competitive environment, thus, firms might be high-performing without introducing service innovations. However, from the point of view of the knowledge economy, the role of business services in generating and circulating new knowledge has been heavily emphasized (e.g., Miles *et al.* 1995; Miles and Boden 2000). As a result, the focus of this study was placed on the effects of contractual arrangements on service innovation activities.

We begin by examining the innovation effects of internal incentive schemes within business-service firms. There are many ways in which firms can establish incentive systems for their employees. Employees might be rewarded for the qualitative success or financial performance of their unit. These rewards might be targeted at individuals, teams, or the whole organization. Employees might also be rewarded either financially or in other ways, such as recognition ('employee of the month' or other types of public praise), promotion, or more desirable work tasks. These various incentive instruments are likely to have different effects on employees' motivation to innovate.

First, qualitative measures of performance tend to be subjective and depend on the manager's assessment of the situation (see Baker, Gibbons, and Murphy 1994). Nevertheless, in order to bring rewards and performance measures to lower levels of activity than the whole company or business units, subjective performance measures are often necessary in rewarding individuals and project teams. Financial measures of performance, on the other hand, may sometimes be available at the project level, but more often these are used in the year end to reward all or most upper-echelon employees for financial success. The problem with this kind of a reward is that it is rather removed from the actual efforts of individuals and teams. The incentive effect is thus likely to be less significant than direct rewards for a project well completed. Hence, incentives based on qualitative (subjective) performance measures are expected to be more closely associated with innovativeness than incentives based on financial performance. This result would also be aligned with descriptive evidence of high-performance innovators by Griffin (1996).

Secondly, incentives may be targeted at individuals, teams or work groups, or all the employees in the organization. While rewarding all employees of the company may create positive feedback in terms of organization culture and cohesiveness, it is not likely to influence efforts or activities on the part of specific employees. The choice between rewarding individuals or teams depends on which unit is more important in completing service projects. It can be argued, however, that in most knowledge-intensive business services teams consisting of employees with complementary skills are the main unit of competence. Individual star designers or consultants may occasionally be significant sources of innovation and profitability, but it is more common that teams of experts are the key source of competitiveness.[1] In particular, achieving service innovation is likely to depend on team effort, simply because of the nature of innovation (Kline and Rosenberg 1986). Therefore, team incentives are hypothesized to be more closely aligned with innovation outcomes than individual-based incentives.

Thirdly, economic theories tend to emphasize profit and monetary compensation as the sources of motivation for the *homo economicus*, but in practice it is not well understood how non-economic incentives affect economic behaviour. In the empirical section to follow I can assess the difference between monetary and other types of rewards in influencing innovation with empirical data.

The empirical data here also enable us to make a comparison of the effects of fixed pricing, time-based (cost-plus) pricing, and performance (incentive) pricing on innovation. Fixed pricing makes the service provider operate efficiently because it is the residual claimant of any revenue over and above its cost of production. In contrast, cost-plus (or, in our case, time-based pricing) is often used because such contracts are less demanding to write. Therefore, it is likely to be used particularly in highly complex or innovative projects. The downside is that it generates relatively low-powered incentives for the service provider. In projects with asymmetric information, which is probably the case in almost all knowledge-intensive business services, pricing based on performance measurement would be ideal, but it is often difficult to set up. Many business service projects involve customization or even customized innovation, which is difficult to specify and quantify ahead of time (Bajari and Tadelis 2001). For instance, what would be appropriate performance measures for the design of an advertising campaign or a new product design? The success of these designs will probably be determined much later in time, and their impact is likely to be confounded by the client firm's own actions. It is thus often very difficult to identify the performance impact precisely. Nevertheless, business services occasionally use these kinds of performance bonuses in their contracts. For example, if the sales of the product increase by 10 per cent or more during the three months following the launch of the advertising campaign, the advertising agency might be rewarded with a bonus. When the relationship between a business service firm and its client is ongoing, these kinds of retrospective rewards may prove valuable (Baker, Gibbons, and Murphy 2002).

While most firms do not regularly use performance elements in their pricing, those that do may tie performance bonuses to different aspects of performance, such as productivity (impact per cost of the project), speed (for example, completion ahead of schedule), quality (low occurrence of mistakes, bugs, or errors), or customer satisfaction (usually measured with satisfaction surveys collected after the project completion). One can argue that these dimensions of performance have different effects on the likelihood of innovation. For example, when speed is emphasized, there is probably little time for 'doodling' and developing uncertain or unfamiliar ideas. Innovation, however, often depends upon these kinds of seemingly unproductive activities. Therefore, speed-based performance bonuses are expected to be negatively associated with service innovation. Customer satisfaction, on the other hand, is expected to be more positively associated with innovation. Business-service providers who will be rewarded based on customer satisfaction are likely to think of new ways to respond to clients' needs and demands. Finally, quality and productivity-based measures of performance might be conducive to improvements in service processes, but do not appear to be related to ideas for new service products. The types of performance measures considered here could thus be ranked with respect to their expected effects on innovation in the following way: speed will have the least positive (or even negative) effect on innovation, quality and productivity measures may have some positive effect on innovation, while customer satisfaction measures are expected to have the strongest positive relationship with service innovation outcomes.

The last contractual elements considered here have to do with intellectual property rights and exclusivity clauses in client contracts. In many areas of business services, firms agree with their clients that as long as they cooperate, and usually for some time thereafter, the business-service firm will not provide services to a certain set of the client's competitors. This reduces potential knowledge spillovers from the current project and client to future projects and clients. Furthermore, the service firm and its client often specify who owns or controls the use of the designs or other outcomes of the service project. In some industries, such as industrial design, the norm is to hand all control rights to the designs to the client, but in many other industries, this aspect is up for negotiation.

Exclusivity of service provision and yielding to clients the control rights to intellectual assets created in joint projects are expected to reduce the incentives to innovate. When service firms cannot control or fully use the intellectual property and competencies created in the current project, they are less driven to generate innovations that could be used in future projects with other clients.

Namely, exclusivity and transfers of control right to clients reduce the returns to developing such innovative new services.

9.2 The survey data on Finnish business-service firms

The empirical analyses to follow are based on a survey dataset of 167 Finnish business-service firms from six knowledge-intensive industries. The industries included here are industrial design, advertising, machine and process engineering, electrical engineering, management consulting, and R&D services.[2] The choice of industries studied is based on their importance in the knowledge economy (for example, see Miles *et al.* 1995) and relative scarcity of existing research into their innovation activities. As a result, the software industry is not included, for example, because many studies have already focused on this industry.

The survey respondents were identified from lists of the 100 largest firms in each industry, with respect to numbers of employees, obtained from the Statistics Finland (the national statistical agency of Finland). The bias towards large firms was intentional because of the focus on organizational features behind business-service innovation. In many business-service industries, the average firm size is very small, and organizational arrangements are not well defined in these kinds of micro-enterprises. The overall survey response rate was 42 per cent, varying between 35 and 50 per cent across the six industries. The survey respondents represented firms that were 20 per cent larger than the mean in the target group. However, in terms of profitability (sales per employee), firms in the sample performed somewhat worse than the targeted group. The sample thus does not seem to be biased towards more successful firms. Moreover, comparison with the CIS 1994–96 sample of technical services suggests that the sample of engineering firms here is not biased (see Leiponen 2007 for more details). Assuming that the other industry samples included here are aligned with the two engineering industries, the total sample is reasonably representative of the Finnish knowledge-intensive business service sector.

To examine the relationships between contractual features and innovation, a host of variables must be held constant in order to identify any relevant co-variation. The control variables used here include a set of fairly standard firm characteristics: firm size (number of employees), structure (whether the firm is subsidiary in a business group), age, export intensity (exports per sales revenue), employee skills (share of employees with higher education degrees), and R&D activities (R&D investments per sales revenue and whether the firm has a permanent R&D team or department). Extant research has found these factors to influence firms' likelihood to engage and succeed in innovation.

The main variables of interest include the dependent variable, whether the firm introduced new or significantly improved services, and explanatory variables that describe relevant features from employee and client contracts deployed by the respondent firms. The dependent variable is formed by combining the data from two survey questions. The first question asked whether the firm introduced any new services (new to the firm, not necessarily to the market) in the preceding three years. A new service is described in the questionnaire as having substantially different features or uses than those previously offered by the firm. The second question asked whether the firm introduced any significantly improved services. These questions align with the Community Innovation Survey questionnaire implemented in several European countries and developed in cooperation with the Eurostat. The dependent variable here, INNOVATIVE, is a binary indicator that obtains the value of 1 if the firm answered 'yes' to either or both of the above questions and 0 if the firm answered 'no' to both questions. 63 per cent of the sampled firms are innovative according to this measure.

The main explanatory variables describe the firms' contractual practices regarding employees and clients. First, we will compare the effects of monetary incentives for individuals against those for teams; monetary incentives based on qualitative performance against those based on financial performance; and monetary rewards against other types of rewards (typically, recognition and praise). Secondly, we will examine the effects of fixed project pricing, time-based cost-plus pricing, and performance-based pricing. If firms indicate that they often use performance bonuses, they were also asked to report whether these are based on productivity, speed, quality or lack of errors, or customer satisfaction. These were hypothesized to have different effects on the willingness to develop new services or improvements to existing ones. Finally, firms were asked whether control rights to designs and other intellectual output tend to be transferred to clients and whether the service firm agrees to some type of exclusivity arrangement whereby it will not provide services to the named competitors of the client for a specified time period. These two aspects are highly correlated and therefore combined to a new variable that is called control rights to client. This binary indicator takes on the value of one if the firm reports that it *always* agrees to either transfer intellectual output to clients or sign an exclusivity clause (or both). If the firm uses these clauses only occasionally or never, then the control rights to client dummy variable is zero.

The descriptive statistics of the main variables of interest and control variables are displayed in Table 9.1. On average, firms in the sample are fairly small (41 employees), highly R&D intensive (R&D investments 5.8 per cent of sales), and employ highly educated people (33 per cent have degrees from tertiary education – they are college or university graduates). These firms are thus indeed highly knowledge intensive. 38 per cent of firms also belong to (or are subsidiaries in) a domestic or multinational business group. In other words, they are partially or wholly owned by a larger entity. However, service units of manufacturing firms are excluded from the sample.

The main explanatory variables are also included in Table 9.1. The survey questions on incentives are binary (yes/no). Thus, 53 per cent of firms offer

Table 9.1 Descriptive statistics

	Variable	*Mean*	*Std. Dev.*	*Minimum*	*Maximum*	*Cases*
Dependent variable	INNOVATIVE (0/1)	0.63	0.48	0	1	167
Control variables	EMPLOYEES	40.53	81.79	1	590	164
	AGE	17.31	13.72	1	90	166
	GROUP (0/1)	0.38	0.49	0	1	166
	EXPORT INTENSITY	0.12	0.26	0	1	167
	HIGHER EDUCATION	32.81	31.06	0	100	163
	R&D DEPARTMENT (0/1)	0.20	0.40	0	1	163
	R&D INTENSITY	0.058	0.33	0	4	162
Incentives for employees	ANY MONETARY INCENTIVES (0/1)	0.74	0.44	0	1	166
	INDIVIDUAL INCENTIVES (0/1)	0.53	0.50	0	1	167
	TEAM INCENTIVES (0/1)	0.19	0.39	0	1	167
	QUALITATIVE INCENTIVES (0/1)	0.42	0.50	0	1	167
	PROFIT INCENTIVES (0/1)	0.71	0.46	0	1	167
	NON-MONETARY INCENTIVES (0/1)	0.34	0.48	0	1	161
Features in client contracts	INTELLECTUAL ASSETS TO CLIENT (0–3)	2.19	0.81	0	3	164
	EXCLUSIVITY (0–3)	1.85	1.16	0	3	162
	CONTROL RIGHTS TO 67 CLIENT (0/1)	0.60	0.49	0	1	167
	TIME PRICING (0–3)	1.78	0.75	0	3	162
	FIXED PRICING (0–3)	1.74	0.73	0	3	163
	PERFORMANCE PRICING (0–3)	0.99	0.89	0	3	155
	PRODUCTIVITY PERFORMANCE (0–3)	1.04	1.05	0	3	165
	QUALITY PERFORMANCE (0–3)	1.17	1.23	0	3	165
	SPEED PERFORMANCE (0–3)	0.81	0.94	0	3	164
	CUSTOMER SATISFACTION PERFORMANCE (0–3)	1.25	1.23	0	3	165

Note: Variables marked (0/1) are binary, those marked (0–3) have a Likert scale ranging from 0 (never) to 3 (always). Other variables are continuous.

their employees monetary rewards based on individual performance, while 19 per cent offer such rewards for teams. Performance is measured in qualitative terms in 42 per cent of firms and the majority, 71 per cent, base their incentives on financial measures of performance. The sum of these numbers exceeds 100 per cent – firms may have both types of incentives in place. In addition 34 per cent of firms use non-monetary incentives to motivate employees.

The survey questions concerning pricing and control rights were on a scale of 0 (never used)–3 (always used). As Table 9.1 attests, it is very common to transfer the rights to the intellectual output to clients – most firms do this often or always. Exclusivity clauses are fairly common too. When these two survey questions are combined to the binary indicator 'control rights to client', 60 per cent of firms always use one or both of these contractual clauses that transfer control rights to their clients.

Business-service firms surveyed here tend most often to use time-based cost-plus pricing (billing by hours or days spent on the project), although fixed pricing (fixed price for completing a pre-specified outcome) is almost equally common. Performance bonuses, on the other hand, are much less common. This probably reflects the difficulty of defining objective performance outcomes in many innovative and highly customized development projects that these types of service firms are hired to provide. If pricing is based on some element of performance, then customer satisfaction and quality measures are slightly more common than productivity and speed.

9.3 Results of empirical analyses

In this section, the survey data introduced in the previous section are used in regression analyses to examine the relationship between business firms' contractual arrangements with employees and clients and their innovation activities. In particular, the contractual variables are used to explain the INNOVATIVE variable that indicates whether firms introduced new or significantly improved services in the previous three years. These statistical relationships are assessed in a multiple regression framework (probit maximum likelihood because the dependent variable is binary)[3] controlling for firm size, age, group membership, export intensity, R&D activities (intensity and permanent team), and skills.

In Table 9.2, the sets of variables relating to each of the contractual dimensions are added one at a time. The final model (5) includes the statistically significant variables from the various regressions to check that the results hold when different aspects of contracting are included. In all models, firm size is measured with the logarithm of the number of employees to allow for a non-linear effect.

Most of the control variables are only marginally significant. As a result, their significance level may change depending upon the specification. Overall, even though few variables are individually significant, the models are able to correctly predict 73–5 per cent of the cases. More specifically, firm size, age, group structure, higher education level, and R&D activities are positively associated with innovativeness, and in some specifications significant at the 90 per cent level. The result regarding R&D activities suggests, in line with Sundbo's (1997) assertion, that formal R&D can be helpful, but is not necessary for service innovations to emerge. In contrast, export intensity is

Table 9.2 The effects of contractual arrangements on business service innovation

	(1)		(2)		(3)		(4)		(5)	
Variable	*Coeff*	*Std. Err.*	*Coeff.*	*Std. Err.*	*Coeff.*	*Std. Err.*	*Coeff.*	*Std. Err.*	*Coeff.*	*Std. Err.*
Constant	−0.921*	0.497	−1.21**	0.529	−0.689	0.852	−0.535	0.537	−0.506	0.578
Log(EMPLOYEES)	0.062	0.138	0.071	0.141	0.175	0.142	0.159	0.130	0.087	0.137
AGE	0.020	0.013	0.023*	0.013	0.016	0.014	0.017	0.013	0.022*	0.013
GROUP	0.510*	0.276	0.482*	0.284	0.428	0.287	0.59**	0.276	0.496*	0.292
EXPORT INTENSITY	−0.648	0.508	−0.508	0.491	−0.779	0.529	−0.809	0.503	−0.662	0.512
HIGHER EDUCATION	0.007*	0.004	0.007	0.005	0.005	0.005	0.007	0.005	0.005	0.005
R&D DEPARTMENT	0.571*	0.333	0.582*	0.346	0.506	0.348	0.573*	0.339	0.595*	0.359
R&D INTENSITY	5.212	3.546	5.397	3.622	4.373	3.612	5.502	3.685	6.782*	3.935
INDIVIDUAL INCENTIVES	−0.136	0.269								
TEAM INCENTIVES	0.515	0.356								
ANY FIN. INCENTIVES			−0.137	0.305						
NON-MONETARY INCENTIVES			0.71**	0.277					0.84**	0.288

(Continued)

Table 9.2 Continued

Variable	*(1) Coeff*	*Std. Err.*	*(2) Coeff.*	*Std. Err.*	*(3) Coeff.*	*Std. Err.*	*(4) Coeff.*	*Std. Err.*	*(5) Coeff.*	*Std. Err.*
PRODUCTIVITY PRICING					0.163	0.179				
SPEED PRICING					−0.44**	0.210			−0.184	0.136
QUALITY PRICING					0.030	0.200				
SATISFACTION PRICING					0.122	0.192				
TIME-BASED PRICING					−0.212	0.191				
FIXED PRICE					0.120	0.209				
CONTROL RIGHTS TO CLIENT							−0.58**	0.261	−0.80**	0.282
Log likelihood	−79.18		−74.08		−73.17		−77.64		−68.05	
% correctly predicted	72.7		77.2		78.0		69.3		77.5	
Observations	150		145		141		150		142	

Notes: Probit ML estimation. Dependent variable: INNOVATIVE. Numbers of observations vary because of item non-response. ** denotes statistical significance at 95% level, * denotes 90% level. Industry dummies are included but not reported.

negatively correlated with service innovation. This result suggests that export orientation is not necessarily a strategy pursued by innovative service firms, in contrast to manufacturing firms (for example, Salomon and Shaver 2005).

Regarding the various financial and non-monetary incentive measures used, only the non-monetary incentives are significantly associated with innovative output (specification 2). Team incentives are also positively associated with innovation output, but only at the 83 per cent level of significance. Interestingly, incentives for individuals are negatively related to innovation, and the same is true for financial incentives in general. Thus, the results here suggest that non-monetary ways to motivate employees work best if the goal is to promote innovation in the firm.

Specifications (3) and (4) include the pricing and control right variables. The coefficients indicate that while performance pricing is positively associated with service innovation, it is not statistically significant. Time-based (cost-plus) and fixed pricing are in negative relationship with innovation but they are also not significant. In contrast, when the different types of performance bonuses are included, performance measured as speed – often a bonus for completing within or ahead of the timetable – is significantly negatively associated with innovation. This is quite intuitive, since being in a hurry is not conducive to the kinds of uncertain explorations often associated with successful innovation. Alternatively, a selection effect may be at play here: firms that offer service projects that can be completed in a pre-specified timetable are not innovation-oriented firms.

The 'control rights to client' variable demonstrates a strong negative relationship with innovation outcomes. This result is in line with the property rights model in the theory of the firm in that giving away ownership or the ability to control the knowledge produced in a service project reduces the incentives to come up with innovative ideas that can be built on in future projects. This aspect is further examined using slightly more sophisticated estimation techniques in a separate paper (Leiponen 2007).

The preferred model (5) summarizes the significant estimation results. As far as contractual arrangements with service employees and clients are concerned, non-monetary incentives appear to be most motivating with respect to innovation, and transferring control rights to intellectual assets to clients reduces the incentives to innovate. In contrast, performance pricing based on the speed of completing the project is now significant only at the 82 per cent level. The result obtained earlier may be affected by endogeneities or multicollinearity in the dataset.

9.4 Conclusions

This chapter has examined the determinants of innovation in knowledge-intensive business services, particularly from the point of view of incentives to innovate generated by contractual arrangements. First of all, it was argued that team incentives and qualitative incentives might work better than incentives based on overall financial performance, given that there is a lot of measurement error in the latter regarding performance of individuals or workgroups. The estimation results are aligned with the hypotheses, but they are statistically not very significant. In contrast, a significant relationship is found between non-monetary incentives, typically public praise and recognition, and innovation outcomes. This result would merit further exploration, especially in respect of organization psychological studies of human motivation in work environments, and how individuals respond to monetary vs. non-monetary incentives.

Secondly, we explored the relationships between innovation and firms' pricing arrangements with clients. According to the only statistically significant result, pricing based on performance, when the performance measure is related to speed of completion of the project, is detrimental to innovation. The result is intuitive in that projects that need to be finished to very tight schedules are not likely to be conducive to innovative ideas. Innovation tends to involve uncertain activities, and projects and ideas can often take time to mature. The speed requirement is probably often orthogonal to this. However, this result is not very robust – it becomes statistically insignificant when other contractual elements are included in the model. Multicollinearity and endogeneity structures in the dataset are the probable reasons behind this.

The third empirical result suggests that contractual specifications which transfer control rights to intellectual assets of output to clients reduce business-service firms' innovativeness. This result is in line with the property rights theory of the firm which argues that property – or control – rights are associated with incentives to invest in un-measurable activities such as learning or innovation. Indeed, business-service firms that regularly transfer rights to the designs to their clients or sign exclusivity arrangements with clients tend to be significantly less innovative.

In future research, the relationships between non-monetary incentives for employees and performance-based pricing, on the one hand, and innovation outcomes, on the other hand, would be particularly interesting to investigate in more detail. Furthermore, the theoretical foundations for the effects of contractual strategies on innovation activities are relatively weak, and would benefit from further work. Hence, there is ample room for both theoretical and empirical contributions in the area of applying the economic theories of the firm in the context of innovation, particularly service innovation.

For management practitioners, the implications of the results are fairly straightforward. First, managers need to balance monetary and non-monetary incentives for employees. The emphasis in economics on profits and monetary compensation may not after all be aligned with human behaviour and motivation. Secondly, if performance pricing is used, managers need to reconcile the firm's innovation strategy with the types of performance measures available. Aspiring to make substantial service innovations while attempting to complete projects with maximum speed may not both be attainable. Finally, service firms should be careful about matching their intellectual property and other control rights strategies to their innovation strategies. Yielding control rights to clients may hamper the attainment of the innovation goals of the organization. From service clients' perspective, this means that maximizing control of intellectual property may not maximize innovative output. If emphasis is on the latter, then clients would be better off pursuing repeated relationships with innovative suppliers rather than attempting to implement very restrictive control rights transfer clauses. Repeated interaction is more likely to both reduce the supplier's incentive to leak valuable intellectual assets to competitors and simultaneously provide incentives for service innovation.

Policy makers in the areas of industrial and technology policy might also want to pay attention to a few issues examined here. First, regarding public procurement programmes, this study argues that contractual forms do matter. In particular, pricing schemes and control right specifications may have significant effects on service firms' incentives to innovate. From a social welfare point of view, policy makers need to optimize both efficiency and innovation activities in the economy. Second, R&D policy makers might need to reconsider how control rights should be allocated in cooperative R&D programmes. Ideally, the most innovative partners should be able to retain the rights to their intellectual assets and their freedom to operate, while losing control rights has less of an effect on non-innovative firms. Finally, R&D policies are usually justified on the grounds that private innovation investments are suboptimal because of the positive externalities on the economy. On this basis, policy makers might want to consider including business services in publicly supported innovation programmes. While business service innovations are usually highly intangible, they nevertheless provide essential new knowledge and ideas for the rest of the economy, as argued by the growing literature on KIBS industries. This study, along with many earlier ones, has demonstrated that many knowledge-intensive business service firms indeed innovate and could therefore usefully be included in public innovation programmes.

Notes

1. For example, in the survey dataset used in the following section, for the question 'How would you rate the following elements as sources of your firm's competitiveness, on a scale of 0 (not relevant)–3 (very important)?' the average score regarding work teams was 2.2, on par with schooling (2.3), on-the-job training (2.4), and improvement of services (2.3). Learning on the job was the highest element (2.8).
2. These industries correspond to the European NACE industrial classification system industries NACE 74841 (graphic design; only industrial design firms were included), 74401 (advertising), 74206 (machine and process engineering and consultancy), 74208 (electrical engineering), 7414 (business and management consultancy), and 731 (research and experimental development on natural sciences and engineering).
3. Logit models tend to yield very similar results, and since probit models are based on the normal distribution rather than the logistic distribution, it is the estimation method of choice here

10

Organizational Innovation, Information Technology, and Outsourcing to Business Services

Werner Hölzl, Andreas Reinstaller and Paul Windrum[1]

Introduction

This chapter examines the relationship between organizational innovation, the introduction of new internet-based ICTs, de-verticalization, and the rapid growth in business-service outsourcing since the early 1990s. We present data on the range of activities that are being outsourced, and discuss a set of potential advantages associated with outsourcing activities to knowledge-intensive service providers (KIBS). We also examine the latest empirical studies which throw up a set of potential disadvantages associated with outsourcing. These suggest that outsourcing may have advantages in the short run, but may also have negative long-run implications for competitive performance.

In order to examine this issue, we develop a model of organizational innovation. In this model, the goal of managers is to identify an organizational design that more effectively integrates all of the administrative activities of the firm. As part of the process of innovation, the managers can choose either to carry out an administrative activity in-house, or alternatively to outsource that activity. A key factor influencing this decision is the relative information costs of organizing activities internally and the information costs associated with setting up and maintaining interfaces with external suppliers. Herein lies the importance of new ICT. The introduction of new ICTs can alter the relative costs of internal and external administration. This captures a key stylized fact about knowledge-intensive business services (KIBS), such as business consultants, financial services, and ICT services: the rapid expansion of KIBS over the last decade is strongly connected the introduction and diffusion of internet-based networking ICTs.

The chapter is organized as follows. Section 10.1 introduces the key concepts of organizational design and organizational innovation. It then outlines the core theoretical approach that is used to conceptualize organizational innovation. This is based on a modular theory of the firm, which is founded on the twin principles of increasing specialization and the modularization of complex organizational structures. Increasing the modularity of the organizational structure not only leads to improvements in efficiency through specialization, but also enables a firm to realize systems economies, thereby pushing ahead the productivity frontier. At the core of the theoretical framework is a transmission mechanism between ICT adoption, organizational innovation and outsourcing. Using this theoretical framework we are able to offer a critical discussion of the long-run implications of outsourcing on productivity. Section 10.2 reviews recent empirical studies in order to identify a set of potential benefits and potential disadvantages associated with the outsourcing of activities to business services. In particular, it addresses new empirical evidence suggesting that outsourcing can be detrimental to the innovative capacity of the firms and, hence, can have a negative impact on its long-run productivity growth. Section 10.3 describes the simulation model and the outputs it has generated. The model is used to investigate the manner in which the outsourcing of activities restricts the long-term opportunities for organizational innovation, leading to lower levels of productivity growth. Section 10.4 pulls together the overall findings of the chapter and highlights some interesting directions for further research.

10.1 Organizational innovation

The goal of organizational change is the identification of an organizational design that more effectively integrates all of the administrative activities of the firm. An organizational design is a hierarchical structure that solves two key problems faced by managers. The first is the 'fundamental coordination problem', namely, how to most effectively organize the value-adding activities and information flows of the firm in order to maximize profit. In addition, managers need to resolve the 'agency problem': to realize and enforce coordination and control in production, both internally and across the boundary of the firm.

Organizational innovation involves the search for new organizational designs that alter the internal organizational structure of the firm, and change the boundary between the firm and markets (verticalization/de-verticalization). As just described, it is a search process that is conducted within a complex search space containing many dimensions, and in which the dimensions are related to one another in highly non-linear ways. Dealing with this organizational complexity requires managers to engage in ongoing strategic experimentation and learning. It is this ongoing problem-solving activity that drives organizational change and innovation over time.

Our analysis is based on a modular theory of the firm, developed in recent work by Langlois and Robertson (1995), Baldwin and Clark (1997), Langlois (2002, 2003), and Marengo and Dosi (2005). The theory brings together Adam Smith's principles of specialization and the division of labour (Smith, 1776), and Herbert Simon's discussion of complexity and the near-decomposability of complex problems (Simon, 1996, 2002), and provides a useful means of discussing organizational change and innovation. We will use this theory to identify the set of conditions under which modularization is associated with outsourcing to specialist KIBS, and to consider the impact of new ICTs on the decision to outsource.

Simon (1996, 2002) provides an important insight into problem-solving activity in general. He provides us with an idea of how problem-solving activity occurs in complex systems. Simon suggested that complex problems can be made more manageable by breaking them down into a set of constituent parts, or 'modular components'. In this way, the number of distinct elements in a system is reduced by grouping them into a smaller number of subsystems. The great advantage of modularization is that improvements can be made to one subcomponent of the system without the need to change all other parts of the system (as would be the case if there were no modularization). There is a cost, however. These are associated with the establishment and maintenance of organizational interfaces between sub-components. These interfaces enable a subcomponent to function compatibly with all other subcomponents. This ensures the organizational structure as a whole functions in an integrated way, while maintaining a high degree of independence for each sub-component. Given these considerations, the task for management seeking a better division of labour becomes the identification of subsystems, establishing linkages between distinct subsystems, and understanding, managing and codifying their interactions. First, they have to find out how to decompose its value-adding activities and, second, how to coordinate the subsystems. Through successful modularization, a complex system is then transformed into a nearly decomposable one.

To this theory we add the concept of 'system economies' introduced by Nightingale *et al.* (2003). Our interpretation of system economies is that they are mostly due to improvements in the control of a given set of productive activities and, hence, operate at the meta level. Managers of the firm seek to improve productivity by reorganizing the way in which these value-adding activities interact. This productivity improvement is gained through the design of a more effective organizational design. Organizational innovation, the process through which new designs are arrived at, involves either splitting the administrative tasks into more organizational modules or, alternatively, the integrating of organizational modules to increase control of the modular elements and their interaction. A superior organizational design improves the coordination and control of goods, traffic, materials, funds, services, and information that flows through the complex supply, production and distribution activities of the firm. In this way, better organizational designs (that is, more effective modularization schemas) increase the productive utilization of the firm's installed productive capacity. Innovation begets further innovation over time. Through organizational innovation, managers gain a more specific view of the different activities of the firm, and see the potential creative opportunities that arise through breaking down 'departmental silos' and creating novel synergies activities (such as new organizational combinations). For example, creating stronger interactions between the sales and production departments can lead to new product opportunities being realized. These in turn may lead to economies of scope and, if able to develop new markets, economies of scale. This picks up on the point made by Baldwin and Clark (1997), that the more modular the organizational design, the greater the likelihood of stimulating new inventions, for example, innovation in products/services, distribution, and the other key value adding activities of the firm.

We suggest that the extent of organization specialization depends ultimately upon a number of demand- and supply-side factors. On the demand side, it will depend on the extent of the market (such as increases in population and income), and the degree of competition (the elasticity of demand) (Young, 1928). On the supply side, it is affected by the availability of ICTs that enable activities to be subdivided and coordinated, and which enable managers to deal with the agency problem. In order to do this, managers must be able to generate information on the parts of the organization for which they are directly responsible, and to exchange between them information about different parts of the organization. Together, the demand- and supply-side factors determine the extent to which activities can be effectively modularized and technical hierarchies established.

A number of issues can be discussed within this theoretical framework. To start with, the framework clarifies the relationship between new ICTs and more effective administrative control leading to system economies. The application of new, improved ICTs enable further modularization of the organization to occur by lowering the cost of managing and controlling information, leading to increased system economies.[2] It was Chandler (1962, 1977) who made the first claims that technology directly affects organizational structure. His observation goes to the heart of our discussion. New ICTs alter the set of feasible technological opportunities in production and the division of labour (the fundamental coordination problem), and the opportunities for effective coordination and control within and across the boundary of the firm (the agency problem). These alter the relative efficacy of holding activities in-house and outsourcing. Depending on the particular vintage of ICTs, technological opportunities and cost reductions may stimulate verticalization or de-verticalization.

Internet-based ICTs enable the external coordination costs of the firm to be reduced significantly. This opens up new opportunities outsourcing within new experimental organizational designs. Over the last decade, a new generation of 'networking' ICTs (built on open web and internet protocols) have provided the means by which firms can radically reorganize interactions with firms along the supply chain. It has opened up previously inconceivable levels of interaction between companies. This includes new opportunities for outsourcing to specialist KIBS providers. The networked corporation has emerged as a consequence of inter-firm networking activities along the supply chain. There is a flattening of the hierarchy of the firm, a tendency towards vertical disintegration, and for individual business units to become smaller in size.

It is important to note that the relationship between new ICTs and outsourcing is not a simple one. Certain types of new ICTs may decrease the costs of internal as well as external communication. Internet technologies, for example, lower the cost of internal administration (through applications such as intranets) as well as reducing the administration cost of external interaction. Others only reduce internal costs. As discussed by Reinstaller and Hölzl (2004), ICTs that were limited in their application to internal administrative activities (such as calculators, typewriters, Hollerith electric tabulating machines, and bookkeeping machines) played an important role in the development of u-form and m-form hierarchies. Chandler (1977) and Yates (2000) have discussed the way in which these technologies were essential for the emergence of the modern hierarchical organization in the period between the 1850s and the 1930s. Large corporations were the key purchasers of these new ICT1 technologies, and these technologies in turn further enhanced their ability to grow in size, with a tendency towards vertical integration and the greater centralization of activities by bringing activities in-house, increasing the hierarchy within the firm.

A second issue that is of central importance in this chapter is the long-run implications of outsourcing for firm performance. On the one hand, as discussed, internet-based technologies reduce the cost of setting up organizational and information interactions with KIBS. This makes it possible to outsource activities that can be delivered more cheaply by the external supplier. At the same time, outsourcing reduces the internal administration overheads of the firm. However, there are limits to the benefits of modularization. To start with, while internal administration overheads are reduced, external administration overheads rise because an effective interface with the external provider needs to be set up and maintained. In terms of administrative overheads, the net benefit depends on whether the cost of the external interface is greater or less than the cost of the internal interface. This is the non-separability effect discussed by Steinmueller (2003) and Miozzo and Grimshaw (2005). They suggest that the governance structures that oversee the interface interactions between client and supplier represent large, sunk investments. Consequently, suppliers are not easily substituted.

A more important potential downside is the impact of outsourcing on the client's long-run potential for organization innovation and, hence, on its long-run productivity growth. To understand this, let us apply the transmission mechanism just discussed. If new, internet-based ICTs significantly reduce external administration costs compared to internal administration costs, there is a stimulus for outsourcing. However, by outsourcing, the set of internal activities under the direct management of the firm is reduced. This reduces the set of modular elements with which managers can experiment and innovate to create new, more efficient organizational designs. In the long run this can lead to a lower productivity growth of the client firm. Prencipe (1997) and Brusoni *et al.* (2001) stress the need to retain control over R&D, not just for the activity itself, but because it is important to maintain control of the coordination of R&D, design and manufacturing activities.

10.2 Potential advantages and potential costs of outsourcing

The 1990s saw a dramatic rise in the number of specialized business-service firms. The sheer variety of activities that are being outsourced is highlighted by McCarthy's 2002 study of outsourcing by US firms. These activities include not only basic back-office activities such as payrolls, but also advanced, back-office activities such as legal services, and client-facing front-office activities in sales and marketing. The purchase of business services from external providers raised the performance of client firms in both services and manufacturing. While acknowledgement of the role played by business services in economic development is not recent (see, for example, Greenfield, 1966), empirical studies of their impact are new. For example, Windrum and Tomlinson (1999) tested the contribution to services and manufacturing sectors of knowledge-intensive business services (KIBS) such as business consultants, financial services, and ICT services. Using input–output data from 1970 to 1990, they examined Germany, Japan, the Netherlands, and the UK. KIBS were found to have a positive impact on both service and manufacturing sectors in all four countries over the twenty-year period. Similar findings have been identified in studies by Drejer (2001), Peneder *et al.* (2003) and Tomlinson (2003). So, while the use of business services has grown rapidly, their use is not new.

A number of studies have sought to identify the key drivers for outsourcing. One of the best known is in the Morgan Chambers study of FTSE 100 firms (Morgan Chambers, 2001). In addition, there is the Outsourcing Institute's study of outsourcing in Japan (Outsourcing Institute, 2005). Taken together, these studies present a remarkably consistent picture, the findings of which are presented in Table 10.1. We see that the top three-ranked drivers are the same in each study. These are, in order, the reduction of operating costs, improving the focus of the business through a reorganization of the activities that are conducted in-house and those that are externally sourced, and access to skills and technologies that are not held in-house. In both surveys, these three drivers together accounted for more than 60 per cent of all responses.

These three key drivers have also been highlighted in the literature on knowledge-intensive business services (KIBS). KIBS provide their clients with high-quality information on new business opportunities, new trends in the marketplace, and the business potential of new technologies, such as new ICTs. Through the outsourcing of specific inputs to KIBS, clients can improve productivity and competitive performance as existing in-house inputs are substituted for higher-quality, externally sourced inputs. Third, KIBS are

Table 10.1 Drivers of outsourcing, by rank

Morgan Chambers study	*Outsourcing Institute study*
Cost saving	Reduce and control operating costs
Focus on core business	Improve company focus
Access to skills and technology	Gain access to world-class capabilities
Risk management	Free internal resources for other purposes
Quality service improvement	Resources are not available internally
Change enabler	Accelerate re-engineering benefits
Business development	Function is difficult to manage/out of control
Other	Make capital funds available
	Share risks
	Cash infusion

exemplars of novel business models. They provide a concrete illustration of new business models and, through their ongoing relationship, introduce clients to these new ways of working and new technologies. Antonelli (1998), for example, has highlighted the role of KIBS on the diffusion of new ICTs. KIBS are leading advocates of new, internet-based technologies because these technologies enable them to interface more effectively with clients and, as a consequence, to more effectively intermediate experience, information and knowledge between clients. In this way, KIBS have become key intermediaries, improving the efficiency and speed of learning within innovation networks.

As noted in section 10.1, there exist a set of potential disadvantages associated with outsourcing. These can have negative long-run implications for organization innovation and, hence, long-run productivity growth. Let us discuss these in detail. An empirical study based on a large-scale survey of large and medium-sized Swedish manufacturing and service firms[3] has been conducted by Bengtsson and von Hartman (2005). They found that companies' evaluations of the direct effects of outsourcing – for example, cost reduction through the reduction of direct personnel – were fulfilled. However, management and administrative functions were not reduced. Indeed the firms report a strongly negative impact of outsourcing on logistics – such as manufacturing lead times, delivery times and accuracy. They also report negative impacts on quality and adaptation to customer demands. These key findings indicate that outsourcing is accompanied by more complex logistics, increasing the internal administrative overhead. Bengtsson and von Hartman report that these logistics problems were more common among amongst companies that outsource to low-cost countries.

These findings are supported by research conducted by other authors. First, it is observed that the contract needs to be monitored and measured carefully. This can prove expensive, and increasingly expensive if skills in the client firm are lost over time (Domberger, 1998). Secondly, governance inseparability between client and supplier means considerable investment in interpersonal and administrative relations between the firms is necessary in order to support the new division of labour (Steinmueller, 2003; Miozzo and Grimshaw, 2005). Thirdly, poorly delivered services will negatively affect the client's production or, where end-user services are delivered, the client's brand and reputation (Hinks and Hanson, 2001). Fourthly, the security of sensitive information needs to be considered, with an increased risk of exposure of the clients' sensitive internal information (Mylott III, 1995). Fifthly, there are well-documented cases of knowledge and information, acquired by the service provider, being shared with the clients' competitor firms. Clients believed that services and information would be proprietary, while the service providers saw the transactions as the basis for further business within the client's industry.

Of course, it is not only low-skilled activities that are being outsourced: Complex production and advanced R&D are also affected. The inseparability of ICT from production means suppliers are not turn-key – that is, they cannot be easily substituted (Miozzo and Grimshaw, 2005). Prencipe (1997) highlights the dangers of outsourcing activities based on simple notions of core and non-core competences. The outsourcing of what today appear to be non-core competences can seriously impair the future development of new (core) technological competences. Separation of development and production hampers innovation. Brusoni *et al.* (2001) emphasize the importance of retaining control over R&D, and the ability to coordinate the R&D, design and manufacturing activities of suppliers.

To summarize, a growing body of empirical research exists which suggests the short-run gains of outsourcing may be more than offset in the longer term, leading to lower long-run productivity growth. We have formulated a theoretical framework for understanding these dangers; one that links organizational innovation with the adoption of new ICTs and with outsourcing opportunities. The framework enables us to identify a specific transmission mechanism between ICT adoption, organizational innovation and outsourcing. Further, the framework explains why outsourcing can negatively impact organizational innovation and productivity in the long run. Specifically, the outsourcing of activities reduces the total set of modular elements that can be subjected to experimental innovation in the future. With fewer components under their control, managers are unable to experiment with all possible organizational combinations. The danger is that this prevents the discovery of more efficient organizational designs. Hence, the firm can become locked in to a suboptimal design space. If this is the case, then the outsourcing firm will suffer lower growth in productivity than if it had not outsourced (and the entire space of organizational designs could have be explored).

10.3 The modelling of organizational innovation, outsourcing strategies and the impact of ICTs

We have developed a model that captures the most important of the recent theoretical developments discussed in section 10.1. Here we use the model to study the effect of internet-based ICTs on outsourcing, organizational innovation and long-run productivity. New possibilities arise because internet-based ICTs reduce external coordination costs. We shall not, in this chapter, examine co-invention and co-production. Instead we focus on the outsourcing to KIBS of knowledge-intensive coordination and management activities, highlighted in the empirical data discussed earlier. This includes, for example, the outsourcing of IT services to specialist KIBS providers. We examine the long-run implications of this type of outsourcing activity on organizational innovation and, consequently, productivity growth.

The model is presented schematically as a flowchart in Figure 10.1. The technical details are presented in Hölzl *et al.* (2005). The model differs from standard economic models in three respects. First, it embodies the idea of a partially non-separable organization and technology for the firm. Secondly, and in line with recent work on the theory of the firm and organization, it views organizational

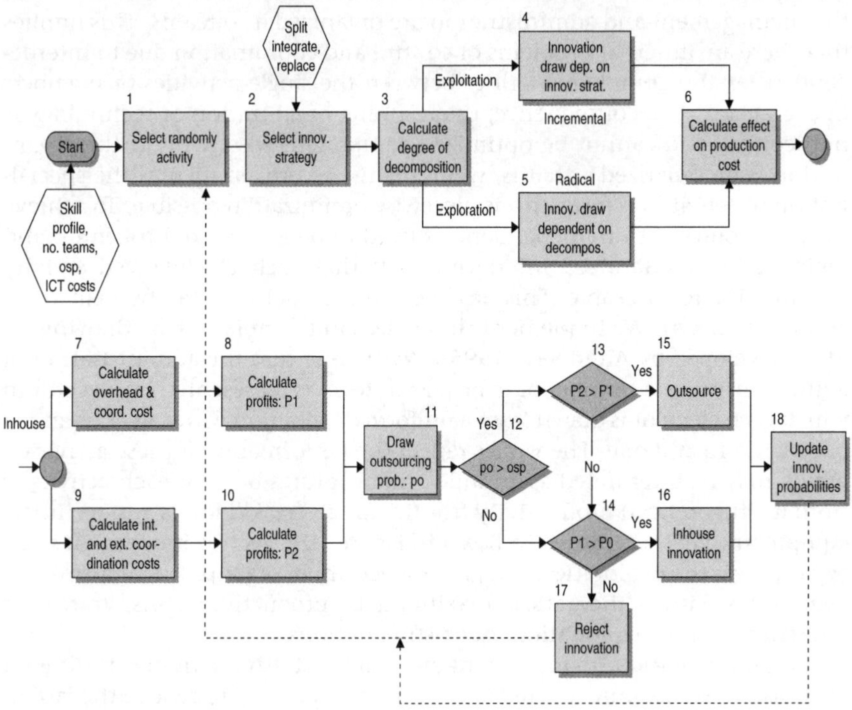

Figure 10.1 Flowchart of the simulation model

Note: rectangular boxes show processes, hexagons exogenous parameters, small squares show some important variables, diamond boxes show decision criteria and squared boxes with inlaying circles reflect the crucial exogenous parameters whose impact on the model behaviour is studied. All processes are numbered in sequence as they are worked off by the computer program.

change as a process of remodularization. Thirdly, it assumes that firms are boundedly rational and learn adaptively from past experience. The first and third assumptions mean the model cannot be solved using closed form analytical techniques but must be investigated through simulation modelling.

In our model, firms are boundedly rational. In this case, we assume that a firm knows the parameters of its demand schedule and all relevant cost parameters at a given moment in time. However, we assume it does not know the characteristics of the stochastic process that generates incremental and radical innovations. They have this information only after the stochastic variables realize some value. As a consequence, they decide optimally after they have this information (see Boxes 7 to 14, where all available information is used to calculate prospective profits for each innovation), but are not able to look forward on the basis of the averages of the realized stochastic variables.

At the heart of this model is the idea that management and business activities deliver services to production activities by fostering their productivity. Therefore, management has an incentive to improve the organization and quality of managerial and administrative processes, or 'services'. We assume that management and administration are organized into teams. This implies that there are inherent problems of control and coordination due to interdependencies and complementarities between the single activities or members in each team. As a consequence, the resulting organization or technology is non-convex and cannot be optimized component-wise. Only if the organization is modularized – that is, when teams are broken up and the specialization of activities is fostered – is piecewise optimization possible. To achieve this, the sources of interdependencies need to be identified, broken up and replaced by standardized interfaces, such that each modularized activity becomes interchangeable. This has been worked out in detail by Reinstaller and Hölzl (2004). We implement these ideas in a simple way by drawing on ideas developed by Altenberg (1995). We assume that the administration of a firm consists of a number of teams. Each team is represented by a vector in which each element is drawn from a uniform distribution with values bounded between zero and one. The values reflect the performance of these activities, which may be interpreted as an index that captures how far each activity is from its (theoretical) productivity frontier for given skill levels and technical equipment. This is captured in Box 4 in Figure 10.1. As this innovation strategy captures the exploration of a given spectrum of organizational forms and techniques with a theoretical maximum in productivity, this strategy is referred to as the 'exploitation' of existing options.

The productivity of management and administrative activities is difficult to measure. We assume it is reflected in their capability to reduce the labour costs of productive (or shopfloor) activities. If one of the elements in the vector (one of the team members or one of the activities in a team) is changed by replacing it with a better-performing element, non-separability means there are changes in all performance values in that vector (that is, for each element a new draw is made). The average performance of a team is given by the average value over all elements constituting it. This implies that it is more difficult to change performance for a larger team than for a smaller team. Hence, the more interdependent and complex the organizational structure of a firm, the more difficult it is to monitor and improve its performance. Modularity in organization helps to alleviate this problem by creating separable subactivities which can then be optimized one by one. A second benefit is that it allows new and old organizational elements to be recombined more easily, thereby augmenting the adaptability of the firm. Note that the standard production functions used in mainstream models to capture the technology of a firm are always assumed to be separable. In the present model, this assumption is endogenized and the management of firms actually seeks an optimal degree of separability of the organizational process. This is introduced into the model through the innovation strategies it can pursue.

In our model, the management tries to solve the problems of coordination and control by introducing organizational innovations which allow it to control single activities in better ways (see Box 2 in Figure 10.1). There are three possible innovation strategies:

1. The first strategy is 'split'. Here a large vector is split into smaller vectors and a neutralizing interface connects the smaller teams within a new organizational process. This division of labour/specialization process enables management to raise performance. With this strategy the modularity of the organizational process increases.
2. The second strategy is 'replace'. Here work performed by an existing team is improved by replacing its old working routines with the new, improved routines. Here the modularity of the organizational process does not change. This strategy may be best thought of as a way to introduce learning-by-doing into the model.
3. The third strategy is 'integrate'. This involves job enrichment strategies, combining activities together and creating beneficial synergies in order to improve productivity. Consequently, the modularity of the organizational process decreases. If they, choose this strategy, firms must trade the gains from beneficial synergies against the losses of a lower modularity of the organizational process.

The probability of choosing any one of these strategies changes endogenously through reinforcement learning, as described by Arthur (1991). This means the weight of the probability of a strategy to be chosen by the management increases or decreases as it proves to be more or less successful in improving the performance of managerial activities. This is represented by Box 18 in Figure 10.1. Another aspect of organizational innovation discussed in section 10.1 of this chapter is that the literature on modularity assumes that innovativeness increases as a function of the degree of decomposition of organizations (see, for instance, Langlois 2002). We therefore assume that as the modularity of the organization increases firms may invest in R&D to explore new innovation possibilities that increase the performance of all management activities. Following Silverberg and Verspagen (1994), these innovations are modelled as a Poisson process where the arrival parameter depends on the modularity of the activities. The latter innovation strategy is assumed to push ahead the theoretical productivity frontier of all the organizational designs the firm can explore. It captures radical innovations in organization. This type of innovation is referred to as the 'exploration' of new techno-organizational designs. It is represented by Box 5 in Figure 10.1.

In line with the discussion in section 10.2 we study the comparative dynamic behaviour of the model with respect to two parameters. The first parameter is the outsourcing propensity of the management (denoted as 'OSP' in Box 12 in Figure 10.1). Altering the value of this parameter enables one to assess its impact on the dynamic behaviour. The outsourcing propensity captures the risk attitude of management – that is, its risk position towards the potential gains of outsourcing set against the loss of in-house managerial/administrative competences. For any given outsourcing propensity we draw a uniformly distributed random variable indicating whether an option to outsource is available. This is represented by Box 11 in Figure 10.1. Business-service providers are assumed to have cost advantages over the firm in the production of certain services (see Box 9 in Figure 10.1). The process of outsourcing involves the service provider and the outsourcing firm negotiating a contract for the delivery of a specific service (for example, the management and delivery of specific IT services), at a specified price. If the outsourcing firm enters this contract, it shuts down its own activities and loses these competences. To simplify, we assume that these are lost forever. This strong assumption is not necessarily unrealistic. Empirical evidence indicates it can be extremely difficult and expensive to reacquire competences, especially in knowledge intense activities.

The second exogenous parameter (see Box 9 in Figure 10.1) captures the impact of internet-based ICTs on outsourcing behaviour. It captures how the reduction of external transaction cost influences the outsourcing decisions, and hence the structure of the firm. The remaining assumptions in the model are standard. We assume that the firm faces a downward-sloping demand curve. Furthermore, the firm is assumed to be able to expand demand whenever it wants, that is, Say's law holds. During each time step, the firm uses all available information to maximize its profits. For each activity that is initially selected for improvement (see Box 1 in Figure 10.1), the firm calculates the profits it would gain if the activity was produced in-house, pre- and post-innovation, and if the resulting services were retained in-house or outsourced. This process is represented in Boxes 7 through 17 in Figure 10.1.

To sum up, there are essentially three stochastic engines driving the productivity dynamics in the model. The first two are represented by Boxes 1 through 6 in Figure 10.1, and the third is represented by Box 11. The first is captured by the process of 'exploitation'. Firms choose some innovation strategy and get some innovation or learning draws which they accept if the overall performance of the firm is improved. The second stochastic engine of the model is a Poisson process with the arrival rate depends on the degree of decomposition or modularity of the organization. A final stochastic element is the probability of outsourcing. For any given managerial propensity to outsource organizational activities, we draw an outsourcing probability. Note that management teams with a low propensity to outsource require more draws before an activity is outsourced than teams with a high propensity to outsource.

We report the results obtained under four different scenarios. These are presented in Figure 10.2. The plots in the top left- and right-hand quadrant of Figure 10.2 show the development of productivity within the firm. The bold line represents the mean over 50 runs for each parameter setting, while the thin dashed lines represent the 95 per cent confidence interval. The plots in the bottom left- and right-hand quadrants show the development of average unit costs over time.

The first scenario, presented in the left-hand side of Figure 10.2, juxtaposes the impact of ICTs on performance, and the average unit costs of the firm given a *high* propensity of managers to choose the outsourcing strategy. The results for low internal, but high external coordination costs are represented by dash-dot-dash lines, while those for equally efficient internal and external communication costs are represented by unbroken lines.

A number of lessons can be drawn from the findings presented in Figure 10.1. First, a firm with a high propensity to outsource tends to perform worse in the long run when new ICTs lead to a reduction in external coordination costs. The explanation for this is as follows. Managers of the firm are learning myopically over time. They do not have information on the payoffs of all possible choices, and are unable to observe the payoffs of firms that choose a different strategy. Hence, they are only able to observe the payoffs associated with their own past choices, i.e. they are engaged in pure learning-by-doing (see above). In practice, this is a reasonable approximation of the reality for managers in the vast majority of firms. Unlike physical products and services, which can be obtained and reverse engineered, managers do not have ready access to information on the other firms' organizational structures, administrative services, and the performance of those organizational structures.

Under these circumstances, the managers of the firm perceive there to be cost-cutting potentials if ICTs lead to a fall in external coordination costs, and proceed to outsource a high number of service activities. As a consequence, the depth of the hierarchy is reduced and in the beginning overhead costs also drop. Initially, productivity grows as well. It grows at a much slower rate than if the firm had not outsourced but, of course, the firm does not actually 'see' this in practice because it has chosen to pursue the alternative trajectory of outsourcing. Unfortunately, as the firm continues along this path, productivity

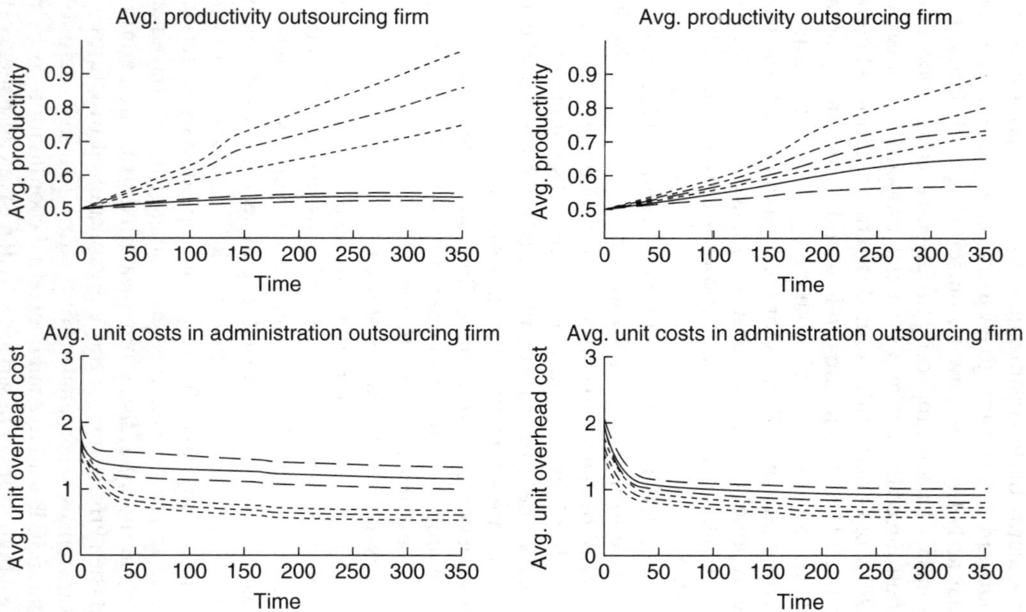

Figure 10.2 Simulation runs
Notes: Left: scenario with high outsourcing propensity by management. Right: scenario with low outsourcing propensity by management. Dash-dot-dash lines represent runs with low internal communication costs, for a given outsourcing propensity. Unbroken lines represent runs with low internal and low external communication costs, for a given outsourcing propensity. The bold lines represent means over 50 runs. The thin dashed lines represent the 95% confidence intervals around these means.

growth continues to fall and can even stagnate. The upshot is that managers focused on the short-run cost-cutting effect will succeed in reducing costs, but will also unwittingly reduce the long-run innovation potential of the firm.

By contrast, where new ICTs lower internal coordination costs relative to external coordination costs, firms engage in less outsourcing and instead focus on the development of increased modularity in their administrative structures. As the activities become more specialized, it is easier to improve the quality of their service to the productive activities. At the same time, the long-run potential for radical organizational innovations is exploited successfully. The long-run productivity of the firm under this scenario outperforms the alternative scenario where new ICTs lower external coordination costs and firms engage in outsourcing. These results support the empirical findings that outsourcing may reduce short term costs but it can have a negative impact on the long run performance and survival of firms.

On the right-hand side of Figure 10.2 we present the results for our third and fourth scenarios – that is, where the outsourcing propensities of management are low. Again, we consider what happens if ICT reduces external coordination costs relative to internal coordination costs, and what happens if ICTs reduce internal external coordination costs relative to external coordination costs. Once again, the finding is that ICTs which stimulate internal organizational innovation outperform the scenario in which ICTs stimulate outsourcing. As before, the reason is that the long-run productivity potential of the firm depends upon the degree of decomposition of administrative activities. Therefore, firms always fare better in the long run if they keep the service activities in-house and reap all the benefits of the process of organizational innovation. Once activities are outsourced, suppliers in our model charge a constant price and no longer improve the quality of the services they deliver. As a consequence, producing services in-house is the dominant strategy in this simulation.

The results support the observations of the empirical studies discussed in section 10.2. However, it is important to observe that long-run productivity of the runs with low external coordination cost comes close to the long-run productivity levels where external coordination costs are high in the upper end of the confidence interval. This outcome depends on the propensity of the firm to invest in radical organizational innovation. It suggests that, if a firm chooses to (moderately) outsource and is inclined to do so by low external coordination costs, it should scale up its investment in radical organizational innovations, which will better exploit the innovation potentials.

10.4 Conclusions and directions for further research

The chapter has investigated the thesis that outsourcing activities to business services (KIBS) can reduce certain administrative costs, but that they may reduce productivity growth in the long run. This is the striking thesis that is emerging from the latest empirical research on the long-term impacts of outsourcing on the innovative capabilities and productivity growth of client firms. The chapter summarized the short- and long-term costs and benefits of outsourcing, and proceeded to place them on a more analytical footing through the development of a framework of organizational innovation that integrates decisions to outsource with the introduction of cost-saving new ICTs. The framework specified a transmission mechanism that explains the links between the adoption of new ICTs, alternative strategies for organizational restructuring, system economies and the decision to outsource.

The framework has been implemented in a novel model of organizational innovation. Simulations conducted on this model enabled us to consider the short- and long-run impacts of outsourcing on administration overheads and on long-term productivity growth. The interesting finding is that managers of a firm can become locked into a low trajectory of productivity growth, associated with the outsourcing of activities, if they are myopic and learn through their own actions. They perceive outsourcing to cut overhead costs in the short run (as expected), and so engage in further outsourcing thereafter. This is to the detriment of long-run productivity gains (system economies) generated though organizational innovation. This occurs because the potential for organizational innovation is reduced when modular components are outsourced, placing them beyond the control of the firms' management. The findings accord well with the empirical data, and provide a salutary warning for managers and policy makers about the potential long-term implications of outsourcing.

Looking forward, there are a number of interesting extensions that can be made to the current model. Future research will also explore the relaxation of certain assumptions of the current model. For instance, outsourcing is purely concerned with access and cost of externally produced services. This accords with empirical findings regarding the main drivers of outsourcing. However, other considerations have been highlighted by the theoretical literature on KIBS, such as co-production and the co-innovation of products and services. These will be explored in future research.

Notes

1. The authors gratefully acknowledge supportive funding through the PUBLIN Project, European Commission's Framework 5 Program.
2. Brynolfsson and Hitt (2000) studied the impact of large ICT investments over the last decades on productivity. They find that, on their own, costly investments have little impact on productivity. They do, however, have very significant impacts on productivity when they are matched with complementary changes in the organizational design.
3. The analysis is based on a set of completed written questionnaires from 267 firms. All firms have more than 50 employees and are drawn from the ISIC sectors 28–35: metal goods, machinery, office equipment and computers, other electronics, telecoms, instrumentation, and the automotive industry.

Part III

Markets and Competition in Business Services

11
Market Structure, Productivity and Scale in European Business Services

Henk Kox, George van Leeuwen and Henry van der Wiel

Prologue

Labour productivity in the business-services industry tends to lag behind the rest of the economy. The present chapter investigates whether or not labour productivity in European business services is affected by unexploited economies of scale. In addition, it analyses whether the incidence of scale suboptimality is related to characteristics of the market or to national regulation characteristics. The econometric analysis is based on a production function model in combination with a distance-to-the-frontier model. A main result is that we find evidence for the existence of increasing returns to scale in business-services firms. Throughout the EU, firms with fewer than 20 persons have a significantly lower average level of labour productivity than the rest of the business-services industry. We find two explanatory factors for the level of scale inefficiency. The first is the level of policy-caused firm-entry costs; higher start-up costs for new firms go along with more scale inefficiency for business-services firms. Secondly, we find evidence that business-services markets tend to be segmented by firm size: firms tend to compete predominantly with other firms of similar size. Scale-related inefficiencies may to some extent be compensated by more competition within a firm's own size segment. If a firm operates in a more "crowded" segment this has a significant and positive impact on its labour productivity. We derive some policy implications from our findings.

Introduction

During the past 15 years, the business-services industries in most OECD countries have experienced comparatively high growth rates. This held in terms of its production, but even more so in terms of employment. Labour productivity in the business-services industry tends to lag behind the rest of the economy. This is a reason for policy concern, because the business-services industry today has become a large part of OECD economies, and is a major supplier of inputs to other industries. Low productivity in a large economic sector may negatively affect macroeconomic growth in a direct way (cf. Part I of this volume). One of the findings of a large Dutch research project on the causes of the sluggish productivity growth in business services was that scale suboptimality may be a source of the poor productivity performance in business services.[1] The statistical evidence then available suggested that the overwhelming majority of firms in this industry operates at a scale where potential scale economies are left unexploited.

The present chapter investigates this hypothesis more profoundly by analysing the scale impacts on productivity in business services in an internationally comparative context. More specifically, we investigate econometrically the following questions:

- is productivity in European business services affected by unexploited economies of scale? if this is the case,
- is the incidence of scale suboptimality related to characteristics of the market or to national regulation characteristics?

The research with regard to these questions will be undertaken mainly based on Eurostat NewCronos data. Section 11.1 presents some descriptive statistics for the business services for the 11 EU countries. Section 11.2 of the chapter sketches the analytical framework. After a brief data description in section 11.3, section 11.4 presents the empirical results with regard to the hypotheses. Section 11.5 summarizes the overall conclusions.

11.1 Stylized facts

The business-services industry consists of a wide range of branches such as accountants, market research, economic consultancy, and industrial cleaning. Large differences in features are related to, amongst others, differences in labour intensity, capital intensity, knowledge intensity and product differentiation. The products of the business-services industry are mostly high value-added products as a result of the large level of knowledge intensity in this industry. Compared with other industries, the business-services industry employs relatively many high-educated employees and employers. In order to limit the amount of sectoral heterogeneity, we focus on the labour-intensive part of the business-services industry.[2]

At first glance, there are a number of similarities across the EU countries with respect to some key statistics. Here, we mention two of them. First, business services in most EU countries is typically a small-firm business with the average number of employed persons well below ten persons (see Figure 11.1). The figure, however, also shows that the share of firms with less than ten employed persons ranges between 17 and 57 per cent of total value added. This indicates that there can be large differences between countries in the firm size-distribution.

Figure 11.1 Average firm size in business services and the share of small firms (<10 employed persons) in total value added, 11 EU countries, 1999
Note: NACE K72 + K74. Firms with less than one employed person are not included. Calculated from Eurostat NewCronos data (Firm demography, Business services by size class). Data for the Netherlands compiled from Dutch production census data, using the New Cronos classification of size classes.

A second similarity across most EU countries is that the average level of labour productivity may differ considerably between size-classes of firms. Figure 11.2 depicts the average labour productivity for all business services per size-class and per country. In the left-hand panel we see that six out of 11 countries display a clear hump-shaped (inverted U) relation between productivity level and firm size. The right-hand panel shows that in two countries (Ireland, Sweden) there is a monotone productivity increase by size-class, and in three countries (UK, France, and Denmark) the relation between labour productivity and scale does not exhibit a clear pattern. Overall, the graphs suggest that scale effects could play a role in the productivity performance of firms. The hump-shaped curvature hints at the existence of an optimal firm size. In the rest of the chapter we will further investigate the nature and causes of the different productivity performance by size class.

11.2 Explanatory models

In this section, we describe the explanatory models that will be tested to locate scale effects in business services, and their main assumptions. Our basic framework is a translog production function. First, we discuss the specification of our basic model. Scale effects are here considered only from a technological

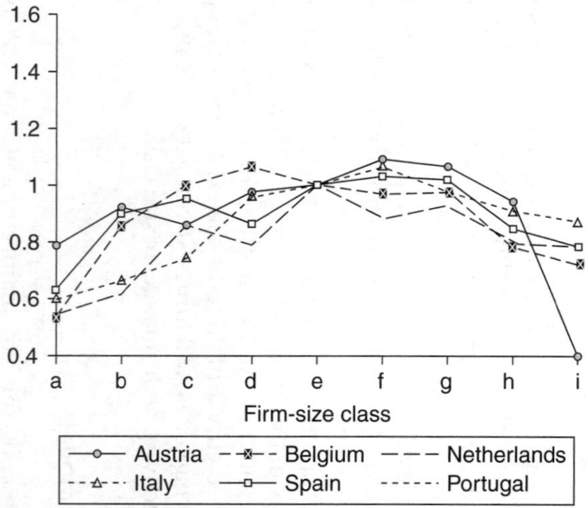

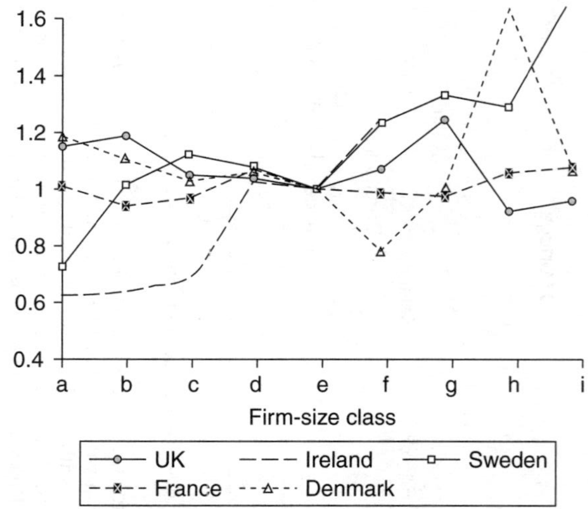

Figure 11.2 Relative labour productivity performance by size-class in business services, 11 EU countries, 1999

Note: Relative labour productivity by size-class (size-class with 50–99 employees is benchmark) for all subsectors. Labour productivity is measured as value added (in 1,000 Euros) per employed person. Legend for firm-size classes, based on employed persons per firm: a) 1–4; b) 5–9; c) 10–19; d) 20–49; e) 50–99; f) 100–249; g) 250–499; h) 500–999; and i) over 1,000 employed persons.

perspective. Next, we widen the perspective of the translog function by augmenting it with variables that control for market-specific factors and country-specific policy factors. Finally, we introduce the main characteristics of a distance-to-frontier model. We apply the generalized stochastic frontier approach of Kumbhakar *et al.* (1991) that simultaneously explains X-inefficiencies and input intensities from market-specific and country-specific characteristics.

Basic production function (PF) model

The presence of scale effects means that an output increase (ΔOUT) is not only a function of increased inputs (ΔIN) but also from the already achieved level of inputs (IN):

$$\Delta OUT = f(\Delta IN\,;\, IN) \tag{11.1}$$

The effect of the marginal unit of inputs on output growth is variable with the already attained level of inputs. If the long-run average-cost function of a firm in an industry displays a U-shape, then the production elasticity of at least one input must be variable. The occurrence of variable or 'local' scale effects can, for instance, occur when there are discontinuities in the technology options, lower efficiency incentives (bureaucracy), or fewer opportunities for internal labour division. It implies that some firm sizes allow more efficiency than other sizes.

To take into account variable input elasticities, we employ the so-called translog production function in which the expansion of one or more inputs may have a non-linear effect on the output level.[3] The translog specification explicitly checks for variable scale effects and the presence of size-class specific complementarity between inputs. The presence of variable scale effects is detected separately by adding a quadratic term for each input.[4] In a logarithmic specification the basic translog production function for a firm's value added reads:

$$\begin{aligned} \ln Y = {} & \alpha_y + \beta_1 \ln K + \beta_2 \ln L + \frac{1}{2}\beta_{11}(\ln K)^2 \\ & + \frac{1}{2}\beta_{22}(\ln L)^2 + \beta_{12}(\ln K \times \ln L) \end{aligned} \tag{11.2}$$

in which Y is value added, K is physical capital inputs, and L represents labour inputs. The parameters β_1 and β_2 reflect the linear effects of more input use on value added. The parameters β_{11} and β_{22} reflect the non-linear effects for both basic inputs. Interaction parameter β_{12} represents local level interactions between the individual inputs.[5] The interaction parameter becomes significant if the output elasticity of a particular input depends on the *level* of the other input (input complementarity). As an example for the business-services sector, we may think of the positive labour productivity effects that come within reach after a fixed-capital investment in a local PC network. The constant α_y

is a catch-up term for the impact of non-observed variables on output, frequently interpreted as the level of 'multi-factor productivity'. In the basic specification we add sector and country dummies that account for unobserved sector-specific and country-specific fixed effects.

Measuring economies of scale. With regard to scale effects on production, three meaningful outcomes for the model described by equation (11.2) can be distinguished. When there are no scale effects (constant returns to scale) we will find that $\beta_1 + \beta_2 = 1$, i.e. the output increase is equal to the increment of combined inputs. There may also be identical scale effects – either diminishing or increasing – for all firm-size classes. That is the case when we find the combination of $\beta_1 + \beta_2 \neq 1$ with $\beta_{11} = \beta_{22} = \beta_{12} = 0$ (no variable scale and input-interaction effects). Finally, if significant non-zero values are found for β_{11}, β_{22} and/or β_{12} it means that differentiated scale effects occur for specific size classes of firms.[6]

Augmented PF-model

In the basic translog specification, it is assumed that the shape of the production function and therefore the scale effects are identical everywhere: for all firms in all subsectors of business services in all EU countries. This is a simplification as there may be other factors that play a role in specific subsectors and in specific countries. We therefore augment our basic translog PF-model with variables that control for market structure and country-specific policy factors.

We distinguish three market-specific factors that may influence the relation between scale and productivity: market segmentation, market concentration, and the degree of product homogeneity. We subsequently discuss each of these factors.

Market segmentation implies that not all firms in a subsector are direct competitors of each other. The existence of market segmentation has potential repercussions for the competitive incentives to remove scale-related inefficiencies. There are some suggestions in the literature that business-services markets may be segmented (at least partly) along firm-size characteristics, and that this is to some extent related to reputation effects.[7] We use a simple procedure to control for the possible impact of firm-size related market segmentation on productivity. Suppose size-related market segmentation is present. In that case, the firm's input choices that govern productivity performance will be geared more towards competition in its own size segment than towards competition with firms in other size-segments of the market. As the measure of competition we take the average firm's market share; this is the inverse of the number of firms (*NOF*) in a relevant market. When segmentation by size class is present, the number of competitors in the firm's own size-class (*SEGM*) will have a stronger impact on the firm's productivity performance than the number of competitors in the rest of the sector's size classes (*SR*). For size class s ($s = 1,\ldots,S$), sector j ($j = 1,..,J$) and country $k(k = 1,..,N)$ the normalized indicators for intra-segment competition intensity and extra-segment competition intensity are:[8]

$$SEGM_{sjk} = \ln(\gamma_{jk}\, NOF_{sjk}) \quad \text{and} \quad SR_{sjk} = \ln\{\gamma_{jk}(NOF_{jk} - NOF_{sjk})\}$$

$$\text{with } \gamma_{jk} = \frac{\frac{\gamma_k}{J}\sum_j^J NOF_{jk}}{NOF_{jk}} \quad \text{and} \quad \gamma_k = \frac{\frac{1}{N}\sum_k^N NOF_k}{NOF_k} \tag{11.3}$$

The segmentation hypothesis can be tested straightforwardly by adding both variables to the production function model. If α_1 and α_2 are respectively the impact parameters of, respectively, *SEGMsjk* and *SRsjk* in the augmented production-function model, the interpretation of the results must be as follows. If *all* firms in the subsector compete with each other, regardless of size segment, the parameter α_1 will either be zero or be roughly equal to the parameter α_2. If, however, market segmentation by size class is important we will find: $|\alpha_1| > |\alpha_2| > 0$. Given the possibility that one of both parameters could directly pick up scale inefficiencies, we apply the segmentation test in an absolute formulation.[9]

Market concentration is a second market characteristic for which we want to control. High concentration implies that imperfect competition prevails in a market, with less pressure on firms to remove scale-related X-inefficiencies, even if markets are not segmented. Fabiani *et al.* (2005) and ECB Task Force (2006) find that European non-trade services firms review and change prices less often than in other industries, indicating the presence of mark-up pricing and imperfect competition. With a higher intensity of competition, firms have fewer opportunities for mark-up pricing, and firm size will be more directly related to their cost and labour productivity levels. We want to control for this possibly disturbing effect on our results. We use (the logarithm of) the Hirschmann-Herfindahl index (*HHI*) as a measure of market concentration. It does not measure competition intensity as such, but it may indicate markets with weak incentives for eradicating scale-related inefficiencies.[10] A high degree of market concentration is expected to cause a lower efficiency pressure. Hence, we expect a negative sign for the estimated *HHI* parameter.

Finally, the degree of *product differentiation* is a final market characteristic that we want to take into account. Descriptive data for the business-services industry in the EU show that some subsectors have a high degree of product differentiation. Product differentiation may affect the input mix and the internal organization of firms. In case of product differentiation, labour-saving and internal division of labour according to the Babbage principle (spreading costs of overhead and management labour across more workers) may become more difficult, thus affecting productivity. Product specialization in business services could have two opposite effects on productivity. The required higher overall qualification level of employees may benefit labour productivity in some elements of the production process. Conversely, the lack of task standardization, specialization and production routines may negatively affect productivity.[11] A priori, it is not obvious which of the two productivity effects is dominant. To isolate the potential impact of product differentiation on productivity, we add subsector dummies to take account of product differentiation and other unobserved factors that vary by subsector.

Apart from market characteristics, the augmented production-function model also accounts for *country-specific differences* in product-market regulation. Regulation of product markets by national governments could possibly explain part of the variation in business services productivity across EU countries. Stricter regulations are found to go along with more mark-up pricing in services (ECB Task Force, 2006); hence, with strict regulations there will be fewer incentives to remove scale-related inefficiencies. In addition, research by Scarpetta *et al.* (2002) and Schiantarelli (2005) supports the expectation that the incidence of scale inefficiencies may be a function of the regulation type and the relative regulation intensity in countries. We explicitly control for two types of national policy indicators:[12]

- intensity of product-market regulation, relative to other countries (*PMR*). We expect this variable to correlate negatively with productivity.
- entry costs for new firms (*EC*). A high entry hurdle diminishes the competitive pressure that newcomers in the market exert on incumbent firms. We expect a negative effect on average firm productivity.

With the addition of market-specific and country-specific regulation factors to equation 11.2, we arrive at the augmented translog PF-model. Since we focus on labour productivity, the equation is further reformulated so that labour productivity is indeed the dependent variable:

$$\begin{aligned} \ln\left(\frac{Y}{L}\right) &= \lambda_L + \beta_1 \ln K + (\beta_2 - 1)\ln L + \frac{1}{2}\beta_{11}(\ln K)^2 \\ &\quad + \frac{1}{2}\beta_{22}(\ln L)^2 + \beta_{12}(\ln K \times \ln L) + \alpha_1 SEGM_{sjk} \\ &\quad + \alpha_2 SR_{sjk} + \alpha_3 HHI + \alpha_4 PMR + \alpha_5 EC \\ &\quad + \alpha_6 D + \mu \end{aligned} \tag{11.4}$$

All β-parameters refer to technological parameters, whereas the α-parameters refer to the control variables of the augmented model. *SEGM* and *SR* are the indicators for within-segment competition respectively competition with other segments, while *HHI* denotes the market concentration. Both are specific for subsector and country. Furthermore, two indicators refer to country-specific policy regulations: product market regulation (PMR) and Entry costs (EC). Vector D contains subsector dummies that account for unobserved sector-specific fixed effects. Finally, λ_L is the regression constant, and μ is the error term of the regression. An important element of the (augmented) PF-model is that the error term μ is thought to contain only white noise.[13]

Distance-to-the-frontier model

The production function models assume a representative 'average' firm with a more or less homogenous input mix. We may get a step closer to reality by allowing for the possibility that firms, size-classes or subsectors can be heterogeneous in their input mixes. The distance-to-frontier model does two things. It identifies a technological efficiency frontier per sector ('best practice').[14] All individual observations can thus be defined as deviations from the frontier. The model at the same time explains from market-structure variables and regulation characteristics why some or even most firms are not on the efficiency frontier. The individual productivity distance to the frontier firm (X-inefficiency) becomes the independent variable. We use the generalized stochastic frontier (GSF) model, an adapted version of the method developed by Kumbhakar *et al.* (1991). The GSF takes into account the fact that both X-inefficiencies and input choices depend on market-specific and country-specific characteristics.

The first part of our GSF-model is again a standard translog productivity equation:

$$\ln\left(\frac{Y}{L}\right) = \lambda_L + \beta_1 \ln K + (\beta_2 - 1)\ln L + \frac{1}{2}\beta_{11}(\ln K)^2 + \frac{1}{2}\beta_{22}(\ln L)^2 + \beta_{12}(\ln K \times \ln L) + \delta B + \varepsilon \tag{11.5}$$

The vector B collects the sector-, country- and size-class dummies that act as control variables for the technology parameters. The error term ε is important for further analysis in the GSF-model, since it is thought to contain a deterministic component (τ), which representing the part of the X-inefficiencies that can be explained from market and regulation characteristics. Apart from that, a white noise component (ω) is present, so that $\varepsilon = \tau + \varpi$.[15] The efficiency frontier is defined as those observations without deterministic X-ineficiencies, so that the distribution of τ is truncated at zero (condition $\tau \leqslant 0$). The second equation of the GSF- model explains the X-inefficiencies in terms of a vector of Z that contains the market and regulation variables:

$$\tau = \gamma' Z + \theta \quad \text{with} \quad \tau \sim N(\gamma' Z, \sigma_\tau^2) \tag{11.6}$$

The equation (11.6) says that X-inefficiencies are drawings from a truncated normal distribution with expectation $\hat{\tau} = \gamma' Z$. This specification implies that

X-efficiencies are deviations from their mean determined by the vector Z.[16] The market and regulation variables in Z are the same as those used in the augmented PF-model. Both equations of the GSF model (11.5 and 11.6) are to be estimated simultaneously. Note that because the last equation explains *in*efficiencies the signs of the explanatory variables must be interpreted in an opposite way (negatively) to find the impact on labour productivity.

The three explanatory models that have been developed in this section are related to each other. They can be considered as stages in diminishing abstraction: the first model (PF) explains possible scale effects only from technological input choices. The second model (augmented PF) allows for the possibility that market characteristics and country-specific regulatory characteristics affect input choices, and hence scale effects. Both models basically assume the homogeneity of all firms, i.e. some representative firm. This homogeneity assumption is dropped in the GSF-model, by identifying a production frontier and explaining the individual firm's deviation to this frontier in terms of market characteristics and country-specific regulatory characteristics. The three models are tested subsequently.

11.3 Data

In order to test our explanatory models empirically we use national production census data for business-services firms, made available through the Eurostat NewCronos database *Firm demography, Business services by size class* (data retrieval August 2005). The data are for 11 EU Member states and cover some 1.9 million individual firms – by subsector and by country – with the reference year 1999.[17] The data are aggregated by size-class of firms, but since the number of firms by size-class is given, we can infer data for the average firm by size-class, by subsector and country. The aggregation level of the NewCronos data does not allow us to deal with firm-level heterogeneity, but we may calculate scale effects for the average firm in each size class in each subsector of the business-services industry.

Firm size is measured in terms of the number of employed persons per firm, a measure that includes the entrepreneur. Nine different size-classes are distinguished, ranging from small firms with one to four employees to very large firms with more than 1,000 employees. The available data allow a cross-section regression for 11 EU countries: Austria, Belgium, Denmark, France, Ireland, Italy, the Netherlands, Portugal, Spain, Sweden, and the United Kingdom. The total number of observations is about 760, from up to 12 different subsectors of NACE 72 (Computer-related services) and NACE 74 (Other business services).

Labour input is measured as the number of employed persons. The amount of depreciation is used as an indicator for capital input. For market concentration, we use a modified version of the HHI.[18] For the variable PMR (intensity product-market regulation) we use the OECD's economy-wide indicator for the relative intensity of competition regulation in reference year 1998 (Nicoletti *et al.* 2000). A high value of the PMR indicates a relatively regulated national economy. Data for variable EC (policy-caused, country-specific costs for setting up a new firm) are derived from a World Bank dataset (Djankov *et al.* 2002). A high value of the indicator refers to a large amount of entry costs.

11.4 Empirical results

We subsequently present the estimation results for the explanatory models, starting with the results for the two PF-models. The dependent variable is, in all cases, the logarithm of the productivity level (value added per employed person).

Table 11.1 presents the results of both the basic and the augmented PF-model applied on the pooled dataset for all 11 EU countries and all available subsectors. The results for the basic PF-model suggest that there are increasing returns to scale in the EU business-services industry. From the magnitude of the technology variables in combination with the levels of capital and labour inputs (not shown) it can be inferred that there are positive scale economies. Since β_{11}, β_{22} and β_{12} are significantly different from zero, we must conclude that these positive scale effects are 'local', i.e. they only occur in some size classes.

We would expect these local effects to pop up in the augmented PF-model where we add dummies for individual size-classes as well as variables for market characteristics and country-specific regulation characteristics. However, the estimation outcomes show that none of the size dummies is statistically significant. This suggests that neither small nor very large firms operate on a less-efficient production frontier scale. A small average market share for firms within a size segment (variable *SEGM*) has a significantly negative impact on labour productivity, but, overall, this effect is dominated by a larger positive productivity impact of competition with firms in other size segments (variable *SR*). Because of the relative size of both effects, the market segmentation hypothesis is rejected in the augmented PF-model: the condition $|\alpha_1| > |\alpha_2|$ is not fulfilled. The estimated coefficients of the market concentration (*HHI*) and policy-caused entry costs (*EC*) have the expected negative sign and are statistically highly significant. The PMR variable is significant at the 10 per cent confidence level, but it has not the expected sign. The positive sign suggests that strict regulation in a country strengthens labour productivity performance. This is at odds with most of the literature, and we do not have a good explanation for this result. The indicator for the intensity of product-market regulation in a country could be too broad to be meaningfully used for explaining the differences in productivity level of the business-services industry.

Both of the preceding models illustrate that capital intensity (parameter β_1) matters for the labour productivity level in business services. The coefficient for capital is, however, much smaller in the augmented PF-model. The

Table 11.1 Estimation results for basic and augmented PF-model based on pooled regression in business services (all sub-sectors, 11 EU countries, reference year 1999)

Independent variables		*Basic PF-model*		*Augmented PF-model*	
	Parameter	*Estimated value*[3]	*t-value*[1]	*Estimated value*[3]	*t-value*[1]
Technology variables					
Fixed capital	β_1	0.51	5.5***	0.35	3.0***
Labour input	β_2	0.63	5.9***	0.60	4.3***
Local scale effects, capital-based	β_{11}	−0.09	−3.9***	−0.09	−3.8***
Local scale effects, labour-based	β_{22}	−0.05	−1.7*	−0.08	−2.5**
Local scale effects, capital-labour interaction	β_{12}	0.06	2.4***	0.09	3.7***
Size-class dummies					
1–4 employed persons				0.13	1.0
5–9 employed persons				0.02	0.2
10–19 employed persons				0.03	0.4
20–49 employed persons				0.06	1.0
50–99 employed persons				0.01	0.2
250–499 employed persons				0.05	0.8
500–999 employed persons				−0.12	−1.3
>1,000 employed persons				−0.09	−1.0
Market-characteristics					
Within-segment competition ($SEGM_{sjk}$)	α_1			−0.06	−3.1***
Competition with non-segment firms (SR_{jk})	α_2			0.08	3.6***
Market concentration, (HHI)	α_3			−0.15	−3.6***
National policy regulation					
Product-market regulation (PMR)	α_4			0.06	1.7*
Entry costs (EC)	α_5			−0.54	−4.6***
Sector dummies[2]		Yes		Yes	
Country dummies[2]		Yes		No	
Other regression statistics					
Regression constant	α_y, λ_L	3.15	8.5***	4.49	7.5***
Number of observations		713		713	
Adjusted R^2		0.63		0.61	
Log likelihood		−176.69		−216.6	

Notes: [1] Asterisks denote the confidence interval (two-tailed) of the estimates: *** at 1% level, ** at 5% level, and * at 10% level. [2] The size reference group is size class 100–249 employed persons, the reference sector is sub-sector NACE K744, and the reference country is Ireland. [3] The use of size-class averages (based on different numbers of firm observations) could create a bias if we used Ordinary Least Squares estimation. To prevent this we apply the Weighted Least Square method, including White Heteroskedasticity-consistent standard errors.

'local effect' parameter β_{11} indicates that capital intensity has decreasing returns to scale in some size classes. Labour input also explains a large part of the variation in the productivity levels. The estimated parameter for β_2 shows that productivity *generically* increases in the number of employed persons, and hence in firm size. As one would expect in labour-intensive industries, the coefficient for labour (labour input elasticity) is higher than the one for capital.

Results for the GSF-model. The basic PF-model and its augmented variant pay no attention to the possibility that firms are heterogeneous in their input mix, and that not all of them operate on the efficiency frontier. The results of the GSF-model indicate that it is important to take firm heterogeneity and X-inefficiencies on board. The model simultaneously explains X-inefficiencies and input intensities from market-structure variables and regulation characteristics. Table 11.2 presents the results for this model.

From the estimated technology parameters and the input levels (not shown) we may conclude that the business-services industry is characterized by increasing returns to scale, once we control for the possibility of X-inefficiencies. In particular, parameters for capital inputs (β_1) and labour inputs (β_2) are substantially larger in the GSF-model than in the augmented PF-model.

The parameters for the non-linear input effect (β_{11}, β_{22} and β_{12}) are significantly different from zero, indicating that there are 'local' scale effects, specific for some size-classes. The size-class now allows us to identify the locus of these local scale effects. Small firms, up to a size of 20 employed persons, experience considerable productivity disadvantages compared to the reference size class (100–249 employed persons). The findings suggest that firms operate on different production frontiers. Recall that Figure 11.2 already suggested such a pattern prevails for a considerable part of the European business-services industry. The GSF results, however, do not confirm the hump-shaped pattern in the size-productivity relation (left panel Figure 11.2). The size-class dummies for the large size-classes turn out not to be significantly different from zero, possibly because larger firms can, on average, compensate a relatively lower labour productivity through a more efficient use of capital inputs. Scale-related productivity effects only occur up to a threshold firm size. A number of 20 employed persons appears to be the minimum efficient firm size in European business services. Beyond a size of 20 employed persons further firm growth on average yields no more significant productivity advantages, if we control for capital input.

The reasons for this minimum firm size can be related to the internal division of labour (in the spirit of Adam Smith's pin factory), human capital specialization, spreading fixed capital costs, routine development, and the Babbage principle (the possibilities for spreading managerial and other overhead costs). Further research would be necessary to assess which of these factors forms the binding constraint that defines the minimum efficient scale in business services.

Table 11.2 Estimation results for GSF-model based on pooled regression in business services (all subsectors, 11 EU-countries, reference year 1999)

Independent variables	*Parameter*	*Estimated value*[3]	*t-value*[4]
Production frontier equation			
Technology variables			
Fixed capital	β_1	0.42	6.3***
Labour input	β_2	0.67	7.3***
Local scale effects, capital-based	β_{11}	−0.08	−3.7***
Local scale effects, labour-based	β_{22}	−0.05	−2.0**
Local scale effects, capital-labour interaction	β_{12}	0.06	2.8***
Size-class dummies			
1–4 employed persons		−0.36	−5.2***
5–9 employed persons		−0.32	−4.5***
10–19 employed persons		−0.21	−3.0***
20–49 employed persons		−0.03	−0.4
50–99 employed persons		−0.01	−0.1
250–499 employed persons		−0.01	−0.1
500–999 employed persons		−0.04	−0.4
>1,000 employed persons		0.03	0.3
Sector dummies[2]		Yes	
Country dummies[2]		Yes	
X-inefficiencies equation			
Market-characteristics			
Within-segment competition ($SEGM_{sjk}$)	α_1	−0.31	−1.8*
Competition with non-segment firms (SR_{sjk})	α_2	0.15	0.9
Market concentration (HHI)	α_3	−0.03	−0.2
National policy regulation			
Product-market regulation (OECD)	α_4	0.06	0.3
Entry costs (OECD)	α_5	1.88	1.7*
Size-class dummies[2]		Yes	
Other regression statistics			
Regression constant	λ_L	3.67	13.0***
Number of observations		713	
Log likelihood		−112.13	

Notes: [1] Asterisks denote the confidence interval (two-tailed) of the estimates: *** at 1% level, ** at 5% level, and * at 10% level. [2] The size reference group is size class 100–249 employed persons, the reference sector is subsector NACE K744, and the reference country is Ireland. [3] Both equations of the GSF model have been estimated simultaneously using the Full-Information Maximum Likelifood estimation procedure (cf Kox *et al.* 2006).

While scale-related inefficiencies are primarily found at firm sizes smaller than 20 employed persons, X-inefficiencies related to suboptimal input choices may also occur at larger firm sizes. The τ-equation of the GSF-model identifies the market characteristics and regulatory environments that tend to be correlated with X-inefficiencies. Size-related market segmentation could be an important characteristic in business-services markets. The market segmentation test $|\alpha_1| > |\alpha_2|$ is satisfied.[19] The estimated parameter is significant at the 10 per cent confidence level; hence the issue warrants further research.

There is a remarkable difference from the findings of Table 11.1. Now that X-inefficiencies are taken into account, the estimated parameter for intra-segment competition (*SEGM*) has a larger value and a different sign. More intra-segment competition has a negative impact on *in*efficiencies, and hence a positive impact on labour productivity. Being in a 'crowded' size segment of the market could therefore, to some extent, compensate any scale-related inefficiencies. Consistent with this is the finding that a high level of policy-caused start-up costs for new firms (*EC*) works out positively on the incidence of X-inefficiencies, and hence negatively on the labour productivity performance. A final result is that, on average, market concentration (*HHI*) and the intensity of competition-related regulation (*PMR*) are not significant factors for explaining the incidence of X-inefficiencies.

11.5 Conclusions and some policy implications

We find clear indications for the existence of increasing returns to scale in business-services firms. The scale effects are not the same for all size classes. Throughout the EU, firms with fewer than 20 persons have significantly lower average labour productivity levels than the rest of the business-services industry. The size of 20 employed persons can be regarded as the minimum-efficient scale in European business services. Beyond that size there are no significant impacts of scale on labour productivity performance.

Likely explanatory candidates for the presence of the minimum-efficient scale size in business services are traditional drawbacks of small scale known from the literature, such as having less efficient division of labour, and having less opportunities for spreading fixed managerial costs, overhead costs, fixed human-capital costs, and fixed-capital costs. Further research could establish the reasons for the presence of the minimum-efficient scale size.

Apart from scale-related inefficiencies, we find evidence that X-inefficiencies related to input choices may occur in all size-classes. Estimation results for the generalized stochastic frontier model (GSF) indicate that X-inefficiencies caused by suboptimal input choices are affected by market characteristics and the regulatory environment of firms. In particular, we find that business-services markets may be segmented by size-class of firms. This means that firms from different size-classes on average only have weak competition with firms in other size-classes. Small firms rarely compete directly against large firms. They possibly serve different market segments, have different clients and also different types of products.

A final result is that more intra-segment competition works out positively on labour productivity of the firms in that size-class. Being in a 'crowded' size segment of the market could thus, to some extent, compensate scale-related inefficiencies. For instance, the relatively intense 'neck-and-neck' competition among small firms may to some extent both compensate their scale-related inefficiencies, for example, by reducing their non-scale inefficiencies, including suboptimal input choice. Consistent with this is the finding that a high level of policy-caused start-up costs for new firms negatively affects labour productivity performance. Higher entry barriers may weaken the stimulus for incumbent firms to be efficient.

Our results are based on cross-section analysis for one year, but we think the results warrant a more comprehensive research programme on scale-effects in European business services, using data from more years (panel data) and real micro-level data instead of size-class averages. In fact, such research is already long overdue, if we take into account that business services is one of the largest sectors in the European economy with an employment share of about 11 per cent, a value-added share of about 12 per cent in the European Union, and a 54 per cent share in EU employment growth between 1979 and 2001 (cf. Chapter 1).

Although we cannot discuss policy implications at length, there are several links between the productivity agenda in business services and government policies in EU countries. Government policies have leaned strongly towards promoting market entry by new entrepreneurs, rather than paying attention to existing scale inefficiencies. The idea was that more entry is good for competition is probably right. Entry by new business-services firm constituted was a major factor major in total EU employment growth during the 1990s. This was (partly) the result of government policies. For the future, further thought must be given to such policies before continuing on the same track. When market segmentation is indeed as important as we think it might be, new entrants will mostly compete with one another, i.e. with the other small and 'young' firms.[20] As with lobsters that try to escape the box in which they find themselves, their mutual competition means that no one escapes. They may remain in operation at a relatively inefficient firm size.

Perhaps a new balance has to be struck between upscaling in order to remove scale inefficiencies and ensuring a constant influx of new entrepreneurs. The question is whether the markets themselves will solve this issue, or whether governments have a role in assisting the market forces. With segmented markets – both within and between countries – competition may not lead automatically to more scale-efficient production sizes. Today Many national and EU policy programmes play at least lip-service to lowering administrative burdens for firms. Perhaps especially the firms below 20 employed persons should get a light administrative burden from government regulation.

This will make it easier for firms to grow beyond the present small-firm business model. In addition, the opening of markets for intra-EU competition may yield more incentives for the upscaling of business-services firms.

Notes

1. Van der Wiel, 1999, 2001; Kox, 2002, 2004.
2. We particularly focus on computer-related services (NACE K72) and Other Business Services (NACE K74). We exclude two capital-intensive branches – real estate (NACE K70) and equipment rental (NACE K71) – since the latter two branches use distinctly more fixed capital per employed person than the rest of the business services. We have also left out the data for contract-research establishments (NACE K73), since this subsector appeared to include data for university institutes where education is an unobserved side-product.
3. Cf. Christensen *et al.* (1971); Fuss and McFadden (1978); Greene (1993); Kim (1992) and Ray (1998).
4. This is done by introducing a second-order Taylor expansion and parametrizing for the quadratic effects of input use. With two inputs, capital (K) and labour (L), the partial derivatives of output with respect to both inputs are evaluated around the sample mean.
5. The cross-derivatives in (11.2) are assumed to be symmetric: $\beta_{ij} = \beta_{ji}$ *for* $i \neq j$. Note that by imposing zero restrictions on each of the coefficients $\beta_{ij}(i,j = 1,2)$ the translog production function reduces to a standard Cobb–Douglas production function.
6. The type of scale economies that prevail can be measured by adding up the derivative of output with respect to the inputs of capital, respectively labour.
7. See O'Farrell and Moffat, 1991; CSES 2001; Eustace, 2000; Kox, 2002.
8. Since we want to apply the model to cross-section data for different subsectors and countries, the normalization factor γ_{jk} is necessary to remove the impacts on the total number of firms per subsector that come from relative country size and relative sector size (within a country). Normalization makes both indicators comparable across countries and markets.
9. The test can also be put in a strong form, i.e. $\alpha_1 > \alpha_2 > 0$, but this fails in case of opposite signs. In the case of excessive entry, the average firm's market share could become smaller than minimal efficient scale, thus depressing the size segment's average productivity and producing a negative sign for one of both parameters.
10. The use of more preferable indicators of competition-intensity like the relative profit measure (cf. Boone 2000) or average price-cost margins is problematic in our case because price and cost data are difficult to obtain for European business services.
11. If branches with a high degree of product differentiation on average have higher-qualified employees this might also mean that part of their jobs consists of elements for which they are overqualified. It may thus have a negative impact on cost efficiency.
12. It turned out that other available indicators such as the national restrictions on foreign direct investment strongly correlates with other explanatory variables.
13 The errors are assumed to be i.i.d. normally distributed around mean zero, $\mu \sim N(0, \sigma_\mu^2)$, i.e. they can have positive or negative values.
14. Technically, the efficiency frontier is the set of all minimum input combinations needed to produce a particular output level. The efficiency frontier is equal to a

theoretical production function that identifies all output-maximising (or input-minimizing) combinations of inputs and output.

15. The white noise component in the error term (ω) is again assumed to be i.i.d. normally distributed around mean zero: $\varpi \sim N(0, \sigma_{\varpi}^2)$. Moreover, τ and ω are assumed to be independent: $\tau(\varpi) = \varpi(\tau) = 0$.
16. In a companion paper we show the derivation of the likelihood function for the GSF model (Kox *et al.* 2006).
17. Lacking data for the Netherlands have been compiled directly from Dutch production census data, ensuring compatibility by the use of the NewCronos aggregation method.
18. In order to avoid multicollinearity with the *SR* variable, we have calculated the *HHI* as the logarithm of summed squares of all size-class shares in a subsector's total value added.
19. The estimated parameter for α_1 is significant at the 10 per cent confidence level (2-tailed), while α_2 is not statistically significant.
20. Cf. the 'neck-and-neck' competition in Aghion and Griffith (2005).

12
Globalization and Global Sourcing in Business Services

Luis Rubalcaba and Desirée van Welsum[1]

Introduction

Most large firms contract or use business services as part of an international strategy. New technologies and liberalization of trade and investment allow their business-services provision from remote locations, thereby contributing to the globalization process. Some business services follow the clients and/or generate cross-border trade while others set up foreign subsidiaries. It is a dynamic process with repercussions on employment and value added, international trade, foreign direct investment (FDI), and service-related intangibles. Business services also play an active role in the internationalization of other sectors.

Technological developments, especially in information and communication technologies (ICTs), have increased the tradability of existing business services; they have also created new tradable business services. The expansion of the ICT-enabled trade in services allows the remote provision of services with huge potential impacts on the organization of economic activity. This trend is reinforced by codification and standardization of IT- and ICT-enabled services tasks.

The relatively recent trend of ICT-enabled business-services (BSS) globalization has generated a lot of debate centred around the issue of offshoring services. Politicians worry about the employment effect of services offshoring and there are media reports citing a wide range of numbers of jobs lost to offshoring. However, these reports tend to be based on interpretations of anecdotal evidence and are not founded on hard facts, and even the largest numbers cited tend to be small in comparison to normal annual job churning (OECD, 2004d). There are currently no official data measuring the extent of services offshoring. Services could follow delocalization trends which have existed in manufacturing for several decades. These trends may result in potential initial employment losses in the country of origin, and job creation in the country that receives the offshored services activities. But in the long run, increased productivity and efficiency should improve growth also in the country of origin and generate new employment opportunities. Furthermore, little is known about the current size and magnitude of that effect and about the substitution effects between new employment created abroad and exiting employment.

Recent works have started to consider the productivity impacts of outsourcing and offshoring of services and find a positive effect (for example, Abramovsky and Griffith, 2005; Amiti and Wei, 2006), although the phenomenon is rather complex and economic results from service offshoring depend on the different models established and 'it is hard to offer robust conclusions, especially about aggregate welfare of countries' (Markusen, 2005).

In a context of globalization, market deregulation and rapid technological developments, firms increasingly resort to new organizational forms in order to face competitive pressures. Firms can reorganize through mergers and acquisitions, joint ventures and strategic alliances, but also by sourcing activities to foreign affiliates or outsourcing them to external suppliers. By concentrating on their core comparative advantages and outsourcing other activities, firms may increase their competitiveness through cuts in labour and capital investment costs and the exploitation of economies of scale. Global sourcing may also lead to the more efficient organization of firms and allow them to share and spread risk.

Services offshoring is a recent development in ongoing globalization as services become increasingly tradable. It involves both international outsourcing (giving rise to unaffiliated trade in services) and international sourcing in foreign affiliates (giving rise to foreign direct investment and affiliated trade in services). Figure 12.1 defines the nature and scope of offshoring, or international sourcing, in terms of a matrix of location and control, viewed from the perspective of the services-using firm. Services can be supplied internally (that is, insourced) or by an external supplier (that is,

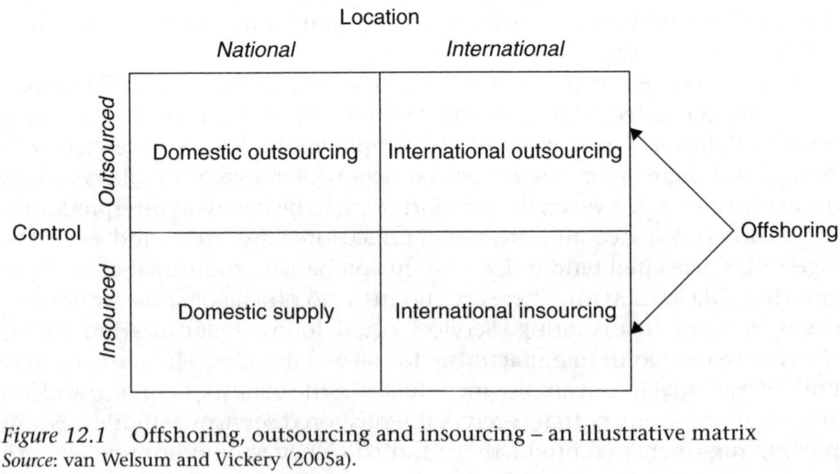

Figure 12.1 Offshoring, outsourcing and insourcing – an illustrative matrix
Source: van Welsum and Vickery (2005a).

outsourced), and they can be supplied from within the country (nationally) or from another country (internationally). Anecdotal evidence suggests that as much as two-thirds of offshoring takes place between related parties, and as much as two-thirds of outsourcing takes place domestically.

To date, most evidence of services offshoring is anecdotal and there are no official statistics measuring the extent of the offshoring phenomenon. This is complicated by important definitional and measurement problems.[2] We may derive indirect indicators from data on trade in services, FDI, and employment. However, these indirect measures are difficult to interpret and in many cases imperfect. Other indirect data sources that may inform the debate include data on trade in intermediates and input–output tables. Data from company surveys may form a useful complement. More references on methodology and measurement of current official statistics can be found in OECD (2002) and van Welsum (2003a).

The benefits of outsourcing, mainly from a domestic framework point of view, are underlined in Chapter 1. There is no firm evidence that there are substantial differences between domestic outsourcing and international outsourcing. Geographical distance may be compensated for by differences in relative costs or skills endowments if the sourcing takes place in lower-wage countries for example. Such purchasing considerations may be similar to those for domestic outsourcing, but they are combined with the gains from trade in services and the efficiency gains obtained through specialization processes.

A major focus in this chapter is on the offshoring, or international sourcing, of IT- and ICT-enabled business services such as customer services, back-office services and professional services. Technological developments and trade and investment liberalization have enabled this phenomenon, creating increased competition and efficiency pressures. The ensuing need to cut costs, combined with skills shortages in certain areas of competency (particularly in IT services) has created a self-reinforcing dynamic. Once one or two firms shifted to lower-cost locations and moved the cost/quality frontier, others had to follow. How long the dynamic will be maintained will depend on the availability of skills and relative wage and other costs. As activities are being moved offshore, relative wages will adjust and change the dynamics of the offshoring process. The extent to which activities can be moved offshore will also depend on the supply of skilled labour overseas and the potential for undertaking service activities at a distance. Quality of service concerns and data security and privacy issues may further limit the extent services will continue to globalize.[3]

The chapter is organized as follows. The first section presents an analytical framework that is useful in understanding the basic ways in which business services and globalization interact, of which service global sourcing presented in the later section is likely the most significant outcome of a wider set of interactions. The second section attempts to identify the key activities and countries leading the trends towards business-service globalization. And the third section examines the current magnitude and potential for growth of the globalization and international sourcing of IT- and ICT-enabled business services.

12.1 The contribution of business services to globalization

Business services are at the heart of the current wave of services globalization. Examples of business services include accounting, legal, management consulting, marketing, R&D, HR, computer and information services. In some cases, companies need services to increase the quality of their products and processes. In other cases companies need services that directly advise them on international strategy. Other services help in marketing abroad or allow companies to concentrate on their most important tasks.

Services may contribute to the integration of markets and to business competitiveness (Rubalcaba, 2007b; Rubalcaba and Cuadrado, 2002a). For example, when the offshoring or outsourcing of business services allows firms to focus on their core competitive activities. In some cases, services bring together entities that are geographically distant (communications, transport, tourism). In other cases, they create links between entities that are distant from economic and socio-cultural points of view (legal services, strategic consultancy, language services, fairs and exhibitions, and so on). Unlike the globalization of the production of goods, which tends to create a substitution effect between what is produced locally and what is produced globally, services benefit from a complementarity. There are services that exist because of economic, social, geographic or cultural diversity. Many services contribute to integrating markets through diversity.

One long-standing definition of a service is 'a change in the condition of a person, or of a good belonging to some economic unit, which is brought about as the result of the activity of some other economic unit, with the prior agreement of the former person or economic unit' (Hill, 1977: 318). Later additions and modifications to this definition accounted for emerging additional aspects of services, including an increasing amount of business services, and have ultimately resulted in a classification of services and of trade in services along 'modes of supply'.[4] This also forms the basis of the General Agreement on Trade in Services (see van Welsum, 2003a, for more details). Mode 1 is closest to the traditional sense of trade in goods. Karsenty (2002) presents some rough estimates of the global importance of each mode of supply, mainly using balance-of-payments categories. The largest mode of supply is mode 3, which if approximated by statistics on turnover of local establishments of multinational firms (FATS database of OECD) is worth approximately $2,000 billion. Mode 1, as approximated by commercial services exports (excluding travel), is estimated to be around $1,000 billion. Mode 2 is evaluated at around $500 billion, based on travel exports. Finally, mode 4, as approximated by the balance-of-payments category 'transferred compensation of employees', is worth around $50 billion.

Services are large promoters of what is known as 'glocalization', reflecting that one of the outcomes of services globalization is improved 'localization' or 're-localization' and better adjustment to the regulatory, economic, social and cultural parameters of the region in which companies operate (Rubalcaba, 1999). Services globalization also offers a type of globalization that may relatively better tailored to local needs. This may be facilitated in particular by the work of consultants, lawyers, trade shows or publicists when they advise on a suitable way of responding to local needs. The differentiation and competitiveness of business services is based on the capacity to distinguish those elements that combine at optimum level what should be global and what should be local.

Table 12.1 shows the principal forms in which business services contribute to the globalization of companies. It explains how business services improve access to productive inputs (capital, labour and knowledge), markets (new and old markets, brands and reputation) and locations (outsourcing, offshoring, communication). Examples of business services are provided for each case.

12.2 Major players of business service trading and recent growth within Europe

The large European countries also tend to account for most international trade and investment in business services. The big three countries – Germany, UK and France – also account for the largest share in total trade, trade in total services, trade in business services and in foreign direct investment. However, certain differences are worth noting. Germany accounts for the largest individual share in most indicators, around 19 per cent of the total EU14 considered[5] in total services trade and business services trade. However, it accounts for as much as 50 per cent of FDI. The UK takes the second place, very close to Germany in terms of both FDI and international trade. However, unlike the situation in total of services, UK business services are much stronger in international trade (16.6 per cent) than in FDI, where the figure is very low (9 per cent). France takes the second place above the UK, with 29 per cent of the total EU15. It is important to note that, taken together, the three leading countries have a much larger share in FDI (88 per cent) than in international trade (46 per cent).

Within EU15, the highest export growth and coverage rate growth over the period 1996–2003 is always for Ireland. However, strong growth also takes place for Romania, Estonia, Sweden, Spain, the UK and Portugal. Other research has shown the increasing position of Baltic States and other new EU countries in business services exports to the EU15 (OECD, 2004d; Stare and Rubalcaba, 2005).

The leading companies in business service trade and FDI are large companies. However, SMEs also play a significant role. Business services are the largest sector in the economy, but in terms of mergers and acquisitions have

Table 12.1 Why business services are important for enterprises facing globalization: The role of business services satisfying global needs

	Needs and opportunities of/for enterprises derived from globalization
Global use of inputs	Global access to capital and production of globally competitive technical innovation (e.g., Financial auxiliary services; Engineering and technical services; Tests and quality control; Research and development Design)
	Global access to labour and use of new global skills in local markets (e.g., Selection and, provision of personnel; Head hunting; Professional training; Outplacement; Temporary work)
	Access to and management of global knowledge (e.g., Computer and other ICT services; Internet and intranet services; Consultancy on information technologies and knowledge management)
	Outsourcing and offshoring to low-costs countries (e.g., High-skilled ICT services, accountancy and reporting; Low-skilled operational services, call centres)
	Transport and communication between different locations (e.g., Logistics and transport services; Communication services)
Global product markets	Access to new markets (e.g., Management consultancy; Market research; Export aid; Fairs and exhibitions; Legal services)
	Adaptation of global products into local needs & creation of new needs (e.g., Advertising and direct marketing; Public relations and press offices; Market research and management; Distributive trades; Services related to Internet: B2B, B2C, web pages)
	Global reputation (e.g., Brands and mark services; Communication services; Environmental services and CSR)

led the number of operations in the last decade (accounting for 18 per cent of all M&As between 1993 and 2003).[6] That means that, on average, some SMEs in business services are extremely dynamic, operating ICT services on a global basis. Engineering and advertising services are more prone to M&A activities than sectors such as those in professional services or facility management (Rubalcaba, 2007b).

12.3 Offshoring and globalization of business services

12.3.1 Trade in services

One way to examine the extent of offshoring using trade data would be to consider countries' imports of services (e.g. van Welsum, 2004). If a country sources services activities internationally, this should result in a return flow of imports of services. For example, van Welsum (2004) finds a clear effect of production relocation in the services sector on US imports of services. Another way is to look at exports of services (for example, Pain and van Welsum, 2004), especially of countries that are host to international sourcing activities (for example, OECD, 2004b; van Welsum and Vickery, 2005a; van Welsum and Reif, 2006a, b).

The extent of international trade in IT- and ICT-enabled business services in international trade statistics is approximated by summing the International Monetary Fund (IMF) balance-of-payments categories 'computer and information services' and 'other business services' (see OECD (2002) for details on which services are included in these categories). These data contain information on international outsourcing and international insourcing combined (see also van Welsum, 2004), although it is not possible to identify the proportion of this trade that results directly from offshoring. Data on computer and information services are not available for all countries. For some, such as India, they are included under 'other business services', along with other services.[7] The 'other business services' category may have variable shares of IT- and ICT-enabled services in different countries. Moreover, the data are reported in current USD and will be affected by currency movements.

Business services account for around 30 per cent of total services trade in EU15 (Eurostat data for 2004).[8] This provides a positive balance, a coverage rate of 1.3.[9] These 2004 figures are significant when compared to 1993. At that time, business services represented only 21 per cent (even 8 per cent in previous years) of total services trade, an increase by eight percentage points over the course of a decade. This is a result of the increasing importance of trade in computer and information services, as well as professional and miscellaneous business services. In terms of total trade (goods and services), business services represent 7.4 per cent, which is still under the expected share of the sector in trading when considering its weight in total employment and value added at around 10–11 per cent (excluding real estate; 12 per cent employment and 22 per cent value added if real estate is included). When considering EU25 the role of business services in total trade is slightly less significant.

Further examination of data on trade in services (in the categories 'other business services' and 'computer and information services' reveals that many of the countries often mentioned in the offshoring debate (for example, China, India, Ireland, and some of the Eastern European countries) have indeed experienced rapid growth of their trade in those services. However, the exports of many of these countries are growing from a low base, and many of the countries with strong export growth have also seen strong import growth (Figures 12.2 and 12.3). Furthermore, the bulk of exports of other business services and computer and information services still originates in OECD countries, although their share has declined over time, from 83.1 per cent in 1990, to 80.3 per cent in 1995 and 79.1 per cent in 2003.[10] The 20 countries that accounted for the largest value shares in 2003, as well as some other selected economies, are shown in Figure 12.3. OECD countries had the top seven shares of these services exports in 2003, with Hong Kong, China, India, Singapore and Israel, that is, the five non-OECD countries in this top 20. Nevertheless, some non-member developing economies are experiencing rapid growth in exports (Figure 12.4), although most are starting from very low levels. Only Ireland is among the ten countries with the largest share (in 2003) and the fastest growth rates (China, Denmark, India, Ireland, Israel, Spain, Sweden and the UK are both among the 20 countries with highest shares in 2003 and the fastest growth rates).

It remains, however, difficult to interpret these data and link them to different sourcing activities. It is not possible to tell what share of these exports results from international sourcing activities. Offshoring can include unaffiliated trade in services (from international outsourcing), affiliated trade (from international insourcing) and also temporary migration (mode 4 trade in services under the GATS; but temporary migration is not captured by balance of payments trade data).

12.3.2 Global FDI

FDI in services has grown rapidly and its stock now exceeds that of FDI in manufacturing in most developed countries. However, the bulk of FDI in services is in categories other than business services – such as financial services. It is difficult to know which category would be most suitable[12] to match the trade categories used in this section (other business and computer and information services), but probably the best approximation would be given by 'business activities', which can be obtained by subtracting 'real estate' from 'real estate and business activities'. Unfortunately, this breakdown is not widely available, but 'real estate' tends to account for a relatively small share of that category.

Business services represented 24 per cent of total services FDI in EU15 in 2004, most of which is covered by the aggregate category 'other business services'. In contrast, in 1996 FDI in goods for the EU15 still exceeded FDI in services, and business services still accounted for 28 per cent of the total FDI. FDI by the financial and telecommunications services over the period 1996–2004 have grown faster than FDI of business services in the EU15. Average annual growth rates between 1996 and 2004 have been very high. The boom of the 'new economy' brought huge investments in telecommunications and computer services, with greater outflows than inflows for Europe. Investment in all services grew strongly.

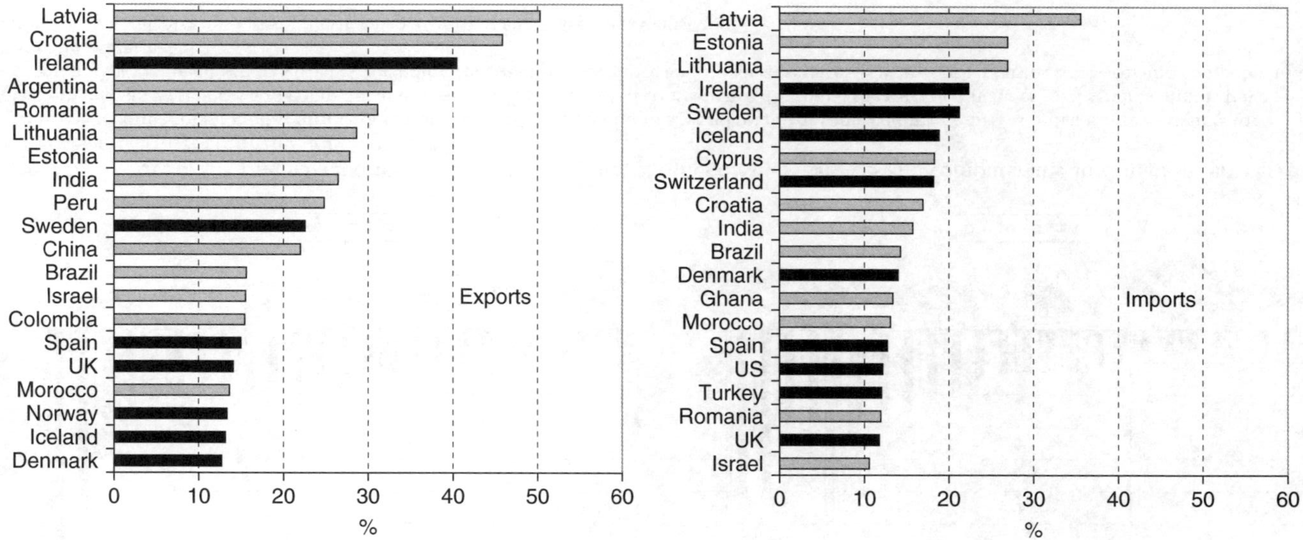

Figure 12.2 Top 20 export and import growth (other business and computer and information services) (CAGR 1995–2003)
Note: Countries in dark shading are members of the OECD.
Source: Authors' calculations based on IMF Balance of Payments Database (August 2005).

Decreasing order of the total reported value share in 2003, percentages

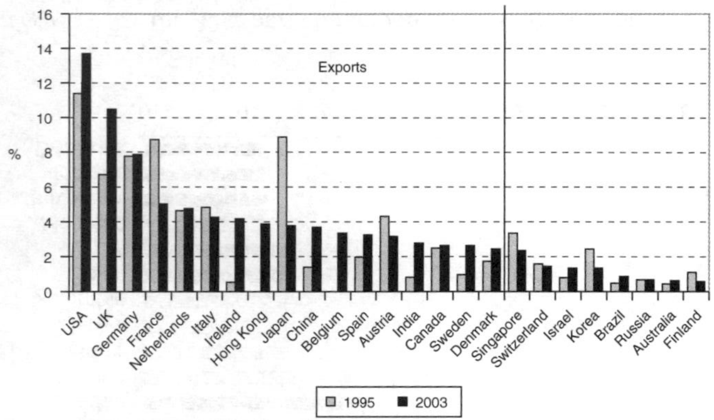

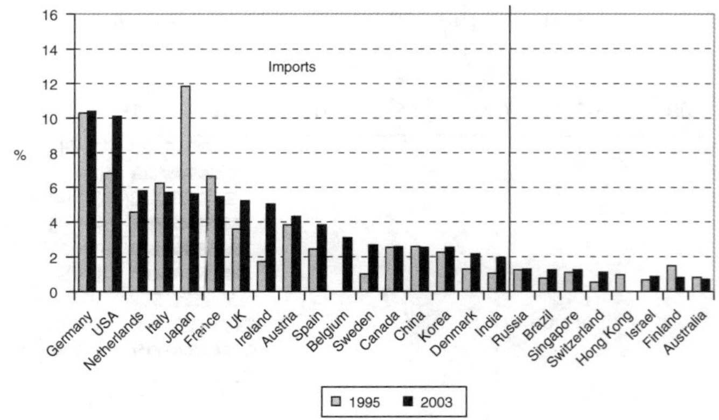

Figure 12.3 Share of the value of reported total[1] value of exports of other business services and computer and information services, top 20 and selected other countries, 1995 and 2003

Note: 1. The reported total for all countries does not necessarily correspond to a world total. For some countries, such as India, it is not possible to isolate other business services and computer and information services. As a consequence, for India, the category includes total services, minus travel, transport and government services (that is, including construction, insurance and financial services as well as other business services and computer and information services).

Source: Authors' calculations based on IMF Balance of Payments Database (August 2005).

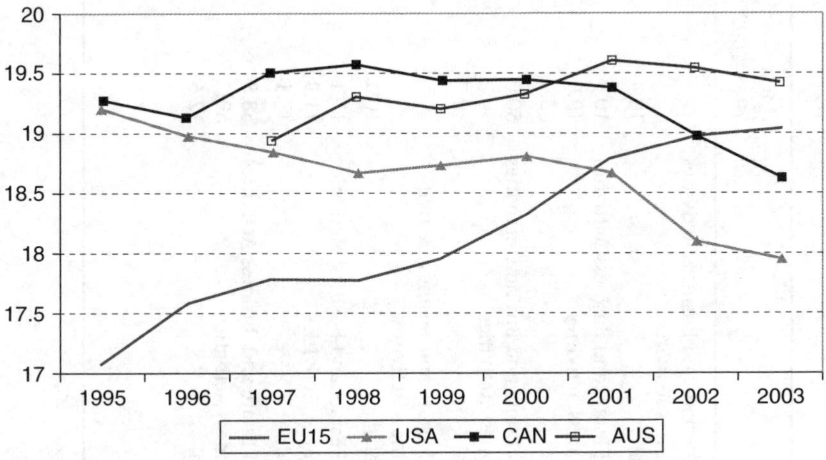

Figure 12.4 The share of employment potentially affected by ICT-enabled business services offshoring: EU15,[1] USA, Canada, and Australia 1995–2003[2] (percentages)
Notes: 1. Includes estimations where a full dataset was not available. 2. Because of classification changes, the number for the US for 2003 is an estimate. Due to differences in classifications the levels are not directly comparable.
Source: Author's calculations and van Welsum and Vickery (2005a), based on EULFS, US Current Population Survey, Statistics Canada and Australian Bureau of Statistics (2004/5).

Table 12.2 shows the average annual growth rate of the outward position in 'real estate and business activities', and 'business activities' alone where available, as well as total FDI. In most countries, except the UK, outward FDI in business services has grown more rapidly than the total FDI stock. While some of this more rapid growth can be explained by this investment position growing from a smaller base, it is also an indication of the globalization of business services.

The ongoing trends towards more global sourcing and more global provision of business services should be understood in a context which goes beyond cost factors. Although most reports state lower relative costs as the main reason for offshoring, other factors, such as quality, international business strategies to penetrate new markets, the need of flexibility and time-savings using 24-hours schemes, also play a remarkable role. There are many drivers of the international sourcing of the business services which take advantage of the new global conditions and ICTs acting as enablers (as shown in Chapter 10). Among the set of relative cost and non-cost drivers the role of employment and skills endowments in a given country is particularly important.

12.3.3 Employment and potential impact of offshoring

Labour costs and skills shortages are among the drivers of international sourcing, and much of the focus of the current media is on the offshoring of

Table 12.2 Outwards FDI growth in business services

		CAGR 1995–2002[1]			*CAGR 1995–2002*[1]
Australia	Real Estate and Business Activities	27.3	Italy	Real Estate and Business Activities	
	Business Activities			Business Activites	
	Total	8.5		Total	10.4
Austria	Real Estate and Business Activities	24.9	Netherlands	Real Estate and Business Activities	10.9
	Business Activities	23.6		Business Activities	19.9
	Total	20.2		Total	12.2
Canada	Real Estate and Business Activities		Portugal	Real Estate and Business Activities	50.0
	Business Activities			Business Activities	50.2
	Total	12.7		Total	32.7
Denmark	Real Estate and Business Activities	29.0	Sweden	Real Estate and Business Activities	
	Business Activities	31.4		Business Activities	
	Total	18.5		Total	10.4
Finland	Real Estate and Business Activities	38.4	United Kingdom	Real Estate and Business Activities	11.1
	Business Activities			Business Activities	11.9
	Total	23.0		Total	17.1
France	Real Estate and Business Activities	38.5	United States	Real Estate and Business Activities	58.8
	Business Activities	39.3		Business Activities	59.7
	Total	20.3		Total	12.6
Germany	Real Estate and Business Activities	21.6			
	Business Activities	21.9			
	Total	13.3			

Note: 1. Except Australia and Denmark, 1994–2002, and France, 1996–2002.
Source: Authors' calculations based on OECD, Direct Investment Statistics Database (2005).

services jobs so it is important to see what can be learnt from employment data – and from occupational employment data in particular. However, most data on changes in employment are anecdotal or based on model projections, which vary widely across sources and studies. These large differences illustrate the difficulty of measuring the international sourcing phenomenon as well as its impact. However, even the largest projections of jobs 'lost' to offshoring are small in comparison to annual job turnover, and most job terminations are not related to offshoring (OECD, 2004c).

While the current debate focuses on the impact on services jobs, this does not mean that services employment would necessarily contract. The offshoring phenomenon itself will also create new jobs in the domestic economy. The efficiency and productivity gains achieved through offshoring are also expected to enhance the overall growth and employment opportunities of both the domestic and host economies and should result in further job creation (see, for example, Global Insight, 2004; Mann, 2003). In addition, jobs created offshore generate demand for developed-country goods and services exports for ICT equipment and communications services immediately and, over time, for a wide range of other goods and services. At the same time, wages and prices in offshore locations are likely to rise, creating wealthier host country consumers and reducing the wage cost differential and arbitrage opportunities.

To get an idea of the 'outer limits' of employment potentially affected by offshoring, van Welsum and Vickery (2005a) calculate the share of people employed who are mainly performing the type of functions that could be potentially carried out anywhere, using data on employment by occupation by industry. The classifications were not harmonized internationally, but the same methodology and rationale were applied to the individual country data sources.[13] As this analysis was carried out in order to obtain an order of magnitude on the share of people employed performing tasks that could potentially be carried out anywhere, no additional assumptions were made as to what proportion of each occupational group was actually likely to be affected by offshoring in practice. Thus, the whole of each selected occupation was then included in the calculations.

Occupations were selected by examining detailed occupational and task descriptions on the basis of the following four criteria, or 'offshorability attributes': (i) intensive use of ICTs, (ii) an output that can be traded/transmitted enabled by ICTs, (iii) high codificable knowledge content, and (iv) no face-to-face contact requirements. The occupational selections that resulted from this exercise and the methodological background are reported in van Welsum and Vickery (2005a, b). This analysis, using occupational data for several OECD countries, suggests that around 20 per cent of total employment carries out the kinds of functions that are potentially geographically footloose as a result of rapid technological advances in ICTs and the increased tradability of services, and could therefore potentially be affected by international sourcing of IT- and ICT-enabled business services.[14] Nevertheless, as classifications are not harmonized internationally, the levels of these estimates are not directly comparable.

The evolution over time of the share of employment potentially affected by offshoring is illustrated in Figure 12.4. Even though the levels of these shares are not directly comparable, the evolution of the trends is interesting. The share of occupations potentially affected by offshoring in the EU15 increased (from 17.1 per cent in 1995 to 19.2 per cent in 2003). For Canada it was more or less flat (around 19.5 per cent) until 2001, after which it declined (to 18.6 per cent by 2003). For the USA the share declined (from 19.2 per cent in 1995 to 18.1 per cent in 2002).[15] In Australia, the share increased at first (between 1996 and 2001, except in 1999) but started to decline in 2001.

While it is difficult to draw inferences from these trends without further analysis, since the trends are affected by a multitude of factors, the evolutions shown in these trends are consistent with some casual observations on the ICT-enabled offshoring that is taking place, such as Canada serving as an offshoring location, mainly from the USA, but less so more recently as other locations, such as India, have started to emerge. Similarly, Australia possibly also experienced competition for attracting, or keeping, activities that can be sourced internationally from India and other emerging locations in the region. Thus, the declining share in the USA, Canada and Australia towards the end of the period could be consistent with the offshoring of IT-related and back-office activities (with some 'potential offshoring' having become 'actual offshoring'), for example, even though this is unlikely to account for the whole of the decline. Another possible explanation could be a differential pace of technological change with a relatively more rapid adoption and integration of new technologies, leading to relatively more jobs disappearing sooner as they become automated and/or digitized. Thus, a possible explanation for the diverging trends could be that European countries are using relatively less technology. The increasing share for Europe is compatible with an overall increase in services employment as well as the finding from surveys that European firms tend to offshore within Europe (see Millar, 2002, and Marin, 2004, for example). At least one EU country, Ireland is also a major destination country of offshoring activities from the USA (IT-related activities in particular). Other factors could also be important, for example, cyclical developments and changes in labour supply and labour quality.

The offshoring phenomenon does not necessarily have to result in a decline in services employment. Many existing services sectors have expanded, new services have emerged, and with ongoing technological developments and services trade liberalization it is likely yet more are to be created. Furthermore, with the elasticity of demand of internationally traded services greater than one (e.g. Pain and van Welsum, 2004; van Welsum, 2004; Mann, 2004), rapid growth in countries such as India and China should also lead to reinforced exports from OECD countries. The offshoring phenomenon itself will also create new jobs in the domestic economy. However, it could be that certain types of occupations will experience slower growth than they otherwise might have done.

As the trends in Figure 12.4 are expressed as shares, there are several possibilities to explain changes in these trends. For example, a decline in the share could be explained by an absolute decline in the number of people employed in the categories identified as being potentially affected by offshoring. Alternatively, it could be that this selection of occupations is growing at a slower pace than total employment. The relatively slower growth of employment potentially affected by offshoring is what in fact explains most of the declines observed in the trends, with the exception of the USA, where the absolute number of people employed in the categories identified as potentially affected by offshoring has declined in some cases (see van Welsum and Reif, 2006b). These observations would therefore tend to support the idea that offshoring may lead to slower growth of employment in occupations potentially affected by offshoring and not necessarily to actual declines in employment.

Factors statistically associated with changes in the share of employment potentially affected by ICT-enabled offshoring of business services are examined in van Welsum and Reif (2006a, b). They find that exports and net FDI are among the key factors that have a positive association with the share of this kind of employment in total employment. They do not find evidence of a negative association with imports of business and computer and information services. Other key factors found to be positively associated with the share of employment potentially affected by offshoring are the comparative size of the service sector, the growing share of ICT investment in total fixed investment, and human capital.

12.4 Concluding remarks and policy implications

Business services play an important role in the wave of current globalization. They contribute to international service flows and they have contributed to the transition from a 'simple' international economy, where trade and transactions occurred on a bilateral and cross-border basis, to a more complex global economy, where multilateral international activities arise. However, it may not always be obvious exactly where and between which parties transactions have occurred (especially since in the case of services that are traded with the help of ICTs there are no physical border crossings like in the case of trade in goods), where inputs and outputs are obtained and distributed in any part of the world and where enterprises start to behave as truly global enterprises. Business services contribute to global access to factors of production (capital, labour, productive inputs and technology), but also to access to new markets. Business services contribute to increased competitiveness when they establish the right link between what should be local and what should be global. Competitive enterprises need competitive business services to globalize and 'glocalize' successfully, in order to fully achieve and exploit comparative advantages.

However, business services have not only contributed to the emergence of the global economy. They have also become more global themselves and therefore contribute directly to international flows. Business services have become global through the four GATS modes of international trade in services, but other factors have also played an important role. The role of intangible resources (reputation, brands, and knowledge transfer) and formal or informal international networking are essential in understanding the process of business-service globalization (Rubalcaba and Cuadrado, 2002b) and further research is needed on this topic.

As measured by balance-of-payments statistics, international trade in services remains constant at around 20 per cent of total trade. This shows that services globalize also in ways other than what is measured in these statistics. There are also other factors such as non-tariff barriers, which are generally thought to be especially important in the case of services (for example, standards, certification, qualifications), as elaborated in Chapter 13 of this book. FDI is another means through which services globalize, and for some services a natural presence is a prerequisite for any trade in services to take place at all. However, recent trends towards more integration of ICTs in services and increasing trade and investment liberalization are enchancing the tradability of existing services and are also creating new tradable services (See Rubalcaba, 2007b).

Despite the recent widespread attention given to services globalization and offshoring of services, little is known about the extent of this phenomenon, or the extent to which it is related to other economic and structural developments. In particular, an explicit link is often made between trade, the activities of multinational firms and changes in employment, but this has not been founded on any solid quantitative evidence. In the absence of any formal and official data measuring the extent of services globalization and offshoring, this chapter has examined three indirect measures: data on trade in services, FDI and occupational employment.

Services trade data show that trade in services has been growing rapidly, and that many of the countries frequently cited as beneficiaries of offshoring have seen rapid growth of their exports of other business and computer and information services. However, many have also seen rapid growth of imports of these services. The FDI data show that even though FDI in business services activities accounts for only a relatively small share of total FDI, it has been growing rapidly, which could be a further indication of the pace of services globalization. The analysis of occupational employment data for selected OECD countries sought to determine the share of total employment that could potentially be affected by the international sourcing of IT- and ICT-enabled services. It suggested that close to 20 per cent of total employment could potentially be affected by offshoring.

Thus far there is no evidence to suggest that the ICT-enabled offshoring of services has led to a decline in employment in the occupations potentially affected in the OECD countries analysed at the aggregate level. However, different types of occupations are likely to be affected in different ways and sectoral and occupational shifts are likely to take place, which will imply some adjustment costs in the short run. However, it is expected that in the long run the benefits of services offshoring may outweigh the costs. Policy reactions to services offshoring should reflect the positive aspects. This includes remaining commitments to trade and investment liberalization and implementing policies that contribute to the overall competitiveness of the economy and improve the macroeconomic framework, in particular those policies that contribute to a sound investment climate, and those policies that improve the skills base and flexibility of the workforce. In Europe, this is particularly important in the context of the many existing obstacles to trade and investment within the EU frontiers and the urgent need for further market integration (see Chapter 13) in the context of the Lisbon Strategy. Europe will never become more competitive if protectionism and defensive policies are taken against trade liberalization, globalization and service offshoring. Positive strategies to reinforce competitive positions and to face global challenges should be considered more appropriate.

Notes

1. The opinions expressed and arguments employed herein are those of the author and do not necessarily reflect the official views of the Organisation (OECD) or of the governments of its member countries.
2. There are many challenges involved in tracking offshoring activities. Difficulties arise from definitional and data collection complications and because there are a number of modes of offshoring. For example, if international sourcing implicitly refers to activities that were previously carried out in the home country and within the firm (in the case of outsourcing), this raises the question of 'when outsourcing stops being outsourcing', that is, 'When does it become just another intermediate purchase?'
3. We do not assess the impacts of service offshoring on productivity (see, for example, Amiti and Wei, 2006; Abramovsky and Griffith, 2006), nor do we here intend to model globalization of services (e.g. Markusen, 2005).
4. Mode 1: cross-border supply; Mode 2: consumption abroad; Mode 3: commercial presence (through local subsidiaries); Mode 4: presence of natural persons.
5. EU15 minus Belgium (excluded because of no enough available data).
6. Masi database, European Commission, DG Economy.
7. For India, the category 'other business services' includes all services except travel, transport and government services. However, Indian firms are now extensively exporting ICT-enabled services and business process services and the remaining services included in the category are likely to be small in comparison. Furthermore, data on overseas revenues from annual reports of top Indian export firms show patterns similar to the IMF data.

8. Royalties and license fees are not included. Business services cover the activities defined in the NACE classification under codes 70, 71, 72, 73 and 74.
9. The coverage rate (or ratio) is defined as exports divided by imports.
10. The share of some services-exporting countries may be understated as they may not have very good data on trade in services to report to the IMF, which will bias their actual share downwards. Furthermore, other countries that export services may not be members and report to the IMF.
11. See van Welsum (2003a) for a discussion. The quality of the data may be variable and there can be very large discrepancies between reported exports and imports (see, for example, OECD, 2004b; Chapter 2; GAO, 2005). Some of the problems with data on trade in services can be explained by factors such as reporting difficulties, collection methods (company surveys rather than customs records for goods), varying timelines of implementing Balance of Payments (BPM5) methodology and rules, the treatment of certain services categories, and the complexity of the structures and operations of multinational firms (OECD, 2004b).
12. 'Real estate and business activities' represents section K of ISIC 3 (minus if available 'of which real estate'), but the connection is loose between service products and service activities determined for large enterprises. Business services can be provided internally within multinationals with main activities elsewhere – for example, in manufacturing.
13. The European data are Labour Force Survey data provided by Eurostat. The occupational classification system in those data is the ISCO – International Standard Classification of Occupations – and NACE – the industrial classification system of the European Union – is used for sectoral classification. For the USA, data from the Current Population Survey were used. The Current Population Survey collects information on both the industry and the occupation of the employed and unemployed. However, beginning with data from January 2003, the 1990 Census Industrial Classification System was replaced by one based on the North American Industry Classification (NAICS), and the 1990 Census Occupational Classification was replaced by one derived from the US Standard Occupational Classification (SOC). Further information is available on the website of the US Bureau of Labour Statistics at: http://www.bls.gov/opub/hom/pdf/homch1.pdf (accessed November 2004): chapter 1: Labour Force Data derived from the Current Population Survey. For Canada Labour Force Data provided by Statistics Canada were used. The occupational classification is in SOC91. For Australia data from the Labour Force Survey provided by the Australian Bureau of Statistics were used. The occupational classification is in Australian Standard Classification of Occupations (ASCO) second edition.
14. Other studies have taken a similar approach. For example, Bardhan and Kroll (2003) produced estimates of 11 per cent of total employment in the USA in 2001 as having been potentially affected by offshoring, and Forrester Research, as reported by Kirkegaard (2004) up to 44 per cent of total employment. The differences in these estimates can be explained by the selection criteria that are applied to the occupational data. Thus, Bardhan and Kroll (2003) only included occupations in which at least some offshoring was already know to have taken place yielding a more conservative estimate of the share of employment potentially affected, whereas the Forrester study used less detailed occupational categories resulting in a larger estimate of jobs potentially affected.
15. The number for 2003 (just under 18 per cent) is an estimate as both the occupational and industrial classification systems were changed in 2003 in the USA.

13
The European Internal Market for Business Services: No Open Borders Yet

Henk Kox and Arjan Lejour

Introduction

A cornerstone of the European Union (EU) is the principle that goods, services, capital and labour can move freely between the member states. The internal market for goods seems to function well, following the implementation of the Single Market programme in 1992. That is, however, not yet the case for the internal market in services. Service providers often experience obstacles if they want to export their services to other EU member states, or when they want to start a subsidiary company in another EU member state. The European Commission (2002a) concluded that these impediments are to a considerable degree caused by national regulations for service exporters, foreign investors in services, and for the service product itself. Such regulations are mostly made for domestic purposes without much regard for the interests of foreign service providers. The result, however, is a European maze of different regulations for firms that provide their services in other EU countries. Especially the markets for knowledge-intensive services – among which many business services – still tend to be highly regulated in national markets, with strong differences in regulation.

In this chapter we conduct an empirical investigation of the effects of the regulatory obstacles for bilateral trade and direct investment in business and other commercial services between EU member states. We quantify how the strictness of regulations and the inter-country variety in regulations affect the operations of the internal market for services.

In section 13.1 we provide descriptive data to characterize the level of international integration in the European market for business services. In section 13.2 we discuss the nature of regulatory obstacles for intra-European trade and direct investment in business services. Section 13.3 quantifies the effects of the regulatory obstacles for bilateral trade, and in section 13.4 the same is done for bilateral direct investment. In section 13.5 we illustrate the policy relevance of our findings by applying them to simulate the effects of the 2004 European Commission proposals for a Services Directive. This directive is to reduce the effects of national regulation differences in the internal market for services.

Table 13.1 Growth rates of intra-EU trade in business services compared to other services trade between developing countries (OECD), 1999–2003

	Average annual growth 1999–2003 (%)		
	Exports between OECD countries	*EU exports to other OECD countries*	*EU exports to other EU member states*
Total services	7.9	11.1	13.1
of which:			
Travel & tourism	4.9	7.2	10.4
Transport & storage	5.9	8.0	8.7
Banking services	13.7	14.6	19.2
Insurance	16.4	15.1	4.0
Business services	3.3	2.9	−0.2
of which:			
Computer services	−3.5	−3.6	−9.5
Other business services	4.3	4.9	3.6

Source: CPB consistent bilateral services trade matrices, developed on the basis of OECD data and the GTAP method for consistency of bilateral trade flows. Annual data in current US dollars. EU data have been calculated for EU25.

13.1 The EU internal market in business services: some data

Whereas about 70 per cent of EU employment is in services, these industries are still to a large extent inward-oriented. Service exports still represents only a very modest one-fifth of total intra-EU trade. Between 1992 – when the EU Single Market programme began – and 2001, the intra-EU share of total European services trade remained stable. Business services accounted for about one-third of the total European services trade in 2001, and a little bit more than half of it was intra-EU trade.[1] The most important components of business services trade are the *Computer-related services*, the *Legal, accounting and consulting services* and the *Architectural and engineering services*. Table 13.1 shows that intra-EU trade in business services recently has stagnated, compared to overall services trade in the EU, and also in comparison with total services trade between OECD countries. Especially trade in computer-related services experienced a setback after strong growth in the preceding decade. But *Other business services* also displayed a relative trade stagnation. Business-cycle effects may have played a role, but other services sectors apparently were less affected.

Across the European Union there are substantial differences between member states with regard to the export orientation of the business-services industry. For a trade-openness indicator we use the value of exports of a service sector divided by its total production (value added). Table 13.2 shows that the export orientation of business-services firms is low in most of the countries. The sector is relatively trade-oriented in the Netherlands, the UK and, to a smaller extent, Spain. Business-services firms in France, Germany and Italy appear to be

Table 13.2 Trade openness (exports as % of domestic value added), selected EU countries, 2001

	France	*Germany*	*Italy*	*Netherlands*	*Spain*	*UK*
Business services	5.8	5.3	7.4	20.8	10.7	15.8
PM, for comparison:						
Transport, communication	20.4	17.7	9.2	70.8	13.1	20.2
Finance and insurance	3.2	7.8	2.2	4.0	6.4	52.6
Personal services	3.1	0.4	1.3	4.1	2.4	3.4

Source: OECD (2003c, 2004e), and own calculations.

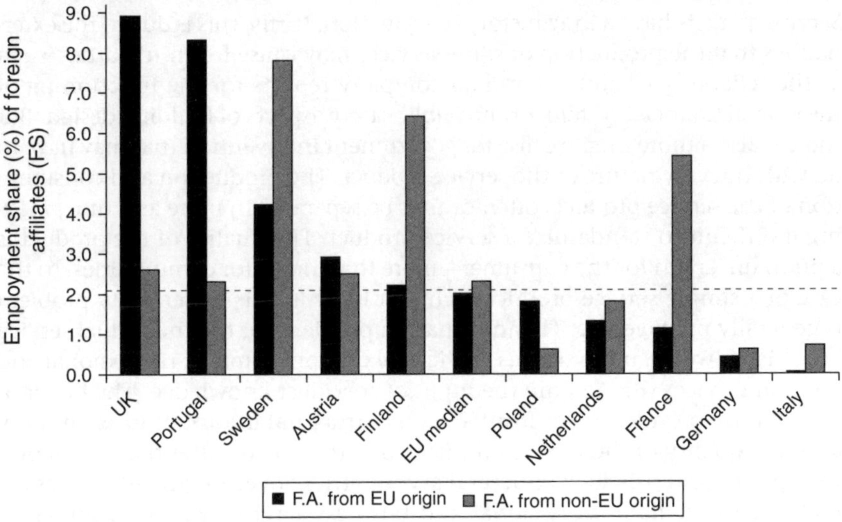

Figure 13.1 Share of foreign affiliates (FA) in domestic business-services employment, selected member states, 1997–1998

Note: Majority-owned foreign affiliates in 'Business activities', of which business services forms the largest part.

Data: calculated from OECD FATS database and OECD STAN database (Kox *et al.* 2004a).

rather inward-oriented. Since the UK and Spain are also relatively large countries, the inward orientation cannot only be caused by the large-country effect (domestic market relatively more important).

Export is only one of the forms in which national business-services markets may open-up for firms from other EU member states. The other major form of internationalization is through setting up a local subsidiary in a foreign market. The degree to which EU business-services markets are open for to such competition can be measured by the share of foreign affiliates (FA) in domestic business-services employment. Figure 13.1 shows again that there are considerable differences between EU member states in this respect. In several large EU countries (France, Germany, Italy) foreign firms from other EU countries account for just a small section of employment, whereas in the UK and Sweden this is much higher.

This short overview indicates that EU markets for business services still remain very inward-oriented. Exposure to competition from other EU member states is weakly developed. The differences between countries suggest that policy differences could well be part of the explanation for this. We set out to explore this.

13.2 National regulatory obstacles for the Internal Market

Service markets have a long history of regulation. Partly, this is due to the externalities that the production of some services may cause for third parties, such as the reliability of audited annual company reports for the functioning of the overall financial system, or the public safety aspects of building design. But there is also a more innate cause for government intervention that may have to do with the very nature of the service product. The production and consumption of the service products often cannot be separated in place and time, making it difficult to standardize a service product. The quality of the product is a priori uncertain for the consumer – more than holds for commodities. In the case of a simple service product such as a haircut, this uncertainty problem is generally manageable. The information problem for the individual service buyer is, however, more serious in the case of more complex professional and medical services that require the input of specialist knowledge. The buyer of such service products is confronted with a structural information asymmetry as to the quality of the service product, sometimes even after the transaction took place. To repair such structural asymmetries government authorities are inclined to regulate professional and business services where information asymmetry may be relevant, even if the services are mainly supplied to companies. As shown in Box 1, many of such regulations for service providers affect fixed costs of service firms.

The fact that a national service market is regulated is not in itself an important barrier to international services trade. This can be shown by a little thought experiment. Suppose that all countries have the same type of regulation – for instance, a qualification requirement for providers producing a particular service product. Since qualification costs are mainly fixed costs, it would cost an exporting firm a one-off effort to comply with the qualification criteria. Once having incurred these fixed costs, it could allow the firm to reap economies of scale by expanding its market into additional EU member states.

However, at the present time there is no such uniform system of regulation for service markets. Countries often have little confidence in the quality of each other's legal regimes and are reluctant to adapt their own regimes where necessary to facilitate cross-border activities. The result is that each authority

Box 1 Examples of national regulations for services providers that affect fixed costs

- Firm start-up licenses and associated authorisation requirements.
- Service-providing personnel must have locally recognised professional qualifications (may necessitate re-qualification).
- Obligatory membership of local professional association.
- Owners or managers of service-providing firm must have local residence or nationality
- Firms must have a specific legal form.
- Requirement that service providers have nationally recognised liability insurance or professional indemnity insurance.
- All service activities in export destination country fully subject to regular administrative and tax procedures.
- Limitations on inter-professional co-operation or on the variety of services provided by one firm (may require unbundling)
- Temporary service personnel from origin country subject to rules of the social security system of the destination country
- Impediments for material inputs, suppliers and personnel from origin country (necessitates search for new local suppliers)

Source: European Commission (2002a).

within the European Union uses its own system of quality safeguards to protect services buyers. That could perhaps be fine in an autarkic system, but it is certainly a great nuisance in a situation with international trade. Service exporters are confronted with different regulations and requirements, leading to additional costs when the firms want to do business in other EU member states. These costs can be a prohibitive barrier for entering export markets.[2]

Moreover, due to the fact that these fixed qualification costs are specific for that national market, the costs cannot be spread out over production that is destined for other EU markets. The consequence is that the regulation heterogeneity limits intra-European economies of scale. Figure 13.2 pictures these effects for a service provider who subsequently enters a number of EU export markets. The presence of national qualification requirements gives rise to country-specific fixed transaction costs for the service exporter. Implicitly, the shaded area in Figure 13.2 shows – from the perspective of the exporting firm – the cost savings of a system that allows firms to achieve more economies of scale in dealing with regulation requirements. Qualification requirements and associated costs for legal and other assistance are mostly independent of firm size. Hence, the market-entry deterring effect will be

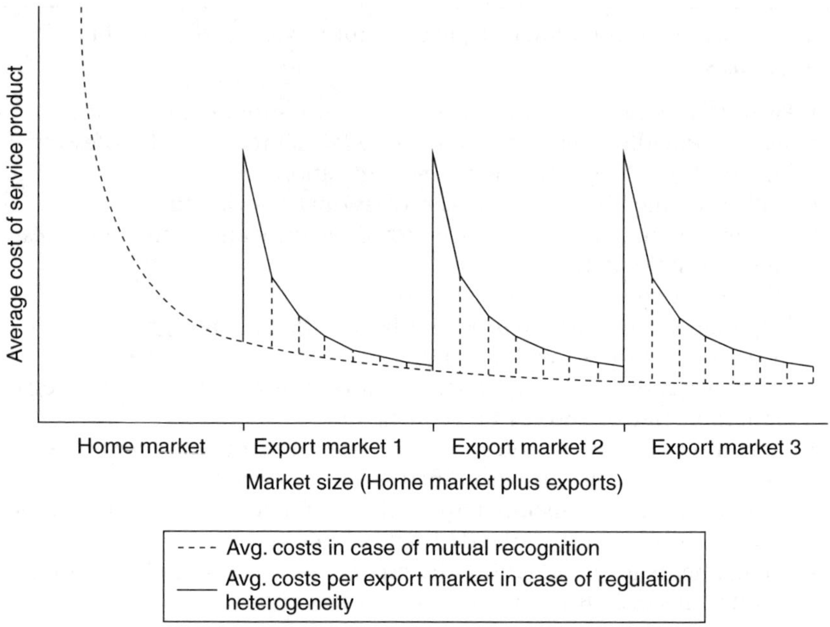

Figure 13.2 Cost effect of regulation heterogeneity in the EU internal market

strongest for small and medium-sized firms. They form the large majority of service providers.

In a survey among a large number of business service firms in the EU, 44 per cent of the firms mentioned costs as a 'very important' barrier to setting up a local operation in other countries (CSES 2001: 43). Those firms that were able to estimate the size of the set-up costs estimated the latter to be of the order of six months, sales proceeds (ibid.: 191). Elsewhere the European Commission (2002a) states:

> Evidence collected from SMEs and SME-supporting organisations suggests that many SMEs back off after initial inquiries about administrative requirements and procedures because they feel they do not have the necessary resources to deal with the current complexity. Such agencies report that micro enterprises in particular were easily dissuaded from engaging in cross-border activities.

Not only service providers are hampered by the heterogeneity in regulatory regimes. Regulation heterogeneity suppresses foreign competition and the influx of foreign service providers with new products and innovative working methods. It implicitly restricts the choice possibilities for domestic firms that want to purchase business services. The domestic price of business services will be higher than necessary (compared to the open-borders case). In the case of producer services, it leads to higher input prices for EU-based firms. Ghellinck *et al.* (1996) found that intra-EU sectoral price differences were largest for the services sector; they attributed this to the existence of non-tariff barriers that effectively fragment intra-EU services markets.

Policy heterogeneity has many dimensions, and does not easily lend itself to a quantitative analysis, let alone in an internationally comparative context. In order to estimate the effect of differences in regulation on international trade and investment in services, we developed a new index for bilateral policy heterogeneity for product-market regulation. As a basic data source we use the OECD International Regulation database, fed by official inputs from governments of OECD member states. It is by far the most detailed and structured dataset on national differences in product-market regulation proving information on hundreds of economic policy items (Nicoletti *et al.* 2000). We made a selection by removing all items that were either too industry-specific, too general or irrelevant for service markets. We preserved 183 detailed aspects of product market regulation, all of a more or less general nature, or at least representative for a country's overall product market regulation approach in commercial services (cf. Kox *et al.* 2004b: annex 1).

Our index for bilateral regulatory heterogeneity builds upon detailed pairwise comparisons between individual countries for specific aspects of product market regulation, regarding both the form and the contents of the regulation. For each item in the cleaned-up database we assess whether two countries are identical or not. It yields information of a binary nature: when the two countries differ in that particular regulation item we assign a value of 1, and when there is no difference we assign the value of 0 to the regulation heterogeneity index. The results per item are aggregated for all relevant items per country pair. The value of the composite indicator ranges between 1 in the case of complete dissimilarity and 0 in the case of identical product-market regulations. The average bilateral policy heterogeneity is lowest between Denmark and Ireland (0.26) and highest between the UK and Poland (0.70). Full data on average bilateral policy heterogeneity are available in Kox and Lejour (2006).

The impact of regulatory heterogeneity on trade may differ by policy area. We have therefore decomposed the overall heterogeneity index into five specific policy areas, following the system of the OECD regulation database. The five sub-domains of product-market regulation are: *barriers to competition*; *administrative barriers for start-ups; regulatory and administrative opacity; explicit barriers to trade and investment;* and *state control*. Disaggregation by policy area allows us to test in which policy areas the international regulatory heterogeneity has its largest trade impact on services.

13.3 Quantifying the role of policy heterogeneity as a fixed-cost trade barrier

We investigate the impact of international regulatory heterogeneity on international trade in business and other commercial services in the context of a gravity model. This model is a 'workhorse' of international trade theory. Helpman and Krugman (1985) and Bergstrand (1989) have shown that the model can be derived from a trade model with differentiated goods and monopolistic competition. Deardorff (1998) demonstrated that it can also be consistent with the Heckscher–Ohlin trade theory. Anderson and Van Wincoop (2004) have recently generalized these findings on the applicability of the gravity model.

Numerous studies have applied the gravity model to total trade or manufacturing trade. Its application to bilateral trade in services is only of recent date.[3] Nicoletti *et al.* (2003) include regulation-intensity variables. They find that a higher regulation level in a country negatively affects bilateral service trade. They only consider the *intensity* level of a country's product-market regulation, so that policy *heterogeneity* between the partner countries is an unobserved variable that may at least partly explain their results. In our application the basic gravity model is augmented with regulation variables, both the intensity level and the bilateral heterogeneity of product-market regulation. In our specification of the gravity model bilateral trade in commercial services is explained by GDP in the country of origin, GDP in the country of destination, physical distance, language distance, and policy variables. The tested gravity equation reads:

$$\begin{aligned}\ln(TRD_{ij}) = {} & \beta_0 + \beta_1 \ln(GDP_i) + \beta_2 \ln(GDP_j) + \beta_3 \ln(DIS_{ij}) + \beta_4 LAN_{ij} \\ & + \beta_5 PMR_i + \beta_6 BEN_j + \sum_k \beta_{7k} HET_{ijk} + \beta_8 D_{00} + \beta_9 D_{01} + \varepsilon_{ij} \end{aligned} \quad (13.1)$$

TRD represents the bilateral exports between region *i* and *j*. The basic explanatory variables are: GDP in the exporting region *i*, GDP in the importing region *j*, and geographical distance (*DIS*) and language distance (*LAN*) between those regions. The level variables are all expressed in logarithms. The added policy variables are: *PMR* represents the level of product-market regulation in the country of origin *i*, and *BEN* the barriers to entrepreneurship in the country of destination *j*, while *HET* represents regulation-heterogeneity indicators for each pair of countries. The suffix *k* represents the five sub-domains in regulation heterogeneity. Year dummies for the year 2000 (D_{OO}) and 2001 (D_{O1}) are added to control for possible time effects. In some of the regressions we also controlled for country-specific fixed effects. The inclusion of the regulation level also allows us to test for the hypothesis that a low level of regulation in home markets has a positive effect on the competitiveness of its service exporters in the world market (e.g. Porter 1990).

Data. Data on bilateral trade in business services between EU member states are not available, so we have to move up to a higher aggregation level in the trade data. We use the data 'Other commercial services': commercial services without transport, without tourism, without government services. Business services form by far the largest component of Other commercial services. Another important component is formed by financial services. The bilateral trade data are from the OECD trade statistics (OECD 2003c) for the period 1999–2001. We have focussed on those countries that were EU members in that period. In case of multiple and conflicting reporting we choose the data of the most reliable reporting countries for our dataset. For the EU countries with missing data we took the data as reported by their bilateral partners. In this way, we only miss bilateral trade data between the countries Denmark, Greece, Ireland, Spain and Sweden. Trade data for 2000 and 2001 are corrected for nominal differences caused by US dollar inflation. GDP data are from the World Bank Development Indicators dataset, and distance data from CEPII (Gaulier *et al.* 2003). The language data are based on linguistic differences between languages, derived from the place of the language on the language classification tree (Belot and Ederveen 2005). Data on the relative intensity of product-market regulation are drawn from the OECD summary indicators for the relative strictness intensity of each country's product market regulation (cf. Nicoletti *et al.* 2000). We constructed the data on bilateral regulatory heterogeneity indicators based upon OECD International Regulation Database for 1998. We refrained from using the 2003 update of these data, because our trade data refer to 1999–2001, and since it is reasonable to expect a time lag before the actual degree of policy heterogeneity is fully taken into account by service exporters. Therefore, we preferred to use data on the degree of policy heterogeneity that prevailed in 1998.

Results. We test the augmented gravity model by ordinary least-squares (OLS) estimation, with and without fixed effects, and by the full-information maximum likelihood (FIML) procedure. The regression results for bilateral trade are summarized in Table 13.3. They will be discussed subsequently, starting with the OLS results.

The OLS results in Table 13.3 show that the estimated coefficients of the basic gravity model are significant, have plausible magnitudes and the expected signs. The market size (GDP) coefficient for the origin country is higher than that for the destination country. The estimated parameters for physical distance and language distance have about the same size, which may be specific for services, because face-to-face communication tends to be more important than for trade in goods. The language variable may also pick up non-regulation trade barriers such as cultural differences. How do the policy variables affect bilateral services trade? The level of product-market regulation in the origin country (PMR) has a significant negative impact on bilateral trade. This is in line with the Porter hypothesis: regulation shields off the home market, and

Table 13.3 Regression results: explaining bilateral trade in other commercial services, EU 14 countries, 1999–2001

	Estimation method				
Gravity variables	*OLS [1)]*	*OLS fixed effects origin country*	*OLS fixed effects destination*	*FIML [2)] DM origin + fixed effects*	*FIML [3)] DM destination + fixed effects*
Ln GDP Origin	0.83*** (0.03)		0.83*** (0.03)	0.83*** (0.04)	
Ln GDP Destination	0.67*** (0.03)	0.70*** (0.03)			0.88*** (0.04)
Ln Distance	−0.76*** (0.07)	−0.71*** (0.07)	−0.82*** (0.07)	−0.85*** (0.09)	−0.85*** (0.09)
Language distance	−0.69*** (0.15)	−0.68*** (0.15)	−0.64*** (0.15)	−0.71*** (0.22)	−0.71*** (0.22)
Regulation level					
Product market regulation Origin	−0.33*** (0.07)		−0.37*** (0.07)	−0.34*** (0.09)	
Barriers for entrepreneurship Destination	0.08 (0.05)	−0.08 (0.05)			−0.03 (0.07)
Regulation heterogeneity					
Heterogeneity, administrative barriers for start ups	0.07 (0.26)	0.27 (0.25)	0.30 (0.25)	0.35 (0.36)	0.35 (0.36)
Heterogeneity, barriers to competition	−3.67*** (0.37)	−2.64*** (0.39)	−3.21*** (0.40)	−3.10*** (0.55)	−3.10*** (0.55)
Heterogeneity, regulatory and administrative opacity	−0.50*** (0.23)	−0.78*** (0.24)	−0.40* (0.24)	−0.23 (0.33)	−0.23 (0.33)
Heterogeneity, state control	−0.14 (0.40)	−0.00 (0.40)	0.31 (0.40)	0.74 (0.58)	0.74 (0.58)
Heterogeneity, barriers to trade and investment	−1.31*** (0.23)	−0.97*** (0.25)	−0.80*** (0.25)	−0.86*** (0.30)	−0.86*** (0.30)
Year dummy 2000	0.11 (0.08)	0.04 (0.07)	0.05 (0.07)	0.01 (0.10)	0.01 (0.10)
Year dummy 2001	0.22*** (0.08)	0.13** (0.07)	0.15*** (0.07)	−0.01 (0.10)	−0.01 (0.10)
Constant	−5.81*** (0.90)				
Country dummies		origin, significant	destination, significant	destination, significant	origin, significant
Number of observations:	481	481	481	481	481
Adjusted R-squared	0.85	0.87	0.87	0.70	0.61

Note: 1. Absolute value of standard error in brackets. Code: *** = coefficient significant at 1% confidence level; ** = coefficient significant at 5% confidence level; * = coefficient significant at 10% confidence level. 2. Full Information Maximum Likelihood (FIML), applying simultaneous estimation of equations for origin and destination countries. All bilateral variables are transformed as deviations from their individual country-wise mean (DM), further explained in the main text.

hampers the international competitiveness of domestic service providers, thus reducing their export possibilities. Interestingly, we found that the regulation level in the destination country (*Barriers to entrepreneurship*) has no significant effect. Three of the indicators for bilateral regulatory heterogeneity are statistically significant and have a substantial negative impact on bilateral services trade. The areas for which this holds are, in order of importance: *Barriers to competition, Explicit barriers to trade and investment,* and *Regulatory and administrative opacity*. Bilateral policy heterogeneity in two other regulation areas (*State control* and *Administrative barriers for start-up firms*) appears not to have a statistically significant impact. Of the time dummies only the one for 2001 is significant.

We check for the possibility that the coefficients of the explanatory variables pick up the effects of unobserved country variables by introducing fixed effects (country dummies) in the OLS regressions. The second and third data columns of Table 13.3 represent the regression results with fixed effects.[4] The country dummies replace the regression constant. The parameter estimates of most heterogeneity variables become slightly smaller, but the pattern of results is otherwise unchanged. After correcting for period effects (time dummies) and country effects (dummies for origin and destination country), there is still the possibility that unobserved country-pair effects affect the results. An excessive loss of degrees of freedom prevents us from including dummies for all country-partner pairs. We solve this by transforming variables as deviations from their individual mean (hence: DM).[5] For each destination country this data transformation highlights the differences between origin countries, and for each origin country it highlights the differences between destination countries. We get two equations for bilateral exports, one from the origin perspective and one from the destination perspective. The 'origin' equation expresses all bilateral variables as deviations from their values for the average origin (=export) country. Say Z_{kj} is a bilateral variable of equation (13.1). Its DM-transformed equivalent in the 'origin' equation becomes:

$$\Delta_k Z_{kj} = Z_{kj} - \frac{1}{I}\sum_{i=1}^{I} Z_{ij} \tag{13.2}$$

in which I and J represent the number of countries for origin and destination. If Z represents exports from country k to j the transformed variable $\Delta_k z_{kj}$ indicates the exports of country k to country j in deviation of the average exports to country j. In the same way, bilateral imports and all bilateral explanatory variables in the 'destination' equation are expressed as deviations from their values for the average destination (=import) country.

After transforming all bilateral variables in this way, we estimate the two equations simultaneously by the full-information maximum likelihood (FIML) procedure. The advantage of the transformed variables is that the origin-specific unobserved effects are accounted for in the origin equation. At the same time we can add explicit country-dummies to take account of the unobserved effects for the destination countries. Similarly, in the destination equations the destination-specific unobserved effects are accounted for by the transformation, and the origin-specific unobserved effects are evaluated by adding explicit country-dummies. Additional degrees of freedom are gained by assuming that in each of the two equations the incremental information provided by the unobserved country-pair effect over the 'pure' origin (or destination) effect is random, and can be included in the error term.[6] In the origin and destination equation we impose identical coefficients for the year dummies, and for those variables that express bilateral differences: physical distance, language distance, and regulatory heterogeneity.

The last two columns in Table 13.3 show the FIML regression results with the transformed (DM) variables. The coefficients of most variables are comparable to the ones found for OLS with fixed effects. The coefficient for physical distance is higher now. The coefficient for policy heterogeneity in *Regulatory and administrative opacity* is no longer significant; apparently it picked up specific country-pair effects in the OLS regressions. The estimated parameters for regulation heterogeneity with respect to the areas *Barriers to competition* and *Explicit barriers to trade and investment* remain invariably negative and significant. The year dummy for 2001 is no longer significant in the FIML estimates.

Summing up, the regression results for bilateral trade in 'other commercial services' are fairly stable over various specifications and estimation procedures. A robust result is that inter-country differences with regard to product-market regulation in the areas of *Barriers to competition* and *Explicit barriers to trade and investment* have a significant negative impact on bilateral service trade. Finally, another firm result is that we consistently find empirical support for the Porter hypothesis that a high level of home-market regulation negatively affects the international competitiveness of exporters from that country.

13.4 Regulation impact on bilateral direct investment

The knowledge-capital model of the multinational enterprise (cf. Markusen 2002) provides a theoretical basis for the hypothesis that direct investment is affected by gravitational factors like market size and distance. The knowledge-capital framework deals explicitly with the firm's choice between exporting and setting up foreign affiliates, thereby distinguishing between resource-seeking (vertical) and market-seeking (horizontal) multinationals. It analyses the direct-investment decision by taking into account the role of factors like market size, firm-level scale economies derived from knowledge capital, plant-level scale economies, and trade costs. Some of these elements are typical gravity factors, and it is no coincidence that the knowledge-capital model has stimulated econometric work in a gravity type framework (for example,

Brainard 1997; Barrios *et al.* 2001; Carr *et al.* 2001). All find support for gravity variables driving cross-border investment.

We apply a gravity analysis to bilateral FDI stocks in order to investigate whether direct investment is affected by policy heterogeneity. On the basis of these results we subsequently analyse the potential FDI impacts caused by the 2004 EU services directive. We include the labour productivity level of the service sector of the origin country to represents the origin-country knowledge asset. For estimating the effect of heterogeneity in regulation on FDI stocks we apply the following reduced-form regression equation:

$$\begin{aligned}\ln(FDI_{ij}) = {} & \beta_0 + \beta_1 \ln(GDP_i) + \beta_2 \ln(GDP_j) + \beta_3 \ln(DIS_{ij}) \\ & + \beta_4 Lan_{ij} + \beta_5 PMR_i + \beta_6 \ln(H_i) + \beta_7 \sum\nolimits_k \beta_{7k} HET_{ijk} \\ & + \beta_8 BEN_j + \beta_9 RFD_j + \varepsilon_{ij}\end{aligned} \tag{13.3}$$

in which FDI_{ij} represents the FDI stock from country i in the reporting county j. This FDI stock is explained by the GDP in the origin country and the destination country, by the physical distance (DIS_{ij}) between the two countries, and the language distance, *Lan*. H_i is the labour productivity in the service sector of the country of origin. Regulation heterogeneity between origin and destination country for domain k of product market regulation is expressed by HET_{ijk}. The variable PMR_i represents the level of product-market regulation in the origin country, while BEN_j and RFD_j represent respectively *Barriers to entrepreneurship* and *FDI restrictions* in the destination country. We add further country-dummies for origin and/or destination country.

Data limitations make it impossible to test the impact of policy heterogeneity on bilateral FDI in business services. No authorized international dataset is available for bilateral FDI stocks in the services sector, let alone for FDI in business services. As an approximation we use total bilateral FDI stocks in all sectors, with 1999 as reference year.[7] Later on we weigh the results with the share of the services FDI in total FDI stocks.

The number of countries is larger than for bilateral service trade; it includes three EU accession countries (Poland, Hungary and the Czech Republic) and the USA, as the EU's largest outside direct investment partner.[8] We have used OLS with fixed effects and the seemingly-unrelated-regression method (SUR) with the DM-transformed variables as estimation methods. The latter method is used to test for possible unobserved variables in the bilateral relations between FDI partner countries.

Results for bilateral FDI. The empirical results are presented in Table 13.4. All estimated coefficients for the typical gravity variables are significant and have the expected sign. In general, the coefficients for the market size proxy (GDP) are similar for the destination country and the origin country. The coefficient for distance is about minus one, but much lower for OLS with

Table 13.4 Regression results: explaining bilateral foreign direct investment (inward), 1999

	Estimation Method [1]			
	OLS, fixed effects origin	*OLS, fixed effects destination*	*SUR*[2] *DM origin + fixed effects*	*SUR*[2] *DM destination + fixed effects*
Variables augmented gravity model				
Ln GDP Origin		0.92***	0.95***	
		(0.10)	(0.09)	
Ln GDP Destination	0.91***			0.74***
	(0.08)			(0.06)
Language	−0.69	−0.46	−0.15	−0.15
	(0.46)	(0.52)	(0.14)	(0.14)
Ln Distance	−0.74***	−1.08***	−1.08***	−1.08***
	(0.15)	(0.16)	(0.13)	(0.13)
Ln (service sector productivity origin country)		2.13***	0.05***	
		(0.30)	(0.01)	
Regulation variables				
Heterogeneity, administrative barriers for start-ups	0.19	−0.38	0.48	0.48
	(0.53)	(0.68)	(0.44)	(0.44)
Heterogeneity, barriers to competition	−2.77***	−3.71***	−3.28***	−3.28***
	(0.96)	(1.21)	(0.84)	(0.84)
Heterogeneity, regulatory and administrative opacity	−0.94	−1.20	−0.89	−0.89
	(0.64)	(0.77)	(0.56)	(0.56)
Heterogeneity, state control	−1.32	−1.47	−1.42*	−1.42*
	(0.89)	(1.04)	(0.77)	(0.77)
Heterogeneity, explicit barriers to trade and investment	0.58	1.48*	0.30	0.30
	(0.48)	(0.81)	(0.54)	(0.54)
Level product-market regulation, origin country		−0.78***	−0.87***	
		(0.20)	(0.18)	
Barriers to entrepreneurship, destination country	−0.45***			−0.21
	(0.15)			(0.13)
FDI regulation indicator, destination country	−4.91***			−8.27***
	(1.78)			(1.42)
Country dummies	Origin, significant	Destination, significant	Destination, significant	Origin, significant
Number of observations	261	196	195	260
Adjusted R-squared	0.80	0.77	0.66	0.47

Notes: 1. Absolute value of standard error in brackets. Code: *** = coefficient significant at 1% confidence level; ** = coefficient significant at 5% confidence level; * = coefficient significant at 10% confidence level. 2. Seemingly Unrelated Regression (SUR), applying simultaneous estimation of equations for origin and destination countries. All bilateral variables are transformed as deviations from their individual country-wise mean (DM, cf. main text).
Data source for OECD regulation data: Nicoletti, Scarpetta and Boylaud (2000); and Golub (2003) for FDI restriction indicators.

fixed effects of the country of origin. The variable for language distance between two countries does not significantly explain the variation of bilateral FDI stocks, as it did in the case of exports. The reason may be that multinationals typically use local personnel in their affiliates. The productivity of services in the origin country – used as a proxy for knowledge-related assets that provide firm-level scale economies for foreign affiliates – is significant in all specifications and it has the predicted sign. This result therefore is consistent with the prediction of the knowledge-capital model.

Now we get to the policy variables. Heterogeneity in *Barriers to competition* and in *State control* (only for the preferred SUR method) have a significant negative impact on bilateral FDI. The effect of heterogeneity in *Regulatory and administrative opacity is* also negative, but not significant. Heterogeneity in *Barriers to start ups* has a small positive effect, but this is not statistically significant. Heterogeneity in *Explicit barriers to trade and investment* has a positive effect, but it is not significant at the 5 per cent level. Interestingly, less heterogeneity in these barriers increases bilateral trade but lowers investment. This resembles the 'tariff jumping' effect: firms serve the foreign market by exports if trade barriers are low, but serve this market by foreign investment is the barriers are high. The estimation result confirms the hypothesis that a high level of product market regulation in the origin country reduces outward investment, because more regulation hampers competitiveness. The same holds for the hypothesis that the level of regulation (*Barriers to entrepreneurship, FDI restrictions*) in the destination country also has a negative impact on direct investment.

13.5 Policy implications: simulating the impacts of the EU Services Directive

We have found firm statistical evidence that policy heterogeneity between EU member states has a negative impact on bilateral trade in business and other commercial services. Also the findings with regard to bilateral FDI, although tested at a higher level of aggregation, indicate that policy heterogeneity between countries has a negative impact on bilateral FDI. This section illustrates the policy implications of these findings by using them for simulating the possible impacts of the EU Services Directive, proposed by the European Commission in 2004.

The European Commission launched a *Proposal for a Directive of the European Parliament and of the Council on Services in the Internal Market* (European Commission 2004a). Its aim is to boost the EU's Internal Market in Services by reducing regulation-based impediments to trade and investment in the service market. This proposal is motivated by the idea that differences in regulation hamper trade and direct investment in services. Anecdotical evidence underpins this idea, but systematic analyses are lacking to date. The proposed directive is intended to become effective from 2010 onwards. It has a 'horizontal' approach: it applies the same principles to a large part of the EU service sector and thus has a large impact on the European service economy.[9] A key element of the 2004 Commission proposals is the 'country of origin' principle: a service firm has to meet the standards set by regulation in its country of origin, but may no longer be confronted by additional regulation in the EU country where the service is delivered. This principle implies mutual recognition of service-market regulation by member states, which would be a breakthrough in Internal Market integration. Other elements of the proposed directive target directly at removing barriers for direct investment in services, by eliminating unnecessary discriminatory elements in national regulations (e.g. nationality and residence requirements), and by obliging member states to create a single point of contact for foreign firms where the foreign service providers can fulfil all their administrative and regulatory obligations.

We first assess how the 2004 Commission proposals would affect the bilateral regulation heterogeneity between EU member states. This is done by close reading of the proposals and all individual policy items that underlie our heterogeneity indices. For each of the five heterogeneity sub-indicators we quantify what impact the proposed measures may have, assuming that they are integrally adopted and implemented. Table 13.5 gives the expected changes per policy sub-domain. The heterogeneity components *Regulatory and administrative opacity* and *Explicit barriers to trade and investment* are heavily affected by the EU directive. The heterogeneity components *Administrative burdens for start-ups* and *Barriers to competition* are moderately affected, while

Table 13.5 Expected impacts of proposed EU measures on intra-EU policy heterogeneity, by sub-domain

Components of heterogeneity indicator and covered policy domains	*Reduction of the components of indicator due to implementation EU Directive (%)*[1]
Regulatory and administrative opacity	66–77
Explicit barriers to trade and investment	73–78
Administrative burdens for start-ups	34–46
Barriers to competition	29–37
State control	3–6
Overall PMR heterogeneity indicator	31–38

Note: 1. Based on detailed item-wise consideration of the match between the proposed EU directive and the 183 specific regulation items selected from the OECD database as basis for calculating the heterogeneity indicators. If all items for a sub-domain would be fully affected by the EU directive, the expected impact would 100%. If no items are affected, the expected impact is 0%. Because of the uncertain impact of the EU directive on some regulatory comparison items – in particular for those items that are partially affected – we use a bandwidth indicating a minimum and maximum effect. *Source*: Kox *et al.* (2004).

the component *State control* is hardly affected. In the latter case, this is mainly due to the fact that network sectors are not included in the proposed EU directive.

We combine the heterogeneity-reduction effects reported in Table 13.5 with the parameter estimates for the policy variables, taking results based on the FIML and SUR estimation of the transformed variables with fixed effects for the country of origin (last column in Tables 13.3 and 13.4) as our preferred results. For every EU-country pair separately we calculate how their bilateral trade and FDI might be changed as a result of the EU proposals. The effect differs by country pair, because the initial heterogeneity in regulation also varies for each country pair.[10] We account for uncertainties by combining the uncertainty effects of the parameter estimates – using a spread between plus and minus one standard deviation around the estimated coefficients – with the bandwidth of the heterogeneity effects in Table 13.5. For direct investment, our scenario includes the effect of a lower *level* of national FDI restrictions in the destination countries.[11] We quantified the effects of full implementation of the EU directive, indicating the bandwidth of the resulting maximal effects on service trade and direct investment. Table 13.6 shows the results. Implementation of the proposals could increase commercial service trade by 30 to 62 per cent, while intra-EU foreign direct investment in services could

Table 13.6 Potential impacts of 2004 EU Services Directive on trade and FDI in (commercial) services

	Minimum effects	*Maximum effects*
Total intra-EU trade increase	**30**	**62**
of which:		
• Increase due to reduced heterogeneity in Barriers to competition	25	51
• Increase due to reduced heterogeneity in Explicit barriers to trade and investment	5	11
Total intra-EU FDI increase	**18**	**36**
(including rounding difference)		
of which:		
• Increase due to reduced heterogeneity in Barriers to competition	7	18
• Increase due to less FDI restrictions (level effect) [1]	11	16
• Increase due to reduced heterogeneity in state control	0	2

Note: 1 Assuming that investors from other EU countries experience a 30% reduction in the destination country's level of FDI restrictions. Our FDI indicator is cumulative direct investment stocks. Since the adaptation of FDI stocks occurs mainly through annual FDI flows, the effect on annual direct investment flows will be much higher. To what extent this is the case depends on the length of the adaptation period.

increase by 18 to 36 per cent. The increase in trade and FDI is mainly caused by a reduction in the heterogeneity of the *Barriers to competition*. For FDI, also the reduced intensity of FDI restrictions is important.

In order to estimate the macroeconomic importance of the SD, de Bruijn *et al.* (2007) have fed the estimated trade impacts of Table 13.6 (not the FDI effects) into Worldscan, a large CGE model, in order to simulate the potential macroeconomic impacts. The Worldscan model, described in Lejour *et al.* (2006), separately models most of the EU countries. The main macroeconomic result from the simulations is that average European consumption could increase by between 0.5 and 1.2 per cent due to the measures. According to the simulations, the mutual-recognition element in the Services Directive (the country-of-origin principle) accounts for about 40 per cent of the Services Directive's potential effects. Note that these effects do not yet account for the positive impacts of the measures on intra-European direct investment in services. All EU member states benefit from the proposals, not only the ones that are specialized in commercial services. Part of the economic effects is caused by shifts in specialization. Integrating of national services markets improves the allocative efficiency of the sectoral structure in the EU. Some of the original EU member states increase their relative specialization in commercial services due to the more open borders. The new member states, however, reallocate more resources to their manufacturing activity. For them, this effect represents a significant part of the GDP increase that they may experience due to the Services Directive. Interestingly, the current process of specialization in manufacturing by the new Member States benefits from being complemented by a more integrated EU services market (de Bruijn *et al.* 2007).

Copenhagen Economics (2005a,b) also analyses the welfare effects of the EU proposals with a CGE model; the latter also considers the FDI effects. They assess that overall consumption in the European Union would increase by 0.6 per cent. This estimate corresponds to the minimum estimate by de Bruijn *et al.* (2007). According to their analysis the CoOP contributes only about 10 per cent to the total welfare effects (including the FDI-induced effects). This is not surprising, since their concept of non-tariff barriers in services is more limited: they look at domestic regulation within a country, but do not consider the impacts of inter-country differences in the form and content of the regulations.

13.6 Conclusions

International trade in business services is hampered by non-tariff barriers that originate from national regulations: not only the level of regulation in home or export country matters, but also the national differences in regulations for service markets. Because regulations often differ by market, the fixed costs of complying with national regulations in an export market cause sunk market-entry costs. A new index of bilateral policy heterogeneity is developed to proxy the extent of these sunk market-entry costs with the EU services markets. The indicator is applied as an explanatory variable in a gravity model for explaining bilateral trade and FDI between EU member states. The empirical results support our theoretical prediction: the degree of regulatory heterogeneity is inversely related to the level of bilateral service trade, and also the level of bilateral FDI. Policy heterogeneity between countries has a negative impact on bilateral service trade and on bilateral direct investment. It indicates that policy heterogeneity is still an important barrier to the development of a real Internal Market for services in the European Union.

We used our results to simulate the potential impacts of the 2004 European Commission proposals for the services markets. The simulations show that if countries make more use of mutual recognition, bilateral trade in commercial services among EU countries could increase by between 30 and 62 per cent. Expressed in terms of total intra-EU trade (goods and services) the increase ranges between 2 and 5 per cent. Supplementary research with a macroeconomic CGE model shows that these trade effects are sufficient to cause average European consumption to rise by 0.5 to 1.2 per cent. Almost half of this effect is accounted for by the mutual recognition element of the proposals, that is, the country-of-origin principle, which is particularly relevant for many of the still highly regulated professional business services. All EU member states benefit from the proposals, not only the ones that are specialized in commercial services.

We derive firm indications that the EU service sector might benefit from the proposed EU directive through a substantial increase in direct investment between member states. FDI in services could also increase by about 18 per cent to 36 per cent, with possibilities for more competition, innovation, lower prices and efficiency in domestic business-services sectors.

Lowering national regulatory differences between member states means that the sunk export costs for individual services firms will fall. This will attract new layers of particularly the more productive medium-sized business-services firms to embark on exporting to other EU member states. An integrated market for business services will particularly benefit SMEs. The burden of red tape is more ponderous for SMEs than big firms, because many of the related costs are fixed costs and therefore hardly related to firm size.

Notes

1. The export contributions of Transport services and Travel together represented about 50 per cent, financial services accounted for 7 per cent of the total, personal service for just one per cent, and construction, communication and insurance each for about 2.5 per cent (OECD 2003c).
2. Kox and Lejour (2005) prove this in a theoretical model using Dixit–Stiglitz type of preferences and fixed production costs.

3. Among them are: Nicoletti *et al.* (2003); Grünfeld and Moxnes (2003); Kimura and Lee (2006).
4. Fixed effects or in this case country dummies represent all country-specific heterogeneity that is not captured by the other country-specific variables (like GDP and PMR) in the first specification (OLS without fixed effects). The disadvantage is that we can not ascribe this heterogeneity to specific economic variables. For analytical reasons it is therefore not attractive to combine country dummies for the origin and destination countries in one specification.
5. It is a 'within' fixed-effect estimator. The method is introduced for bilateral trade by Erkel-Rousse and Mirza (2002).
6. Thus assuming that the deviations of bilateral fixed effects from their means are i.i.d. random terms.
7. Sectoral data on FDI stock and flow data are available on a country basis, but not on a bilateral basis with countries of origin and destination specified. The data cover inward FDI stocks, that is, the stock of direct investment reported by a particular host country as stemming from a particular country of origin. We used OECD data on bilateral FDI stocks, to which we applied a consistency check, similar to that applied to bilateral services trade, for identifying the most reliable reporting country, see Kox *et al.* (2004a). Bilateral FDI stocks are used rather than annual FDI flows, for three reasons. The first reason is a very practical one: to our knowledge there is no authorized international dataset available for bilateral FDI flows. The second reason is that stock data are closer to the level of actual production by foreign affiliates than annual flow data. Thirdly, bilateral FDI flows are very volatile from one year to another; a few large transactions like mergers may cause large swings in the annual data, sometimes causing negative flows.
8. We have also included a country-dummy for the USA and for the EU's accession countries in our country set. These dummies are not significant. The regression results with country dummies are available upon request.
9. Including the commercial service sectors Trade and Distribution, Business Services, Hotels and Restaurants, Personal Services, Construction. Not covered by the proposed Directive are: Banking, Insurance, Transport, and Medical Services.
10. Note that exports and FDI stocks are estimated in logs. So the new export or (FDI stock) level equals the old level times the exponent of the product of the change in heterogeneity and the estimated coefficient. We have calculated this for each country-pair and averaged these results to derive the total EU-effect, using the size of bilateral services trade and FDI stocks, respectively, as weights.
11. For the level effect we assume a 30 per cent reduction for investors from other EU member states. This is a conservative estimate, since the directive aims at abandoning discriminatory regulation.

14
A Segmentation Approach to Understanding Business and Professional Services in City-regions: Shifting the Horizon Beyond Global Cities

John R. Bryson and P. W. Daniels

Introduction

In an increasingly globalized world successful economic activity, in both manufacturing and services, is founded upon the exploitation of four sources of competitive advantage – price, quality, design and knowledge/expertise. These are not mutually exclusive (Bryson, Daniels and Rusten 2004). As a result, manufacturing production in developed market economies has fragmented into increasingly smaller components that are outsourced or offshored to increase efficiency, profits, and value (Gage and Lesher, 2005). The manufacturing that remains in the developed market economies must compete by targeting sectors and markets that require client customization, niche manufacturing or fashion-driven fast production. These require significant inputs of knowledge and expertise, whether provided internally or externally by independent firms, and these 'changes have redefined the way in which many manufacturing firms use services and interact with service suppliers' (Gage and Lesher, 2005: 7). Knowledge inputs are also required by service providers, while final consumers utilize the services of a range of knowledge providers, from accountants to image consultants (Bryson and Wellington, 2003). The net rise in importance of knowledge has been accompanied by a dramatic growth of independent business and professional service (BPS) firms that provide intermediate inputs to the production system.

Against this background it is intriguing to find that much of the literature on BPS has really only explored their rise, role and organization in key global cities (Sassen, 2001; Keeble and Nachum, 2002). There is an underlying perception that 'the things a global city makes are highly specialized services and financial goods' (Sassen, 2001: 5) and that global cities are the 'most *advanced* production sites for creating these services' (Sassen, 2001: 6). While Sassen and others (Duffy, 1995; Rubalcaba, 1999; Beaverstock *et al.*, 1999) have identified business services as one of the most important economic sectors in advanced western economies, only limited attention has been given to understanding their role and dynamics outside the global cities (Beyers and Lindahl, 1996b; Daniels and Bryson, 2005). This raises a number of major conceptual and empirical questions about the role performed by BPS firms located elsewhere in regional and national economies. In second- or third-tier city-regions do they primarily fulfil local market demand or do they also supply their expertise to non-local clients? Do such firms only provide 'general' expertise to clients wherever they are located, leaving BPS firms located in the global cities to provide 'specialist', 'advanced' expertise? These are important issues that must be explored in the European context and especially in city-regions.

This chapter begins to address such questions using evidence drawn from the Birmingham city-region (UK). It is one of a number of similar European city-regions that incorporate a mix of large urban centres and areas dominated by rural activities; all have experienced deindustrialization and restructuring in recent decades. While the share of manufacturing in the Birmingham city-region remains higher than elsewhere in the UK, its recent history is dominated by the contraction of blue-collar jobs and the growth of service employment (especially BPS, consumer services, tourism). Between 1995 and 2004 employment in BPS increased by 46,000 (+1.3 per cent) while manufacturing employment declined by 158,000 (−7.7 per cent). By 2005, 312,000 people were employed in BPS compared with 463,000 in manufacturing; the region now has the second largest concentration of BPS firms in the UK.

Parts of this chapter draw upon the results of a telephone survey of 218 BPS firms in ten sectors that was undertaken during 2002: banking and financial services; legal services; property services, quantity and rating surveyors; insurance and pension services; marketing, advertising and public relations services; computer services, telecommunications and multimedia consultants; consultancy services; design-related services; employment consultants and agencies and accountants and accountancy services (for details, see Daniels and Bryson, 2005). This was complemented by a small number of in-depth interviews with a sub-sample of the telephone survey respondents. The survey population comprised 9,547 BPS firms listed in the *Yell Business Directory* and grouped by sector and listed in alphabetical order. In order to achieve a representative cross-section, potential respondents were selected systematically from the top of each list, using the total in that category divided by the target number. Thus, starting with first entry every 47th firm in the list of banks and financial institutions was sampled; returning to the second firm in the list and repeating the procedure when the first tranche had been completed. A successful response was obtained from every seventh firm approached.

14.1 Business and professional services beyond global cities

Global cities are advocated in the literature as the 'command and control' centres of the world economic system. In this capacity, they not only operate as arenas of interaction based on face-to-face contact, but also facilitate political connections, high-quality artistic and cultural functions, and enable business, entertainment and other elites to rub shoulders easily. While other cities such as Paris, Toronto, Los Angeles, Osaka, Hong Kong, and Singapore can certainly lay claim to being national/international (or second-tier) cities in the global economy, the trio (or triad) of New York, London and Tokyo has played a disproportionate role in the production and transformation of international economic relations in the late twentieth century. Internationalizing service firms have been in the forefront of this process (Roberts, 2002).

Sitting at the top of the international urban hierarchy, truly global cities are simultaneously:

(i) Centres of creative innovation, news, fashion, and culture industries.
(ii) Centres for raising and managing investment capital.
(iii) Centres of specialized expertise in advertising and marketing, legal services, accounting, computer services (amongst others).
(iv) The location for the management, planning and control centres for corporations and nongovernmental organizations (NGOs) that operate with increasing ease over the entire planet.

The *raison d'être* of global cities is the facilitation and enhancement of the specialized knowledge and expertise upon which so much of the current global economy depends. Each city is inextricably linked via an extensive web of investment, trade, migration, and telecommunications to clients and markets, suppliers and competitors, located throughout the world (Taylor, 2001). All three metropolises are endowed with state-of-the-art telecommunications infrastructures that enable corporate headquarters to maintain and monitor global networks of branch plants, back offices, customers, subcontractors, subsidiaries, and competitors.

That global cities have experienced impressive rates of new BPS firm formation as well as rapid growth in employment is not in doubt. But similar growth has also occurred in cities lower down the hierarchy, and even in some rural areas. Sassen suggests that the growth of BPS in smaller cities is a function of the growing demand for their inputs by firms in all sectors. However, she notes the existence of a dual economy whereby the 'best' expertise is located in the global cities and only 'adequate' expertise is located elsewhere. Thus:

> When these services are for global firms and markets their complexity is such that global cities are the best production sites. But when the demand is for fairly routine producer services, cities at various levels of the urban system can be adequate production sites. (Sassen, 2001: 359–60)

This statement provokes three observations. First, Sassen overlooks the possibility that significant, global market, BPS firms are located in places other than global cities. This is an important oversight in that some BPS firms located outside the global cities are able to out-compete firms operating from such high-cost locations. A large law firm located in Birmingham, hereafter known as *Birmingham Law*, noted that:

> There are no disadvantages to being in Birmingham as a national practice. The advantages, in comparison to London, are those that help keep our overheads low – labour and office costs. This has a direct impact on hourly rates and we are able to offer a cost differential, but we sell ourselves on our distinctive services and the quality of our people. (Interview, managing partner)

In the European context this is important because it suggests that BPS providers outside the 'global' urban centres are still able to compete nationally rather than regionally.

Second, by focusing her analysis on global cities she underplays the crucial role of the production networks that are utilized by BPS to deliver expertise to client firms; her analysis does not, therefore, incorporate the ways in which firms located beyond the global cities contribute to the evolving BPS global production system. The key to this is the role that branch offices play in a large BPS firm's spatial division of expertise (Bryson, Daniels and Warf 2004; Bryson and Rusten, 2005). Third, Sassen's arguments are underpinned by research undertaken in the key global cities that is not complemented with investigations into the role, function and markets of BPS activities located in other places.

Part of the rationale for the research bias towards global cities is that BPS firms accumulate significant benefits from agglomeration or close proximity to other service providers. These benefits include the availability of skilled staff as well as opportunities for inter-firm collaboration. Thus, advanced producer services 'are only weakly dependent on proximity to consumers served (and that) such specialized firms benefit from and need to locate close to other firms who produce key inputs or whose proximity makes possible joint production of certain service offerings' (Sassen, 2001: 11). This provokes two observations.

First, weak dependence on client proximity is a justification for the role global cities play in the world economy, but there is evidence that the client base of a BPS firm is closely related to its location (Bryson and Daniels, 1998, Rusten, 2000). This is no less likely to be the case for BPS firms located in the global cities. Within the Birmingham city-region BPS firms are extremely dependent on close proximity to clients; just under one-third (32.8 per cent) were located within ten miles of the BPS provider. A further 27 per cent of clients were located elsewhere in the city-region, 33.8 per cent in other regions of the UK, and 5.3 per cent were overseas. It is also not necessarily the case that smaller firms rely more on local markets (within ten miles) than larger firms, although micro-businesses (one person firms) do have 75 per cent of their clients within the city-region (Table 14.1). A total of 43 firms identified at least one important overseas market and 25 firms listed up to three in order of

Table 14.1 Location of BPS service firm clients, by share (per cent) of sales/fees and size of firm as well as sector Birmingham city-region

a) Size

Location of client	*Size of firm (no. of employees)*							
	1	*2–6*	*7–12*	*13–50*	*51–100*	*102–499*	*>500*	*Total*
Local (within 10 miles)	29.8	32.9	38.2	27.8	38.1	33.2	24.0	32.8
Rest of city-region	44.8	29.4	14.7	23.9	27.7	20.0	27.0	27.0
London & the South East	4.6	9.7	17.2	13.9	12.7	14.0	10.0	11.3
Rest of the UK	16.1	21.2	21.1	29.1	21.7	18.0	39.0	22.5
EU	0.5	1.5	5.0	2.8	1.2	5.8	0.0	2.3
Rest of World	0.0	4.3	2.6	2.2	0.5	7.3	0.0	3.0

b) Sector

Location of client	*Banking and insurance*	*Consultancy and accountancy*	*Computer, marketing and design*	*Legal and property services*	*Total*
Local (within 10 miles)	34.9	35.7	18.7	38.3	32.8
Rest of WM	27.8	26.7	25.7	27.7	27.0
London and the South East	4.0	17.0	14.4	7.7	11.3
Rest of the UK	29.8	15.0	30.7	20.1	22.5
EU	0.9	2.1	3.9	2.2	2.3
Rest of World	2.8	2.1	6.3	1.7	3.0

Source: Daniels and Bryson, 2002.

importance. The proportion of sales/fee income attributed to their most important overseas market (29 firms) typically did not exceed 10 per cent, but for a very small number of firms (four) the proportion exceeded 60 per cent. The average is highest (8.3 per cent) amongst computer, marketing and design service firms.

Such is the flexibility now offered by information and telecommunications technology that the costs of arm's-length transactions with clients are not prohibitive. For many aspects of these transactions the quality of the service is not necessarily compromised by an inability to work face-to-face with clients or collaborating firms on a regular basis. It is important, however, not to understate the ongoing relevance of face-to-face contacts for the conduct of BPS transactions. Such close geographical ties persist for historical reasons in that many of the existing relationships amongst small and medium-sized firms (SMEs) will have been obtained via recommendation, word of mouth, and local contacts. Such relationships often endure even though firms have grown and extended their markets (Rusten *et al.*, 2005). It is also the case that ease of access to clients, including the ability to visit them as well as them visiting the supplier of a service, also encourages proximity between supplier and client.

Secondly, a key justification for agglomerations of BPS in global cities is the opportunities they provide for collaboration and co-production of expertise. In their efforts to retain market share or the loyalty of clients, BPS must often collaborate with other firms to co-produce a service. The increasing complexity of service 'products' that incorporate complex specialized knowledge or expertise also requires firms to seek partners so that they can deliver the quality or kind of service expected by large clients who are themselves more discriminating about what to expect from their service providers. Collaboration is also encouraged as individual firms become more specialized in response to tighter regulation, as in financial services, or in response to client demand and expectations.

It is assumed that this type of collaborative relationship between BPS providers must be founded upon close proximity. The evidence from BPS firms in the Birmingham city-region suggests that close proximity between collaborators is not always required. Larger firms can increase their scope by recruiting and retaining appropriate expertise in-house, but for smaller firms collaboration is the principal option. Larger firms need to collaborate with BPS providers located beyond their area of direct operation. In the Birmingham city-region one in three BPS firms had collaborated with a non-affiliated establishment in the form of a joint venture, co-licensing agreement, team project or some other formal or informal association during the last year. More than half of legal and property services had engaged in some form of collaboration and slightly less than half of consultancy and accountancy firms. It is important to note that the location of collaborators was not confined to the region (Table 14.2). Just under half of the partner firms were located outside the region, while 13 per cent were based overseas. Information and communication technologies (ICT), for example, now enables collaboration with overseas partners and is just as likely to involve firms elsewhere in the UK as in London and the South East. Collaboration with overseas partners is often driven by, or follows from, the needs of local clients with overseas interests. Thus, one of Birmingham's most important law firms, Wragge & Co., has established a network of preferred law firms around the world. This enables the company to maintain and develop its legal expertise in the UK, while working with partners to provide advice to clients on international matters. Wragge's refers clients to suitable overseas lawyers and advisers and also project manages or acts as an intermediary for international projects. It is also the case that affiliates of firms located in the Birmingham city-region, in activities such as management consulting, corporate accounting, or banking, will refer business to their partners and this fosters further collaborative activity. This suggests that the geography of joint

Table 14.2 Location of three most important collaborating firms, BPS by sector, Birmingham city-region

Sector	*Birmingham*	*Rest of city-region*	*London/ South East*	*Other UK*	*Overseas*	*Total*
Banking and Insurance	5	3	4	3	2	17
Consultancy and Accountancy	4	10	6	9	3	28
Computer, Marketing and Design	2	5	2	3	3	15
Legal and Property Services	11	9	5	6	4	35
Total	22	27	13	21	12	95

Source: Daniels and Bryson, 2002.

production by BPS is much more complex than has previously been assumed. This is a topic that urgently requires further detailed research.

14.2 A segmentation approach to business and professional services

The activities that comprise the BPS sector of the economy are both diverse and complex. They include several distinctive sectors (such as law, accountancy, market research and technical consultancy) as well as a very broad size-range of firms. The latter is extremely significant in that it makes comparatively little sense to compare the activities of a micro firm with those of a large company employing several thousand staff. During the late 1970s segmentation theory developed in economics and sociology as a conceptual framework for exploring the complexity of economic activity. This approach begins by postulating the existence of two or more basic segments (sectors or markets) that reflect different modes of organising production and work (Berger and Piore, 1980). Segmentation theory was introduced to economic geography by Taylor and Thrift (1982a, b) but was essentially neglected and relegated to the analysis of labour markets (Atkinson, 1984; Doeringer and Piore, 1971; Piore and Sabel, 1984; Fine, 1998).

Central to Taylor and Thrift's analysis is an appreciation that small firms act in different ways to large firms. Small firms can be classified as 'leaders' (innovators), 'niche players', 'satellites' and 'the satisfied' while large firms are 'leaders', 'intermediates', 'laggards' and 'supports' (providing specialized service inputs) (Taylor, 2000: 216). These categories are derived from research undertaken on manufacturing and cannot be transferred in their totality to BPS. The key difference is that the manufacturing research was founded upon the conceptualization of power in enterprise relations and, in particular, inequalities in resource control. Allocation to the segments was on the basis of size and the on-site presence of R&D. For BPS firms' initial allocation to segments is based on size and, subsequently, by orientation within the marketplace (local, regional, etc.). For smaller firms the reputation of individual professionals is a key driver behind the localization of a BPS firm's activities; the client network is forged on the back of individual reputations. Larger firms have developed reputations based around the construction and articulation of identifiable brands. This means that their geographical reach, facilitated by ICT and a branch network, can be much more extensive than small firms.

Segmentation theory highlights the diversity of economic actors and draws attention to the different characteristics of small and large firms. Nevertheless, Berger and Piore (1980: 2) stressed that 'the significance of dualism is not that a society is divided into two autonomous and discontinuous segments, but that a society is divided segmentally'. Segmentation theory needs to be revisited and developed as its application to the service economy would highlight important differences in the operation and activities of different segments (by size as well as business model) of BPS. The application of this approach would overcome many of the problems that exist in the global cities literature. It would highlight the complexity of BPS firms by identifying those firms that provide specialist compared to general expertise as well as draw attention to the diversity of different business models in operation in this sector. We argue that the majority of BPS firms in London are providing fairly routine services (Bryson, Daniels and Rusten 2004) and that a small minority of firms are involved with the provision of complex expertise. This is also the case for the Birmingham city-region.

14.2.1 Segmentation by market

Within the Birmingham city-region three basic segments or units of analysis for BPS can be identified using the data from the 2002 survey. These segments reflect different business models, especially 'satisfier' smaller firms and 'leaders'. First, *heavily localized small firms* (59.8 per cent of responses) service a local need by providing generic or general expertise – for example, small local accountancy firms, predominately targeted at individuals as well as SMEs. Such firms have no intention of growing or establishing an export base outside their area of operation. The main reasons for their localization rests on the importance attached to face-to-face interaction for service delivery and owners' limited aspirations to expand the firm. These firms fulfil local demand and are an essential underpinning for the production system as a whole in the city-region. Their business and employment growth prospects are very much linked to the performance of their local client companies.

Secondly, there are *cross-region (or regionalized) firms* operating from more than one site within the city-region. These firms have evolved from heavily localized firms and have grown organically or by merger and acquisition.

Some are starting to provide services to clients that are located outside the city-region, usually in contiguous regions or in London.

Thirdly, *national/international firms* provide services from the Birmingham city-region to regional, national and international markets. A significant proportion of these organizations are branch offices (19.6 per cent of responses). This exposes the region to many of the problems usually associated with manufacturing branch plants: the centres of control, strategy and innovation are located elsewhere. Nevertheless, a small number of BPS firms in the city-region are developing a national, and, increasingly, an international, reputation for the supply of advanced business or professional services. Of particular importance is a group of marketing, legal and environment service suppliers that have successfully developed export revenues and fees built on the quality of their expertise, local reputation, and strategic development and management of their national and international client base. These are the firms that are competing, innovating and, in many instances, out-competing their global city, London-based rivals by providing advanced rather than routine services. Some of these companies are growing extremely rapidly (20–40 per cent per annum during the four years prior to 2002), in terms of turnover, client base, and as providers of professional and support employment. A firm with around 70 employees supplying corporate legal services noted that 'Birmingham is now at the northern edge of the southern prosperity belt – the 'economic heart of the country is moving south'. This company is increasingly disengaged from the city-region, with most of its clients based in areas to the south of Birmingham and in London and the South East. Some 20 to 25 per cent of the work handled by its office in central Birmingham arises from referrals by the firm's overseas offices. For example, its Dallas office will refer a client to Birmingham which will then take over responsibility for the ongoing relationship with the client – including invoicing the work in whatever currency the client prefers. The location of the work is explained by long-term relationships that exist between individual professionals and the client base.

14.2.2 Segmentation by motivation and business model

Local, regional and national/international BPS firms have different geographies, clients, recruitment practices and impacts on the regional economy. This research identified three additional motivational or business model-driven sub-segments in the BPS economy of this city-region: local, proactive and reactive. First, there are firms *that think and act locally*; they have no desire or motivation to develop a client base beyond the region. These *locally engaged and embedded firms* perform an important role, providing expertise to local companies, some of which will be involved in the export of services and products. In this way *localized firms* make an indirect contribution to the export base of a city-region (Daniels, 2000).

Secondly, a select and small number of BPS firms in the region are servicing local demand whilst simultaneously, and increasingly, *proactively* developing strategies to attract national and international clients. These firms are trying *to think and act regionally, nationally and internationally* whilst still maintaining a strong local client base. These are companies trying to *disengage* from the city-region to become national and international providers of BPS expertise.

Thus, Birmingham Law has been systematically transformed into a national and international practice with strong local underpinnings. According to the managing partner:

> [...] to develop a national client base you cannot just be in Birmingham [...] We thought we could build a strong firm from a Birmingham base and what one needed to look at to build a national profile was the quality of your people and the quality of your product. We thought that it would be perfectly possible to attract quality people and to develop quality products from a law firm with a single office and a lot of our strength comes from having so many people under one roof. (Interview, managing partner, May 2002)

During the 1980s and early 1990s the strategy was concerned with the development of a national profile, but in the late 1990s this altered to include a global presence. By 2004, around 25 per cent of the firm's work was international. The firm altered its geographical strategy as it considered that:

> For certain product lines and in certain markets then it is possible, in order to have a credible offering internationally, that we might need a London office because of the way international markets and clients perceive the UK – they won't know where Birmingham is, but this is not proven. (Interview, managing partner, May 2002)

In order to develop a global presence the firm decided to focus on the development of niche products, for which it was known as one of the top five providers in the UK. This strategy proved to be extremely effective, but there came a time when one of the niche teams reached a threshold beyond which they could not develop without a London presence. The firm therefore merged with a small niche London practice that had a reputation for the relevant product. Part of the strategy was about 'pushing out the boundaries of the quality and people in our team' (Interview, managing partner, May 2002). Birmingham Law is now able to out-compete London law firms, not on price but rather on the quality and distinctiveness of the services it provides to clients.

Thirdly, there are a small number of BPS firms that *react* to the activities of key clients. These firms are, in effect, forced to provide services to existing clients that have expanded beyond the West Midlands. For example, an existing local client may encourage a local BPS firm to develop strategic relationships with BPS firms located outside the region and, in exceptional cases, might make the firm open an office in another locality in order to maintain the business relationship. The important point is that such firms are reacting to the demands of clients rather than acting proactively.

There is a development progression experienced by newly established BPS firms from being dependent upon local clients to establishing a wider client base. In policy terms, it might be possible to develop mechanisms that would encourage BPS firms to adopt a proactive approach to business development. The strategy of proactive BPS firms is based on targeted client identification and development; such techniques could usefully be introduced to other firms in the region. An important caveat, however, is that it will still be important to recognise that the majority of BPS firms in the Birmingham city-region will always primarily, if not exclusively, service local demand. It is the activities of the proactive firms that will play the most important role in structuring the dynamic relationship between second-city and global-city BPS.

14.3 Conclusions

Business and professional services are an essential component of all European regional economies. The expertise that they provide enables local client companies to retain or enhance their competitiveness. At the most basic level BPS firms may actually only help their clients to cope with the requirements of new regulations, for example, in employment law or environmental legislation, by providing a standard service (Sundbo, 2002) or recipe knowledge (Bryson, Daniels and Rusten 2004). It is difficult, however, to differentiate between BPS firms that provide routine knowledge and those that are providing heavily customized, extremely high-value expertise. In many cases, a firm will customize or appear to customize recipe knowledge; evidently a contradiction, but by definition much professional and other forms of business-service expertise is actually embedded in established technical expertise.

The segmentation approach to BPS that is outlined in this chapter enables a number of generalizations to be made about services across the European Union. The approach draws attention to the diversity that exists within the BPS business community. The majority of BPS firms are heavily localized, which is unsurprising since the majority are small, typically employing fewer than ten people (professionals and support staff). Nevertheless, a significant proportion of BPS firms in the Birmingham city-region provide services to clients located elsewhere in the UK, while a small number also work with clients located in other countries. It is also the case that BPS professionals are relatively well paid and thus generate comparatively high local economic multipliers. Further research is required to ascertain both the extent and determinants of these multipliers.

Our exploratory research suggests that it is essential to look even more closely at the BPS firms found in places other than the global cities. Some of the BPS firms located in the Birmingham city-region are closely integrated into the economies of London and the South East. By doing so they are implementing a dual geographical business strategy that simultaneously involves *engagement* with local clients and *disengagement* from the city-region as they endeavour to obtain clients that may not have a business presence in the region. The BPS firms in this group are not just providing routine expertise; they are offering specialist expertise that matches that provided by BPS firms located in the global cities.

The dichotomy between a significant majority of BPS firms that are predominantly locally engaged and a small group that is attempting to disengage from the regional marketplace highlights the segmentation of BPS in the economy. Segmentation theory needs to be revisited, developed and applied to the service world. It is an approach that highlights the complexity and diversity of economic activity and which encourages researchers to consider the different ways in which firms are organized. If it is applied to research on the relationship between BPS and global cities segmentation theory would perhaps reveal that their service worlds are extremely localized and that, in common with the Birmingham city-region, only a small proportion of BPS firms are in fact acting globally.

15
Policy Implications

Henk Kox and Luis Rubalcaba

Introduction

The growth of business services since 1990 has absorbed about half of the growth in European employment. In addition, the business-services industry has also had impacts on aggregate productivity and innovation. In the movement towards a more competitive Europe the role of business services in economic growth needs to receive particular attention. The evidence from the USA about the use of business services suggests that there is additional room for growth. The contributions of the business-services industry to innovation, to scale economies in respect of human capital and knowledge, to efficiency spillovers and their impacts on productivity growth have all served to bring about a more productive and competitive EU economy. Most of the quantitative empirical evidence on these contributions points to very positive results.

Since these facts all touch upon the EU's Lisbon goals, the business-services sector is an interesting enough domain for policy makers. But is there a real need for policy intervention at EU level? Most of the recent developments in the business-services sector have been driven by markets and private initiatives. The free development of an industry does not automatically generate the best possible welfare outcomes. There may be 'banknotes left on the sidewalk', which the business-services sector itself is unable to pick up. Targeted, stimulating action can in some cases seize welfare opportunities that otherwise would have remained underdeveloped. Welfare theory suggests that policy intervention is only called for if markets do not work properly. Moreover, if policy intervention is called for, at what level should it take place? The subsidiarity principle indicates that EU policies are required when national market problems have a European dimension. These elements will be used to discuss whether EU policy intervention is required in the development of the business-services sector. For a proper discussion, this chapter splits the issue into two questions, each of them calling for an answer:

1. Are there market failures in connection with the expanding business-services sector and, if so, are they such that the welfare outcomes could be improved upon by policy intervention?

2. If indeed market failures exist, is there a need for EU-wide policies beyond what national governments do (or can do) to improve the market outcomes of national business-services sectors? Put another way, do market failures in the business-services sector have a European dimension?

Both questions will be dealt with in separate sections, and a final section will present the general conclusions and the possible policy solutions.

15.1 Potential market failures in the business-services sector

Welfare theory highlights several reasons for market failure. Market failure exists when the private-market prices for business services would systematically differ from the marginal costs and benefits of these services for society as a whole. The achievement of socially optimal outcomes by the free development of business-services markets can be disturbed by the three types of market failures, or combinations thereof:

- *Markets do not account for social externalities*, either positive or negative. Intervention may be required to suppress negative social externalities, or to sustain a sufficient provision of positive social externalities.
- Existence and abuse of *market power* results in socially undesirable outcomes. In markets with entry barriers, monopolist or strategic oligopolist behaviour by market parties results in suboptimal allocation of resources or too high prices for consumers. This means that the private market prices for a substantial group of firms are systematically higher than marginal costs.
- *Information asymmetry* causes undesirable outcomes in markets for information-sensitive goods. Less-informed parties may systematically find themselves in a disadvantaged position, and – being aware of this risk – may also deliberately reduce their exposure to being deceived. This reduces total transaction volume below the level that would prevail without the information asymmetry problem.

The three groups of market failures will be dealt with one by one, although there are clear overlaps between some aspects.

Social externalities. External effects arise when transactions between suppliers and buyers of business services have welfare effects for other producers or consumers that are not taken into account by the transaction partners. External effects are not reflected in the costs and prices of the business-services products. As a consequence, the market price for the delivered service is – from the social perspective – either too high or too low. We first mention some branch-specific externalities, and afterwards turn to more general externalities, positive and negative.

Intervention in markets for a number of knowledge-intensive business-services products has long been based on the social externalities that go along with these services. Specific examples of such services and the social externalities involved are:

- accountancy: important for the safeguarding of reliable financial information, which is essential for trust in capital markets and the financial system as a whole;
- legal services (lawyers, notaries): important for upholding the legitimacy of the constitutional state and the legal system;
- engineering: safeguarding the liability of technical systems;
- architects: special role in upholding the amenity value of the urban environment, and the quality and aesthetic value of housing and other buildings.

Prevention of charlatanism and concern for the independence, reliability and accountability of providers of these professional services partly explain why policy makers hesitate to remove regulation barriers and 'red tape' with regard to multi-professional cooperation. This concern, real or exaggerated, also played a role in the recent debate on the EU Services Directive.

The growth of the business-services industry has had several positive external effects outside the industry itself, particularly in the areas of innovation and productivity development. This is especially true if innovation is understood in the broad sense of the word and not only in the traditional sense of R&D carried out for certain products. Innovation of both processes and organization proves to be very important in providing those innovative services that can lead to productivity gains.

The sector makes its own, direct contribution to technological innovation, particularly in the areas of software and engineering. It also contributes directly, through non-technological innovations, to labour productivity development in client industries. The availability of external business services makes it possible for small and medium-sized enterprises to surmount scale problems (and associated set-up costs) for knowledge inputs. Finally, the business-services sector contributes to the diffusion of production-frontier knowledge among client firms, with regard to many competence areas of business development. Through the latter contribution, business services contribute to the general speed of technological and non-technological innovation in the European economy.

Many of these effects can be regarded as externalities, because the business-services industry itself cannot appropriate all associated benefits for client industries. Intellectual property rights in the business-services industry are underdeveloped. Clients, competitors and employees that leave the business-services firm often have few problems in applying the same idea for their own account and benefit. The positive external effects are increasingly acknowledged by national governments and international organizations. Recent policy documents mention business services as a crucial factor for enhancing the productivity and competitiveness of client industries.[1] Given these positive externalities, it can be taken for granted that economic welfare in the European economy is served by having a strong and innovative business-services industry.

Under-provision of innovation-related positive externalities can occur for several reasons. Consider first the yield in terms of original innovations. Several business-services branches in EU countries spend only a small share of their turnover on innovation expenditure. Such expenditure is essential for the creation of original innovation by the business-services industry. The incentive structure, institutional structures, bureaucratic procedures and fiscal climate for original innovations with an immaterial character deserve to be screened for this reason (Rubalcaba, 2006). Intellectual property rights for services products, such as brand names and copyrights, are underdeveloped in the EU. Many business services products, even though innovative, are difficult to patent. Under-provision of positive externalities in the area of knowledge diffusion may occur when the knowledge assets upon which diffusion must rest become obsolete. Constant maintenance and renewal of such human capital assets is necessary. The problem in this respect lies with the large majority of small business-services firms. Many of them entered the markets in the second half of the 1990s. Entrepreneurs and their employees (if there are any) are often so engaged in daily business services that they do not have the opportunity to keep their knowledge up-to-date, and certainly not to acquire new knowledge and skills that go beyond their current activities. Projected into the future, this could lead to exhaustion of the knowledge base in important parts of the business-services industry.

A major negative externality of business-services development on general economic welfare derives from this industry's own sluggish rate of productivity development. A stagnating productivity development in a large sector such as the business-services industry could become a drag on economic growth. Efficiency stagnation in intermediary industries has economy-wide effects, because most transactions in the final-goods market are preceded by several intermediary transactions. A low level of efficiency in business-services markets causes prices that are too high, that are then passed on downstream throughout the entire economy. This precise argument is mentioned in a report to the EU Industry Council. The EU Commission stresses that 'a great number of the cost pressures on the industry are generated not only within manufacturing, but in the service sectors. These input services to manufacturing are in many cases not competitive in Europe. The resulting negative downstream externalities effectively reduce the competitiveness of Europe's manufacturing industry.' The report adds that 'the most important obstacle to enhanced competitiveness of business services is represented by national market access restrictions' (European Commission, 1997).

How do the positive and negative externalities of business-services growth add up? Present data do not allow cost-benefit quantification. If we consider only the overall effect of business-services growth on macroeconomic labour productivity, there are two diverging effects. The positive effect runs through the impact on client industries. The negative effect comes from productivity stagnation in the business-services industry itself. A double-edged policy would therefore seek to improve the productivity growth of the business-services industry itself, while at the same time grasping opportunities to foster the productive impact of this sector for its client industries.

Market failure resulting from market power and monopolistic competition. Product markets in the business-services sector differ in their competitiveness. Table 15.1 provides some EU-wide data on market structures. Markets for standardised products are relatively transparent, characterized by limited product differentiation, and product prices are important competitive tools. Table 15.1 shows the market position of the leading firms (at EU level) in relation to the position of all other companies. The market hybridity factor measures the gap between the average leading firm and the average 'other' firm. A salient difference emerges between the branches with client-specific and standardized business-services products. When judged by the relatively small combined market

Table 15.1 Hybrid market structure in European business services industries, selected markets, 1992

Business services branch	*Number of firms (×1,000)*	*Number of leading firms*	*Combined market share (%)*		*Market hybridity factor*[1]
			Leading firms[2]	*All other firms*	
Standardized services					
Inspection and control	5.0	20	18	82	69
Temporary work agencies	7.6	6	35	65	682
Security services	5.0	7	62	38	1165
Cleaning services	40.0	200	35	65	108
Car hire	12.0	5	50	50	2400
Other equipment rental	72.0	47	20	80	383
Client-specific services					
Management consulting	8.0	20	8	92	35
Legal services	200.0	15	2	98	272
Accounting/auditing serv.[3]	150.0	6	10	90	2778
Industrial engineering	15.0	10	7	93	113
Computer services	16.0	10	9	91	158
Market research	1.5	10	—	—	—
Advertising	20.0	13	55	45	1880

Notes: 1. The market hybridity factor is calculated as the average market share of large, leading firms divided by the average market share of the small firms. 2. Market share is based on turnover value. 3. Data did not allow differentiation between simple administration shops and more knowledge-intensive services like certified accountants.
Sources: Data compiled by Rubalcaba (1999: 46, 430) from EU, Panorama of the EU Industry and industry sources; Kox (2002: 39).

share of the leading firms, markets for client-specific products are far more fragmented. It would seem that firms in the standardized business-services branches are better able to exploit some scale economies. In most branches for standardized services products, a small number of large and often international firms together account for a sizable market share, often in the range of 20 to 50 per cent of the market. This opens up the possibility for strategic and collusive behaviour by leading oligopolists. Since the markets for standardized products are reasonably transparent, competition-surveillance authorities will probably be able to deal relatively easily with collusive behaviour.

A different story holds for those business-services branches characterized by client-specific business services. The existence of concentrated market shares is not a widely present market failure problem here.[2] The leading firms often have smaller combined market shares than in the markets for standardized business-services products. Rather, market failure stems from the fact that these product markets are non-transparent and segmented, with prices playing a smaller role in competition. Distinctive knowledge-based inputs have come to be the key element in the reputations and competitiveness of firms in these markets for client-specific services.[3] Market segmentation occurs by region and by reputation of the provider. A proliferation of different product varieties is offered in different regional markets. Monopolistic competition, sometimes approaching localized monopolies, makes up the dominant form of competition.[4] A widespread complaint among users of these client-specific services is that the buyers find the tariff structure of the providers to be not very transparent. Buyers of knowledge-intensive services often have little insight into the real quality of the service providers – certainly not before buying the service. The standard market-failure problem – that prices diverge from marginal costs – must necessarily occur whenever demand is not perfectly price-elastic (Eaton and Lipsey 1989). Since demand for client-intensive business-services products is not perfectly price-elastic, market failures must be omnipresent in this instance. Switching-costs on the clients' side lower the price-elasticity of demand and contribute to the opacity of these markets.[5]

Policy attention seems required in order to address the lack of market transparency, and the prevalence of imperfect competition in knowledge-intensive business-services branches. Around a decade ago, the European Commission called on member states to take steps to promote transparency in the supply and demand sides of the business-services market (European Commission, 1998). The need for this is stressed again by the Commission more recently (European Commission, 2003a).

Market failure due to information asymmetry. Many knowledge-intensive business services products can be considered as credence goods – in other words, before and perhaps even shortly after purchasing the service, the client firm may be unable to judge its quality adequately. This creates information asymmetry. The market-based correction mechanism for this problem is the reputation premium. A client firm has to rely on information on the business-services firm's past performance. Basically, a reputation is nothing other than the expectation that an economic agent will act in the same way as he did in the past. Business-services firms with a proven reputation for being able to supply a high-quality service product can earn a price premium. The premium is a reward for time-consistent behaviour by the business-services provider. Building up a broad reputation for being able to supply high-quality services products is a lengthy and precarious process. Reputations in the business-services industry form implicit market-entry barriers, causing market segmentation. The established reputations of incumbents form a barrier to entering the premium segments of their market, with the reputation-barrier sheltering them from competition by newcomers. Hence, the reputation mechanism forms a barrier in the competition process, preventing direct competition between established, large incumbents on the one hand and new entrants or SME firms with local reputations on the other. In a market with reputation-based segmentation, increased entry of new firms in the market does not necessarily mean that the total business-services market becomes more competitive, nor that incumbents have a stronger incentive to reduce X-inefficiencies, and exploit any possible scale economies in order to gain cost-price advantages. For client firms, the reputation mechanism means that they often pay too high a price.[6]

The general conclusion from this section is that the development of the European business-services industry goes along with several market failures – social externalities, market power, information asymmetry and market non-transparencies – that may result in socially undesirable outcomes. This means that there may be a case for policy intervention in business-services markets. The next question is for which market failures policy intervention should perhaps be left in the hands of national authorities, and which elements deserve to be taken up at EU level.

15.2 Scope for EU-wide policies in business-services markets

A few simple rules may help in deciding which policy interventions in business-service developments are most appropriately made at the national level, and which issues might more auspiciously be tackled at the European level. The following criteria may help in delineating the most efficient policy level for dealing with issues related to market failures in business services:

Does the issue at hand form a clear issue provided for in the *acquis communautaire* of the European Union?[7]

Do the market failures in business-services development have a common European dimension?

For all other aspects: is there a positive reason to deviate from the subsidiarity rule that leaves policy intervention in principle at the level of member states?

Table 15.2 indicatively presents some market-failure issues that most likely pertain to particular elements in the *acquis communautaire*. Indicatively, because in the new 25-member Union there is likely to be debate between EU member states on any specific policy interference.

Creating a common ground for national business-services firms in the internal market is a policy area where market failures may have a clear European dimension. One particular European challenge relates to the role of market integration and the elimination of obstacles in the internal market for services. This is a political challenge that would allow European business services to compete in better positions and take advantage of wider and less fragmented markets.

European business-services markets are still dominated mainly by domestic competition, as is shown in Figure 15.1. The IT consultancy, equipment renting and personnel-recruitment branches are the most exposed to foreign competition, while those that are currently most sheltered from foreign competition are accountancy and tax consultancy. The international firms active in these branches operate in specific market segments, but the overwhelming majority of firms report that they have only domestic firms as competitors. Nonetheless, increasing the exposure of domestic firms to foreign competition would probably result in a number of beneficial effects: more pressure to improve labour productivity; more products; and process innovation. These positive externalities will have a European dimension. Innovation policies and the technology-transfer policies may have an unbeatable ally in business services. Business services produce innovative effects in companies and generate a change in the state of their technological knowledge. However, at the same time, they are carriers of the most important technological advances in society. This makes them possible pivots in EU policies that seek to stimulate and disseminate innovations.

Other policy areas that concern market failures with an EU-wide dimension include the protection of intellectual property rights and the creation of a system of innovation incentives for European business-services firms. Though national preferences can play a role here, it is clearly in everyone's interest to prevent national systems from being set up according to a 'beggar-my-neighbour' principle. The Kok Report (2004: 20) recognised the importance of business services, calling for sectoral policies: 'business *with a fast growth potential must be better supported*' and for the role of knowledge-intensive services to be recognised among other key sectors.

The same holds for quality standards for business-services firms: all EU member states may gain by agreeing on the use of more mutual recognition and some harmonization of national quality standards for business-services firms. Foreign competition can be suppressed artificially by national regulations that offer shelter to domestic business-services firms vis-à-vis foreign providers. Market regulations can operate as effective trade barriers, even if that was not the intention of the policy maker. In some knowledge-intensive

Table 15.2 Market failure issues in business-services development and the *acquis communautaire:* indicative correspondence

Market failure type	*Causative factor*	*Relevant elements of the acquis communautaire*	*Examples of relevant aspects*
Information asymmetry	Non-transparency of markets for client-specific business services	Freedom to provide services Right of establishment	• Different national quality standards, intra-EU trade
		Competition policy Consumers and health protection	• Transparent price and tariff structure • Quality guarantees law • Quality certification system • Reduce switching costs
Too few positive externalities	Market and system failures in innovation-related policies	Science and research, enterprise innovation policy	• Orientation of tangible products and processes • Under-recognition of organizational innovation and other intangible elements
	Lack of intellectual property rights for BSS products		• EU patent bureaucracy, innovation incentives
	Limited use of KIS	Small/medium-sized enterprises	• Intensity of KIBS use
Too many negative externalities	Slow productivity growth of BSS firms	Small/medium-sized enterprises	• Permanent education SME firms • Administrative burdens SME • Preconditions for scale effects
		Education and training	• Availability qualified personnel
		Science and research, industrial policy	• Positive incentives for innovative start-ups
		Competition policy	• Abate market collusion • Transparent prices/tariffs
		Freedom to provide services	• Free movement firms EU • Opening up national markets
		Regional policy	• New regional policies oriented to innovation spillovers
		Telecom and information technology	• Communication infrastructure
	Employment in business services	Training and education	• Relevant skills and expertise for KIBS activities
		Regional policy, social policy and employment	• Assist business services policies in new member states

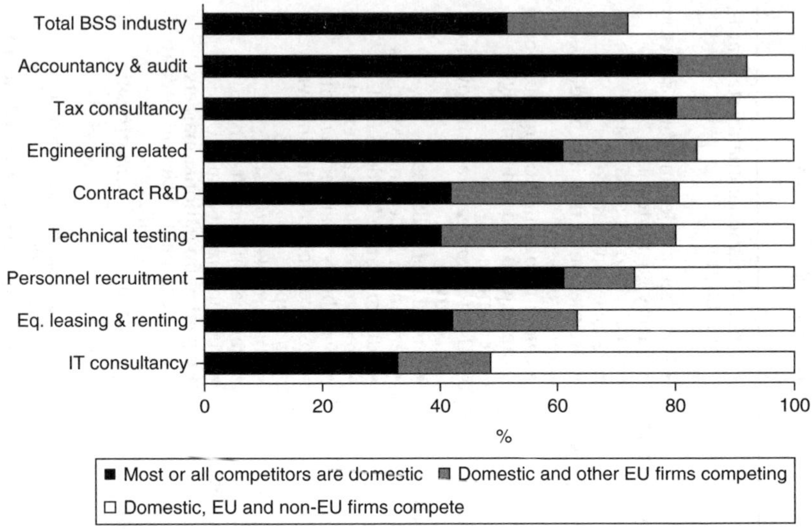

Figure 15.1 Exposure of domestic business services markets in the EU to international competition
Source: Results of a European survey among BSS firms. CSES (2001: 143).

business services, several market-affecting regulations are left that might function as effective non-tariff barriers to imports and direct investment. In 1993, European industrial organization specialists observed that service industries are highly affected by specific regulations and that 'in many countries services are subject to more government interventions than most other activities' (Sapir, Buigues and Jacquemin, 1993). There has been some improvement since then, but the situation in the business-services industry is still characterized by a relatively strong presence of market regulation by governments. The integration process of the Internal Market in an enlarged Europe may offer new opportunities to improve the qualifications and mobility of business-service professionals. Ensuring competitive and transparent markets for business services is an issue that obviously has EU-wide elements, if only because part of competition policies must be based on European competition law.

For some other policy areas, such as the promotion of business-services employment, it is far from obvious that this is an area where European policies should prevail over national policy interventions. Since labour market conditions and industrial structure still differ considerably between EU countries, it might be more efficient if national policies have precedence over EU policies. Insofar as business services have constituted the most dynamic sector in job creation in recent years, an active job policy may be contributing to the acceleration of this market process in some countries. It might reduce current levels of unemployment. Jobs generated in the sector will in turn create indirect jobs through positive spillovers: more services and greater competition. Hence, there may be good reasons for national policies to enhance business-services employment, e.g. by allowing more scope for part-time jobs, thus creating better conditions for women to take up jobs in business-services firms. European policies in this area may be supportive to national policy efforts, but should not replace the latter.

A similar argument holds for removing rigidities in labour markets. The latter may disturb business-services growth, because flexible working conditions appear to be a requirement for the growth of some business-services branches. Flexibility encourages the appearance and expansion of advanced services, many of which develop with very little structure, part-time jobs and in conditions of high job rotation. If market rigidities are not removed, more business-service jobs may migrate to low-wage countries. Given the specific national character of market failures in the relevant labour markets, national policies should – also here – have precedence over EU policies. The Kok Report (2004) calls, *inter alia*, for a re-examination of certain non-wage labour costs.[8]

To sum up, an affirmative answer can be given to the question 'Is there a need for EU-wide policies beyond what national governments do (or can do) to improve the market outcomes of national business-services sectors?' There is certainly scope for EU-wide policies in this area, but dealing with market failures in business-services development sometimes means that EU policies need to be formulated with a cooperative eye to member states' national policies. This may pertain, for instance to quality standards, recognition of professional qualifications, and tax treatment of business-services firms. Some policy issues, such as employment policies for the business-services industry, might perhaps more efficiently be left to the governments of EU member states, although some Commission activities and policies could help to promote employment-related actions at regional and national level.

In conclusion, there is room for policy actions – at the national and the EU level – that boost and encourage the contribution of business services to economic growth. It is beyond the scope of this study to discuss in detail all the market failure items mentioned in Table 15.2. However, several policy elements can be envisaged which will boost the role of business services in European economic growth. This may help to achieve some of the ambitious Lisbon goals with respect to employment, productivity and innovation.

Notes

1. According to the OECD: 'The provision of strategic business services is considered key to enhancing performance across the economy, in manufacturing and services alike'. Increased efficiency in the provision of services will have positive spillover effects on both large and small firms' (OECD, 1999: 8). A similar judgement stems

from the European Commission: 'The key importance of business services lies in their dynamic links and their contribution to the competitiveness of EU industry. An important element in EU competitiveness policy is to promote intangible investments (knowledge creation, quality, innovation, management, etc.). Business services are often required to supply key elements of such investments' (European Commission, 1998).

2. An exception may be the market for certified accountancy services, in which the international market is characterized by a small number of very large firms. However, due to lack of data, Table 15.1 is unable to distinguish this sub-market from that of the much more standardized administration services.
3. Distinctive assets are often intangible in nature (cf. Eustace, 2000), and as such it is difficult to separate them from the organizational fabric of the company and its workers.
4. Balkanization is the label used in industrial organisation theory for the proliferation of product varieties. In a survey article, Eaton and Lipsey (1989: 760) note: 'Market failure is ubiquitous in [...] models with balkanisation and localised competition since in free-entry equilibrium the position of each product is very much like [...] a natural monopoly'.
5. Client firms necessarily invest labour time and other resources in identifying, communicating and sometimes jointly solving specific business problems with the external business-services provider.
6. The clients may also have higher switching costs than necessary. In the case of proven reliability by a familiar business-services supplier, client firms may 'put all their eggs in one basket' by purchasing other services from the same supplier without the latter being the best or the cheapest supplier. The problem of market failure as a result of asymmetric information creates additional market-information costs, and hence stands in the way of the most cost-effective business solutions.
7. During the process of the enlargement of the European Union, the *acquis* was divided into 31 chapters for the purpose of negotiation between the EU and the candidate countries. Some of the relevant 'Chapters' are: Free movement of persons, Freedom to provide services, Free movement of capital, Company law, Competition policy, Taxation, Statistics, Social policy and employment, Industrial policy, Small and medium-sized enterprises, Science and research, Telecom and information technologies, Culture and audio-visual policy, Regional policy and coordination of structural instruments, Consumers and health protection, Cooperation in the field of Justice and Home Affairs.
8. The ideas in the Kok Report (2004), the work on the European Employment Strategy, and the ideas collected at the Forum on Business-Related Services and the Internal Market may bring about new policy actions that will boost employment growth in business services (e.g. European Commission, 2003b).

References

Abramovsky, L. and Griffith, R. (2006) 'Outsourcing and Offshoring: How Important is ICT?', *Journal of the European Economic Association*, 4, 2–3, April/May.

Aghion, P. and Griffith, R. (2005) *Competition and Growth: Reconciling Theory and Evidence*. Cambridge, MA: MIT Press.

Aiginger, K. (2001) 'Speed of Change and Growth of Manufacturing', in M. Peneder *et al.* (eds), *Structural Change and Economic Growth*. Vienna: WIFO.

Alange, S., Jacobsson, S. and Jarnehammar, A. (1998) 'Some Aspects of an Analytical Framework for Studying the Diffusion of Organizational Innovations', *Technology Analysis and Strategic Management*, 10, 3–21.

Altenberg, L. (1995) 'Genome Growth and the Evolution of the Genotype–Phenotype Map', in W. Banzhaf and F.H. Eckman (eds), *Evolution and Biocomputation*. Berlin and Heidelberg: Springer-Verlag, pp. 205–59.

Amable, B. and Palombarini, S. (1998) 'Technical Change and Incorporated R&D in the Services Sector', *Research Policy*, 27, 655–75.

Amiti, M. and Wei, S. (2006) 'Service Offshoring and Productivity: Evidence from the United States', National Bureau of Economic Research, *Working Paper No 11926*, January.

Andersen, B., Howells, J., Hull, R., Miles, I. and Roberts, J. (eds) (2000) *Knowledge and Innovation in the New Service Economy*. Aldershot: Edward Elgar.

Anderson, J. and van Wincoop, E. (2004) 'Trade Costs', *Journal of Economic Literature*, 42, September, 691–751.

Antonelli, C. (1998) 'Localized Technological Change, New Information Technology and the Knowledge-Based Economy: the European Evidence', *Journal of Evolutionary Economics*, 8, 2, 177–98.

Antonelli, C. (1999) *The Micro Dynamics of Technological Change*. London: Routledge.

Antonelli, C. (2000) 'New Information Technology and Localized Technological Change in the Knowledge Based Economy', in M. Boden and I. Miles (eds) *Services and the Knowledge-Based Economy*. London and New York: Continuum, pp. 170–91.

Antonelli, C. (2006) 'Diffusion as a Process of Creative Adoption', *Journal of Technology Transfer*, 31, 211–26.

Archibugi, D. and Lundvall, B.A. (2001) *The Globalizing Learning Economy*. Oxford: Oxford University Press.

Argyres, N.S. and Silverman, B.S. (2004) 'R&D, Organization Structure, and the Development of Corporate Technological Knowledge', *Strategic Management Journal*, 25, 929–58.

Arnold, J., Javorcik, B.S. and Mattoo (2006) 'Does Services Liberalization Benefit Manufacturing Firms?', *CEPR Discussion Paper 5902*. London: CEPR.

Arthur, B.W. (1991) 'Designing Economic Agents that Act like Human Agents: a Behavioural Approach to Bounded Rationality', *American Economic Review*, 81, 353–9.

Atkinson, J. (1984) 'Manpower Strategies for Flexible Organisations', *Personnel Management*, August, 29–31.

Autor, D., Levy, F. and Murnane, R. (2003) 'The Skill Content of Recent Technological Change: an Empirical Exploration', *Quarterly Journal of Economics*, 118, 4, 1279–33.

Bajari, P. and Tadelis, S. (2001) 'Incentives versus Transaction Costs: a Theory of Procurement Contracts', *RAND Journal of Economics*, 32, 3, 387–407.

Baker, G.P., Gibbons, R. and Murphy, K.J. (1994) 'Subjective Performance Measures in Optimal Incentive Contracts', *Quarterly Journal of Economics*, 109, 1125–56.

Baker, G.P., Gibbons, R. and Murphy, K.J. (2002) 'Relational Contracts and the Theory of the Firm', *Quarterly Journal of Economics*, 117, 1, 39–84.

Baldwin, C.Y. and Clark, K.B. (1997) 'Managing in an Age of Modularity', *Harvard Business Review*, 75, 5, 84–94.

Baldwin, R. (2006) 'Globalisation: the Great Unbundling(s)', Contributed paper to project Globalisation Challenges for Europe and Finland, Prime Minister's Office, Helsinki, 20 September.

Bandt, J. de (1995a) 'Indirect Productivity of Business Services, Through Non-material Investments', in E. Felli *et al.* (eds), The Service Sector: Productivity and Growth. Heidelberg: Physica Verlag, 157–73.

Bandt, J. de (1995b) *Services aux entreprises: informations, produits, richesses*. Paris: Economica.

Bandt, J. de (1999) 'The Concept of Labour Competence Requirements in a Service Economy', *The Service Industries Journal*, 19, 1, 1–17.

Bardhan, A.D., and Kroll, C. (2003) 'The New Wave of Outsourcing', University of California Berkeley, Fisher Centre for Real Estate and Urban Economics, Fisher Centre Research Report No. 1103.

Barrios, S., Görg, H. and Strobl, E. (2001) 'Multinational Enterprises and New Trade Theory: Evidence for the Convergence Hypothesis', *CEPR Discussion Paper 2827*. London: CEPR.

Bartelsman, E.J., Scarpetta, S. and Schivardi, F. (2003) 'Comparative Analysis of Firm Demographics and Survival: Micro-Level Evidence for the OECD Countries', *OECD Economics Department Working Paper No. 348*. Paris: OECD.

Baumol, W. (1967) 'Macroeconomics of Unbalanced Growth: The Anatomy of Urban Crisis; *American Economic Review*, 57, 415–26.

Baumol, W. et al. (1989) *Productivity and American leadership: The Long View*. London: MIT Press.

Baumol, W. (2007) 'On Mechanisms Underlying the Growing Share of Service Employment in the Industrialized Economies', in M. Gregory *et al.* (eds), *Services and Employment: Explaining the US–European Gap*. Princeton: Princeton University Press, 63–80.

Beaverstock, J., Taylor, P.J. and Smith. R.G. (1999) 'A Roster of World Cities', *Cities*, 16, 6, 445–58.

Belot, M. and Ederveen, S. (2005) 'Indicators of Cultural and Institutional Barriers in OECD Countries', CPB Memorandum, The Hague.

Bengtsson, L. and von Hartman, L. (2005) 'Outsourcing Manufacturing and its Effect on Firm Performance', Paper presented at CINet, Brighton, 4–6 September.

Berger, S. and Piore, M. (1980) *Dualism and Discontinuity in Industrial Societies*. New York: *Cambridge University Press*.

Bergstrand, J. (1989) 'The Generalized Gravity Equation, Monopolistic competition, and the Factor-Proportions Theory of International Trade', *Review of Economics and Statistics*, 23.

Beyers, W.B. and Lindahl, D.P. (1996a) 'Explaining the Demand for Producer Services: Is Costdriven Externalisation the Major Factor?', *Papers in Regional Science*, 75, 3, 351–74.

Beyers, W.B. and Lindahl, D.P. (1996b) 'Lone Eagles and High Fliers in Rural Producer Services', *Rural Development Perspectives*, 12, 3, 2–10.

Bilderbeek, R., Hertog, P. den, Marklund, G. and Miles, I. (1998) 'Service in Innovation: Knowledge-Intensive Business Services (KIBS) as Co-Producers of Innovation', SI4S Synthesis Papers, TSER program, STEP Group, Oslo.

Blind, K. *et al.* (2003) 'Patents in the Service Industries', Final Report to European Commission DG Research, Fraunhofer Institut für Systemtechnik und Innovationsforschung, Karlsruhe.

Boden, M. and Miles, I. (eds) (2000) *Services and the Knowledge-Based Economy*. London: Continuum.

Boone, J. (2000) 'Competitive Pressure: The Effects on Investments in Product and Process Innovation', *RAND Journal of Economics*, 31, 3, 549–69.

Brainard, S. (1997) 'An Empirical Assessment of the Proximity-Concentration Trade-off between Multinational Sales and Trade', *American Economic Review*, 87, 4.

Bresnahan, T. and Trajtenberg, M. (1995) 'General Purpose Technologies: Engines of Growth', *Journal of Econometrics*, 65, 83–108.

Bresnahan, T., Brynjolfsson, E. and Hitt, L.M. (2002) 'Information Technology, Workplace Organization and the Demand for Skilled Labor: Firm-level Evidence', *Quarterly Journal of Economics*, 117, 1, 339–76.

Brown, T.L. and Potosk, M. (2001) 'The Influence of Transaction Costs on Municipal and County Government Choices about Alternative Modes of Service Provision', School of Public Policy and Management Ohio State University, Paper presented at the 6th National Public Management Research Conference, Indiana University.

Browning, H. and Singelmann, J. (1978) 'The transformation of the US Labor Force – the Interaction of Industry and Occupation', *Politics and Society*, 8, 3/4.

Bruijn, R. de, Kox, H. and Lejour, A. (2007) 'Economic Benefits of an Integrated European Market for Services', *Journal of Policy Modeling*, 29.

Brusoni, S., Prencipe, A. and Pavitt, K. (2001) 'Knowledge Specialization, Organizational Coupling, and the Boundaries of the Firm: Why do Firms Know More Than They Make?', *Administrative Science Quarterly*, 46, 597–621.

Brynolfsson, E. and Hitt, L.M. (2000) 'Beyond Computation: Information Technology, Organizational Transformation, and Business Performance', *Journal of Economic Perspectives*, 117, 339–76.

Bryson, J.R. and Daniels, P.W. (1998) 'Business Link, Strong Ties and the Walls of Silence: Small and Medium-sized Enterprises and External Business Service Expertise', *Environment and Planning: Government and Policy*, 16, 265–80.

Bryson, J.R. and Rusten, G. (2005) 'Spatial Divisions of Expertise: Knowledge Intensive Business Service Firms and Regional Development in Norway', *The Services Industries Journal*, 25, 8, 959–77.

Bryson, J.R. and Wellington C. (2003) 'Image Consultancy in the United Kingdom: Recipe Knowledge and Recreational Employment', *The Service Industries Journal*, 23, 1, 59–76.

Bryson, J.R., Daniels, P.W. and Rusten, G. (2004) 'Design Workshops of the World: The Production and Integration of Industrial Design Expertise into the Product Development and Manufacturing Process in Norway and the United Kingdom', *Working Paper 61/02*, Institute for Research, Economics and Business Administration, Bergen, November.

Bryson, J.R., Daniels, P.W. and Warf, B. (2004) *Service Worlds: People, Organisations, Technologies*. London: Routledge.

Burda, M. and Dluhosch, B. (2000) 'Cost Competition, Fragmentation and Globalization', *CESifo Paper No. 393*. Munich: Center for Economic Studies & IFO Institute for Economic Research.

Caballero, R. and Hammour, M. (1991) 'The Cleaning Effects of Recessions', *NBER working paper*. Washington DC: NBER.

Carmeli, A. and Tishler, A. (2004) 'The Relationship Between Intangible Organizational Elements and Organizational Performance', *Strategic Management Journal*, 25, 1257–78.

Carr, D.L., Markusen, J.R. and Maskus, K.E. (2001) 'Estimating the Knowledge Capital Model of the Multinational Enterprise', *American Economic Review*, 91.
Chandler, A.D. (1962) *Strategy and Structure*. Cambridge, MA: MIT Press.
Chandler, A.D. (1977) *The Visible Hand: The Managerial Revolution in American Business*. Cambridge, MA: Belknap Harvard University Press.
Christensen, L.R., Jorgenson, D.W. and Lau, L.J. (1971) 'Conjugate Duality and the Transcendental Logarithmic Production Function', *Econometrica*, 39, 255–6.
Chun, H. (2003) 'Information Technology and the Demand for Educated Workers: Disentangling the Impacts of Adoption Versus Use', *The Review of Economics and Statistics*, 85, 1–8.
Clark, C. (1938) 'Australian Economic Progress Against a World Background', J. Fisher Lecture.
Coe, N.M. (2000) 'The Externalisation of Producer Services Debate: the UK Computer Services Sector', *The Services Journal*, 20, 2, 64–81.
Collechia, A. (2001) 'The impact of Information Communications Technology on output growth', STI Working Paper. Paris: OECD.
Conway, P., Janod, V. and Nicoletti, G. (2005) 'Product Market Regulation in OECD Countries: 1998 to 2003', *OECD Economics Department Working Paper No. 419*. Paris: OECD.
Copenhagen Economics (2005a) 'Economic Assessment of the Barriers to the Internal Market in Services', Commissioned by the European Commission, Copenhagen/Brussels. Available at www.copenhageneconomics.com.
Copenhagen Economics (2005b) 'The Economic Importance of the Country of Origin Principle in the Proposed Services Directive', Commissioned by UK presidency of the EU, Copenhagen.
Creplet F., Dupouet, O., Kern, F., Mehmanpazir, B. and Munier, F. (2001) 'Consultants and Experts in Management Consulting Firms', *Research Policy*, 30, 1517–35.
Crépon, B., Duguet, E. and Mairesse, J. (1998) 'Research and Development, Innovation and Productivity: an Econometric Analysis at the Firm Level', *Economics of Innovation and New Technology*, 7, 115–58.
CSES (2001) 'Barriers to Trade in Business Services, Final report', Report commissioned by the European Commission, Centre for Strategy and Evaluation Services. Brussels: European Commission. Available at: http://europa.eu.int/comm/enterprise/services/business_services/documents/studies/barriers_to_trade_bs.pdf.
Cuadrado, J.R. and Río, C. del (1993) Los servicios en España. Madrid: Pirámide.
Czarnitzki, D. and Spielkamp, A. (2000) 'Business Services in Germany: Bridges for Innovation', *ZEW Discussion paper 52*. Mannheim: ZEW.
Damanpour, F. and Evan, W.M. (1984) 'Organizational Innovation and Performance: the Problem of Organizational Lag', *Administrative Science Quarterly*, 29, 392–409.
Daniels, P.W. (2000) 'Exports of Services or Servicing Exports?' *Geografiska Annaler*, 82B, 1–15.
Daniels, P.W. and Bryson J.R. (2005) 'Sustaining Business and Professional Services in a Second City Region: The Case of Birmingham, UK', The Service Industries Journal, 25, 4, 505–24.
Daniels, P.W., Dinteren, J.H.J van and Monnoyer, M.C. (1992) 'Consultancy Services and the Urban Hierarchy in Western Europe', *Environment and Planning A*, 24, 1731–48.
Daveri, F. (2002) 'The New Economy in Europe, 1992–2001', *Oxford Review of Economic Policy*, 18, 23–48.
David, P. (1990) 'The Dynamo and the Computer: an Historical Perspective on the Modern Productivity Paradox', *American Economic Review*, 80, 355–61.

Davies, A. (2001) 'Integrated Solutions: the New Economy Between Manufacturing and Services' Falmer, Sussex: SPRU/EPSRC/CENTRIM, PowerPoint presentation at: http://www.beonline.co.uk/Activities/Conference/conf2003/AndyDavies.ppt.

Davies, A. (2003) 'Are Firms Moving Downstream into High-Value Services', in J. Tidd and F.M. Hull (eds), *Service Innovation: Organizational Responses to Technological Imperatives and Market Opportunities*. London. Imperial College Press.

Dawson, R. (1999) *Developing Knowledge-Based Client Relationships: The Future of Professional Services*. Boston: Butterworth-Heinemann.

Deardorff, A.V. (1998) 'Determinants of Bilateral Trade: Does Gravity Work in a Neoclassical World?', in J.A. Frankel (ed.), *The Regionalization of the World Economy*. Chicago: University of Chicago Press.

Denison, E. (1967) *Why Growth Rates Differ*. Washington: The Brookings Institution.

Djankov, S., La Porta, R., Lopez, F. and Shleifer, A. (2002) 'The regulation of entry', *Quarterly Journal of Economics*, 117, 1, 1–37.

Djellal, F. (2000) 'The Rise of Information Technologies', Non-Informational Services, Vierteljahrshefte zur Wirtschaftsforschung 69, Jahrgang, Heft 4, 646–56, available at: http://www.diw.de/deutsch/publikationen/vierteljahrshefte/docs/papers/v_00_4_12.pdf.

Doeringer, P.B. and Piore, M.J. (1971) *Internal Labor Markets and Manpower Analysis*. Lexington, MA: D.C. Heath.

Domberger, S. (1998) *The Contracting Organization: A Strategic Guide to Outsourcing*. Oxford, Oxford University Press.

Drejer, I. (1999) 'Technological Change and Interindustrial Linkages: Introducing Knowledge Flows in Input–output Studies'. PhD dissertation, Aalborg University, Aalborg.

Drejer, I. (2001) 'Business Services – a Driver of Innovation and Technological Development?' Paper presented at The Future of Innovation Studies Eindhoven, University of Technology, September.

Drejer, I. (2002) 'Business Services as a Production Function', *Economic Systems Research*, 14, 4, 389–405.

Duffy, H. (1995) *Competitive Cities: Succeeding in the Global Economy*. London and New York: E. and F.N. Spon.

Eaton, B.C. and Lipsey, R.G. (1989) 'Product differentiation', in R. Schmalensee and R. Willig (eds), *Handbook of Industrial Organization*. Amsterdam: North-Holland, I, 725–68.

ECB Task Force (2006) 'Competition, Productivity and Prices in the Euro area Services Sector', Task Force of the Monetary Policy Committee of the European System of Central Banks, Occasional Paper Series No 44, European Central Bank, Frankfurt.

ECORYS-NEI (2004) 'Business Services: Contribution to Growth and Productivity in the European Union', Technical report prepared for the European Commission, Enterprise Directorate-General.

Edwards, B.K. and Starr, R.M. (1987) 'A Note on Indivisibilities, Specialisation and Economies of Scale', *American Economic Review*, 77, 1, 192–4.

Elfenbein, D. and Lerner, J. (2003) 'Ownership and Control Rights in Internet Portal Alliances, 1995–1999', *RAND Journal of Economics*, 34, 2, 356–69.

Elfring, T. (1988) *Service Sector Employment in Advanced Economies*. Aldershot: Gower.

Empirica GmbH, DIW Berlin and Databank Consulting spa (2003) 'ICT & e-business in the Business Services Sector', E-business watch, European Commission, Enterprise Directorate General, e-Business, ICT Industries, and Services, Bonn/Brussels, March.

Erkel-Rousse, H. and Mirza, D. (2002) 'Import Price Elasticities: Reconsidering the Evidence', *Canadian Journal of Economics*, 35, 282–306.

European Commission (1989) 'The Efficiency of Business Services Used by Manufacturing Industries', MRB-Study, Brussels and Luxembourg, European Commission.

European Commission (1997) 'Industrial Competitiveness and Business Services: Report to the Industry Council', Working Document from the Commission Services, IIIA.0/OG D(97)pw//bs/workpap. Brussels: European Commission.

European Commission (1998) 'The Contribution of Business Services to Industrial Performance: a Common Policy Framework', Communication from the Commission to the Council, COM(1998)534final. Brussels: European Commission.

European Commission (2000) '*European Competitiveness Report*'. Brussels: Commission of the European Communities.

European Commission (2002a) 'Report from the Commission to the Council and the European Parliament on the state of the internal market for services', COM (2002) 441 final. Brussels: European Commission.

European Commission (2002b) 'Europe's Response to World Ageing: A Contribution of the European Commission to the 2nd World Assembly of Ageing', COM (2002) 143 FIN. Brussels: European Commission.

European Commission (2003a) 'Third European Report on Science and Technology Indicators – Towards a Knowledge-Based Economy', Luxembourg: European Commission.

European Commission (2003b) 'The Competitiveness of Business-Related Services and their Contribution to the Performance of European Enterprises'. Communication from the European Commission 747(2003) final. Brussels: European Commission.

European Commission (2004a) 'Proposal for a Directive of the European Parliament and of the Council on Services in the Internal Market', SEC (2004) 21. Brussels: European Commission.

European Commission (2004b) 'Innovation in Europe – Results for the EU, Iceland and Norway, Data 1998–2001, 2004 Edition'. Brussels: European Commission/Eurostat.

European Commission (2005) 'Key Figures 2005 on Science, Technology and Innovation: Towards a European Knowledge Area DG Research'. Brussels: Commission of the European Communities.

Eurostat (2000) 'Report of the Task Force Price and Volume Measures for Real Estate, Renting and Business Services'. Luxembourg: Eurostat B1/CN 438e.

Eurostat (2001) 'Handbook on Price and Volume Measures in National Accounts', Luxembourg: Office for Official Publication of the European Communities.

Eustace, C. (2000) 'The Intangible Economy – Impact and Policy Issues', Report of the European High Level Expert Group on the Intangible Economy, European Commission, Brussels.

Evangelista, R. (2000) 'Sectoral Patterns of Technological Change in Services', *Economics of Innovation and New Technology*, 4, 183–221.

Fabiani, S., Druant, M. and Hernando, I. (2005) 'The Pricing Behaviour of Firms in the Euro Area: New Survey Evidence', *Working Paper Series No. 535*. Frankfurt: European Central Bank.

Feenstra, R.C. and Hanson, G.H. (1999) 'The Impact of Outsourcing and High-technology Capital on Wages: Estimates for the United States, 1979–1990', *Quarterly Journal of Economics*, 114, 3, 907–40.

Filardo, A. (1997) 'Cyclical Implications of the Declining Manufacturing Employment Share', Federeal Reserve of Kansas City, Economic review 2Q.

Fine, B. (1998) *Labour Market Theory: Constructive Reassessment*. New York: Routledge.

Fisher, A.G.B. (1939) 'Production, Primary, Secondary, Tertiary', *Economic Record*, 15, June, 24–38.

Fixler, D.J. and Siegel, D. (1999) 'Outsourcing and Productivity Growth in Services', *Structural Change and Economic Dynamics*, 10, 177–94.

Fontaine, C. (1988) 'Le development des activités de service aux enterprises et dans les enterprises', *Revue d'Economie Industrielle*, I trimester.

Francois, J.F. (1990) 'Producer Services, Scale and the Division of Labour', *Oxford Economic Papers*, 42, 715–29.

Francois, J.F. and Reinert, K. (1995) 'The Role of Services in the Structure of Production and Trade: Stylised Facts from a Cross-Country Analysis', *CEPR Discussion Paper No. 1228*. London: CEPR.

Fuss, M. and McFadden, D. (eds) (1978) *Production Economics: a Dual Approach to Theory and Applications*. Amsterdam: North-Holland.

Gadrey, J. and Gallouj, F. (1998) 'The Provider–Customer Interface in Business and Professional Services', *The Services Industries Journal*, 18, 2, 2–15.

Gadrey, J., Gallouj, F. and Weinstein, O. (1995) 'New Modes of Innovation: How Services Benefit Industry', *International Journal of Service Industry Management*, 6, 4–16.

Gage, J. and Lesher, M. (2005) 'Intertwined: FDI in Manufacturing and Trade in Services', *OECD Trade Policy Paper No. 25*. Paris, OECD.

Gallouj, C. (1997) 'Asymmetry of Information and the Service Relationship: Selection and Evaluation of the Service Provider', *International Journal of Service Industry Management*, 8, 1, 42–64.

Gallouj, C. and Gallouj, F. (1996) L'innovation dans les services. Paris: Editions Economica.

Gallouj, F. (1997) 'Asymmetry of Information and the Service Relationship: Selection and Evaluation of the Service Provider', *International Journal of Service Industry Management*, 8, 1, 42–64.

Gallouj, F. and Weinstein, O. (1997) 'Innovation in Services', Research Policy, 26, 537–56.

GAO – Government Accountability Office (2005) 'International Trade – US and India Data on Offshoring Show Significant Differences', *Report to Congressional Committees*, October. Washington DC: GAO.

Gaulier, G., Mayer, T. and Zignago, S. (2003) 'Notes on CEPII's distances measures'. Available at Paris, www.cepii.fr.

Ghellinck, E. de, *et al.* (1996) 'Price Competition and Price Convergence: The Single Market Review Series, Impact on Competition and Scale Effects'. Brussels: DRI/European Commission.

Ghosh, A. (1958) 'Input–Output Approach to an Allocative System', *Economica*, 25, 58–64.

Ghoshal. S. and Moran, P. (1996) 'Bad for Practice: A Critique of the Transaction Cost Theory', *Academy of Management Review*, 21, 1, 13–47.

Global Insight (2004) *The Comprehensive Impact of Offshore IT Software and Services Outsourcing on the US Economy and the IT Industry*. March. Lexington, MA: Global Insight.

Glückler, J. (1999) 'Management Consulting – Structure and Growth of a Knowledge Intensive Business Service Market in Europe', Institut für Wirtschafts- und Sozialgeographie, Department of Economic and Social Geography, Johann Wolfgang Goethe-Universität Frankfurt, IWSG Working Papers 12-1999.

Golub, S. (2003) 'Measures of Restrictions on Inward Foreign Direct Investment for OECD Countries'. OECD Economic Department Working paper no. 357. Paris: OECD.

Granovetter, M.S. (1985) 'Economic Action and Social Structure: The Problem of Embeddedness', *American Journal of Sociology*, 91, 3, 481–510.

Greene, W.H. (1993) *Econometric Analysis*, 2nd edn. Englewood Cliffs, NJ: Prentice Hall.

Greenfield, H.I. (1966) *Manpower and the Growth of Producer Services*. Columbia, NY: Columbia University Press.

Greenhalgh, C. and Gregory, M. (2000) 'Labour Productivity and Product Quality: Their Growth and Inter-industry Transmission in the UK 1979–90', in R. Barrell, G. Mason and M. O'Mahoney, (eds), *Productivity, Innovation and Economic Performance*. Cambridge: Cambridge University Press.

Griffin, A. (1996) 'PDMA Success Measurement Project: Recommended Measures for Product Development Success and Failure.' *Journal of Product Innovation Management*, 13, 478–496.

Griliches, Z. (1979) 'Issues in Assessing the Contribution of Research and Development to Productivity Growth', *Bell Journal of Economics*, 10, 92–116.

Grimshaw, D. and Miozzo, M. (2006) 'Institutional Effects on the Market for IT Outsourcing: Analyzing Clients, suppliers and staff transfer in Germany and the UK', Organization Studies, 27, 1229–590.

Grossman, G. and Rossi-Hansberg, E. (2006) 'The Rise of Offshoring: It's not Wine and Cloth Anymore', MIMEO Princeton University, Lecture at Jackson Hole, 25 August.

Grubel, H. (1995) 'Producer Services: Their Important Role in Growing Economies', in E. Felli, F.C. Rosati and G. Tria, (eds), *The Service Sector: Productivity and Growth*. Heidelberg: Physica-Verlag.

Grubel, H.G. and Walker, M.A. (1991) 'The Dominance of Producers' Services in the US Economy', *Banca Nazionale del Lavoro Quarterly Review*, 1976, 57–68.

Grünfeld, L.A. and Moxnes, A. (2003) 'The Intangible Globalization: Explaining the Patterns of International Trade and Foreign Direct Investment in Services'. Mimeo, Norwegian Institute of International Affairs.

Guerrieri, P., Maggi, B., Meliciani, V. and Padoan, P. (2005) 'Technology Diffusion, Services, and Endogenous Growth in Europe: Is the Lisbon Strategy Useful?', *IMF Working Paper WP/05/103*. Washington: IMF.

Hansen, N. (1994) 'The Strategic Role of Producer Services in Regional Development', *International Regional Science Review*, 16, 187–95.

Hargadon, A. and Sutton, R.I. (1997) 'Technology brokering and innovation in a product development firm', *Administrative Science Quarterly*, 42, 718–49.

Hauknes, J. (2000) 'Dynamic Innovation Systems: What Is the Role of Services?', in M. Boden and I. Miles (eds), *Services and the Knowledge-based Economy*. London: Continuum, pp. 38–63.

Heeks, R. (1996) *India's Software Industry*. Thousand Oaks, CA/London: Sage Publications.

Helpman, E. and Krugman, P. (1985) *Market Structure and Foreign Trade*. Cambridge, MA: The MIT Press.

Hempell, T. (2002) 'What's Spurious, What's Real? Measuring the Productivity Impacts of ICT at Firm-level', ZEW Discussion Paper 02-42. Mannheim: Center for European Economic Research.

Hertog, P. den, (2000) 'Knowledge Intensive Business Services as Co-Producers of Innovation', *International Journal of Innovation Management*, 4, 4, 491–528.

Hertog, P. den and Bilderbeek, R. (1998) 'The New Knowledge Infrastructure: The Role of Technology-Based Knowledge Intensive Business Services in National Innovation Systems', *SI4S Topical Paper*. Oslo: STEP Group.

Hicks, J. (1973) *Capital and Time, a neo-Austrian theory*. Oxford: Clarendon Press.

Hill, T.D. (1977) 'On Goods and Services', *Review of Income and Wealth*, 4, 23, 315–38.

Hinks, J. and Hanson, H. (2001) 'In-house or Outsourced? Making the Decision', in J. Hinks and J. Reuvid (eds), *Strategies for Outsourcing and Facilities Management: Managing Business Support Service*. London: Kogan, pp. 41–9.

Hipp, C., Tether, B. and Miles, I. (2000) 'The Incidence And Effects Of Innovation In Services: Evidence From Germany', *International Journal of Innovation Management*, December, 417–54.

Hislop, D. (2002) 'The Client Role in Consultancy Relations During the Appropriation of Technological Innovations', *Research Policy*, 31, 657–71.

Hodrick, R. and Prescott, E. (1980) 'Post-war US Business Cycles: an Empirical Investigation'. Carnegie/Mellon University Working Paper.

Hollenstein, H. (2002) 'Innovation Modes in the Swiss Service Sector: a Cluster Analysis Based on Firm-level Data', *Research Policy*, 32, 5, 715–885.

Hölzl, W., Reinstaller, A. and Windrum, P. (2005) 'Organizational Innovation, Information Technology, and Outsourcing to Business Services'. Maastricht: MERIT-Infonomics Working paper 2005-030. Available at: http://www.merit.unu.edu/publications/rmpdf/2005/rm2005-030.pdf.

Howells, J. (2001) 'The Nature of Innovation in Services', in D. Pilat (ed.), *Innovation and Productivity in Services*. Paris: OECD, pp. 55–79.

Howells, J. (2002) 'Innovation, Consumption and Services: Encapsulation and the Combinatorial Role of Services'. Paper for 12th RESER Conference (Services and Innovation, Manchester). Manchester: CRIC/Prest.

Howells, J. and Tether, B. (2004) 'Innovation in Services: Issues at Stake and Trends', Inno Studies Programme (ENTR-C/2001). Brussels: Commission of the European Communities.

Hughes, A. and Wood, E. (1999) 'Rethinking Innovation Comparisons between Manufacturing and Services: the Experience of the CBR SME Surveys in the UK', *Working paper no. 140*. Cambridge: ESRC Center for Business Research, Cambridge University.

Illeris, S. (1994) 'Proximity between Service Producers and Service Users', *Tijdschrift voor Economische en Sociale Geografie*, 85, 4, 294–302.

Inklaar, R., O'Mahony, M. and Timmer, M. (2005) 'ICT and Europe's Productivity Performance: Industry-Level Growth Account Comparison with the United States', *Review of Income and Wealth*, 51, 505–26.

Itami, H. and Roehl, W.T. (1987) *Mobilizing Invisible Assets*. Cambridge, MA: Harvard University Press.

Jorgenson, D.W. and Griliches, Z. (1967) 'The Explanation of Productivity Change', *Review of Economic Studies*, 34, 249–83.

Jorgenson, D.W. and Stiroh, K.J. (2000) 'Raising the Speed Limit: US Economic Growth in the Information Age', *Brookings Papers on Economic Activity*, 1, 125–211.

Jorgenson, D.W., Gollup, F.M. and Fraumeni, B.M. (1987) *Productivity and US Economic Growth*. Cambridge, MA: Harvard University Press.

Jorgenson, D.W., Ho, M.S. and Stiroh, K.J. (2005) 'Growth of US Industries and Investment in Information Technology and Higher Education', in C. Corrado, J. Haltiwanger and D. Sichel, (eds), *Measuring Capital in a New Economy*. Chicago: University of Chicago Press.

Kamien, M.I., Muller, E. and Zang, I. (1992) 'Research Joint Ventures and R&D Cartels', *American Economic Review*, 82, 5, 1293–306.

Karsenty, G. (2002) 'Trends in Services Trade under GATS Recent Developments', Presentation prepared for the Symposium on Assessment of Trade in Services, WTO, 14–15 March.

Katsoulacos, Y. and Tsounis, N. (2000) 'Knowledge-Intensive Business Services and Productivity Growth: the Greek Evidence', in M. Boden and I. Miles (eds), *Services and the Knowledge-based Economy.* London: Continuum, pp. 192–208.

Keeble, D. and Nachum, L. (2002) 'Why do Business Service Firms Cluster? Small Consultancies, Clustering and Decentralization in London and Southern England', *Transactions of the Institute of British Geographers*, 27, 1, 67–90.

Kim, H.Y. (1992) 'The Translog Production Function and Variable Returns to Scale', *The Review of Economics and Statistics*, 74, 546–52.

Kimura, F. and Lee, H. (2006) 'The Gravity Equation in International Trade in Services', *Review of World Economics*, 142, 92–129.

Kirkegaard, J.F. (2004) 'Outsourcing – Stains on the White Collar?' Washington DC: Institute for International Economics.

KISINN (1998) 'Knowledge-intensive Services and Innovation: A Review of European Developments', Final report available at: http://improving-ser.sti.jrc.it/default/page.gx?_app.page=entity.html&_app.action=entity&_entity.object=TSER----000000000000001B8&_entity.name=Executive_summary.

Kline, S.J. and Rosenberg, N. (1986) 'An Overview of Innovation', in R. Landau and N. Rosenberg (eds), *The Positive Sum Strategy: Harnessing Technology for Economic Growth.* Washington, DC: National Academy Press, pp. 275–305.

Klodt, H., Maurer, R. and Schimmelpfennig, A. (1997) 'Tertiarisierung in der deutsche Wirtschaft: Schwerpunkstudie zur Strukturberichterstattung fur den Bundesminister fur Wirtschaft'. Kiel: Institut fur Weltwirtschaft.

Kok, W. (2004) 'Facing the Challenge: The Lisbon strategy for growth and Employment'. Report from the High Level Group chaired by Wim Kok, November. Brussels: European Commission.

Kongsrud, P.M. and Wanner, I. (2005) 'The Impact of Structural Policies on Trade-Related Adjustments and the Shift to Services', Enhancing the Performance of the Services Sector. Paris: OECD.

Kox, H. (2001) 'Sources of structural growth in business services', *CPB Research memorandum No. III/2001/12,* The Hague. Available at http://www.cpb.nl/eng/pub/cpbreeksen/memorandum/12/memo12.pdf.

Kox, H. (2002) 'Growth Challenges for the Dutch Business-services Industry: International Comparison and Policy Issues', *Special study No. 40.* The Hague: CPB Netherlands Bureau for Economic Policy Analysis.

Kox, H. (2004) 'The Contribution of Business Services to Aggregate Productivity Growth', in G. Gelauff *et al.* (eds), *Fostering Productivity Growth – Patterns,* Determinants and Policy Implications, Contributions to Economic Analysis Series No. 263, June. Amsterdam/Boston: Elsevier Science, pp. 245–64.

Kox, H. and Lejour, A. (2005) 'Regulatory Heterogeneity as Obstacle for International Services Trade', *CPB Discussion Paper 49.* The Hague: CPB.

Kox, H. and Lejour, A. (2006) 'The Effect of the Services Directive on Intra-EU Trade and FDI', *Revue Economique*, 57, 4, 747–69.

Kox, H., Leeuwen, G. van and Wiel, H. van der (2006) 'Scale, Market Structure and Productivity in European Business Services', *Discussion Paper.* The Hague: CPB.

Kox, H., Lejour, A. and Montizaan, R. (2004a) 'The Free Movement of Services Within the EU', *CPB Document 69.* The Hague: CPB.

Kox, H., Lejour, A. and Montizaan, R. (2004b) 'Intra-EU Trade and Investment in Service Sectors and Regulation Patterns', *CPB Memorandum 101.* The Hague: CPB.

Kraft, K. (1990) 'Are Product- and Process-innovations Independent of Each Other?', *Applied Economics*, 22, 1029–38.

Kumbhakar, S., Gosh, S. and McGucking, J. (1991) 'A Generalized Production Frontier Approach for Estimating Determinants of Inefficiency in US Dairy Firms', *Journal of Business and Economic Statistics*, 9, 279–86.
Kutscher, R.E. (1988) 'Growth of Services Employment in the United States', in B.R. Guile and J.B. Quinn (eds), *Technology in Services: Policies for Growth, Trade and Employment*. Washington DC: National Academy Press.
Kuusisto, J. (2000) 'The Determinants of Service Capability in Small Manufacturing Firms'. PhD thesis, Kingston University Small Business Research Centre, Kingston, UK.
Lacity, M. and Hirschheim, R. (1993) *Information Systems Outsourcing: Myths, Metaphors and Realities*. New York: Wiley.
Langlois, R.N. (2002) 'Modularity in Technology and Organization', *Journal of Economic Behaviour and Organization*, 49, 19–37.
Langlois, R.N. (2003) 'The Vanishing Hand: the Changing Dynamics of Industrial Capitalism', *Industrial and Corporate Change*, 12, 2, 351–85.
Langlois, R.N. and Robertson, P.L. (1995) *Firms, Markets and Economic Change*. London: Routledge.
Lawrence, P.R. and Lorsch, J.W. (1967) *Organization and Environment*. Homewood, IL: Irwin.
Lay, G. (2002) 'Service provider Industry: Industrial Migration From Manufacturing to Selling Products and Services – Trends and Impacts', ISI report 8 (ISI-A-13-02). Karlsruhe: Fraunhofer Institute for Systems and Innovation Research.
Lee, J. (1996) 'Do Services Temper Business Cycles?: Implications of the Rising Service Sector'. University of California Irvine, Department of Economics.
Leeuwen, G. van, and Wiel, H. van der (2003) 'Do ICT Spillovers Matter? – Empirical Evidence for the Netherlands', CPB Discussion Paper 26. The Hague: CPB.
Leiponen, A. (2001) *Knowledge Services in the Innovation System*. Helsinki: ETLA/SITRA.
Leiponen, A. (2005) 'Organization of Knowledge and Innovation: The Case of Finnish Business Services', *Industry and Innovation*, 12, 2, 185–203.
Leiponen, A. (2006) 'Managing Knowledge for Innovation: The Case of Business-to-Business Services', *Journal of Product Innovation Management*, 23, 3, 238–58.
Leiponen, A. (2007) 'Control of Intellectual Assets in Client Relationships: Implications for Innovation', Manuscript under review.
Leiponen, A. and Drejer, I. (forthcoming) 'What exactly are technological regimes? Intra-industry heterogeneity in the organization of innovation activities'. Forthcoming in Research Policy 2007. Paper presented at the DRUID Tenth Anniversary Summer Conference 2005 on Dynamics of Industry and Innovation, Organizations, Networks and Systems.
Lejour, A.M., Verweij, G., Veenendaal, P.J.J. and Leeuwen, N.I.M. van (2006) 'WorldScan: a model for International Policy Analysis', *CPB Document 111*. The Hague: CPB.
Lerner, J. and Merges, R.P. (1998) 'The Control of Technology Alliances: An Empirical Analysis of the Biotechnology Industry', *Journal of Industrial Economics*, 46, 2, 125–56.
Lesher, M. and Nordås, H. (2006) 'Business Services, Trade and Costs', TD/TC/WP(2006)32. Paris: OECD.
Lewis, J. (1988) 'Services: Post Industrial Transformation or Flexible Production', in J.N. Marshall, (ed.), *Services and Uneven Development*. Oxford: Oxford University Press.
Machlup, F. (1962) *The Production and Distribution of Knowledge in the United States*. Princeton: Princeton University Press.
Maddison, A. (2004) 'Macromeasurement Before and After Colin Clark', *Australian Economic History Review*, 44, 1, 1–34.

Mahnke, V., Overby, M.L. and Vang, J. (2005) 'Strategic Outsourcing of IT Services: Theoretical Stocktaking and Empirical Challenges', *Industry and Innovation*, 12, 2, 205–53.

Mairesse, J. and Sassenou, M. (1991) 'R&D and Productivity: a Survey of Econometric Studies at the Firm Level', *The Science Technology and Industry Review*, 8, 317–48.

Malerba, F. (2004) *Sectoral Systems of Innovation*. Cambridge: Cambridge University Press.

Mann, C.L. (2003) 'Globalisation of IT Services and White Collar Jobs: The Next Wave of Productivity Growth', *Institute for International Economics Policy Brief No. PB03-11*, December.

Mann, C.L. (2004) 'The US Current Account, New Economy Services and Implications for Sustainability', *Review of International Economics*, 12, 2, 262–76.

Mansfield, E. (1965) 'Rates of Return from Industrial Research and Development', *American Economic Review*, 55, 310–22.

Marengo, L. and Dosi, G. (2005) 'Division of Labor, Organizational Coordination and Market Mechanisms in Collective Problem-solving', *Journal of Economic Behavior and Organization*, 58, 303–26.

Marin, D. (2004) 'A Nation of Poets and Thinkers – Less so with Eastern Enlargement? Austria and Germany', *Department of Economics Discussion Paper No. 2004–06*, April, Munich: University of Munich.

Markusen, J.R. (2002) *Multinational Firms and the Theory of International Trade*. Cambridge, MA: MIT Press.

Markusen, J.R. (2005) 'Modelling the Offshoring of White-collar Services: From Comparative Advantage to the New Theories of Trade and FDI', National Bureau of Economic Research, *Working paper 11827*.

Martini, M. (1990) 'Implicazioni statistiche dell'analisi dei servizi resi alle imprese. Criteri di identificazione e classificazioni', Internal Document of Eurostat, Luxembourg.

Mason, G. and Wagner, K. (1999) 'Knowledge Transfer and Innovation in Germany and Britain: Intermediate Institution Models of Knowledge Transfer under Strain?', *Industry and Innovation*, 6, 1, 85–110.

Mathé, H. and Shapiro, R.D. (1993) *Integrating Service Strategy into the Manufacturing Company*. London: Chapman and Hall.

McCarthy, J.C. (2002) '3.3 Million US Service Jobs go Offshore', *Techstrategy Brief*, Forrester Research Inc., November.

Meade, J. (1955) *The Theory of Custom Unions*. Amsterdam: North Holland.

Meyer, A.D. and Goes, J.B. (1988) 'Organizational Assimilation of Innovations: a Multilevel Contextual Analysis', *Academy of Management Journal*, 31, 897–923.

Miles, I. (1996) *Innovation in Services: Services in Innovation*. Manchester: Manchester Statistical Society.

Miles, I. (2005) 'Knowledge Intensive Business Services: Prospects and Policies', *Foresight*, 7, 6, 39–63.

Miles, I. and Boden, M. (2000) 'Introduction: Are Services Special?', in I. Miles and M. Boden (eds), *Services and the Knowledge-Based Economy*. London: Continuum, pp. 1–20.

Miles, I., Kastrinos, N., Bilderbeek, P., Hertog, P. den, Flanagan, K., Huntink, W. and Bouman, M. (1995) 'Knowledge Intensive Business Services: Their Role as Users, Carriers and Sources of Innovation', Report to the EC DG XIII Sprint EIMS Programme, Publication 15. Luxembourg: European Innovation Monitoring Service, Directorate General for Telecommunications, Information Market and Exploitation of Research, Commission of the European Communities. Available at: http://les.man.ac.uk/PREST/Publications/KIBS1995.htm.

Milgrom, P. and Roberts, J. (1990) 'Complementarities and Fit: Strategy, Structure and Organisational Change in Manufacturing', *Journal of Accounting and Economics*, 19, 2/3, 179–208.

Millar, J. (2002) 'Outsourcing Practices in Europe', STAR Issue Report 27. Available at: www.databank.it/star/list_issue/e.html

Miozzo, M. and Miles, I. (eds) *Internationalization, Technology and Services*. Cheltenham: Elgar, pp. 161–83.

Miozzo, M. and Grimshaw, D. (2005) 'Modularity and Innovation in Knowledge-Intensive Business Services: IT Outsourcing in Germany and the UK', *Research Policy*, 34, 1419–39.

Mohnen, P., Mairesse, J. and Dagenais, M. (2006) 'Innovativeness: a Comparison Across 7 European Countries', *Economics of Innovation and New Technologies*, 15, 4/5, 391–413.

Morgan Chambers (2001) 'Outsourcing in the FTSE 100', The definitive study, available at: www.cw360.com/outsourcingreport.

Müller, E. and Zenker, A. (2000) 'The Contribution of Knowledge-Intensive Business Services to Regional Innovation Capacities'. Karlsruhe: Fraunhofer Institute.

Müller, E. and Zenker, A. (2001) 'Business Services as Actors of Knowledge Transformation: the Role of KIBS in Regional and National Innovation Systems', *Research Policy*, 30, 9, 1501–16.

Mylott, III, T.R. (1995) *Computer Outsourcing: Managing the Transfer of Information Systems*. New Jersey: Prentice Hall.

Nählinder, J. (2005) 'Innovation and Employment in Services: The Case of Knowledge Intensive Business Services in Sweden', Doctoral thesis, Department of Technology and Social Change, Linköping University, Sweden.

Nicoletti, G., Golub, S., Hajkova, D., Mirza, D. and Yoo, K.-Y. (2003) 'Policies and International Integration: Influences on Trade and Foreign Direct Investment', *OECD Economic Department Working paper no. 359*. Paris: OECD.

Nicoletti, G., Scarpetta, S. and Boylaud, O. (2000) 'Summary Indicators of Product Market Regulation with an Extension to Employment Protection Legislation', *OECD Economic Department Working paper no. 226*. Paris: OECD.

Nightingale, P., Brady, T., Davies, A. and Hall, J. (2003) 'Capacity Utilization Revisited: Software, Control and the Growth of Large Technical Systems', *Industrial and Corporate Change*, 12, 3, 477–517.

Nonaka, I. (1994) 'Dynamic Theory of Organizational Knowledge Creation', *Organization Science*, 5, 1, 14–37.

Nonaka, I. and Takeuchi, H. (1995) *The Knowledge-Creating Company*. New York: Oxford University Press.

Nordhaus, W.D. (2002) 'Productivity Growth and the New Economy', *Brookings Papers on Economic Activity*, 2, 211–65.

O'Farrell, P.N. and Moffat, L. (1991) 'An Interaction Model of Business Service Production and Consumption', *British Journal of Management*, 2, 205–21.

O'Mahony, M. and Ark, B. van (2003) 'EU Productivity and Competitiveness: an Industry Perspective. Can Europe Resume the Catching-up Process?', Enterprise publications, European Commission.

OECD (1999) *Strategic Business Services*. Paris: OECD.

OECD (2001) *OECD Productivity Manual: A Guide to the Measurement of Industry-Level and Aggregate Productivity Growth*'. Paris: OECD.

OECD (2002) 'Manual on Statistics of International Trade in Services', released by the European Commission, International Monetary Fund, Organisation for Economic Co-operation and Development, United Nations, United Nations Conference on

Trade and Development, the World Trade Organisation. Available at: http://www.oecd.org/dataoecd/32/45/2404428.pdf
OECD (2003a) *Science, Technology and Industry Scoreboard*. Paris: OECD.
OECD (2003b) *ICT and Economic Growth: Evidence from OECD Countries, Industries and Firms*. Paris: OECD.
OECD (2003c) *Statistics on International Trade in Services by Partner Countries*. Paris: OECD.
OECD (2004a) *The Economic Impact of ICT: Measurement, Evidence and Implications*. Paris: OECD.
OECD (2004b) *OECD Information Technology Outlook 2004*. Paris: OECD.
OECD (2004c) *OECD Economic Outlook*, Vol. 2004/1, No. 75, June. Paris: OECD.
OECD (2004d) *Promoting Trade in Services: Experience of the Baltic States*. Paris: OECD.
OECD (2004e) *Statistics on International Trade in Services by Partner Countries*. Paris: OECD
OECD (2005a) *Growth in Services – Fostering Employment, Productivity* and *Innovation*. Paris: OECD.
OECD (2005b) 'Promoting Innovation in Services', DSTI/STP/TIP(2004)4/FINAL. Paris: OECD.
Oliner, S.D. and Sichel, D.E. (2000) 'The Resurgence of Growth in the Late 1990s: Is the Information Technology the Story?', *Journal of Economic Perspectives*, 14, 3–22.
Oosterhaven, J. and Hoen, A.R. (1998) 'Preferences, Technology, Trade and Real Income Changes in the European Union – an Intercountry Decomposition Analysis for 1975–1985', *The Annals of Regional Science*, 32, 505–24.
Oulton, N. (2001) 'Must the Growth Rate Decline? Baumol's Unbalanced Growth Revisited', *Oxford Economic Papers*, 53, 605–27.
Outsourcing institute (2005) 'New Workplace: Outsourcing in Japan'. Available at: www.outsourcing.com.
Oxley, J.E. (1997) 'Appropriability Hazards and Governance in Strategic Alliances: A Transaction Cost Approach', *Journal of Law, Economics and Organization*, 13, 2, 389–409.
Pagano, P. and Schivardi, F. (2003) 'Firm Size Distribution and Growth', *Scandinavian Journal of Economics*, 105, 255–74.
Pain, N. and Jaumotte, F. (2005) 'Innovation Policies: Innovation in the Business Sector – Evidence on Innovation Determinants from the Community Innovation Survey', ECO/CPE/WP1(2005)2/ANN4. Paris: OECD.
Pain, N. and Welsum, D. van (2004) 'International Production Relocation and Exports of Services', OECD Economic Studies, 38, 2004/1.
Papaconstantinou, G., Sakurai, N. and Ioannidis, E. (1998) 'Domestic and International Product-embodied R&D Diffusion', *Research Policy*, 27, 301–14.
Pavitt, K. (1984) 'Patterns of Technical Change: Towards a Taxonomy and a Theory', *Research Policy*, 13, 343–73.
Peneder, M., Kaniovski, S. and Dachs, B. (2000) 'External Services, Structural Change and Industrial Performance', Background report for the European Competitiveness Report 2000, *Working Paper*. Brussels: DG Enterprise.
Peneder, M., Kaniovski, S. and Dachs, B. (2003) 'What Follows Tertiarization?: Structural Change and the Role of Knowledge-Based Services', *The Service Industries Journal*, 23, 2, 47–66.
Perry, M. (1990) 'Business Services Specialization and Regional Economic Change', *Regional Studies*, 24, 195–209.
Perry, M. (1992) 'Flexible Production, Externalisation and the Interpretation of Business Service Growth', *Service Industries Journal*, 12, 1–16.

Petersen, B. and Strongin, S. (1996) 'Why are Some Industries More Cyclical than Others?' *Journal of Business and Economic Statistics*, April, 12, 2.
Pilat, D. and Lee, F. (2001) 'Productivity Growth in ICT-producing and ICT-using Industries: A Source of Growth Differentials in the OECD?', *STI Working Paper 2001/4*. Paris: OECD.
Pilat, D. and Wölfl, A. (2005) 'Measuring the Interaction Between Manufacturing and Services, *STI Working Paper 2005/5*. Paris: OECD.
Piore, M.J. and Sabel, C. (1984) *The Second Industrial Divide*. New York: Basic Books.
Pisano, G.P. (1991) 'The Governance of Innovation: Vertical Integration and Collaborative Arrangements in the Biotechnology Industry', *Research Policy*, 20, 237–49.
Porter, M. (1990) *The Competitive Advantage of Nations*. London: Macmillan.
Porter, M. (1996) 'What is Strategy?', *Harvard Business Review*, 74, 6, 61–78.
Posthuma, A. (1987) 'Offshore Office Services Falmer', Brighton, SPRU Occasional Paper.
Prencipe, A. (1997) 'Technological Competencies and Product's Evolutionary Dynamics: a Case Study from the Aero-engine Industry', *Research Policy*, 25, 1261–76.
Prencipe, A., Davies, A. and Hobday, M. (eds) (2003) *The Business of Systems Integration*. Oxford: Oxford University Press.
Rajan, A. (1987) *Services: The Second Industrial Revolution?* London: Butterworths.
Ray, S.C. (1998) 'Measuring Scale Efficiency from a Translog Production Function', *Journal of Productivity Analysis*, 11, 183–94.
Reinstaller, A. and Hölzl, W. (2004) 'Complementarity Constraints and Induced Innovation: Some Evidence from the First IT Regime', in J. Foster and W. Hölzl (eds), *Applied Evolutionary Economics and Complex Systems*. Cheltenham: Edward Elgar, pp. 133–54.
Rivkin, J.W. (2000) 'Imitation of Complex Strategies', *Management Science*, 46, 824–44.
Roberts, J. (2002) 'From Markets to Resource-oriented Overseas Expansion: Re-examining a Study of the Internationalisation of UK Business Service Firms', in M. Miozzo and I. Miles (eds), *Internationalisation, Technology and Services*. Cheltenham: Elgar, Edward pp. 161–83.
Rodrigues, M.J. (2002) *The New Knowledge Economy in Europe: A Strategy for International Competitiveness and Social Cohesion*, Cheltenham: Edward Elgar.
Rodríguez, M. (2003) 'Services and Innovation: Towards the Knowledge Economy', PhD thesis, University of Granada.
Rogers, E.M. (1983) *Diffusion of Innovations*, 3rd edition. New York, Free Press.
Rubalcaba, L. (1999) 'Business Services in European Industry: Growth, Employment and Competitiveness'. Luxembourg: Office for Official Publications of the European Community, European Commission.
Rubalcaba, L. (2006) 'Which Policy for Innovation in Services?', *Science and Public Policy*, 33, 10, 745–756.
Rubalcaba, L. (2007a) *The New Services Economy: Challenges and Policy Implications for Europe*. Cheltenham, UK and Northampton, MA: Edward Elgar Publishing.
Rubalcaba, L. (2007b) 'Business Services in the Global Economy: New Evidence form a European Perspective', RESER Working Paper, forthcoming.
Rubalcaba, L. and Cuadrado, J.R. (2002a) 'A Comparative Approach to Internalisation of Service Industries', in J.R. Cuadrado, L. Rubalcaba and J.R. Bryson (eds), *Trading Services in the Global Economy*. Cheltenham: Edward Elgar.
Rubalcaba, L. and Cuadrado, J.R. (2002b) 'Services in the Age of Globalization: Explanatory Interrrelations and Dimensions', in J.R. Cuadrado, L. Rubalcaba and J.R. Bryson (eds), *Trading Services in the Global Economy*. Cheltenham: Edward Elgar.

Rusten, G. (2000) 'Geography of Outsourcing: Business Service Provisions Among Firms in Norway', *Tijdschrift voor Economische en Sociale Geografie*, 912, 122–34.

Rusten, G., Bryson, J. and Gammelsæter, H. (2005) 'Dislocated versus Local Business Service Expertise and Knowledge and the Acquisition of External Management Consultancy Expertise by Small and Medium Sized Enterprises in Norway', *Geoforum*, 36, 4, 525–39.

Ruyssen, O. (1990) 'La situation et le role des business services dans la CE', Rapport à l'attention du Comité des Directeurs Généraux de l'industrie, Commission of the EC. DG III, Brussels.

Salomon, R. and Shaver, J.M. (2005) 'Learning from Exporting: New Insights from Examining Firm Innovation', *Journal of Economics and Management Strategy*, 14, 2, 431–60.

Sapir, A., Buigues, P. and Jacquemin, A. (1993) 'European Competition Policy in Manufacturing and Services: A Two-Speed Approach?', *Oxford Review of Economic Policy*, 9, 2, 113–32.

Sasaki H. (2007) 'The Rise of Service Employment and its Impact on Aggregate Productivity Growth', Graduate School of Economics and Management, Tohoku University, Japan.

Sassen, S. (2001) *The Global City*, 2nd edition. Princeton, NJ: Princeton University Press.

Savona, M. and Lorentz, A. (2005) 'Demand Technology Determinants of Structural Change and Tertiarization'. An input–output structural decomposition analysis for four OECD countries, LEM Working Paper Series 2005/25, December.

Scarpetta, S., Hemmings, P., Tressel, T. and Woo, J. (2002) 'The Role of Policy and Institutions for Productivity and Firm Dynamics: Evidence from Micro and Industry Data', Economics Dept. *Working Paper No. 329*. Paris: OECD.

Schiantarelli, F. (2005) 'Product Market Regulation and Macro-economic Performance: a Review of Cross-country Evidence', *IZA Discussion Paper No. 1791*. Bonn: Institute for the Study of Labor (IZA).

Schreyer, P. (2000) 'The Contribution of Information and Communication Technology to Output Growth: a Study of the G7 Countries', STI Working Paper 2000/2. Paris.

Schulman, J. (1969) *Remaking an Organization*. Albany, NY: SUNY Press.

Schulz, C. (2000) 'Environmental Service-providers, Knowledge Transfer, and the Greening of Industry', Presented at IGU Commission on the Organization of Industrial Space Annual Residential Conference: Industry, Knowledge and Environment, Dongguan, China, 8–12 August.

Shrimpton, M. and Johnson, S. (1998) 'Small Places, Big Ideas: Exporting Knowledge-Based Services from the Atlantic Periphery', Centre for International Business Studies, Faculty of Business Administration, Memorial University of Newfoundland. Available at: http://www.mun.ca/cibs/EKBS/ekbs1.htm.

Siggelkow, N. (2002) 'Evolution Toward Fit', *Administrative Science Quarterly*, 47, 125–59.

Siggelkow, N. and Levinthal, D.A. (2003) 'Temporarily Divide to Conquer: Centralized, Decentralized, and Reintegrated Organizational Approaches to Exploration and Adaptation', *Organization Science*, 14, 6, 650–69.

Silverberg, G. and Verspagen, B. (1994) 'Collective Learning, Innovation and Growth in a Boundedly Rational, Evolutionary World', *Journal of Evolutionary Economics*, 4, 207–26.

Simon, H.A. (1996) 'The Architecture of Complexity: Hierarchical Systems', in H.A. Simon (ed.), *The Sciences of the Artificial*. Cambridge MA: MIT Press, pp. 183–216.

Simon, H.A. (2002) 'Near Decomposability and the Speed of Evolution', *Industrial and Corporate Change*, 11, 587–99.

Sjøholt, P. (2001) 'Transfer of Managerial Knowledge by Business Related Services', *Working Paper No. 247*, Department of Geography, University of Bergen, Norway. Presented at RESER Conference, New Information Technology and Service Activities, Grenoble, October.

Smith, A. (1776) *An Inquiry into the Nature and Causes of the Wealth of Nations*, University of Chicago Press (1976), Reprint of the 1776 edition.

Solow, R.M. (1957) 'Technical Change and the Aggregate Production Function', *Review of Economics and Statistics*, 39, 312–20.

Stare, M. and Rubalcaba, L. (2005) 'Outsourcing of Services from the CEEC – Current Potentials and New Challenges', XV International RESER Conference, Growth, employment and location of services in the new global world, Granada, 22–4 September.

Steinmueller, W.E. (2003) 'The Role of Technical Standards in Co-ordinating the Division of Labour in Complex System Industries', in A. Principe, A. Davies and M. Hobday (eds), *The Business of Systems Integration*. Oxford: Oxford University Press.

Stigler, G.J. (1951) 'The Division of Labour is Limited by the Extent of the Market', *Journal of Political Economy*, 59.

Strambach, S. (2001) 'Innovation Process and the Role of Knowledge-Intensive Business Services', in K. Koschatzky, M. Kulicke and A. Zenker (eds), *Innovation Networks – Concepts and Challenges in the European Perspective*. Heidelberg and New York: Physica-Verlag, pp. 53–68.

Sundbo, J. (1997) 'Management of Innovation in Services', *Service Industries Journal*, 17, 3, 432–55.

Sundbo, J. (2002) 'The service economy: standardisation or customisation?', *The Service Industries Journal*, 22, 4, 93–116.

Taylor, M.J. (2000) 'Enterprise, Power and Embeddedness', in E. Vatne and M.J. Taylor (eds), *The Networked Firm in a Global Environment*. Aldershot: Ashgate, pp. 199–234.

Taylor, M.J. and Thrift, N.J. (1982a) 'Industrial Linkage and the Segmented Economy: 1 Some Theoretical Proposals', *Environment and Planning A*, 14, 1601–13.

Taylor, M.J. and Thrift, N.J. (1982b) 'Industrial Linkage and the Segmented Economy: 2 An Empirical Reinterpretation', *Environment and Planning A*, 14, 1615–22.

Taylor, P.J. (2001) 'Specification of the World City Network', *Geographical Analysis*, 33, 2, 181–94.

Teece, D.J. (1980) 'The Diffusion of an Administrative Innovation', *Management Science*, 26, 464–70.

Teece, D.J. (1986) 'Profiting from Technological Innovation', *Research Policy*, 15, 6, 285–306.

Teece, D.J. (1992) 'Competition, Cooperation, and Innovation-Organizational Arrangements for Regimes of Rapid Technological Progress', *Journal of Economic Behavior and Organization*, 18, 1–25.

Tether, B. (2005) 'Do Services Innovate (Differently)? Insights from the European Innobarometer Survey', *Industry and Innovation*, 12, 2, 153–84.

Tether, B. and Hipp, C. (2002) 'Knowledge Intensive, Technical and Other Services: Patterns of Competitiveness and Innovation', *Technology Analysis and Strategic Management*, 14, 163–82.

Tether, B. and Metcalfe, J.S. (2003) 'Horndal at Heathrow? Capacity Creation Through Co-operation and System Evolution', *Industrial and Corporate Change*, 12, 3, 437–76.

Tether, B., Hipp, C. and Miles, I. (2001) 'Standardisation and Particularisation in Services: Evidence from Germany', *Research Policy*, 30, 7, 1115–38.

Tether, B., Miles, I., Blind, K., Hipp, C., Liso, N. de and Cainelli, G. (2001) 'Analysis Of CIS Data On Innovation In The Service Sector: Final Report', Final Report to European Commission by CRIC/IDSE/ISE.

Timmer, M.P. and Ark, B. van (2005) 'Does Information and Communication Technology Drive EU–US Productivity Growth Differentials?', *Oxford Economic Papers*, 57, 693–716.

Tomlinson, M. (1997) 'The Contribution of Services to Manufacturing Industry', *CRIC Discussion Paper No. 5*. Available at: http://les1.man.ac.uk/cric.

Tomlinson, M. (2000a) 'Information and Technology Flows from the Service Sector: a UK–Japan Comparison', in M. Boden and I. Miles (eds), *Services and the Knowledge-Based Economy*. London and New York: Continuum, pp. 209–21.

Tomlinson, M. (2000b) 'The Contribution of Knowledge-Intensive Services to the Manufacturing Industry', in B. Andersen, J. Howells, R. Hull, I. Miles and J. Roberts (eds), *Knowledge and Innovation in the New Service Economy*. Cheltenham: Edward Elgar.

Tomlinson, M. (2003) 'A New Role for Business Services in Economic Growth', in D. Archibugi and B. Lundvall (eds), *The Globalizing Learning Economy*. Oxford: Oxford University Press.

Tordoir, P.P. (1993) 'The Professional Knowledge Economy: the Management and Integration of Professional Services in Business Organizations', Academisch Proefshrift. Amsterdam: University of Amsterdam.

Tordoir, P.P. (1994) 'Transactions of Professional Business Services and Spatial Systems', *Tijdschrift voor Economische en Sociale Geographie*, 85, 322–32.

Tordoir, P.P. (1995) *The Professional Knowledge Economy: The Management and Integration of Professional Services in Business Organizations*. Dordrecht: Kluwer Academic Publishers.

Tremblay, D.G. (1998) 'Industrial Districts and Innovation Networks: New Theories and Concepts for Entrepreneurship Development', MIMEO, Tele-Universite, Université du Quebec. Available at: http://www.usasbe.org/knowledge/proceedings/1998/20-Tremblay.PDF.

Triplett, J. and Bosworth, B. (2004) 'Productivity in the US Service Sector. New Sources of Economic Growth', The Brookings Institution, Washington, DC, 18, 345–62.

Tschetter, J. (1987) 'Producer Services Industries: Why are They Growing so Rapidly?', *Monthly Labour Review*, 110, 31–40.

van Ark, B. (2005) 'Does the European Union Need to Revive Productivity Growth?', Research Memorandum GD-75, Groningen Growth and Development Centre.

van Ark, B. and Inklaar, R. (2005) 'Catching Up or Getting Stuck? Europe's Troubles to Exploit ICT's Productivity Potential', Research Memorandum GD-79, Groningen Growth and Development Centre.

Varjonen, S. (2005) 'OECD–Eurostat 2004 Inquiry on National Collection of Services Producer Prices'. Paris: OECD.

Vernon, R. (1966) 'International Investment and International Trade in the Product Cycle', *Quarterly Journal of Economics*, 80, 190–207.

Veugelers, R. (1997) 'Internal R&D Expenditures and External Technology Sourcing', *Research Policy*, 26, 303–15.

Veugelers, R. and Cassiman, B. (1999) 'Make and Buy in Innovation Strategies: Evidence from Belgian Manufacturing Firms', *Research Policy*, 28, 63–80.

Viner, J. (1950) *The Custom Union Issue*. New York: Carnegie, Endowments for International Peace.

Webb, I. (2002) 'Knowledge Management in the KIBS–Client Environment: A Case Study Approach', PREST Discussion Paper DP02-12, September. Available at: http://les1.man.ac.uk/prest.

Welsum, D. van (2003a) 'International Trade in Services: Issues and Concepts', *Birkbeck Economics Working Paper 2003 No. 4*. London: Birkbeck College.

Welsum, D. van (2003b) 'Foreign Direct Investment and Exports of Services', *Birkbeck Economics Working Paper 2003 No. 3*. London: Birkbeck College.

Welsum, D. van (2004) 'In Search of Offshoring: Evidence from US Imports of Services', *Birkbeck Economics Working Paper 2004 No. 2*. London: Birkbeck College.

Welsum, D. van and Reif, X. (2006a) 'Potential Offshoring: Evidence from Selected OECD Countries', in S. Collins and L. Brainard (eds), *The Brookings Trade Forum 2005 on Offshoring White-collar Work – The Issues and Implications*. Washington DC: The Brookings Institution.

Welsum, D. van and Reif, X. (2006b) 'The Share of Employment Potentially Affected by Offshoring: An Empirical Investigation', DSTI Information Economy Working Paper, DSTI/ICCP/IE(2005)8/FINAL, OECD, Paris. Available at: http://www.oecd.org/sti/offshoring.

Welsum, D. van and Vickery, G. (2005a) 'Potential Offshoring of ICT-intensive Using Occupations', DSTI Information Economy Working Paper, DSTI/ICCP/IE(2004)19/FINAL, OECD, Paris. Available at: http://www.oecd.org/sti/offshoring.

Welsum, D. van and Vickery, G. (2005b) 'New Perspectives on ICT Skills and Employment', *DSTI Information Economy Working Paper*, DSTI/ICCP/IE(2004)10/FINAL, OECD, Paris. Available at: http://www.oecd.org/sti/ICT-employment.

Wiel, H.P. van der (1999) 'Firm Turnover in Dutch Business Services: The Effect on Labour Productivity', *CPB Research Memorandum No 159*. The Hague: CPB.

Wiel, H.P. van der (2001) 'Innovation and productivity in services', *CPB Report 2001/1*. The Hague: CPB.

Williamson, O.E. (1981) 'The Economics of Organization: the Transaction Cost Approach', *American Journal of Sociology*, 87, 3, 548–77.

Windrum, P. and Tomlinson, M. (1999) 'Knowledge-Intensive Services and International Competitiveness: a Four Country Comparison', *Technology Analysis and Strategic Management*, 11, 3, 391–408.

Wölfl, A. (2003) 'Productivity Growth in Service Industries: an Assessment of Recent Patterns and the Role of Measurement', DSTI/DOC(2003), *OECD Working Paper*. Paris: OECD.

Wölfl, A. (2004) 'The Interaction Between Manufacturing and Services: Some Preliminary Findings', *DSTI Working Paper* DSTI/EAS/IND/SWP/AH(2004)7. Paris: OECD.

Wölfl, A. (2005) 'The Service Economy in OECD Countries', *Chapter 2 in Enhancing the Performance of the Services Sector*. Paris: OECD.

Wood, P. (1998) 'Services & Internationalisation Report to the RESER Network'. Available at: htttp://www.reser.net/gb/rapportgb.html.

Wood, P. (2002) *Consultancy and Innovation: the Business Service Revolution in Europe*. London: Routledge.

Yates, J. (2000) 'Business Use of Information and Technology during the Industrial Age', in A.D. Chandler and J.W. Cortada (eds), *A Nation Transformed by Information*. Oxford: Oxford University Press, pp. 107–36.

Young, A.A. (1928) 'Increasing Returns and Economic Progress', *Economic Journal*, 38, 527–42.

Zambon, S., Lev, B. *et al.* (2003) 'Study on the Measurement of Intangible Assets and Associated Reporting Practices', Prepared for the European Commission (DG Enterprise), Ferrara/Melbourne/New York.

Index